Chile

LATIN AMERICAN HISTORIES

JAMES R. SCOBIE, EDITOR

Chile

THE LEGACY OF HISPANIC CAPITALISM

SECOND EDITION

BRIAN LOVEMAN

New York • Oxford University Press • 1988

Soc
F
3081
L68
1988

Oxford University Press

Oxford   New York   Toronto
Delhi   Bombay   Calcutta   Madras   Karachi
Petaling Jaya   Singapore   Hong Kong   Tokyo
Nairobi   Dar es Salaam   Cape Town
Melbourne   Auckland

and associated companies in
Beirut   Berlin   Ibadan   Nicosia

Published by Oxford University Press, Inc.,
200 Madison Avenue, New York, New York 10016

Oxford is a registered trademark of Oxford University Press

Library of Congress Cataloging-in-Publication Data
Loveman, Brian.
Chile: The legacy of Hispanic capitalism / Brian Loveman. — 2nd ed.
p. cm.
Bibliography: p.
Includes index.
ISBN 0-19-505218-8
ISBN 0-19-505219-6 (pbk.)
1. Chile—History. I. Title.
F3081.L68 1988   983'.064—dc19   87-34891

9 8 7 6 5 4 3 2 1

Printed in the United States of America

Preface

Chile is a nation where historians and social theorists have participated actively in public life as well as in scholarship. Presidents, ministers of state, legislators, and party leaders have contributed to Chile's historical tradition, to its literature, and to its art. No historian, Chilean or foreign, can undertake a new look at Chilean history without returning, first, to the great intellectual contributions of Chile's national writers. While this book departs in some important ways from conventional interpretations of Chile's past, it owes much to the insight and thorough research of generations of Chilean writers.

To the intellectual debt I owe to Chilean writers must be added the use I have made of the studies of hundreds of non-Chilean "Chileanists" who have dedicated their attention to Chilean history. As the format of this book generally precluded systematic footnote citations, I have attempted to note appropriately those works upon which I relied extensively in the selective bibliography at the end of this volume.

As I wrote this study, my friend, teacher, and general editor of Oxford University Press's Latin American Histories Series, James Scobie, offered his advice, encouragement, and critical reviews of the manuscript for which I am extremely grateful. The manuscript has also benefitted from the comments and suggestions made by Jacques Barbier, Harold Blakemore, Simon Collier, Thomas M. Davies, Jr., Philip Flemion, Henry Landsberger, Sharon Loveman, Vincent

Padgett, William Sater, William Sherman, and John Whaley. Larry Stickell generously allowed me to read chapter drafts of his doctoral dissertation on the development of the nitrate industry in Chile and to use data from his research in the present volume. While the insights of these scholars have greatly improved the present book, I am, of course, responsible for any errors of fact or interpretation that remain in the volume.

I have been fortunate to have help from a number of people in the preparation of the manuscript. Special thanks go to Veva Link, Helen Triller, Jeri Haddon and Paula Forrester, and to Phoebe Hoss for her careful copy-editing. Nancy Ferris provided invaluable assistance in preparation of the bibliography as did Michael Arguello in construction of the index.

A final thank you must also go to my friends in Trovolhue who taught me the political meaning of life's daily struggle against the legacy of four centuries of Hispanic Capitalism.

San Diego   B.L.
August 1978

Preface
to the Second Edition

I have completed the second edition of this book at a time when Chileans are in their fourteenth year under an authoritarian, military-dominated dictatorship. This dictatorship, led by General Augusto Pinochet, has effected radical changes in many aspects of Chilean life.

Unlike the military-dominated governments in Argentina, Uruguay, Brazil, and Peru during the 1970s and early 1980s, the Chilean government came to be identified ever more closely with the personalist control of one officer rather than the institutional control of the country by the armed forces. For this reason, an appropriate conclusion to the last chapter of this edition of the book would have been the departure of General Pinochet and the transition to another sort of political leadership. Unfortunately, while the passage of time and the many changes that have transpired in Chile made a second edition essential, the proper conclusion of the last chapter still has not occurred—though it is inevitable.

As in preparation of the first edition of this book I have had the advantage of relying upon the important research and historical analysis of a number of Chilean writers and intellectuals too numerous to identify individually. In addition, conversations and discussions with Alejandro Foxley, Manuel Antonio Garretón, Sol Serrano, Gonzalo Tapia, Francisco Tomic, Maria Elena Valenzuela, and Augusto Varas have assisted me greatly in understanding the last fourteen years. Luis Ortega's valuable published critique of parts of the first edition and suggestions offered by him for improvement have also proved useful in making revisions. Likewise, an extensive set of suggestions for revision by Michael Monteón assisted me in preparing the second edition.

Thomas M. Davies Jr., Paul Drake, Iván Jaksić, Sharon Loveman, Frederick Nunn, Michael Stanfield, and Augusto Varas have all struggled through drafts of new material for the second edition, and spared me errors of fact or interpretation. Naturally, the errors that remain are my responsibility.

I have also been fortunate to have the assistance of Iliana Sonntag in revising and updating the bibliography, Melinda Wedgewood in preparing new maps, Kirsten Mulvey and Cecilia Ubilla in copyediting, and Helen Kanavel in preparation of the new tables. Michael Arguello once again constructed the index.

San Diego   B.L.
July 1987

Contents

Maps

Tables

Chile

Introduction

Harsh exploitation of the labor force in mines, farms, and industry has been the most persistent characteristic of Chilean society since the arrival of European conquerors in the sixteenth century. Despite the recurrent efforts by progressive Church officials or government reformers to improve the lot, first, of Chile's indigenous population and, then, of the ethnically mixed working classes, the Chilean economy continued to rely upon forced labor, agricultural service tenants, and then a highly mobile but miserable wage proletariat. From the first years of conquest and into the 1980s Chilean society and culture reflected the tensions between attempts to better the living and working conditions of the majority of the Chilean people and the realities of an economic and political order resting upon the foundation of conquest, subjugation, and coercion of labor.

In 1620, more than eighty years after the first Spanish expedition to Chile, the king of Spain ordered Chilean encomenderos and settlers to end compulsory labor and to pay farm workers a minimum daily wage. Resistance by the propertied classes and lack of enforcement efforts by public officials prevented implementation of this legislation. More than three centuries later (1953) a Chilean national government enacted a minimum wage for agricultural workers and sought to regulate rural labor conditions. Landowners successfully resisted the feeble enforcement efforts of the Ministry of Labor.

In 1620 Indian and mestizo laborers living on the haciendas of Spaniards were required to work 160 days a year. In 1953 Chilean rural tenants and laborers typically worked well over 200 days a year and provided landowners not only their own labor but also that of family members or other hired hands.

The quest for liberty, justice, and human dignity is a recurrent theme in Chilean history. But in the era of the conquistadors as in modern Chile, the quest has been subordinated inevitably to the requirements of order and material gain for a small privileged minority. Whether the conflict joined Jesuits and encomenderos, or Marxists, reformers, and conservatives, the outcome has repeatedly been a return to pragmatic repression to uphold the economic, social, and political foundations of the Chilean version of Hispanic capitalism—a complex adaptation of neofeudal political and economic institutions to the New World. Relying initially upon slave or forced labor, Hispanic capitalism represented a unique response of the Spanish colonial elite to the expansion of European capitalism.

Some Spaniards called out for social justice almost from the outset of colonization. Clerical and secular precursors of twentieth-century reformers and revolutionaries opposed decimation and abuse of the native population. If the conqueror Pedro de Valdivia came to subjugate and exploit the Indians, the Jesuit Luis de Valdivia urged peaceful conquest and abolition of slavery and compulsory labor. But in a frontier region at perpetual war, efforts by the crown and some churchmen to ameliorate the conditions of the Indians through protective legislation met consistent failure. Governors, soldiers, encomenderos, and even some religious leaders built a Chilean economy from venturesome private initiative and the sweat and suffering of the Indian work force.

For the conquistadors Chile was not the prize of Mexico or Peru. Instead of the vast wealth of the Aztecs and Incas, the Chilean conquerors encountered a people with little more to defend than their land and liberty. Between 1598 and 1612, after more than half a century of warfare and settlement, the Araucanians forced the Spanish to abandon the principal towns south of the Bío Bío River. In 1655 another Indian uprising again destroyed almost all the new and re-established Spanish outposts in Araucania. To survive, to establish a semblance of order, and to achieve some economic returns the Spaniards adopted a de facto policy of pragmatic repression. Ignoring or circumventing royal edicts or colonial legislation designed to protect the Indians, the colonial bureaucracy, soldiers, and encomenderos prevailed. In the words of an Indian cacique: "The King is good and he legislates justly, but your governors and captains do not comply and there is no justice for the Indians."

Thus the struggle between parchment justice and the realities of Chilean society offers a permanent tension in the historical development of the Chilean nation. A war for independence against Spain carried out in the name of liberty, culminated in the establishment of an autocratic order inspired by a merchant deprived of his government-authorized tobacco monopoly. In the tradition of the Spanish governors and captains, Diego Portales used fear and repression to establish political order.

The creation of the Portalian state after 1830 spared Chile the destructive anarchy experienced by most of South America in the first half of the nineteenth century. Portales accomplished this task through harsh, authoritarian treatment of any political opposition. An aphorism attributed to Portales set the tone for the struggle between liberty and autocracy that characterized Chilean development in the nineteenth and twentieth centuries: "The stick and the cake, justly and opportunely administered, are the remedies with which any nation can be cured, however inveterate its bad habits may be." As Portales observed, the social order in Chile was preserved by the "weight of the night . . . the masses' near universal tendency to repose was the guarantee of public tranquility." In case the "weight of the night" should lighten, Portales and his successors never hesitated to use "the stick" to secure that tranquility.

The second half of the nineteenth century brought modernization to Chile as it did in varying degrees to most of Latin America. The steamship, telegraph, railroad, increased labor mobility, and urbanization, as well as expansion of commerce and industry, altered the socio-economic institutions of the nation. Political parties played the game of liberal democracy and mouthed the rhetoric of social justice. Eloquent speeches in the Chilean congress promised relief to the working classes, while laborers and rural workers organized to challenge the propertied interests. New laws guaranteed justice and equality. By the end of the nineteenth century the old order seemed to be coming apart. Growing awareness by the working classes of alternatives to their poverty and misery threatened to end the era of the stick and the cake.

Then in the period 1924-31, in the name of order and justice, a new class of conquistador sought to re-establish authority and to reimpose the "weight of the night" on the Chilean masses. In the tradition of Portales, government-stimulated economic growth accompanied repression of all who voiced opposition to the incumbent regime.

A few years later Chile nevertheless was acclaimed a democracy. Along with Uruguay and Costa Rica, Chile escaped the coups, rebellions, and revolutions that afflicted most of Latin America after the Great Depression. Until 1973 the military did not overtly intervene in Chilean politics. Elections took place as scheduled, and votes were fairly counted. Freedom of the press brought a wide range of viewpoints to the Chilean population and spared the incumbent government no criticism. In contrast to the authoritarian pattern of the Portalian state, Chilean presidents failed to control their own political parties, let alone congressional elections or deliberations. No Chilean president in the period 1932-70 could name his own successor. Great legislative strides were made in the direction of popular participation, social justice, and democratization. But the tension persisted between legislative proclamations and the traditional foundations of Chilean society—autocracy, social stratification, and repression of popular activism. The tension gave a special character to Chilean democracy.

In the early 1960s a Chilean president initiated a "revolution in liberty." Priority was given to increased participation of the popular classes, to removing social and economic inequality, and to stimulating the Chilean economy. It soon became evident that removing the "weight of the night" from the Chilean working classes could not be reconciled with maintenance of the existing socio-economic order. Chilean democracy had concealed but not eliminated the conflicts between liberty and participation and the authoritarian tenets of conquerors and twentieth-century capitalists.

By 1970 the struggle was explicit. Revolutionaries and reformers joined in an effort to destroy the institutions and values of the old order. Ironically, but not surprisingly, the principal vehicle they chose to carry out this radical transformation of Chilean society was an updated model of that employed by conquistadors and Portales: a centralized bureaucracy imbued with the prejudices and defects of Hispanic viceroys, governors, and notaries. The attempt did not prosper. Landlords, capitalists, bureaucrats, and soldiers stifled the "revolution" as they had implementation of the king's mandate in 1620.

In 1973 a military coup terminated a three-year effort to restructure Chilean society. Again owing to pragmatic repression in support of an updated version of Hispanic capitalism, opponents of the incumbent regime lived in an atmosphere of fear. The new military government proclaimed: "In every soldier there is a Chilean; in every Chilean a soldier." In answer to this apparent return to the spirit of conquest, a Christian Democratic politician seemed to echo the Jesuit Luis de Valdivia: "We are convinced that it is not possible to build a lasting order on repression."

From the time of the conquest Chile has been distinctive in Spanish America. Chileans largely avoided the anarchy and dislocation common to the new nations of Latin America in the early nineteenth century. They have believed themselves to be unique, even referring to themselves as the English of South America. The visitor to Chile has repeatedly heard this theme, summed up in the phrase *No somos tropicales* ("We aren't like those other Latin Americans"). Yet the motto on the national emblem, *Por la razón o la fuerza* ("By reason or by force"), has served as a reminder that the present has not escaped the past. It proclaims that national objectives will be attained "by reason or by force."

For the present generation of Chileans, as for their ancestors, the basic dilemmas persist: how to make Chile a land of liberty while maintaining political order; how to achieve economic progress without exploitation of the working classes; how to maintain social order and create social justice without imposing the terrible "weight of the night" on the Chilean people. This is the historical legacy and current challenge of Chile.

Chapter 1 • Land and Society

The territory occupied by the Chilean nation is the prize of military conquest. From Copiapó south to the Bío Bío River, Spanish conquistadors took the land from a variety of indigenous peoples in the sixteenth century. From an undefined point somewhat north of Copiapó (lat. 27° 22′ S), nineteenth-century Chilean armies extended the national domain by defeating Bolivian and Peruvian forces in the War of the Pacific (1879-83). The territory Chile acquired then has remained a source of friction and potential conflict among the three countries. South of the Bío Bío River the Araucanian Indians successfully impeded consolidation of Spanish and then Chilean rule until after 1880, when modern weaponry finally overcame the descendants of the Indian groups that had offered the most determined resistance to the Spanish conquistadors. Only at the end of the nineteenth century, therefore, did the political unit that is now Chile effectively achieve its present boundaries, extending some 2600 miles from the northernmost city of Arica (lat. 18° 28′ S) past the Strait of Magellan to latitude 56° S. Chile also claims substantial portions of Antarctica (lat. 53° W-90° W).

For most of its history Chile did not include the great northern desert containing the vast mineral wealth for which the country became known around the world. Nor did the territory south of the Bío Bío River form an integral part of European settlement. In colonial times (1535-1810) Chile meant a small number of semi-urban places, from La Serena through the central valley (see Map 3), in addition to the precarious frontier fort towns south of the Bío Bío River which Araucanian Indians periodically destroyed. Bounded on the east by the Andes Mountains, on the west by the coastal mountain range and the Pacific Ocean, and on the north by one of the world's driest deserts, the Chilean colony was little more than a backwater of the Spanish Empire.

Between Copiapó and the Bío Bío River the Andes chain occupies from one-third to one-half of the width of present-day Chile (though certain areas in what is now western Argentina—Tucumán in the early colonial period and Cuyo until the late eighteenth century—also belonged to Chile). Moving south from Copiapó, the Andes narrow and become a single dominant cordillera, with some of the highest peaks in South America. In Argentina at the headwaters of the Aconcagua River, Mt. Aconcagua, the loftiest peak in the western hemisphere, rises some 22,835 feet (7000 meters). In Chilean territory in the same Andean region, Mt. Salado reaches over 22,500 feet (6900 meters). The Andean passes as far south as the central valley town of Curicó (lat. 35° S) are typically found at more than 10,000 feet. Los Leones, Lagarto, and Casa de Piedra are located at more than 13,000 feet, and less than ideal weather makes passage extremely difficult. Near Aconcagua, the pass at Los Patos (4,720 meters) served as a conduit for the liberating army of the independence movement led by General San Martín in 1817. Through the gap at Juncal, almost due east of the city of Los Andes, lies the railroad between Chile and the Argentine city of Mendoza. In general, however, the Andes represent a significant barrier to transport and communication, thereby isolating Chile from eastern South America and Europe.

South of the Bío Bío River, the Andes lose height and passes are found at lower elevations. Permanent snow levels are also lower, so that inland from the city of Valdivia (lat. 40° S) snow persists above 5000 feet year round. In this area beautiful yet treacherously active snow-capped volcanoes edge magnificent lakes. Southern Chile is a region of cereal production, diversified agriculture, cattle raising, and dairies set within the forested cordilleras, islands, and fjords. At the southern extreme are the inhospitable Patagonian plains and Tierra del Fuego, where the Strait of Magellan affords a perilous transit around the tip of South America. Before the opening of the Panama Canal in 1914, this southern passage made Valparaíso a commercial competitor of Lima-Callao for the Pacific shipping trade.

In the late nineteenth century Chile incorporated much of the Atacama desert into the national domain and consolidated control over the provinces south of the Bío Bío River. This gave the country more territory with great natural resources, but these northern and southern territories remained sparsely inhabited. To this day some 70 percent of Chile's population resides between Aconcagua and the Bío Bío River. On a map, the nation that emerged in the twentieth century looks like a long, irregularly scalloped ribbon trimming south-western South America. Seen from the air the country is an indentation of varying depths between the Andes on the east and the coastal mountains to the west.

Chile's major urban centers—Santiago, Valparaíso-Viña del Mar, Concepción-Talcahuano—and the regional and provincial capitals from Arica in the north, through the central valley to the southern cities of Temuco, Valdivia, and Puerto Montt (see Table 2) are situated in one of the world's most geologically active regions and over the centuries they have been repeatedly damaged or destroyed by earthquakes and tidal waves. In the 1960s and 1970s severe quakes damaged cities in southern Chile and in the north and the port of Valparaíso. Indeed Chileans assume that "every president will have his earthquake." More recently, in March 1985, a strong quake in central Chile damaged the country's busiest ports of San Antonio and Valparaíso, destroyed thousands of homes, a number of colonial buildings, and modern office structures and condominiums. Highways, bridges, and other public facilities also suffered significant damage. As in the past, Chile began reconstruction almost immediately, though preliminary estimates of almost $2 billion in damages sorely pressed the country's economy. Beyond earthquakes, floods and droughts make agriculture risky in the south as well as in the north and the central valley. Landslides, volcanic eruptions, and avalanches add to the natural violence that persistently threatens Chilean lives and property.

Nature provides Chile not only a continual challenge but also an incredible variety of landscapes, climates, and natural ecologies, ranging from the arid northern deserts to the Chilean antarctic in the south. This diversity is tied together by the Pan American Highway running through the middle of the country some two thousand miles from Arica to Puerto Montt. For most of the distance the highway runs parallel to the longitudinal railroad, much of which the national government built and has operated since the late nineteenth century. Airline service also connects most major cities, though on a reduced scale after 1973 as part of an economy move by the military government.

Prior to 1974 Chile was divided into twenty-five provinces for purposes of internal administration. Departments, subdelegations, and districts formed progressively smaller jurisdictions of each province. An *intendente*, appointed by the Chilean president, served as the chief administrator of each province. In turn a *gobernador* directed administration in the departments, *subdelegados* of the subdelegations, and *inspectores* of each district. Each of these officials served at the pleasure of the Chilean president. In addition, locally elected mayors and municipal councilpersons (*regidores*) had political and administrative responsibilities for local government with *comunas*.

Administrative reforms introduced by the military government after 1974 in efforts to decentralize and rationalize national planning and public administration, as well as to depoliticize regional and local government, reorganized the country into twelve regions plus the Santiago metropolitan area. (See Map 5). *Intendentes* now headed regions, and *gobernadores* administered fifty-one provinces into which the regions were divided. Municipalities (*municipalidades*) were charged with local administration of 335 jurisdictions called communes (*comunas*) under the direction of mayors. The mayors were subordinate to the provincial *gobernador* and the regional *intendente*. The Organic Law of Municipalities (Decree Law 1289, 1976) specified three types of *comunas* (urban, rural-urban, and rural) along with the legal authority, functions, and administrative organization of each type of local entity. While it is unclear that these reforms significantly decentralized public policymaking, they did limit political participation at the regional and local levels and extended the control of the central government over local administration.

From north to south the variety of Chilean landscapes may be illustrated by comparing Chile's several natural subdivisions with the strip of land running from the desert of Baja California to the Yukon and Alaska: the deserts of the Chilean "great north" or *norte grande* (regions I, II, and part of III—Map 2); the transitional steppes and transversal river valleys of the "little north" or *norte chico* (part of region III, region IV, and part of region V—Map 2); the fertile central valley (part of region V south, including part of region VIII—Map 3); the "frontier" region of cereal production and forests south of the major industrial center of Concepción (most of region VIII and all of region IX—Map 3); the lake region (most of region X, excluding Chiloé—Map 4); and the sparsely settled region of southern continental Chile (Chiloé and regions XI, XII—Map 4).

The Chilean *norte grande* is part of South America's western coastal desert which extends northward through Peru and into Ecuador. In much of this region the coastal range amounts only to

Long. 70°	Lat.	Mean Annual Temperature (C)	Rainfall in Millimeters	Major Economic Activities
Iquique	20°	18.3	25	Oasis cultivation, mining, nitrate, fishing and limited industry.
Antofagasta				
La Serena	30°	14.4	114	Early vegetables, fruit, limited vines and cereals, goats, sheep, limited cattle mining, fishing.
Viña del Mar Valparaíso Santiago Rancagua Talca Chillán		13.9	359	Central valley agriculture, fruits, vines, wheat, corn, hemp, tobacco, vegetable oils, diversified livestock —70% of all Chilean industry.
Concepción		13.5	1319	Coal, steel, petro-chemicals, forest products, cereals, potatoes, dairy and cattle, limited vegetables, orchards and vineyards.
Temuco Puerto Montt	40°	11.8	2511	
Aisén		8.9	2865	Forest industries, livestock, subsistence agriculture, fishing, sheep.
	50°			
Punta Arenas		6.2	2754	Sheep and livestock, wool, coal, oil, and natural gas.

CHILE:
Climate and Major Economic Activities

MAP 1: Chile: Climate and Major Economic Activities

MAP 2: *The Norte Grande* and the *Norte Chico*

MAP 3: Central Chile and the Frontier Region

rounded hills which drop sharply to the Pacific. From the Loa River south, the first major surface water to reach the Pacific flows in the Copiapó. The major urban concentration and farming belt around Copiapó (almost 90 miles long) is often taken as the southern limit of the Atacama desert. At the time of the initial Spanish expedition of conquest from Peru into Chile (1535), Copiapó marked the northern boundary of the territory that became Chile.

This northern region is a vast desert. Scattered oases and river valleys provide slight relief from the barren landscape. Charles Darwin's description of a part of this region near Santa Rosa and Huantajaya as a "complete and utter desert," in which he saw only cacti and lichen, matches that of Preston James in the twentieth century: "No part of the west coast of South America is more forbidding, more utterly desert-like in aspect than the stretch of about 600 miles between Arica and Caldera." Despite the fact that weather stations in some parts of the *norte grande* have never recorded rainfall, there are noticeable differences in climate between the coastal and the interior regions. The coast experiences much greater relative humidity and often cloudiness, due to the cooling effects of the Humboldt Current. Inland, skies are cloudless and humidity much less. For example, humidity in the coastal city of Iquique averages about 81 percent, while in Calama, to the southeast, it averages about 48 percent.

For thousands of years small groups of people lived as fishermen along the coast or took advantage of the limited water resources in this region for oasis valley agriculture, especially in the fertile valleys of Azapa and Lluta. Available evidence suggests that the site of Chile's northernmost city, Arica, supported small population clusters many centuries before the Spanish conquistadors came south from Cuzco. To the present, lack of water and the ecological constraints of the desert environment severely limit agricultural activity in this region. Of the 1.1 million hectares of the national territory classified by the 1975-76 Agricultural and Livestock Census as irrigated, less than 15,000 irrigated hectares* corresponded to the *norte grande*. The few irrigated valleys and oases such as Azapa and Belén, east of Arica, and Pica, southeast of Iquique in Region I, and Calama, southwest of the port of Tocopilla (near the copper mine at Chuquicamata), as well as San Pedro de Atacama and Toconao, northeast of Antofagasta in Region II, contribute olives, fruit, herbs, and a variety of food and specialty crops to the regional economy.

* One hectare equals approximately 2.47 acres.

MAP 4: The Lake Region and the Far South

16

REGION	CAPITAL
I	IQUIQUE
II	ANTOFAGASTA
III	COPIAPO
IV	LA SERENA
V	VALPARAISO
	SANTIAGO METROPOLITAN AREA
VI	RANCAGUA
VII	TALCA
VIII	CONCEPCION
IX	TEMUCO
X	PUERTO MONTT
XI	COIHAIQUE
XII	PUNTA ARENAS

CHILEAN ANTARCTIC TERRITORY

90° 33°

POLO SUR

0   300   600 km

MAP 5: Administrative Subdivisions and Regional Capitals, 1987

17

Many of the population centers in the *norte grande* owe their origins to the mining activity made possible by the great mineral wealth of the desert. The major ports—Iquique, Antofagasta, Tocopilla—as well as minor ports and interior cities arose, and prospered or declined with mineral finds (silver, gold, nitrates, copper, iron). Iquique owed its colonial significance to silver strikes at Huantajaya and its nineteenth-century boom to nitrates. In 1870 a silver strike at what came to be called Caracoles, 200 kilometers northeast of Antofagasta, attracted some 10,000 miners in its glory days and transformed Antofagasta into an urban and commercial center. Tocopilla and Antofagasta both prospered from copper mining, and then from nitrates in the nineteenth and twentieth centuries. Other settlements briefly flourished and then died when the mineral deposits to which they owed their existence were exhausted. The remains of mining camps and settlements that litter the desert are reminiscent of the ghost towns of the western United States in an even bleaker setting.

In the late nineteenth century the ports of the *norte grande* served as service centers and transshipment outlets for the nitrate works (*oficinas*) and copper mines. At the time these ports seemed more like overgrown villages than real cities, though in several, particularly Iquique and Antofagasta, luxurious mansions and new public services gave the wealthy a sense of living in modern comfort. This was made possible by importing fuel, food, and even topsoil for plazas while piping water over great distances. An early twentieth-century description of these mining ports tells us that they were sometimes "mere collections of tin shanties crowded at the base of cliffs . . . connected by little lines of railways with the mines in the interior."

The nitrate deposits themselves occur at elevations between 3000 and 9000 feet above sea level, at distances varying from 10 to 80 miles from the Pacific coast. Layers of *caliche* or raw nitrate sometimes lie on the surface of the earth; at other times they are found 20 to 30 feet below the surface. In addition to the nitrate itself, important by-products of processing include iodine, salt, sulphur, and sulphuric acid. Nitrate production and iodine as a by-product played a reduced but still significant role in the *norte grande* in the 1980s, accounting for approximately $80 million per year in exports from 1980 to 1985. In 1986 the Chilean Chemical and Mining Company, SOQUIMICH, entered into new contracts for nitrate sales to China which, along with Japan (Chile's second leading trade partner), had become an important destination for Chilean mineral and seafood exports.

Though the *norte grande* occupies about one-third of the national territory (Antofagasta is as large as the territory from Santiago to the

Bío Bío River), it contains less than 8 percent of the country's population. Despite its sparse population, the region has played an extraordinary role in determining Chilean economic development since the nineteenth century. The extraction of silver, nitrates, nitrate byproducts, and copper allowed foreign investors and Chilean capitalists to accumulate incredible wealth. It also allowed Chilean politicians and governments to avoid fundamental political and institutional issues well into the twentieth century, as they could depend upon revenues from the desert to finance public service and projects instead of devising rational and equitable systems of internal taxation and public finance.

While the desert was yielding wealth to foreign investors and a Chilean elite in the nineteenth and the early twentieth century, its ports, rail lines, and mining camps were the principal battleground of class struggle for Chile's emergent proletariat. Both the wealth of the desert and the experience of working-class organization and struggle came south to influence the rest of Chile. Nitrate revenues and the earnings from copper financed the public sector of the Chilean economy, providing funds for public works and government services. Peasant workers returning south with the new experience of class organization, strikes, blacklists, and sometimes massacres by police or military, brought a new consciousness to the wheat fields of the frontier or the grape harvest of the central valley. Union organizers in the north became national leaders of the Chilean working classes and spread their message from the deserts to the centers of economic and political power in the cities and countryside of the "real" Chile to the south.

Even with the decline of the nitrate industry after World War I, and the depression of the 1930s, the minerals (especially copper), and byproducts such as molybdenum) of the *norte grande* still constituted the principal source of foreign exchange for the Chilean economy. Most of the country's copper came from the *norte grande*, though to the south there are significant deposits in the coastal cordillera and the lower elevations of the Andes. The largest open-pit copper mine in the world, Chuquicamata, is located inland almost due east from Tocopilla and slightly north of Calama. Until the early 1970s, when the leftist coalition government of President Salvador Allende nationalized the largest copper operations, this mine, like most of Chile's largest copper mines, was controlled by United States companies. Other important mines in the area include Exótica (closed in 1975) and Mantos Blancos. Numerous small and medium-size copper operations also contribute to the *norte grande*'s copper output and provide full or part-time employment for thousands of the region's inhabitants. Gold and silver are among the important byproducts of the copper refining process. Copper in the 1960s and 1970s accounted for 70 to 80 percent of the value of Chilean exports, making the economy highly sensitive to small changes in the international price of this commodity. In 1974-77 drastic declines in copper prices played a significant role in exacerbating the substantial economic depression of 1974 to 1976 in the first years of the military government headed by General Augusto Pinochet.

Economic recovery from 1977 to 1980 brought expansion of copper production to over one million tons in the early 1980s. At the same time, however, a new emphasis on exports of fruit, fish products, wood and paper products, and other non-traditional Chilean exports reduced the relative share of the value of copper exports ($1.6 billion to $2 billion in the early and mid-1980s) to approximately 50 percent of the value of all Chilean exports. The Chilean National Copper Corporation, CODELCO, the largest copper company in the world in the 1980s, controlled most of the large copper mines, called the *gran minería*, including Chuquicamata and El Salvador in the north, as well as El Teniente and Andina to the south. CODELCO accounted for some 80 percent of the country's production. In the years after 1974, liberalized foreign investment legislation and new mining laws allowed millions of dollars of new foreign investment in the copper sector and in other mining operations. This portended the evolution of the private *gran minería* alongside the state-controlled mining firms.

The extensive coastline of the *norte grande* makes fishing and fish-related industries of great potential importance. In the early 1960s fishmeal production rapidly expanded, only to decline after 1965 as the *anchovetas*, the small fish whose processing induced large investments in plants at Iquique and Arica, seemed to disappear. Renewed emphasis on the fishing industry in the mid 1970s brought dramatic results. Between 1975 and 1983 the fish and shellfish catch more than tripled, reaching some 4 million tons. After 1980, Chile passed Peru as the world's leading producer of fishmeal and fish oil. More than 80 percent of this production came from the northern coast, with the port of Iquique concentrating some 60 percent of the catch. The Chilean government claimed that Iquique had become the largest fishing port in the world in terms of volume handled. Impressive expansion in fish product exports contributed significantly to the increasingly diversified composition of Chilean exports and, even with declines in prices for fishmeal, accounted for over 450 million dollars

TABLE 1. EXPORTS OF GOODS BY ECONOMIC SECTOR, 1980-84
(MILLIONS OF DOLLARS)

	1980	1981	1982	1983	1984
Total	4,670.7	3,906.3	3,709.5	3,835.5	3,657.2
Mining	2,771.9	2,261.3	2,155.8	2,296.6	1,982.5
Copper	2,152.5	1,714.9	1,731.4	1,835.7	1,586.6
Iron	157.6	161.9	158.2	112.0	110.6
Nitrate and Iodine	89.2	82.9	74.6	83.7	74.3
Molybdenum	129.3	106.7	—	0.4	38.1
Silver (metallic)	120.0	82.0	81.5	114.4	87.2
Other Mineral Products	123.3	112.9	110.1	150.4	85.7
Agricultural (includes fresh fruit, vegetables, flowers and seeds)	244.3	268.0	278.1	253.7	345.6
Animal Products	36.9	29.1	33.5	26.4	29.1
Forestry	1.6	2.1	2.2	2.3	1.6
Fishing	57.1	66.2	61.1	45.1	51.8
Industrial*	1,558.9	1,279.6	1,178.8	1,211.4	1,246.6

* Includes fishmeal, processed and canned fish, fruit, wine, wood products, paper and cellulose, chemicals, elaborated minerals).

(Source: INE: *Compendio Estadístico*, 1985, pp. 171-72.)

in export sales in 1985. Other efforts to industrialize the *norte grande* included installation of vehicle assembly plants in Arica, expansion of copper refineries, smelters, and other mineral-related industries, and the processing of agricultural commodities. Above all, however, the *norte grande* remains a copper-mining region which, in the words of ex-President Salvador Allende, provides the "salary of Chile."

South of the *norte grande*, part of the province of Atacama, Coquimbo, and part of Aconcagua form a transition from desert to steppes and then to the fertile central valley. Here, in the *norte chico*, the desert gives way to scrub and brush vegetation which increases toward the south. The transitional character of this region is well illustrated by the average rainfall for selected stations from Arica in the *norte grande* to Quillota at the southern margin of the *norte chico*. Average annual rainfall increases from 1 to 2 millimeters (mm) in Arica or Iquique to 28 mm at Copiapó. It is 65 mm at

Vallenar and 133 mm in La Serena. Copiapó and the surrounding region are a transition between the arid desert and the semi-arid *norte chico*. At the Aconcagua Valley around Quillota, where average annual rainfall exceeds 400 mm, there is another transition to the temperate climate of central Chile (see Map 3).

Once called the "region of ten thousand mines," the *norte chico*, like the desert to the north, contains great mineral wealth. In 1811 silver discovered near Vallenar, inland from Huasco, led to the opening of some 150 mines. From 1830 to 1850 mining activity in the region reached a peak with new silver strikes at Chañarcillo, south of Copiapó. Production continued here until the 1890s. In this region, in July 1851, Chile inaugurated one of the first three railroads in South America, to transfer ore from the inland mines to the port at Caldera.

While not as large as the Chuquicamata deposits, copper from Potrerillos and then El Salvador has contributed significantly to Chilean copper production. The smelter at Paipote, just south of Copiapó, serves what is called the small and medium copper sector, which gives employment to thousands of Chileans though it accounts for only 15 to 20 percent of total copper production (see Map 6).

In the *norte chico*, unlike the *norte grande*, a number of rivers cross the otherwise arid region, making possible important agricultural activities and the existence of a number of important interior urban concentrations. Still, this region contains only 3 percent of Chile's arable land. During the colonial period, tiny coastal settlements served as collection points for gold or silver brought down from the cordillera and the inland valleys for shipment to Lima and Spain. English, French, and Dutch buccaneers repeatedly menaced these towns and occasionally sacked them, terrorizing their inhabitants.

Initially agriculture in the *norte chico* met the needs of a limited local market and of the workers in nearby mines. Only later did agriculture expand to supply wheat, specialty crops, and fruits to southern and foreign markets. Always, however, the interdependence of agriculture and mining persisted and has dominated the economy of the *norte chico* to the present.

Like the *norte grande*, although to a lesser extent, the *norte chico* has played a disproportionate role in shaping the development of Chilean labor movement and working-class organizations while at the same time exporting its products to support the Chilean economy. Owing to the tendency of many rural laborers and peasants in this region to work alternately in agriculture and mining, depending upon

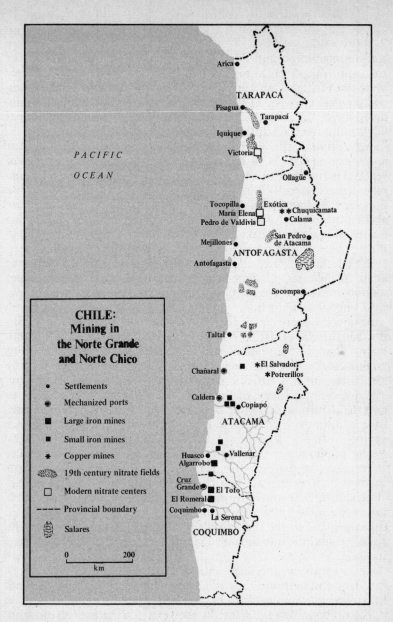

MAP 6: Chile: Mining in the *Norte Grande* and the *Norte Chico*
(Source: Harold Blakemore, "Chile" in *Latin America: Geographical Perspectives*,
Metheun & Co. Ltd., London, 1971.)

23

weather conditions and access to cultivable land, the militancy of the mine workers spread to the rural regions. In the valley of Choapa, southeast of Illapel, and in much of Aconcagua, the natural ecology and political economy of the region forged a rural working-class militancy in the early twentieth century; it spread to the rest of rural Chile only after the 1930s.

Agriculture in the *norte chico* combines pastoral activities (goats and sheep especially) in the cordillera with intensive cultivation of vegetables and fruit like tomatoes and melons. These products command excellent prices in urban centers, particularly Santiago, because they arrive before the harvests in the central valley. Cereal crops are also cultivated, but the region's susceptibility to periodic droughts makes all agriculture risky. Experiments with drought-resistant pastures in recent years have given good results in some areas for sheep and goat forage. After the mid-1960s expanded plantings of fruit orchards increased production of apricots, peaches, avocados, and walnuts in selected area of Coquimbo to complement chirimoya, papaya, and olive production.

Also in the *norte chico*, especially Coquimbo, there prevails a distinctive pattern of partially communal land tenure called *comunidades*. Many of the *comunidades* originated in colonial times with mining concessions. Depletion of minerals or failure to strike pay dirt turned the laborers' attention to agriculture and animal husbandry. Today the limited land of the *comunidades* forces young adults to migrate in search of better opportunities. Thus the *comunidades* have a disproportionate number of the very young and of older adults.

The *comunidades* typically contain large extensions of dry, hilly or cordillera land which the members, called *comuneros*, use as a common pasture. In addition, the *comuneros* have small amounts of permanently or seasonally irrigated land divided into parcels which they work individually. Wheat, barley, potatoes, corn, and beans are cultivated, and in the higher valleys (Limarí, Hurtado, Rio Grande, Rapel) fruits and vineyards play an important part in the *comunero* economy.

Goats constitute the main animal resource, providing dairy products, hides, and meat to the *comuneros* along with some cash income. Intensified goat husbandry has produced significant erosion of soils in the common pasture lands. In the years 1968-71 serious droughts in this region reduced goat herds by more than 75 percent and drastically decreased yields of wheat, thereby impoverishing the region's rural population. Since in all of Coquimbo and Aconcagua there are little more than 100,000 hectares of irrigable land, agriculture in and out of the *comunidades* remains at the mercy of variations in annual rainfall. Irrigation, where practiced, requires heavy investments in water works and dams. The average *comunero* family in Coquimbo (of whose area *comunidades* occupy about 17 percent) in the early 1970s had access to nearly 60 hectares of dry land and only 1/5 hectare of irrigated land.

As in the rest of Chile before 1964, large rural estates called *haciendas* or *fundos* controlled most of the region's agricultural land outside the *comunidades*. These estates usually controlled access to irrigation water and competed with the *comunidades* or with the smallholders for this scarce resource. In most cases the *comuneros* or other smallholders obtained only the water not used by the haciendas, which made small-scale agriculture even more precarious and difficult. Agrarian reforms after 1964 altered the distribution of land and water rights, but the counterreforms under way in the mid-1970s left unclear the future of both the *comunidades* and the agrarian reform cooperatives on the large estates expropriated from 1964 to 1973.

The circumstances of the small and medium-size mining operations and of agriculture in the *norte chico* make stable employment a considerable problem for its population. In the dry years *comuneros* seek work in the nitrate fields, the gold, copper, or iron mines in order to support their families who remain on the land. The variety of minerals in the *norte chico* has allowed small enterprises and individual miners to develop beside the giant firms that historically have dominated the nitrate and copper industries. Numerous small and medium-size firms participate in mining activities supported in part with credit and technical assistance from the Empresa Nacional de Minería (ENAMI).

ENAMI, a public enterprise established in 1960, has served the small and medium mine sector by purchasing, smelting, refining, and marketing the ore mined by thousands of small operators. In addition to its role in the copper economy, ENAMI accounted for approximately 78 percent of the value of Chile's growing gold exports in the 1980s. However, increased foreign investment in this sector, for example, the St. Joe Minerals Corporation's investments at the El Indio and Tambo mines and processing plants (at 4200 meters elevation in the *cordillera* east of La Serena) portended a relatively more important role for industrial mining in relation to the previous dominance of artisanal and medium-size mining operations. In 1985 only Brazil, of all the Latin American nations, exceeded Chile's gold output of 18 metric tons, and Chile ranked among the top ten gold producers in the world.

Despite their poverty, the desperate hope of striking it rich holds many peasant-prospectors in the region. From the exploitation of iron, however, the small miners are essentially excluded. Large foreign interests (Bethlehem Steel) have dominated ore production beginning in 1921 at El Tofo, 68 kilometers north of La Serena, and then, when the ore at El Tofo was practically depleted in the early 1960s, at El Romeral, also to the north of La Serena some 25 kilometers. From these sites the ore is sent south to the steel mill at Huachipato near Concepción for processing or is exported. Other centers of iron production include Cerro Imán, southeast of Caldera and Algarrobo, some 40 kilometers southwest of Vallenar (see map 6). The value and quality of iron exports increased significantly from the mid-1970s until 1981 when it reached over $160 million; international recession reduced this to around $100 million from 1984 to 1986. In the 1980s Japan became a principal market for Chilean iron exports.

Apart from processing of agricultural commodities, pisco* production, fruit drying and canning, fishing, and mining, the *norte chico* lacks significant industrial establishments. Periodic droughts and the limited agricultural resources of the region, notwithstanding some increase in irrigation and vineyard as well as fruit production near Copiapó in the 1980s, make rural poverty endemic. This leaves many inhabitants dependent for survival upon part-time mining endeavors, government make-work projects, and food distribution for survival. Extremely large investments in irrigation, crop development, and agricultural extension are necessary before the *norte chico* can overcome the obstacles to economic development imposed by nature.

At the southern extremity of Aconcagua province, the fertile region known as the "Vale of Chile" marks the northern boundary of Chile's heartland (Map 3). The central valley of Chile contains some 70 percent of Chile's population, provides more than 70 percent of industrial employment, and even accounts for 20 percent of copper production from mines in Santiago, Valparaíso, and especially O'Higgins province. Within a 100-mile radius of Santiago lives more than 50 percent of Chile's population. At its widest the central valley measures some 45 miles between the Andes and the coastal mountains or the sea, and only along the Bío Bío River at its southernmost boundary does the flat valley floor extend all the way to the Pacific.

* A clear South American brandy made out of grapes.

Valparaíso, the major port in the region, is the primary doorway for imports to the Santiago market. To the south, Chile possesses only two other major ports—Talcahuano (Concepción) and Valdivia.

The Chilean central valley has a mediterranean climate with rainfall increasing gradually toward the south. The climate and the fertility of the soil, reminiscent of central California, are ideal for intensive truck farming, orchards, and vineyards in addition to cereal crops and livestock. With the advantage of a harvest season that occurs during Europe's and North America's winter months, the central valley offers Chile a potential source of foreign exchange through export of high-quality fruits, vegetables, wines, dairy products, and specialty crops.

Despite this potential, extensive wheat cultivation and cattle operations, along with vineyards located in a relatively small number of large estates, have dominated the valley's agricultural history. Into the mid-1960s only a minority of these estates had moved to more modern agricultural practices, making the backwardness of Chilean agriculture a critical obstacle to economic development. After 1964 massive agrarian reform programs disrupted traditional agricultural and land tenure patterns by creating agrarian cooperatives operated by *campesinos* under the not always benevolent tutelage of government administrators. After the military coup of 1973, former owners recovered many of the large farms (perhaps 30 percent of those expropriated from 1964 to 1973), and the new government made efforts to break up the production cooperatives into individual family farms.

This resulted in the creation of some 35,000 to 40,000 *unidades agrícolas familiares* (UAF) of approximately ten basic irrigated hectares (BIH)—an amount of land equivalent to ten irrigated hectares in the central valley which supposedly would provide a family with reasonable income and employment opportunity. More than half of the residents of the farms in the reformed sector of agriculture failed to receive land allotments under the military government's scheme. As a result the policies created a group of over 35,000 landless rural workers who resorted to occasional, seasonal, and migratory labor in agriculture, artisanship, or movement to towns and cities in order to survive. Others sought shelter in small makeshift settlements (*villorrios*) which sprang up in the countryside. At the same time a new group of relatively prosperous small- and medium-size commercial farms emerged both as a result of the creation of the UAF sector and as a consequence of restitution or partial restitution of farms that the government determined had been illegally expropriated from 1970 to 1973. Auctions of land from the reformed sector still controlled by the land reform agency, CORA (before its abolition in 1978), added additional units to the small and medium farm sector.

The policies of the military government emphasized creation of an active land market to encourage efficient utilization of farm land. These policies, accompanied by the overall focus on export promotion and on opening the Chilean economy to international trade, altered old patterns of production and discouraged reconstitution of the archaic *hacienda* system. Output of traditional agricultural crops such as wheat, sugar beets, potatoes, corn, oats, and barley grew slowly or declined, though production of some food crops, such as beans and rice, experienced notable increases. Fruits, vegetables, flowers (and lumber products from the south-central and southern regions), and other commodities previously of relatively little importance were responsible for huge increases in Chilean agricultural exports. In 1986 Chile satisfied 27.5 percent of total consumption of table grapes in the United States, and exports of grapes, apples, nectarines, plums, pears, and peaches, along with other assorted fruits and vegetables, amounted to over 58 million boxes.

The dynamism in speciality crop and timber exports to Europe, Japan, Korea, other Latin American countries, and the United States was accompanied by a trend toward importation of more and more of the basic foodstuffs consumed internally—including as much as 40 percent of the country's wheat requirements in the early 1980s. Justifying this trend and the government policies that encouraged it, an ex-Minister of Agriculture noted in 1983 that fruit production from only 34,000 hectares would produce enough foreign exchange to purchase more than one million tons of wheat. To produce this same wheat in Chile would have required more than 200,000 hectares of agricultural land. Nevertheless, under pressure of international recession, growing indebtedness, and declines in foreign exchange earnings, the military government reversed policy by strengthening price supports and introducing barely disguised import barriers to protect local agricultural producers. In the 1985-86 crop year, after five years of steep declines in production, wheat output again reached some 800,000 tons. According to government sources this covered 90 percent of domestic consumption.

With cropping patterns and land values highly responsive to international demand and radical shifts in domestic agricultural policies, the Chilean countryside experienced considerable economic and social instability in the years after 1973. Agro-industrial firms linked to urban capital and transnational firms and markets increased in importance at the same time that small- and medium-size farm units also played a more significant role in the rural sector. Seasonal labor requirements in the production of fruit, vegetables, and in the vineyards induced unprecedented levels of labor mobility and social dislocation. With the gradual disappearance of the old pattern of resident rural labor on the traditional haciendas and continuing rural-urban migration (over 80 percent of Chile's population was considered urban in the mid-1980s), it appeared that social, economic, and political domination of the central valley by the large traditional agricultural estates had finally ended.

The large rural estates in Chile's central valley have influenced much more than agricultural production. Historically, they constituted the single most important political and social institution in Chile. Their owners belonged to a small social elite that has controlled most of Chile's best agricultural land as well as its political institutions. As late as 1930, from 60 to 75 percent of Chile's rural population resided on the haciendas. The tremendous power exercised by landowners or proprietors over the rural labor force made each rural estate a quasi-political unit. The landowner controlled access to land, housing, and employment. The resident rural laborer who disobeyed the landlord's orders risked being fined, whipped, dispossessed, or otherwise punished. In the mid-twentieth century the service-tenant, or *inquilino*, worked the landlord's land in exchange for access to perhaps half an acre or an acre of land, a house and garden plot, and various in-kind payments or perquisites, such as food rations, firewood, or permission to graze a designated number of animals on the *fundo*'s pasture.

After adoption of minimum wage legislation for agriculture in 1953, landowners theoretically paid these workers a minimum wage established by the government, provided minimally decent housing, and obeyed a number of labor laws intended to protect the workers. In practice, landowners successfully ignored or evaded the minimum wage legislation as they had previously evaded other labor laws; workers who complained or registered protests with the Labor Department faced reprisals or dismissals. In 1952 an inspector of the Chilean Labor Department reported:

> In the *fundo* Las Pataguas, owned by the Archbishop of Santiago but rented to Mr. Dario Pavez, the administrator Ramiro Ramírez, aided by the foreman [*mayordomo*], applied about 100 lashes to the worker [*voluntario*], Roberto González. The same administrator has also whipped other workers [four named] and for this has been nicknamed "The Lash" [*El Azotador*]. In fundo

La Carlina, owned by Carlos Aspillaga Sotomayor, and administered by Vicente Salazar, if workers ask for their social security
booklets so they can go to the health service, they are insulted
and offered a kick in the ass. . . .

Families who had lived for generations on a *fundo* could be fired
and evicted at the landowner's whim, with no compensation for improvements they had made to their residence or to the land by way
of fences, fruit trees, or outbuildings.

The dependence of the central valley's agriculture upon a rigidly
stratified social system and the economically inefficient *fundos* permeated Chilean society and made relations between the upper classes
and working classes authoritarian, patronizing, and exploitative. This
situation prevailed after 1932 as the Chilean political system apparently developed into a functioning formal democracy. The inherent
contradictions between a truly democratic political and economic
system and maintenance of the centuries-old hacienda system generated intense political conflict in Chile in the years 1964-73, leading
to profound agrarian reforms and then to renewed, if modified, subjugation of the rural working classes after 1973.

It is difficult to understand the pervasive influence of the haciendas
of the central valley on Chile's politics, economy, and social relations
unless one has witnessed the ritual subservience of the campesino
listening to his landlord's orders—the bowed head, eyes toward the
ground, hat held over the genital area—all symbolic admissions of
the huge gap separating the hacendado from "his" workers. It is also
difficult to understand the deceptive calm of rural Chile after 1973
unless one has witnessed the joy and energy of liberation expressed
by campesinos from 1964 to 1973. In those years the hacienda system
seemed destined for the scrapheap of Chilean history, and the future
of Chilean agriculture appeared tied to thousands of newly formed
peasant organizations. Then, in a manner typical of Chilean history,
the struggle for social change and justice confronted the reality of
naked force defending the interests of the landowners and their allies.
While this defeat of the campesinos left unclear the future structure
of central valley agriculture, it reconfirmed and perpetuated the essential character of the struggle for the land and subjugation of the
labor force initiated in 1535 by the Spanish conquistadors against the
native Chilean peoples.

Lack of opportunities in the countryside, and the stifling hacienda
system in the central valley in the mid-nineteenth century, pushed

rural workers to northern mining camps, railroad construction gangs, and the cities in search of employment and a better life. The rural to urban trend has continued throughout the twentieth century. By the mid 1980s the Santiago metropolitan region accounted for approximately 40 percent of Chile's population, while over 75 percent of all Chileans lived in cities with over 20,000 inhabitants—most of these in the central valley (see Table 2).

Not only have agriculture and the hacienda system made the central valley the political, economic, and social heartland of Chile, but historically, industrial activities (other than the mines) have been concentrated in Santiago, Valparaíso, and Concepción. Modern industry in Chile resulted largely from import-substitution through World War II, but later expanded considerably into secondary products, heavy industrial products, and capital goods. In the mid 1950s over 70 percent of all manufacturing centered in Santiago (51%) and Valparaíso (20%). Since that time planned decentralization has resulted in the emergence of a major steel and petrochemical complex in Concepción-Talcahuano, at the southern extreme of the central valley. Lumber industries, manufacturing based on processing of agricultural products, textile firms in southern Chile, and limited industrialization in the north, typically based on mineral processing, food production, or canning, complement the core industrial establishments of the central region.

Industrialization has not been able to provide employment for all of the thousands of migrants to the urban areas. Squatter settlements, called *callampas* ("mushroom" settlements) or *campamentos*, surround the major cities of the central valley and house large numbers of Chile's urban poor in dwellings constructed of tin, cardboard, and wood, shelters which barely protect their inhabitants from the whims of nature. These settlements often lack such urban services as electricity, potable water, and sewers. They constitute, in this respect, a massive urban village rather than an integrated part of an urban community. As more and more Chileans move to the cities of the central valley, the strains of hyper-urbanization increase, presenting a problem yet to be solved by any Chilean national government.

Indeed, the insistence of the military government after 1974 upon dismantling the system of protective tariffs and other subsidies that supported industrialization in Chile from 1930 onwards, led to numerous bankruptcies in the manufacturing sector, plant closings, and burgeoning levels of unemployment. Cutbacks in government investments in housing and public services further exacerbated the grim

TABLE 2. ESTIMATED POPULATION OF MAJOR CITIES
AND METROPOLITAN AREAS, DECEMBER 1985

City	Estimated Population
Santiago (metropolitan area)	4,364,497
Concepción	280,713
Valparaíso	273,213
Viña del Mar	261,118
Talcahuano	217,660
Antofagasta	203,067
Temuco	168,120
Arica	158,422
Rancagua	157,209
Talca	137,621
San Bernardo	136,224
Chillán	126,531
Iquique	127,491
Puente Alto	126,297
Punta Arenas	107,064
Valdivia	104,910
Osorno	101,948
Quilpué	94,080
La Serena	89,998
Calama	90,056
Puerto Montt	85,058
Los Angeles	76,276
Copiapó	75,791
Coquimbo	70,461
Coronel	70,157
Curicó	65,357
San Antonio	65,027
Villa Alemana	61,365
Linares	48,467
Lota	46,110
Ovalle	46,066
Quillota	45,202
Peñaflor	42,901
La Calera	40,797
Vallenar	39,887
Melipilla	38,352
Los Andes	37,599
Tomé	35,258

Source: INE, *Compendio Estadístico*, 1985.

conditions of the urban poor. The rings of misery constituted by the shanties and *poblaciones* of Santiago swelled with the ranks of the unemployed.

At the Bío Bío River the central valley gives way to the frontier region (see Map 3), marked by year-round rainfall. Instead of the central valley's irrigated fields on alluvial fans sloping toward the sea, the cereal and pasture lands of the frontier region still bear the scars of forest clearing, which makes cultivation possible. From Arauco to Cautín, the overgrazed, overutilized land of the Mapuche Indians and other smallholders present a red-brown image of eroded soil on the increasingly denuded coastal mountains and the valley floor. To the east the Andes continue to dominate but are not as high as they are north of the Bío Bío River. The climate in this region is comparable with the Pacific Northwest of the United States, with stormy wet winters and cool, less damp summers. The region takes its name from the historical role it played in the struggle between the Spanish invaders and the indigenous Indian population. Until late in the nineteenth century the Bío Bío River marked the limits of Spanish and then Chilean control (see Chapter 2). In a social and economic sense it also remained a frontier region with very limited urban population, agricultural production or industry into the late nineteenth century.

Concepción dominated the development of the frontier provinces from the time of the conquest, serving first as the main base of the frontier garrison and later as the Bío Bío region's commercial center. Livestock and cereal production, which supplied the raw materials for mills and other processing industries, paced economic development. Mining activities, principally coal, also played a role, and the mines around Lota remain in the 1980s important economically.

Agriculture in the frontier region depends much less on irrigation than is the case in the central valley of Chile with its Mediterranean climate. Farms in the frontier provinces accounted for around 40 percent of Chile's wheat production in the mid-1980s—a relative increase since the 1970s—attributable in part to a 40 to 50 percent decline in national wheat output in the period 1976-77/1982-83. The region also contributed some 35 to 40 percent of the country's cattle output, while an often backward timber industry provides seasonal employment for numerous rural workers and raw material for Chile's expanding paper and cellulose manufacturers in the region around the Arauco, La Laja, Nacimiento triangle. Expanded hydroelectric capacity installed in the *cordillera* near Lake La Laja to the east of Los Angeles, including plants at El Toro, El Abanico, and the newer facility slightly to the west at Antuco, supported the agro-industrial complex of the region and exported power to the central valley.

Fishing also contributes significantly to the regional economy. The port at Talcahuano is the most important in the region, accounting for around 8 to 10 percent of the country's fish catch and also approximately 10 percent of the fishmeal exported by Chile in the 1980s. From 1980 to 1987 Chile became the world's leading exporter of fishmeal products. The fishing industry of the Concepción-Talcahuano area also provided much of the fresh fish for the central valley and the Santiago metropolitan area.

Also found in the frontier provinces are the remaining communal landholdings (*reducciones*) of the Araucanian (Mapuche) Indians. Deprived of much of their land by the Spanish conquest, and further despoiled by speculators and politicians in the nineteenth century, many Mapuche continue to eke out a livelihood through pastoral, agricultural, and artisan activities. Estimates of the number of Mapuche in the reducciones vary considerably, but there are probably between 300,000 and 500,000. Some reducciones are located in Valdivia, but most are in the provinces of Bío Bío, Arauco, Malleco, and Cautín—the last alone accounts for almost 200,000 Mapuche. In Cautín the reducciones contain some 343,000 hectares, accounting for 22 percent of the agricultural land in the province, and 86 percent of all agricultural units.

The Mapuche on the *reducciones*—or sometimes "ex-reducciones," or *comunidades* without legal title—are family groups that exploit the land, both in common and on individual parcels. Data from an investigation carried out in 1966 by the Dirección de Asuntos Indígenas on 493 *reducciones* indicated that the average reducción amounted to 290 hectares with a population of 83 persons. Economic activity in the reducciones includes fishing and seaweed collection along the coast, lumbering, charcoal making, and extensive production of pigs, sheep, chickens, and cattle, as well as crops. Household manufactures include basketmaking, weaving, and metal working.

The Mapuche are a poor people subjugated by outsiders after a four-century struggle to maintain their independence. The bravery of the Mapuche, celebrated in Alonso de Ercilla's epic poem *La Araucana*, may afford a source of national pride for educated Chileans, but the persisting poverty of these Indians seems to have little effect on the national conscience. Chileans adore Indian heroes such as Lautaro and Caupolicán who defeated the conquistadors but, like their North American counterparts, ignore the present-day plight of the Mapuche. One study of the Mapuche in the 1970s concluded: "The Mapuche works his depleted lands and waits. For a long time he has lived . . . in a world not under his control. He has lost his land. . . . He lives exploited, submerged in poverty." From 1965 to 1973 agrarian reform programs mobilized many Mapuche for land occupations or "recuperations." After 1973 the return of land to former owners and repression of organized rural militancy have restored "calm" to the region, but at the cost of the assassinations of Mapuche leaders and the deaths of Indian farmers.

As part of its program to modernize Chilean agriculture and create a national land market, the military government implemented a new law in 1979 promoting subdivision of the Mapuche reservations. At the time this decree-law took effect the government estimated that some 58,000 Indian families controlled 2066 "properties" consisting of a total of 375,500 hectares. To encourage subdivision the government offered property tax exemptions of up to twenty years; by the end of 1982 the government reported that more than 42,000 Mapuches had requested "regularization" of their land titles, and that more than 30,000 had already received title to individual parcels. Systematic studies of the impact of this legislation on the Indian communities remain to be completed, but initial indications suggest that intracommunity conflict and social dislocation have resulted, along with intensified outmigration to towns and urban centers. Many of the Indians work as day laborers on neighboring farms or seasonal hands during peak agricultural periods. Beyond the economic consequences of the subdivision law, however, parcelization of the Indian reducciones threatened the cultural foundations of the Mapuche community, based as it was on kinship relations and communal land-tenure patterns. Indicative of the plight of these Indian peoples was the title of a revealing study of the Mapuche published in 1983: "Poverty and Subsistence in Contemporary Mapuche Society."

Often little better off than the Mapuche, thousands of campesinos work their small parcels throughout the frontier provinces, barely scratching out a subsistence from depleted soil. During the winter rains long periods of relative idleness are spent around wood-burning stoves in small houses built from the native trees of the region. Larger farms also exist, but they lack the large resident populations characteristic of the central valley.

While most of the frontier region is rural and agricultural, more than 50 percent of the population resides in urban places—with Concepción-Talcahuano and the capital of Cautín province, Temuco, being the most important. Significant industrial activities of the region include Chile's steel industry at Huachipato, paper and cellulose manufacture, textiles, coal mines, petrochemicals, and processing of lumber, flour, beet sugar, matches, cooking oil, cheese, and butter. The coal mined in Arauco and Concepción is of poor quality, necessitating its mixture with imported coal for use in the steel complex. Like the nitrate fields earlier, in the twentieth century the coal mines have been the scene of many labor conflicts that forged working-class consciousness among the Chilean proletariat. They also are the setting for Chilean author Baldomiro Lillo's stories (*Subterra*, 1904) of social protest, describing the lives and suffering of the coal miners.

The lake region—the provinces of Valdivia, Osorno, and Llan-quihue—begins south of the Toltén River and is an extension of the frontier provinces (Map 4). Storminess increases as one moves south and is greater, latitude for latitude, in Chile than in North America. Valdivia (lat. 39° 48′ S) receives almost three times the annual rainfall of Tacoma, Washington. Founded by Pedro de Valdivia in 1552, the city of Valdivia witnessed one of the most memorable amphibious military operations in South American history when, in 1820, Lord Cochrane led a seemingly suicidal assault against Spanish fortifications to capture the port for the independence movement.

Renowned for its natural beauty, the lake region contains numerous snow-capped volcanoes; the tourists it draws supplement agricultural activities. Valuable natural hardwood forests as well as plantations of Monterey pines are the basis for a developing timber industry. Depletion of the natural forests, however, meant that by 1965 some 40 percent of all lumber came from the pine plantations. Dairy farms, beef cattle, and other livestock dominate the agrarian economy, though cereals and diversified small-scale farming also contribute. Together with the frontier provinces the lake region supplies over half of the country's cereal production, over 90 percent of the oats, and 50 percent of the potatoes.

Valdivia, Osorno, and Puerto Montt are the most important urban centers in this region, where almost half of the population still lives in the rural sector. Most of the industries, like that in the frontier provinces, depend upon agrarian production—lumber, wood products, flour mills, textiles, canneries, beer, beet sugar, leather products—or else upon the harvest of the sea. From the remaining native forests and pine plantations of the region comes high quality lumber, while the sea yields a variety of fish and shellfish, thereby supporting a number of canneries and processing plants in Puerto Montt, Calbuco, Quellón (in Chiloé), and Valdivia.

Many industries owe their existence to the influence of German immigrants enticed to Chile in the mid-nineteenth century. When the newly formed Society for Industrial Development (Sociedad de Fomento Fabril, 1883) published a preliminary list of industries in Valdivia and Osorno in 1884, all the breweries, tanneries, brick factories, bakeries, machine shops, furniture manufacturers, and mills (except one) belonged to persons with non-Spanish (mostly German) surnames. While this was the principal region of Chile in which the national government actively intervened to promote colonization in the nineteenth century, the relatively small number of immigrants (perhaps 3000) heavily influenced the economic and cultural development of the provinces from Cautín south, and especially Osorno, Valdivia, and Llanquihue. For example, in 1902 a list of the rural estates in the commune of Valdivia valued at over 40,000 pesos contained not a single Spanish surname. The descendants of these immigrants who cleared dense forest land and prospered through their toil and intellect are still a dominant force in the economy of the lake region.

The territory south from the Gulf of Reloncaví, comprising almost a third of continental Chile, contains no more than 3 percent of the nation's population. This is a region of cold driving winds, great storminess and rainfall, and rough seas. In places rainfall exceeds 200 inches a year. Between Puerto Montt and about latitude 44° S the main structural features of central Chile continue—though the coastal mountain range now runs partly beneath the sea or becomes a chain of forested islands. The snowfall in the eastern cordillera descends to only 2300 feet above sea level at Tierra del Fuego.

The island of Chiloé (lat. 42° S), in a geographical position similar to Vancouver Island in North America, is a densely forested territory where smallholders and a small number of indigenous peoples engage in subsistence agriculture, sheep raising, lumbering, fishing, and potato cultivation. Chiloé makes no great economic contribution to the national economy. Its main towns are Ancud and Castro.

Aisén province is made up of canals, lakes, islands, and mountains, though grasslands and plains support thousands of sheep. Aysén, along with Magallanes, is Chile's last frontier. Punta Arenas, located on the Strait of Magellan, is Chile's most southerly city (pop. 107,000 [1985]). It supports a number of industries based on the thousands of sheep raised on the Patagonian plains. Oil wells and natural gas exploration have increased the economic importance of Magallanes in recent years. Most of the petroleum is shipped to Concón, near Valparaíso, or to Concepción for refining, though a topping plant at Manantiales supplies Magallanes with gasoline, kerosene, and diesel fuel.

In the early 1980s oil wells in the Strait of Magellan accounted for over 70 percent of total output. New oil production in the years after 1980, combined with expanded coal production, made possible by exploration and investment by foreign firms, allowed Chile to cover approximately 50 percent of its hydrocarbon requirements. Development of new coal mines in the Peckett deposits, 36 miles northeast of Punta Arenas, promised to alleviate to some degree Chile's deficit of fossil fuels, with output destined to a great extent for the CODELCO thermoelectric plant at Tocopilla. Increased production and exports of natural gas along with large-scale foreign investment in the Cape Horn Methanol plant near Punta Arenas also gave increasing importance to Magallanes in the national economy. Nevertheless, Chile still imported annually between $500 million and $980 million worth of fuel—the equivalent in value to 25 to 40 percent of the value of copper exports (1980-85).

The vast majority of Chileans descend from the European invaders of the sixteenth and seventeenth centuries and the Indian peoples resident in Chile at the time of Spanish conquest. Africans and non-Iberian Europeans contributed much less to the formation of the Chilean nationality. As elsewhere in Spanish America, Spanish racism and social prejudices have generally reserved the highest social and political positions for those who claimed "purity of blood" (*limpieza de sangre*), thereby creating caste-class stratifications that distinguished Spaniards from "white" mestizos, "Indian" mestizos, Indians, blacks, mulattoes, and *zambos* (offspring of Indian and black). From generation to generation stratification could become quite complex within the *castas* (racially mixed peoples), but customs and legal practices sought to ensure the "integrity" of the ruling class, especially after the massive miscegenation of the sixteenth and seventeenth centuries.

Legal suits filed in the late eighteenth century by family members who feared that a proposed marriage might put a stain on the family honor reveal the fundamental racial and social biases of colonial society. Royal officials were asked to prohibit marriages on the legal grounds of "inequality of castes." An irate mother could "charge" a would-be son-in-law with being the grandson and great-grandson of blacks, "mulatto-colored," or "a pure mulatto" with "obviously Negro hair." While official Spanish policy declared that "being an Indian is not a rational or just motive for denial of parental consent," Chilean colonists looked with disfavor upon "staining the family honor" with marriage to Indians or "Indian mestizos." But these attitudes no more prevented widespread concubinage and miscegenation in the later colonial period than they had in the formation of Chilean nationality in the *mestizaje* of the first century and a half of conquest.

While Chilean national mythology claims descendancy from Spaniards and Araucanians, the Indian component of Chilean racial stock was somewhat more varied than this simple union of the heroic

Araucanian Indians with their European enemies. About the indigenous population in Chile at the time of the conquest much less is known than about the Indians of Mexico, Central America, and Peru. Some investigators believe all originated in a single racial stock, differentiated in customs, language, and organization over time in response to local conditions. Other researchers affirm the diversity of the indigenous groups in Chile, noting differences in language, culture, farming implements, weapons, and political organization. The nomenclature adopted to describe Indian groups often referred merely to their location—for example, *puelches* (people of the east, eastern *cordillera* down to Mendoza); *picunches* (people of the north—though those south of the *puelches* called them *picunches*). Less gradually the Spaniards came to refer to *los pencos, los quillotanos, los mapochos,* and so on, but again these names simply denote Indians of Penco, Quillota, and Mapocho.

As there are neither important archaeological sites south of Copiapó, nor a written language, nor any large territorial political units, we are unlikely to have any great clarification of the evolution of pre-Hispanic Indian cultures in Chile except in the north, where the desert has preserved artifacts and cemeteries thousands of years old. Conventional designations of major Indian groups in Chile at the time of the conquest depend upon the work of a limited number of scholars, most notably Ricardo Latcham. Latcham adopted the generic terms *Diaguitas* (valley of Copiapó to the Choapa River), Mapuche or Araucanian (Itata River to Toltén River), and *Huilliches* (south of Toltén River). In reality no such clear-cut divisions are possible since Araucanian is an independent linguistic family, and each region or tribal group in Chile apparently had only small differences of dialect. The authoritative *Handbook of South American Indians* divides the Araucanians into the following main groups: Picunche, Mapuche, Huilliche, and Cunco (west of the Andes), Pehuenche (Andean Highlands), Argentine Araucanians (east of the Andes). Present-day usage in Chile refers to the major Indian groups south of the River Itata as Araucanos or, more frequently, simply Mapuche. Estimates of the Araucanian population at the time of the Spanish conquest range from 500,000 to 1,500,000.

Prior to the arrival of the Spanish, Inca influence and tribute collection extended as far south as the Itata River or perhaps the Bío Bío River, but gradually diminished toward the south. Despite initial resistance and occasional revolts, by the mid-seventeenth century the Spaniards had pacified, enslaved, or exploited most of the Indian groups north of the Maule River, exacting tribute and recruiting military auxiliaries, as had the Incas. From the River Maule south and into what became the frontier provinces (south of the Bío Bío River), the Araucanians effectively resisted Spanish domination, as they had that of the Incas. By 1568 the Araucanians were making significant use of cavalry in battle against the Spaniards, and well before the end of the sixteenth century they had adopted Spanish firearms, swords, armor, and any other armaments they could capture. By 1600 the Indian stock of horses, estimated at over 10,000, greatly exceeded the horses available to the Spanish settlers and frontier garrisons. Though a simple people with limited handicrafts, a subsistence agriculture, and highly dispersed settlement patterns with no centralized political authority, the Araucanians developed a complex system for organizing large-scale military forces to defend their territory. Indeed, their very dispersion and lack of centralized political structure made virtually impossible either a definitive "victory" or the administration of a Spanish conquest on a scale like that of Peru.

Though they attained no definitive military victory, the Spanish did subjugate thousands of Indians to work in mines, fields, or households. In addition, many Spaniards transferred "their" Indians (Huarpes) from Cuyo (including the towns of present-day Mendoza, San Juan, and San Luis in Argentina) to Santiago or La Serena. Miscegenation and the gradual reduction in the number of "pacified" Indians meant that by the mid-seventeenth century *mestizos* constituted a majority of the rural population. Population data on Chile in the colonial period must be viewed with great caution since contemporary writers provided widely disparate estimates. Chilean historian Francisco Encina estimated that at the end of the seventeenth century the population of Chile, north of the Bío Bío River, consisted of 110,000 Spanish and "mestizos classified as such," 20,000 Indians and "Indian" mestizos, 15,000 blacks, mulattoes and *zambos*, and 7000 pacified Indians in Chiloé. Most Chileans lived in rural districts on the vast haciendas or encomiendas. According to the educated estimate of Chilean researcher Rolando Mellafe, as early as 1620 "white" mestizos already outnumbered European and *criollo* settlers by a ratio of some four to one.

As in the rest of Spanish America, the total population of Chile was substantially reduced due to the effects of the conquest on the native peoples. Mortality among the Spaniards was also high; at the close of the sixteenth century 20 to 25 percent of the Spanish population were killed in the Indian uprising which liquidated eight of the twelve "cities" then in existence. Disease and natural disasters, including earthquakes and floods, also contributed to the losses. Only in the mid-nineteenth century (1843) did the population of Chile (including the unconquered Indians south of the Bío Bío River) approximate what it had been in 1540—about one million! Of these, historian Luis Galdames has estimated that no more than 40 percent were of European descent and the remainder were Indian and *castas*, including several thousand Negro slaves.

From the outset the towns were the centers of European civilization in Chile, but none could really be called cities until the eighteenth century. When the colonial period ended (1810), Chile contained thirty or more so-called cities; Santiago had some 40,000 inhabitants, and the next largest town, Concepción, some 5000 to 6000. Increasingly, however, the population of Chile moved to towns and cities, so that by 1875 over 25 percent of the population could be found in "urban" places; by 1907 this had increased to 43 percent. According to official estimates in the mid-1980s, over 80 percent of all Chileans lived in urban areas.

Unlike Argentina and Brazil, Chilean population growth in the nineteenth and twentieth centuries depended little upon the waves of European immigration that also greatly changed the composition of the United States's population during these years. In 1895 only 2.9 percent of Chile's 2,687,985 inhabitants were foreign born, and

TABLE 3. ESTIMATED POPULATION OF CHILE, JUNE 30, 1985
BY RURAL AND URBAN DISTRIBUTION AND SEX, BY AGE GROUPS

Age Groups	Urban			Rural		
	Both Sexes	Men	Women	Both Sexes	Men	Women
Total	10,092,652	4,912,955	5,179,697	1,981,825	1,065,834	915,991
0 to 4 years	1,095,754	557,752	538,002	259,782	130,175	129,607
5 to 9 years	1,018,661	516,283	502,378	236,792	120,496	116,296
10 to 14 years	952,202	479,584	472,618	206,823	108,641	98,182
15 to 19 years	993,498	492,231	501,267	184,100	103,842	80,258
20 to 24 years	1,035,445	509,227	526,218	174,619	100,867	73,752
25 to 29 years	938,388	461,544	476,844	156,681	88,520	68,161
30 to 34 years	758,151	372,879	385,272	126,509	70,356	56,153
35 to 39 years	681,645	330,933	350,712	116,234	63,126	53,108
40 to 44 years	583,211	281,723	301,488	103,488	55,803	47,685
45 to 49 years	465,639	222,601	243,038	88,524	47,937	40,587
50 to 54 years	387,298	181,764	206,534	78,197	43,053	35,144
55 to 59 years	350,662	160,478	190,184	74,165	41,455	32,710
60 to 64 years	264,020	117,536	146,484	57,015	31,673	25,342
65 to 69 years	211,350	90,717	120,633	44,864	23,994	20,870
70 to 74 years	159,821	65,397	94,424	33,389	17,054	16,335
75 to 79 years	108,010	42,190	65,820	22,404	10,951	11,453
80 years & over	88,897	30,116	58,781	18,239	7,891	10,348

Source: INE, *Compendio Estadístico*, 1985.

in 1907 this had increased but to 4 percent of a total population of 3,114,755. While by the early 1900s hundreds of thousands of Italians had become agricultural laborers or tenant farmers or had settled in urban areas in Argentina, from 1889 until 1914 total net immigration to Chile reached only about 55,000. The largest foreign contingents arrived from Peru, Bolivia, and Spain. Despite their small numbers, however, European immigrants owned nearly one-third of Chile's commercial companies (1907), 20 percent of the 554 most valuable rural estates (1908), and, by 1914, 49 percent of all industrial establishments. European, Syrian, and Lebanese immigrants to Chile rarely became rural laborers or urban workers, as in Argentina, but instead formed an upper-middle-class commercial element which often intermarried with Chilean social elites.

The role of the immigrants was most apparent in the mining districts of the north, in the major cities of Antofagasta, Santiago, Valparaíso, Concepción, and Valdivia, and in the farming regions of the south, heavily influenced by Germans. The immigrants' role in Chilean urban society continued into the 1960s, when estimates indicated that three-fourths of Santiago's major industrial establishments were owned by immigrants or their offspring. Emigration to Chile, consequently, little affected the race and class stratifications that grew out of the miscegenation and politics of conquest, and only served to insert a small, heterogeneous, non-Hispanic, upper- and upper-middle-class group between the upper castes of Hispanic society and the mass of Indian, mestizo, and *casta* laborers in the fields, mines, docks, and factories.

Class and caste stratifications have also produced certain Chilean stereotypes which serve both as national symbols and pejorative epithets, particularly the *roto* and the *huaso*. The huaso is the Chilean cowboy but connotes much more. The flesh and blood huaso is a campesino on horseback or in the fields, who works from sunup to sundown, frequently barefoot or in crude sandals called *ojotas*, and wearing an apron or a flour sack around his waist. When not at work he sports a jacket inherited from his father or older brother and a well-worn hat. There is also the tourist's huaso, dressed for the rodeo in a three-colored *manta* and a sash around his waist (red, white, and blue like the Chilean flag). He rides a strong, well-kept horse which he prods with silver spurs. This is the hacendado, or his hireling, dressed in his best huaso outfit to visit the countryside at the harvest or to make sure the campesinos attend to their labors. The first huaso, the rural worker, bears the brunt of hundreds of country bumpkin jokes. The latter, the postcard huaso, typifies the historic rural basis of the wealth and power of many of Chile's leading families. Together they are the story of Chile—a national symbol which denotes hard work, sacrifice, and struggle to the campesino, and power, leisure, and privilege to the hacendado.

The *roto* is the urban counterpart of the huaso. The roto is the Chilean worker, courageous, strong, persistent, quick to take advantage of a favorable opportunity (*Vivo!*). But *roto* also means "broken one." The command *!No sea roto!* lets one know that he is lacking in social graces, that his behavior is out of line. Perhaps only the typically southern Chilean insult *!No sea indio!* ("don't act like an Indian") is as denigrating a way to put someone "in his place" as to call him roto. Yet used among family and friends, with the right tone of voice, with the appropriate adjective—*roto chorro*—roto becomes a compliment, even a sign of affection.

Joaquín Edwards Bello, a leading twentieth-century Chilean novelist, published *El Roto Chileno* just after World War I. It depicts the underworld of Santiago society—the brothel, the gambling den, the police station . . . the Senate. There was a bit of the roto at all levels of Chilean society, but while the working-class roto languished in prison or died in the streets, the upper-class roto, the Senator and his collaborators at the police station, lived the good life. Edwards Bello's *El Roto* makes clear that the good life of these latter depended upon the exploitation and suffering of the former. Like the huaso then, the roto is a complex symbol of *chilenidad* ("Chilean nationality") which signifies both the misery of the poverty-stricken worker and the *viveza* ("opportunism") of those who benefit from the sweat of his toil.

Since the conquest this tension between the powerful minority and the Indian, the miner, the farm worker, the fisherman, the factory worker has been at the core of Chilean history. It is a history that began with the Spanish expeditions of conquest and the subjugation, enslavement, and decimation of the Indian peoples despite their fierce resistance. It is a history that continued after independence with the violent repression of rural laborers, port and rail workers, miners, and nitrate workers who resisted the exploitation of nineteenth-century capitalism. And it is a history whose most recent chapter involves the "reconquest" of Chile's working classes in the 1970s by a military government proclaiming its loyalty to Christianity and the Hispanic tradition. In the more than four centuries between the Spanish conquest of Chile and this most recent reaffirmation of Hispanic capitalism by the Chilean military, the majority of the Chilean people have been engaged in a daily struggle to achieve a better life for themselves and to overcome the dominance of a small elite which has controlled the territory's political and economic life.

Chapter 2 • The Politics of Conquest

In the sixteenth century Spanish soldiers, ecclesiastics, and administrators created a vast colonial empire in North and South America. Moving from their initial bases in the Caribbean—Haiti, Santo Domingo, Cuba—the Spanish and their Indian allies conquered and despoiled the major indigenous civilizations of Mexico, Central America, and the west coast of South America. In the name of the monarchy and the Church they sought to Christianize the native peoples of America while exploiting their labor in the mines and on the land of the "new world" they called *las indias*. Shiploads of treasure came back to the Iberian peninsula as the Spanish exacted tribute from the new subjects of the king of Spain. After each new conquest, groups of Spaniards who failed to make their fortunes, or who lost the booty acquired, or who dreamed of obtaining even greater wealth and power in new expeditions, sought to extend the empire still farther to as yet unknown lands. From Cuba to Mexico, to Central America, and then to Peru, the Spanish conquistadors reaped the spoils of the conquest as rewards for their daring and their brutality.

As a political and economic venture the Spanish conquest initially combined national-imperial aggrandizement with a semi-feudal form of private enterprise. Individual conquistadors raised armies and financed their own expeditions by authority of the Spanish monarch. In exchange for authorization to collect tribute from the subjugated natives, to operate mines, to use the land for crops or livestock, or to engage in commerce, the king claimed for the royal coffers a share of all the spoils of conquest and of the production of colonial enterprises. In Mexico, Peru, and parts of Central America booty from the accumulated wealth of sophisticated indigenous civilizations constituted a source of quick fortunes for the first Spanish expeditions. Afterward, however, the accumulation of wealth and capital depended upon large-scale exploitation of labor in mining, agriculture, and commercial enterprises.

Social attitudes of fifteenth- and sixteenth-century Spain reserved manual labor and even craftsmanship to the "lower orders." As the Spanish invaders had no intention of working either the mines or the land themselves, this made control over or access to Indian laborers critical for any productive endeavor. Where the Indians had no tradition of daily work obligations or, still less, of contractual or wage labor, the success of conquest as an economic enterprise turned upon somehow mobilizing Indian labor or importing African slaves to work the mines, tend livestock, and cultivate the land. Consequently, despite the flow of bullion and commodities from the colonies into intercolonial and international markets, and the predominance of "private" enterprise in the conquest economy, the earliest modes of production in Spanish America, including Chile, were less capitalistic (in the sense of relying upon wage labor) than they were bastardized or transitional forms of feudal labor dues, fixed-term labor contracts for "indentured" servants (asientos de trabajo), forced labor, or slavery.

Over time Spain created an elaborate administrative apparatus to direct the conquest and the government of las indias. All authority emanated from the Spanish monarch who claimed a divine right to rule. From 1524 the crown governed the new territories through the Supreme Council of the Indies, which began as a handful of officials and expanded to about twenty under the Hapsburg monarchs. The Council of the Indies legislated for the colonies and supervised administration. The royal patronato extended by the Pope granted the Spanish kings the right to name religious functionaries in the New World, thereby extending the authority of the Council of the Indies to matters of religious concern.

In practice the great distances between Spain and the New World left daily or, more accurately, yearly governance of the colonies in the hands of appointed officials. To govern the largest administrative units, the viceroyalties, the king named viceroys, and to lesser territories, captains-general or governors. In addition, a royal judicial council or *audiencia*, composed of judges called *oidores*, and ecclesiastical authorities shared and to some extent checked the power of viceroy or governor. Local officers responsible to the viceroy or governor—or, in their absence, to the *audiencia*—governed smaller jurisdictions or Indian districts. In the towns and cities, municipal councils called *cabildos* legislated and administered regulations of local concern, including fixing prices of commodities, granting licenses to engage in business, and regulating the activity of artisans. Wealthy colonial-born Spaniards (*criollos*) tended to dominate the *cabildos*, while the higher administrative posts usually were reserved for native-born Spaniards or *peninsulares*. Some peninsular officials, however, established local roots, founded prominent criollo families, and acquired interests that conflicted with their bureaucratic duties. From the late seventeenth century onward, sale of offices to criollos accentuated tensions between royal policies and their implementation in the colonies. Moreover, in some cases the cabildos sought to extend their authority and frequently found themselves in conflict with royal officials. Eventually the cabildos would become a rallying point for national independence movements in the nineteenth century.

On paper the government of the empire resembled a strictly hierarchical, neatly arranged chain of command. In reality overlapping authority and conflict between the Council of the Indies, viceroys, governors, ecclesiastical officials, and the cabildos made for continual bureaucratic maneuvering, evasion of royal decrees, and corruption. Though justified by the "donation" to the Spanish monarchy of most of the so-called New World by Pope Alexander VI—in his role as Vicar of Christ—in order to expand the realm of Christendom, the Spanish conquest gave rise to numerous doctrinal and theological conflicts over appropriate treatment of the indigenous peoples. Did the Indians have souls? Could they achieve salvation? If so, could they be forced to accept Christianity, or should conversion be accomplished only through persuasion? Could the Indians be enslaved? Could they be forced to pay tribute? If so, could tribute take the form of forced labor? Everywhere in Spanish America, Church officials and theoreticians debated these questions. In every colony and administrative sub-unit the conquistadors and those who came after them resisted efforts by royal officials and certain churchmen to regulate the exploitation of the conquered peoples. Nowhere did the idealism of the reformers effectively prevent the abuse and eventual decimation of the native American peoples, as economic realities won out over spiritual and humanitarian objections to the exploitation of Indian labor.

By the time Pedro de Valdivia undertook the conquest of Chile (1540) the formal resolution of numerous doctrinal questions had already resulted in official policies prohibiting many of the early abuses of the Indian peoples by the Spanish. For example, a decree signed by Charles V in 1528 prohibited enslavement of the Indians as well as the widespread practice of using the Indians as pack animals or for other "personal services." It also required that the conquerors provide Indians laboring in the mines with religious instruction, including Mass on Sundays and feast days. Later ordinances outlawed the removal of Indians from cold climates to work in hot climates, and vice versa, as well as the "renting out" of Indians by those commended to supervise their care and religious instruction. But the Spanish colonials evaded or violated these restrictions and the hundreds of others adopted in the protolabor codes contained in the royal decrees and ordinances that regulated taxation or tribute paid by the Indians to Spanish officials. Thus, the history of the Spanish conquest in Chile and elsewhere must be seen on three levels: Church doctrine and official policy, administrative implementation or non-implementation, and the reality of everyday life—or death—for the native population.

As a primary institution of conquest and colonial economy in Chile as throughout the Spanish empire, the *encomienda*, with all its variations, illustrates the tremendous gap between Church doctrine or official policy and its implementation upon the subjugated peoples of America. As a reward for military service, and with the obligation to provide for Christianization of the Indians, the crown or its representative "commended" the care of groups of Indians for a specified time—for example, two or three generations—to selected Spaniards and their heirs. The crown insisted that the Indians were free peoples, not to be enslaved except as punishment for rebellion or for resisting Spanish authority. As free vassals, however, the Indians were subject to tribute or taxation. This gave rise to the questions of the form of the tribute and how it could be collected. Concessionary, rather than proprietary, rights to Indian tribute or labor provided incentives to exact *quickly* whatever profits could be made from Indian labor. A new governor might give the encomienda to someone else; a court proceeding could alter the terms of the grant; a new decree might effectively limit the tribute or restrict forced labor. Quick profits through intensive exploitation of the labor force became the main endeavor of individual conquistadors.

A year after the foundation of Chile's first settlement at Santiago in 1541, the New Laws, issued by the Spanish king to control the

ambitions of the encomenderos in the American dominions, prohibited enslavement of Indians even as punishment. They also forbade the granting of new encomiendas and ordered ecclesiastics and
royal officials to give up any encomiendas they held. Existing encomiendas could be retained but not passed on to heirs; tribute was to
be strictly fixed and regulated by crown officials to avoid abuses by
the encomenderos. The encomenderos rebelled against these laws in
Peru and other parts of the empire, defending the spoils of conquest.
Although the crown partially repealed these laws, it subsequently
enacted a succession of legal codes and ordinances that specifically
defined the obligations of encomenderos and limited demands upon
the Indians.

The history of Chile for its first two centuries as a Spanish colony
centered upon the implacable resistance of the encomenderos to
regulation of their exploitation of the native Chilean peoples and
the never-ending struggle of these peoples to maintain their freedom
against the Spanish invaders. This struggle shaped the social and economic structure of colonial Chile and its development within the
Spanish Empire. Formation of the Chilean ethnic stock, race relations, social stratification, and economic development depended upon
the ebb and flow of warfare. No other Amerindian peoples resisted
Spanish conquest as did the Araucanians. No other Spanish colony
drained the royal treasury and expended the lives of thousands of
Spanish and mestizo troops for more than two centuries after initial
contact with indigenous peoples. Nowhere else in the Spanish Empire did warfare or the threat of warfare so significantly shape the
development of the colonial economy or influence the fate of Spanish
towns. Only in Chile did pillage and slave raids, or *malocas*, constitute an important source of wealth for colonial administrators and
military personnel into the mid-seventeenth century. In Chile alone
among the South American colonies did provisioning a standing army
become a principal stimulus to colonial production and internal
commerce, buttressed continually by a military subsidy, the *situado*,
from Peru and Spain.

Perpetual warfare and the periodic destruction of Spanish settlements gave a unique character to the Chilean colony. Plunder, illegal
trade with the Indians, slave raids, and profiteering from the military
budget provided unique opportunities for social and economic mobility, at the same time that the risks of an uprising or reprisal raid
made economic enterprises in the southern regions insecure. The
insecurity of the southern territory encouraged concentration of the

Spanish population in the central valley, thereby promoting the development of a relatively homogeneous, geographically integrated society to the north of the Maule River.

Episodic warfare also perpetuated Indian slave labor and the encomiendas in Chile long after these institutions had declined in the rest of Spanish America. In contrast to the more established colonies, Chilean military leaders and soldiers in the seventeenth and eighteenth centuries could still obtain booty, privileges, and rewards from the king for their efforts to subjugate the indigenous population. In a sense, the prolonged resort to violence as a means of acquiring fame, position, and wealth made physical brutality and coercion an integral part of daily life on the Chilean frontier among Spaniards, mestizos, and the subject Indian peoples. This coercion, or threat of coercion, carried over into the encomiendas and haciendas and became the principal mechanism governing relations between the workers and their masters. The inability to enforce the royal decrees regulating these relationships merely added disrespect for law, evasion, and cynicism to the other legacies of the Chilean colonial experience.

The conquest of Chile was an extension of the Spanish victory, led by Francisco Pizarro and Diego de Almagro, over the Inca empire in Peru. In 1534 the Spanish crown divided the land south of Ecuador into four political units (gobernaciones): Nueva Castilla, assigned to Pizarro; Nueva Toledo, 200 leagues from Ica to latitude 25° 31′ S, assigned to Almagro; and two others assigned to Pedro de Mendoza and Simón de Alcazaba. Mendoza sold his claim to Almagro, and Alcazaba led a disastrous expedition, which was to go by sea to the Strait of Magellan and from there overland to the north but only reached Puerto de los Leones on the east coast. Almagro contested Pizarro's control of Cuzco but agreed to lead an expedition south to explore the rest of Nueva Toledo while awaiting the king's resolution of the conflicting claims.

The Peruvian Indians, who were plotting a rebellion against the conquering Spaniards, had told exaggerated tales of the wealth of the land to the south. These tales, along with Pizarro's prodding, had persuaded Almagro. In organizing the expedition to Chile, he rapidly depleted the fortune he had acquired in the Peruvian conquest. He assembled a force of more than five hundred Spaniards (almost half cavalry)—a larger army than Cortés had led into Mexico or Pizarro into Peru. Many of these Spaniards had participated in earlier expeditions to Mexico, Guatemala, and, of course, Peru. According to various estimates, 10,000 to 15,000 Indian auxiliaries and a small number of Negro slaves accompanied the Spaniards on the first expedition to Chile.

After sending out advance parties—including Inca emissaries to collect tribute from the Indian subjects to the south—as well as some forces by sea, Almagro left Cuzco in July 1535. The main expeditionary force, more than two hundred Spaniards and thousands of Indian auxiliaries, crossed the Bolivian plateau through the Andes range bordering Lake Titicaca. After much privation the expedition reached Tupiza, where it rested for about two months. Here Almagro received a message informing him of the arrival in Cuzco of an emissary from Spain authorized to settle the dispute with Pizarro. The message urged Almagro to return to Cuzco to defend his interests, but he decided to go on to Chile. He led his forces on to Chicoana, near the present Argentine city of Salta; there they encountered hostile Indian activity while reprovisioning themselves and preparing for the Andes crossing.

Upon leaving Chicoana, many of the Indian bearers fled. Rivers flooded from the melting snow, and summer rains drowned numerous llamas, used as pack animals, and destroyed provisions, so food had to be rationed. Almagro's force crossed the Campo del Arenal desert and pushed into the cordillera at the San Francisco pass. In this part of the cordillera the Andes average more than 13,000 feet. There was no pasture for the animals, and often no firewood could be found. *Soroche* or *puna*—a condition of nausea, headaches, and sometimes convulsions produced by the altitude—and frostbite added to the misery of the expedition. Many of the scantily clad Indians froze to death, as did horses—to be "defrosted" and eaten five months later by other Spaniards coming to join Almagro in Chile.

Almagro's forces stayed in Chile until the end of 1536, exploring as far south as the Maule River or perhaps the Itata. Periodic skirmishes with hostile Indians, as well as the Indians' strategy of hiding food and possessions, hindered Almagro's efforts to establish control. Exploratory expeditions found no gold, no silver, no cities. Failure to find a new Peru, combined with news that Cuzco apparently fell into the jurisdiction of Nueva Toledo, persuaded Almagro and his lieutenants to return to Peru. At the end of 1536 they joined forces at Copiapó, and then crossed the desert in small groups, from water hole to water hole, as a ship followed them up the coast.

Upon arrival in Peru, Almagro found the Indians in rebellion and Cuzco under control of Pizarro's brothers. Almagro liberated the city but proved unable to resolve the conflict with the Pizarros. Civil war

The Routes of the Conquest

———— Almagro's Route

----- Valdivia's Route South

All towns are
post-conquest settlements

PERU

Cuzco

BOLIVIA

Lake Titicaca

Arequipa

La Paz

Mollendo

Tacna

Paria

Arica

Lake
Poopó

Tarapacá

Iquique

Tupiza

Chiu-Chiu

ATACAMA

San Pedro
de Atacama

Antofagasta

DESERT

Chicoana

Copiapó

Pass of
San Francisco

Huasco

La Serena

PACIFIC OCEAN

Coquimbo

ARGENTINA

Aconcagua Valley
Uspallata Pass

Valparaíso

Santiago

Río Maule

Reinogüelen

Río Ñuble

Concepción

Río Itata

0   Miles   200

MAP 7: The Routes of the Conquest

(Source: H. R. S. Pocock, *The Conquest of Chile*, Stein and Day, New York,
1967.)

ensued. At the battle of Las Salinas in 1538, Almagro was taken prisoner and executed by the Pizarros.

The tales of Almagro's men discouraged further expeditions to Chile for nearly five years. As the historian Barros Arana wrote, "After the return of Almagro this country [Chile] was the most discredited of the Indies in the minds of the conquistadors . . . a cursed land without gold . . . inhabited by savages of the worst kind and incapable of repaying the costs occasioned by the conquest." The failure of Almagro's expedition also meant that Chile's Indians could not again be surprised or intimidated. They now knew that the Spanish were human, not gods, that they could be barbaric and treacherous, and that their horses could be killed or captured.

It therefore came as somewhat of a surprise to the Spanish elite in Peru when the commander of Pizarro's forces at the battle of Las Salinas, Pedro de Valdivia, gave up his valuable encomienda and a silver mine at Porco in exchange for permission to explore and conquer Chile. Valdivia's motivation cannot be known with certainty, but it seems clear that it went beyond mere wealth, as he sacrificed an immense fortune to organize his Chilean expedition.

In 1540 Valdivia left Cuzco with a few Spanish soldiers (from 5 to 20 according to various estimates), his mistress, Inés de Suárez, and perhaps a thousand Indian auxiliaries. Along the way from Cuzco to Arequipa other Spaniards joined him, among them some former members of the Almagro expedition. At Tarapacá, Valdivia waited for reinforcements, but when the army set out across the Atacama desert, it numbered fewer than 110 Spaniards including two priests. After eleven months of hardship, skirmishes with Indians, and internal conflicts Valdivia's forces arrived in the valley of the Mapocho. Almost immediately they were attacked by an Indian army led by the local chief Michimalongo. The Spaniards eventually drove off the Indian warriors and soon thereafter convinced the local Indians to aid in the construction of Chile's first "city"—Santiago—founded in February 1541. Less than a month later Valdivia created a cabildo, which, in turn, called upon Valdivia to make himself governor of Chile in the name of the king of Spain rather than as Pizarro's lieutenant. After appropriate objections Valdivia acquiesced. Seven months later (September 11, 1541) the Indians of the region attacked Santiago, burned the straw-roofed houses to the ground, and left the Spaniards little more than grain for seed and some livestock. The battle for Chile had begun in earnest.

From 1541 until 1553, Valdivia's forces pushed south from Santiago, warring against the Indians and establishing a number of fort towns. These included Concepción, La Imperial (at the site of present-day Carahue), Valdivia, and Villarrica. In addition, on the other side of the Andes, Francisco de Aguirre governed Santiago del Estero. With the foundation of each "city," Valdivia handed out encomiendas to selected conquistadors, thereby granting them authority to collect tribute from the Indians in their jurisdiction and take charge of the Indians' Christianization. Since the Chilean Indians had little accumulated wealth, tribute typically took the form of forced labor in the mines or gold washings that the Spaniards "discovered." Of course, if the Indians were to be forced to work, they had first to be subjugated; and south of the Maule River this proved no easy task. Instead of a unified Spanish army, each encomendero had to pacify the Indians in his own grant, and his fortunes depended upon his success at this, not upon a salary from a government treasury.

On Christmas day 1553, the Araucanians, led by the cacique Lautaro—who, in his earlier service as Valdivia's groom, had acquired knowlege of Spanish tactics and limitations—lured the Spanish leader into a trap and obliterated his force of about fifty men at the still smoldering ruins of Tucapel. There were no survivors. Although a legend has the Indians capturing Valdivia and pouring molten gold—the metal so sought after by the Spaniards—down his throat, it is more likely that his decapitated head ended up on the point of an Araucanian lance, the Indians' customary treatment of conquered enemies. Following up the victory at Tucapel, the Indians defeated an army led by Francisco de Villagra at Marigüeñu, despite Villagra's use of six small cannon and thirty' harquebuses.* The defeated survivors abandoned Concepción. After twelve years of "conquest," a fearful group of Spanish at Santiago welcomed the refugees from the southern towns fleeing the Araucanian armies.

The Spanish, under Pedro de Villagra, maintained a presence in the south only at Valdivia. Between 1555 and 1557 efforts to resettle the other southern towns met with further defeats at the hands of the Indians, and were complicated by a struggle for power among Valdivia's lieutenants. At first the *audiencia* at Lima left matters in the hands of the local cabildos, but the ensuing chaos led to the appointment of Francisco de Villagra as the ranking officer in Chile. As Lautaro marched toward Santiago, Villagra's forces and Indian auxiliaries surprised the Araucanians at Peteroa, killed Lautaro, and after a gruesome battle, emerged triumphant. This victory avoided

---

* A harquebus was an early type of fuse-fired gun.

total liquidation of the Chilean colony, just as a new governor, García Hurtado de Mendoza, the twenty-one-year-old son of the Peruvian viceroy, arrived at La Serena with 500 soldiers. This was only the first installment in the continuing and costly flow to Chile of reinforcements and war materiel from Peru and Spain.

By authorizing the expenditure of funds from the royal treasury at Lima, the viceroy also recognized the inadequacy of the private seigniorial model of conquest in Chile. Despite the crown's general policy of relying upon private financing of the conquest, by the mid-1560s Chilean governors expended small sums from the royal treasury to help feed and equip soldiers on the Indian frontier. And while Philip II continued to insist upon the traditional policy of avoiding crown expenditures for the conquest of new territories, by 1572 he had authorized the viceroy at Lima to spend moderate sums from the royal coffers to support the war effort in Chile. Until 1600 most financing for the Chilean venture came from the private fortunes of royal officials, encomenderos, and merchants; but the crown gradually moved toward assuming financial responsibility as it became clear that private resources could not pay for the armaments and soldiers necessary to maintain Chile and Peru secure against the threat of Spain's European rivals and the Araucanians.

Shortly after his arrival, Hurtado de Mendoza arrested Aguirre and Francisco de Villagra in order to assert his own control, and then continued the war against the Araucanians. Numerous brutalities followed, including the torture of the *cacique* Galvarino, immortalized in Alonso de Ercilla's epic *La Araucana*. In 1558 Mendoza ordered the resettlement of Concepción, for the third time. Ensuing military engagements reestablished a line of southern forts. Just as Mendoza believed he had pacified Araucania, the king decreed his dismissal at the same time his father was removed as viceroy of Peru. Powerful conquistadors had complained that Mendoza was rewarding his own followers and, more important, was enforcing measures devised by his legal adviser to regulate forced Indian labor.

Replaced by Francisco de Villagra, García Hurtado de Mendoza would return to the colonies as viceroy of Peru some twenty years later. But Mendoza's hope that the Araucanians had been pacified proved illusory, though a terrible smallpox epidemic from 1561 to 1563 certainly reduced their war-making capability. The best estimates available suggest that 20 to 25 percent of the Indian population perished, though reliable data do not exist. Renewed warfare and persistent conflict among the conquistadors and royal officials led the king to decree the establishment of a royal *audiencia* in Chile in

August 1565. The *audiencia* failed to resolve either the internal political or the military problems of the colony. While the encomenderos resisted any restriction on their exploitation of the Indians, and refused to subordinate private interests to public necessities, the Araucanians renewed their struggle against the European invaders.

The Araucanians' relative success against the Spanish invaders resulted largely from their adaptability and ingenuity in warfare. When the Spaniards arrived, Araucanian armaments consisted of bows and stone-tipped arrows, hardened wooden spears or lances, clubs, and slings. For protection they wore helmets and coats of sealskin or whalebone and carried thick skin shields. Like other Amerindians their initial encounters with horses and the Spaniards' killer dogs provoked panic and dismay. The Araucanians, however, quickly modified their weapons and their tactics. They constructed new weapons to fight the Spanish cavalry, including lances tipped with pieces of Spanish swords and nooses to yank the Spanish from their mounts. By the late 1560s the Indians frequently used horses and were improving as cavalrymen. A system of double-mounting allowed a lancer and an archer to ride a single horse. Near the end of the sixteenth century the Araucanians even occasionally utilized captured harquebuses, though having learned the limitations of the fuse-fired weapons they attempted to confront the Spaniards when rain or surprise prevented the lighting of fuses.

To avoid the Spaniards' scorched earth tactics, the Indians began to sow hidden fields and to retaliate in kind—waiting until the harvests of the fort towns reached maturity and then trampling the fields at night in cavalry raids. By the end of the sixteenth century the Araucanians had become accomplished guerrilla fighters, effectively harassing the cumbersome Spanish armies, in which each soldier traveled with several Indian servants to do his cooking, bear his weapons, and wait upon him in the fashion of a medieval lord. Lack of mobility combined with scarcity of munitions and artillery to assist Indian resistance. At the time of the general uprising at the end of the sixteenth century, Chilean historian Crescente Errázuriz claimed that in Chillán, Concepción, Angol, Arauco, and Santa Cruz the Spaniards had only 282 harquebuses, 44 muskets, and 26 cannon and lacked sufficient powder and fuses for even these. But above all, the Indians' determination, inventiveness, and courage stifled the enterprise of conquest.

Half a century after Pedro de Valdivia's forces entered Chile, the colony remained a frontier, governed by military officers who re-

peatedly took to the field against the Araucanians. The population resided in dispersed fort towns that increased or decreased in number
according to the vicissitudes of warfare. Initially, the only significant
source of wealth for the conquerors other than crafts in the towns,
consisted of limited placer gold mines and the exploitation of Indian
labor. Control of the mines and Indians or permission to engage in
industry or commerce stemmed from rights vested in the conquistadors by the governor or the cabildos as the reward for military service
or simply as personal patronage. Whether in the form of an encomienda grant or a concession for a flour mill, economic opportunity and
wealth originated in the manipulation and control of the law and of
political authorities. If Indian labor made possible agricultural production, manufacturing, and mining activities, only "politics" determined the distribution of the booty—including the Indian workers
themselves. Valdivia granted encomiendas to his followers shortly
after founding Santiago and rewarded other conquistadors as well as
religious orders with encomienda grants of Indians surrounding all
the towns and forts founded between 1541 and his death in 1553. In
contrast to the more established colonies such as Mexico or Peru, his
successors continued to grant encomiendas until almost the end of
the eighteenth century—though by that time their importance had
greatly diminished in relation to the large rural estates employing
tenant labor.

The perpetual state of war in Chile led the crown to put the
Chilean Indians in a "special" category which, through contorted
legal and doctrinal reasoning, made them subject after 1608 to legal
enslavement as well as to the usual abuses of the conquistadors. This
eventually made war not only a fact of life in Chile but a great
business venture—based on raids of pillage or "slave hunts" called
campeadas or *malocas*. Before such slave hunts became legal, however, over half a century of warfare had led the Spanish monarch to
establish a permanent Chilean garrison and a yearly budget to sustain
the war against the Araucanians. The Chilean encomenderos, the
royal officials stationed in Chile and Peru, and the small merchant
class would soon owe a portion of their wealth and power to the
Araucanian war and the budget associated with maintenance of
the Chilean garrison. Thus the war that periodically devastated the
Concepción-southern region, made livestock and agricultural enterprise insecure, and deprived the colony of its richest gold mines, enriched royal officials and merchants in Santiago, La Serena, and Lima.

Following continued defeats at the hands of the Araucanians, despite more reinforcements from Peru, and an earthquake that de-

stroyed Concepción in 1570, King Philip II abolished the *audiencia* in Chile in 1573 and named a veteran conquistador, Rodrigo de Quiroga, as governor of the territory. Quiroga, a lieutenant for both Valdivia and García Hurtado de Mendoza, actually assumed office in late January 1575. Two months later another earthquake destroyed La Imperial Villarrica, Osorno, Castro, and Valdivia and also affected Santiago and Valparaíso. Nevertheless, Quiroga pressed forward with a brutal campaign of terror against the Indians in order to end the war. Supported by the viceroy of Peru, Quiroga executed captured caciques and deported prisoners to the north to work the mines in Coquimbo. In order to prevent their escape, Quiroga ordered that their feet be mutilated with a machete or a chisel; to avoid loss of blood and subsequent death, each stump was thrust into a pot of boiling tallow. The governor's concern with the lawfulness of this policy is enlightening. Legal proceedings against the Indians, in their absence, had condemned them to death for rebellion against the empire—and then Quiroga generously reduced the sentence to mutilation and forced labor. The king also instructed Quiroga to ship rebellious Indians to Peru, but the latter replied, on behalf of Chile's encomenderos, that the Indians would survive neither the trip nor the change in climate. The king reconsidered his decree and thus saved most of the human booty for the Chilean conquerors. In the meantime the English corsair Francis Drake sacked Valparaíso and attacked La Serena, thus increasing the military pressure upon the colony. Despite Quiroga's victories against Indian armies, conflict continued to rage.

Between 1580, when Quiroga died, and 1598 three more governors sought to combine warfare and conciliation in order to pacify Araucania. The last of these three, García Oñez de Loyola, was a nephew of the Peruvian viceroy and also a relative of Ignatius de Loyola, founder of the Jesuit order. When Oñez de Loyola arrived in Chile, a major economic activity of the southern-based army garrisons consisted of hunting down Indians for personal use or for sale. Since the soldiers found it easier to capture Indians from pacified tribes, many more of them were seized and sold into slavery than rebel Indians captured in war. Despite the new governor's decrees outlawing such practices, Chilean historian Domingo Amunátegui Solar wrote that the whole territory of the Bishopric of Imperial "had been converted into an immense human 'meat market,'" where the soldiers enriched themselves through the sale of Araucanians, and where the encomenderos and wealthy residents of Santiago and Serena found their domestic servants or replaced the personnel of their *encomiendas* as the local natives died off from overwork or disease. In January 1598, Oñez de Loyola wrote to the king that throughout the country one saw multitudes of lame or mutilated Indians, Indians without hands, noses, or ears, and blind Indians whose tragic condition "incites the others to die rather than surrender."

Ironically, García Oñez de Loyola attempted to end deportation of Indian prisoners beyond the Maule River and otherwise to moderate the abuses of the encomenderos, yet he ended up like Pedro de Valdivia, decapitated after the massacre of his soldiers at the battle of Curalaba in 1598. The defeat at Curalaba marked the beginning of a general uprising by the Araucanians. All major Spanish settlements south of the Bío Bío River were destroyed or abandoned: Santa Cruz and Valdivia in 1599; La Imperial and Angol in 1600; Villarrica in 1602; Osorno and Arauco in 1604. At about the same time Dutch pirates attacked Valparaíso and Chiloé. Four governors succeeded one another in rapid succession, and the efforts to subdue the Araucanians continued to no avail.

In 1600 the king of Spain established a permanent military subsidy, or *situado*, for Chile, and war in Chile became a permanent, institutionalized business of the Lima merchants and shippers until almost the end of the seventeenth century. The *situado*, a symbol of the poverty of the Chilean colony, also freed the encomenderos from most financial and military obligations of the war. Conquest and pacification thus became largely a public venture instead of a private semi-feudal imitation of the Spanish reconquest of their homeland from the Moors.

Exasperated by the loss of all the towns and mines of southern Chile after 1598 and the continued fighting, including the loss of more than a hundred Spanish soldiers at Boroa in 1606, the Council of the Indies proposed the *legal* enslavement of all captured Indian males over ten and one-half years old and females older than nine and one-half years; captured children would be commended to "virtuous" Spaniards to serve them and to be instructed in the Faith until the age of twenty. On May 26, 1608, the Spanish king signed a royal decree that legalized, indeed encouraged, the enslavement of "rebellious" Indians in Chile. Though in practice, enslavement of Indian captives was common from 1570 onward, this royal decree legitimated slave raids and pillage by the Chilean garrisons. Interim governor and *audiencia* judge, Luis Merlo de la Fuente, promulgated the decree in Santiago in August 1610, and then led a force to the south which took nearly a thousand Indian prisoners.

By 1610, seventy years after Valdivia's entry into the country, Chile boasted five "cities": La Serena, with 46 adobe houses, 11 with tile roofs and the rest of straw; Santiago, 200 houses; Chillán, 52, eight with tile roofs, 39 with straw, and five *ranchos* of wood and thatch roofs; Concepción, 76 houses, 36 wooden with straw roofs; and Castro, on Chiloé, with 12 straw-covered houses. The rest of the Chilean population resided in the countryside on the immense territories of the encomiendas* where subjugated Indians panned gold, tended flocks of sheep and cattle, and cultivated the land. With the loss of the encomiendas south of the Bío Bío River, gold mining near La Serena, Santiago, and Concepción took second place to agriculture and livestock as the major source of occupation for the Chilean work force.

Accustomed by the Inca conquest to the idea of tribute long before the arrival of the Spanish, many of the Indians of northern Chile (Copiapó to Maule) gradually submitted to Spanish domination. They provided the labor that produced gold, food, hides, and tallow—the major exports to Peru—to enrich the encomenderos. As forced labor, mistreatment, and disease (especially smallpox) decimated the encomienda Indians, their periodic replacement was necessary in order to maintain the conquest economy. The war against the Araucanians, as well as the capture of the Huarpe peoples in the eastern cordillera, provided the main source of this replenishment and of concubines for Spanish males; it also supplied Indian labor to Peru. The cruel treatment of captured Indians, in "peacetime" or in war, reinforced their will to resist. The Spaniards used the struggle of the Indians to justify their enslavement, mutilation, "commendation," or "deposit" for use by the encomenderos. Even as the war persisted, so did the never-ending succession of decrees, taxes, and ordinances, which the Chileans applied, appealed, or ignored as suited their convenience.

From 1558 until the general uprising after 1598, the crown's major representatives enacted numerous tribute regulations aimed at controlling the encomenderos and protecting the Indian laborers. In each case Catholic clerics influenced adoption of these codes. But in each case Chilean encomenderos subverted or prevented their implementation.

In 1557, Hernando de Santillán, an adviser to Governor García

---

* Strictly speaking, the encomienda grant did not involve title to land; it merely conveyed the right to exact tribute from the Indians. Nevertheless, encomenderos in Chile often exercised a patrimonial authority within the territory of a grant.

Hurtado de Mendoza, promulgated in Chile the royal decrees that prohibited using Indians as pack animals, forbade the encomenderos to employ more than one-fifth of "their" Indians in the gold washings or mines, and ordered them to pay the Indians one-sixth of the gold they mined. In addition, they were to free pacified Indian servants and, if these Indians voluntarily worked the mines, to give them one-fourth of the ore extracted as well as adequate food and tools. Further decrees sought to regulate the conditions of the Indians laboring in the fields, the vineyards, the artisan industries, and even in households. A similar tribute was promulgated in mid-1558 for the region of Concepción and the south.

Taking account of the recent rebellions in Peru, Santillán did not seek to abolish the encomiendas themselves. Nevertheless, the Spanish settlers had no intention of ameliorating the lot of the subjugated Indians and thereby decreasing their own income. In a communication to the Council of the Indies after his departure from Chile in 1560, Santillán described the brutality of conquest from the first entry of the Spanish: "[They] killed, maimed and set dogs upon the Indians, cut off feet, hands, noses and teats, stole their lands, raped their women and daughters, chained them up and used them as beasts of burden, burned their houses and settlements and layed waste their fields." In La Serena in 1557, Santillán had reported that the encomenderos sent the Indians to the mines as pack animals, as well as employing them in other personal services, leaving them not an hour to rest.

In the tradition of Bartolomé de Las Casas, the best-known clerical defender of the New World Indians against the abuses of conquest, another Dominican, Fray Gil de San Nicolás, provided more ammunition for the growing "black legend" of Spanish barbarism:

> They take the Indian men and women prisoners in chains and use them for "dog bait," watching the dogs tear them apart for sport.
> They destroy the crops, burn the houses and villages full of Indians, shutting the doorways [of the houses] so none can escape.

Describing the mines, he wrote that at first the Indians were to receive a sixth part of the gold they extracted and then an eighth part, but they often received nothing at all. In any case, the regulations obligated the Indians to pay the salary of their "protector" from their "earnings." Either purchased in Spain or acquired from a royal official, the post of "protector" allowed venturesome Spaniards to make their fortunes in the New World by mediating between the encomendero and the native peoples. From limited evidence it appears that the gold earned by the Indians was often actually a source of risk capital for Spanish pastoral and commercial enterprises as the "protectors" and encomenderos colluded in defrauding the Indians.

In 1563 Pedro de Villagra promulgated a dozen new tribute ordinances, including provisions that limited the work period in the placer mines to six months, reaffirmed payment of one-sixth of the gold mined to the Indians, prohibited use of Negro taskmasters, and required the "protectors" of the Indians to buy sheep for them with their gold. The new ordinances also split the obligation of the *protector*'s salary between the Indians and the encomendero and increased the number of "protectors." Once again, the encomenderos largely evaded the new regulations. However, the recently created posts did provide a source of income for the new "protectors" authorized to defend the Indians' rights.

Another major reform of the tribute system in 1580 was the *tasa* of Gamboa, which also failed to halt the encomendero's abuse of Indian labor. The *tasa* of Gamboa sought to substitute a fixed money or commodity tax for forced labor. The encomenderos and even some churchmen opposed the new tax as "prejudicial to the colony and the Indians." Its principal innovation consisted of a commutation of labor tribute for a money or commodity tribute. This innovation in no way benefited the encomenderos since it fixed the tribute at seven to nine pesos a year—one-fourth to one-twelfth the value that an Indian could produce in a normal work cycle of eight to twelve months.

Despite the resistance of the encomenderos, the *tasa* of Gamboa merely appeared benign in contrast to previous policies. Illustrative is the tribute owed by the Indians to Luis Jufré, who inherited from his father the encomiendas of Macul near Santiago, Peteroa and Mataquito in Curicó, and Pocoa north of the Maule River. The Macul grant contained 22 tributary Indians; Mataquito, 142; and Pocoa, 57. These Indians owed collectively to their encomendero the following monies and commodities each year.

Macul: 110 gold pesos plus two gold pesos to pay the priest, *corregidor*,* and the administrator of the encomienda; 30 *fanegas*† of wheat, 20 fanegas of barley, and 20 fanegas of maize delivered to the

---

* The corregidors were representatives of royal authority in towns and rural districts. *Corregidores de Indios* were responsible in particular for Indian settlements or areas of Indian population.

† A fanega is approximately equivalent to 1½ bushels.

house of the encomendero; sufficient fish, chickens, or sheep necessary to equal 44 pesos. In addition, the Indians of Macul were to supply nine household servants who would receive a salary and not pay tribute.

Peteroa: In addition to two gold pesos for administrative costs, 985 gold pesos; 394 pesos worth of fish and agricultural commodities, including 200 fanegas of wheat, 100 of barley, 120 of corn, and six of beans; 11 household servants to the encomendero.

Mataquito: two pesos each for administrative costs; 710 gold pesos; 284 pesos in foodstuffs: 150 fanegas of wheat, 80 of barley, five of maize, four of beans, and sufficient quantity of fish, tools, sheep, vegetables, or other commodities to complete the tribute; 10 servants for the encomendero's household.

Pocoa: In addition to two gold pesos for administrative costs, 285 gold pesos; four domestic servants; 114 pesos in commodities, including 80 fanegas of wheat, 40 of barley, and 50 of maize.

Ruiz de Gamboa prohibited any tribute beyond that specified, but allowed the encomenderos to purchase, at a "just price," commodities to eat and drink or other necessities. In order to avoid abuses, copies of the tribute regulations were given to the encomenderos and the Indian caciques; and to ensure compliance, Gamboa appointed new officials to inspect the mines of Coquimbo and Quillota. The Indians could, of course, choose "personal service" instead of paying the tribute. Around La Imperial continual war made enforcement of tribute largely academic, but north of Maule initial implementation of the tribute aroused the animosity of the encomenderos.

The encomenderos emerged again victorious when the king sent a new military expedition and a new governor, Alonso de Sotomayor, with the charge to defend the colony and the wealth of Peru against the attacks of English pirates and to pacify the Araucanians. Sotomayor reinstated forced labor, thereby gaining the encomenderos' cooperation for a new campaign to the south. In this campaign he ordered that the hands and noses of Indian prisoners be cut off before they were released, in order to terrorize their fellows. Terror again failed to intimidate the Araucanians, who fought back with vigor. According to García Oñez de Loyola some years later, Sotomayor's policies forced the Indians to produce more than 100 pesos in goods and services in exchange for garments worth at most three to four pesos. Sotomayor also appointed to the Indian districts new corregidores whose salaries consisted of one-fourth of the grain and livestock raised by the natives, and approved a work cycle or *demora* of eight months instead of the six established by Pedro de Villagra. To "benefit" the Indians, the governor named clerics to the rural districts; their salaries also came out of the Indians' sweat and blood in the fields and the mines.

Although encomenderos continued to evade the regulations intended to improve the conditions of the Indians, the periodic rebellions, and then the disaster following the defeat of the Spaniards at Curalaba in 1598, gave increased credibility to the voices of those few clerics who sought "justice" for the Indian peoples. The best known of these, the Jesuit Luis de Valdivia, finally persuaded the Spanish monarch to introduce a policy of "defensive warfare," which had been suggested earlier by officials in Lima. After 1612 official policy forbade sorties or settlements across the Bío Bío River—except by Jesuit missionaries. Luis de Valdivia returned to Chile with a new military governor, Alonso de Ribera, and with comprehensive authority to impose the policy of defensive warfare. This included pardons for rebellious Indians, suspension of the decree permitting slavery of captured Indians, prohibitions on selling outside of Chile those previously captured, dismantling the forts of Angol and Paicaiví, and a recommendation to the *audiencia* to suspend the labor obligations of the Indians and replace them with money and commodity tribute.

Frontier garrisons resisted defensive warfare for both professional and economic reasons. Encomenderos and most other colonials also sought to reverse governmental policy. Governor Ribera openly violated his charge, while other Spanish violations made a mockery of the defensive warfare policy. New instructions from the king, at the insistence of Luis de Valdivia, reaffirmed this policy, but Alonso de Ribera had died by the time these arrived in Chile (1617).

His interim successor received explicit instructions to comply in all respects with the defensive warfare policy; but when the next governor arrived in Concepción, he wrote to the king that forced Indian labor still had not been eliminated from Chile. At the instruction of the viceroy of Peru, still another tribute regulation, the *tasa* of Esquilache, attempted to limit the encomenderos' abuse of the Indians, while officials also suggested that the importation of one thousand black slaves to be sold "at cost" would help to liberate the Indians from *their* slavery. The *tasa* of Esquilache prohibited *any Indian*, whether peaceful or not, from providing "personal service"; it specified a new formula for taxation or tribute, it limited the percentage of encomienda Indians obligated to work to one-third each year; and it freed the others to sell their labor if they desired. If the encomendero did not need all his laborers, he could rent them to other encomenderos or deserving Spaniards.

The encomenderos, nevertheless, resisted all prohibitions against Indian slavery or forced labor in the mines, and any limit on the number of days that Indians could be forced to work. Luis de Valdivia's departure for Spain in 1619, along with the deaths of the Chilean governor and King Philip III, soon eliminated even the pretense of defensive warfare. Chile's governor from 1625 to 1629, Luis Fernández de Córdoba y Arce, boasted to King Philip IV that he had captured more than 250 Indians in fighting near Imperial in 1627 and had killed or captured more than 2500 in Yumbel and Arauco. According to this governor:

> I entered in the province of Imperial and thereabouts, where Spanish have not trod since the uprising twenty-eight years ago, with such good results that I burned many houses and more than 14 or 15 thousand fanegas of food of all sorts, and destroyed 4 or 5 thousand head of livestock. . . . Despite the obstinate resistance of the enemy we have only lost thirty Spanish dead and some hundred Indian allies. . . .

Still, the governor attempted to ameliorate somewhat the condition of non-hostile Indians—by prohibiting the branding of Indians who were not, within three months of their capture in war, registered in the appropriate government office! Araucanian counteroffensives, led by the cacique Lientur, inflicted important defeats on the Spanish in the La Imperial region, including a total rout of Spanish forces at Las Cangrejeras. The Indians killed 70 Spaniards or mestizos and took 36 Spanish prisoners, including Francisco Nuñez de Pineda y Bascuñan, who later described the battle and his long captivity in a diary of his life with the Indians called *Cautiverio Feliz* ("Happy Captivity").

The long history of war, brutality, pillage, and unenforced decrees "protecting" the Indians continued as Governor Laso de la Vega (1629-39) persisted in the offensive in Araucania. An initial Spanish victory at Albarrada in 1633 ended with butchery or enslavement of the routed Indians—812 dead and some 600 prisoners—and halted the Indian advance into the central valley, blunting yet another threat to Concepción and Santiago. The new governor also faced a new royal order abolishing "personal service" or forced labor "wherever and in whatever form." Despite the determined resistance of the cabildos of Santiago and Concepción, this reform and others emerged in yet another decree—the *tasa* of Laso de la Vega in 1635.

The new *tasa* consisted of sixteen regulations, including the elimination of "personal service," although the Indians still were to pay tribute to the encomenderos in money or commodities each year in the presence of the "protector" and the priest in the encomiendas, or of the administrator and priest in the Indian villages. In general, this new legislation was meant to complement, not replace, the *tasa* of Esquilache by giving the Indians a choice of paying tribute with either labor or commodities and by adding more paternalistic supervision and enforcement. The Indians could pay tribute in labor if they so informed the corregidor, who would also evaluate the commodities delivered by the Indians to the encomendero. In addition, the Indians were authorized to "rent" themselves, with preference to their own encomendero during the time necessary to pay the tribute, and after that to anyone whose property was located within four leagues of the town or hacienda where they resided.

The new restrictions on the encomenderos met with resistance and were little enforced. In 1639 a judge of the *audiencia* of Chile reported to the crown that while some of the poorer Spaniards observed the *tasa*, the rich and powerful continued as always "using the natives as if they were slaves, treating them harshly, without paying them the small wage of their sweat and labor . . . bringing them from as far as Tucumán and Río de la Plata . . . and working them day and night in the copper mines at La Serena or . . . to mine gold at Andacollo." The judge also noted that due to the brutality of the soldiers and the venality of the corregidors and priests, as well as to the exploitation of the encomenderos, most of the Indian villages had been depopulated and the lands gradually appropriated by Spaniards. In a classic understatement concerning the judges' report, Chilean historian Amunátegui Solar suggested:

> From this exposition, it can be deduced that the *tasa* of Laso de la Vega was as inefficacious as those of Santillán, Ruiz de Gamboa, Sotomayor, Ribera and Esquilache; and that at the end of his [Laso de la Vega's] government the Chilean natives were subjugated to forced labor with the same harshness as in the times of Pedro de Valdivia. The orders of the king and the ordinances signed by viceroys and governors came to nothing.

In 1639 another professional soldier—Francisco López de Zúñiga, who had fifteen years' experience in Flanders and Germany—replaced Laso de la Vega as governor. Faced with continued Indian resistance, the new governor attempted to carry out a modified policy of defensive warfare by arranging the Pact of Quillín, in which Spaniards and Mapuche celebrated a "peace treaty." The Spanish formally recognized Indian sovereignty south of the Bío Bío River with the exception of the fort at Arauco and the region thereabouts. In all the enterprise of conquest since 1492, Spain had never before recognized the sovereignty of an Indian people. The Spanish also agreed to discontinue the slave hunts and forced labor. In exchange the Indians agreed to return Spanish captives, to allow missionaries to preach in Indian territory, and to ally themselves with the Spanish against English and Dutch corsairs. King Philip IV approved the pact in 1643. But despite the governor's half-hearted efforts, the frontier garrisons as well as other royal officials and encomendero-commercial interests refused both to observe the *tasas* and to comply with the terms of the Pact of Quillín. Indian labor was too valuable to give up merely because of a peace treaty or official policies.

The soldiers on the frontier continued slave hunts and pillage as their principal source of enrichment. Events slowly led to still another general uprising on the scale of the butchery between 1598 and 1606, as Araucanian resistance to "Christianization," especially to the ban on polygamy, frustrated clerics and governors alike.

Despite reaffirmation of the Pact of Quillín in March 1651, Indians in the region of Cunco killed the shipwrecked survivors of the Spanish vessel bringing the military subsidy to Chile. A punitive expedition slaughtered a number of Indians and sent many women and children north as slaves. Then a series of raids led by the governor's two brothers-in-law provoked increasing Indian retaliation.

The governor and his brothers-in-law took over provisioning of the troops, stole supplies, and launched a large-scale commerce in Indian slaves, with the Boroa fort town serving as a clearing house. The 1608 decree allowing enslavement of rebellious Indians provided the basis for a lucrative "certification" business, in which frontier officials certified that the Indians were captured in battles with rebellious tribes.

In February 1655, a mestizo called Alejo, an ex-soldier in the Spanish garrison, led an Indian uprising and at the same time inspired rebellion by the prisoner-slaves still in the frontier region. The Indians again destroyed the towns and forts south of the Bío Bío River and forced the abandonment of towns as far north as Chillán. According to the historian Carvallo y Goyeneche in the years following the uprising, the Indians captured 1300 Spaniards, sacked 396 estates, took over 400,000 head of cattle, horses, and sheep, and caused property damage estimated at 8 million pesos. The Spanish lost Arauco, San Pedro, Colcura, Buena Esperanza, Nacimiento, Talcamávida, San Rosendo, Boroa, and Chillán, along with over half the armaments in the region. An angry mob in Concepción—shouting, "Long live the king! Death to the bad governor!"—temporarily deposed the corrupt governor, and he was officially replaced in 1656. By then the Spanish held only the town of Concepción in all the Bishopric of Imperial, and communication with Santiago was possible only by military patrols. For all practical purposes Chile consisted of the towns of La Serena, Santiago, and Concepción, along with the encomiendas, mines, and rural estates from the valley of Coquimbo to the Maule River.

From 1657 to 1662 Spanish and Indian soldiers battled each other without resolution, until a Spanish army of 600 soldiers surprised and defeated 1500 Indians led by the cacique Misqui near Curanilahue. Soon thereafter the interim governor ordered the resettlement of Chillán and requested still more troop reinforcements to press the war against the Araucanians. In the meantime the king named a new royal governor and, in order to secure another force of 1000 soldiers in Spain, promised the recruits for Chile the same benefits enjoyed by soldiers who served in Flanders.

Governor Francisco de Meneses came to Chile in 1664 and ruled it as a Hispanic robber baron until 1668. Taking full advantage of the warfare economy, the governor demanded heavy bribes for renewal of encomienda grants, sold military and civilian government posts, and made those he promoted pay him in gold; he taxed ships carrying on commerce between Valparaíso and Callao before they left port—unless they carried his merchandise; and he appropriated for sale in his own retail outlet a large part of the goods arriving as part of the military subsidy. Supported by the Peruvian viceroy's desire to increase the flow of Indian slaves to the mines and fields of Peru, Meneses renewed expeditions to the south, especially against the pacified tribes, where it was easier to obtain human merchandise. In a single raid around Paicaví, Cayucupal, and Tucapel, the Spaniards obtained 400 *piezas* (a weighted equivalent of four hundred Indians, allowing for the lesser value of the labor of children or the old) and assassinated twenty chiefs who spoke out against these "military" operations. Meneses's arbitrary, corrupt rule also adversely affected the interests of important Chilean colonists. Eventually he was replaced owing to their letters of protest and after an unsuccessful attempt on his life.

With a permanent force of some 2500 soldiers, Meneses's successor Juan Henríquez vigorously carried the war into Araucanian territory and also withstood attacks by English Corsairs, including Bartholomew Sharp's sack and burning of La Serena in 1680. He also accumulated vast wealth from slaving, despite the royal decree of 1674 prohibiting Indian slavery. Chilean historian Luis Galdames claims that during his tenure Governor Henríquez took prisoner some 800 Indians and sold them as slaves. The governor set the price at 500 fanegas of wheat for each Indian, with the fanega valued at 50 centavos (in the mid-seventeenth century a first-class Indian, *pieza de lei*, sold for 200 to 300 pesos and lesser valued Indians, *piezas de servidumbre*, for 150 to 200 pesos). When he had accumulated 400,000 fanegas of wheat, he sold the grain to the contractors of his own army at two pesos a fanega and was paid from the royal treasury. War was good business! Henríquez left office after almost twelve years (1682) with a fortune estimated at close to one million pesos.

In 1674 and 1679, during Governor Henríquez's tenure, new decrees abolishing Indian slavery challenged the ingenuity of Chilean encomendero and business interests. In response the Chileans adopted a legal device called the *depósito*, which placed captured Indians in the custody of encomenderos or landowners who agreed to supervise them in exchange for the right to use their labor. An Indian under the *depósito* did not legally "belong to" a particular Spaniard as did a slave, but in practice he might as well have. The Chilean economy continued to depend upon warfare, slave hunts, pillage, and exploitation of the rural labor force.

At the end of the seventeenth century, not only the Indians but also the Spanish-mestizo troops manning the frontier outposts suffered the consequences of government corruption. As Chilean author Benjamín Vicuña Mackenna noted, the military subsidy became "an open bag of money into which everybody dug with both hands, except those [the soldiers] for whom the subsidy had originally been established." The war budget profited Lima merchants, royal officials, and Chilean colonials, while the human booty of the continual raids "stocked" the mines, farms, and *obrajes*. Until 1685 the *situado* consisted largely of commodities, many of which were of no use at all to frontier garrisons which lacked shoes, clothing, and munitions. Moreover, the purchase of oil, salt, and soap in Lima for shipment to Chile benefited only the Lima military contractors, since these commodities were generally available in Chile. The shipwreck of the *San Juan de Díos*, which was bringing the *situado* to Chile, provided the pretext for a request by Chile's governor that the subsidy be sent overland from Potosí—in coin of the realm—thereby avoiding the risks of loss at sea and attack by pirates. The approval of this request in 1685 meant that the soldiers were to be paid in cash and buy their supplies at lower costs in Chile. Unfortunately, however, from the mid-1680s onward the subsidy often arrived late if at all.

An earthquake which shattered Lima-Callao and led to the loss of the Peruvian wheat crop in 1687 induced a temporary boom in Chilean wheat exports and also a considerable increase in prices (see

Chapter 3). This made it difficult to buy the needed provisions for the Chilean garrison within the constraints of the military budget. By the time the last seventeenth-century governor of Chile (1692-1700) took over, the Chilean frontier army could not depend upon the annual subsidy as a sure source of support. From 1692 to 1697 the export boom allowed the governor to maintain the army with loans from colonial merchants. But with the military subsidy almost seven years in arrears, Chile's governor wrote the king in August 1697 that the soldiers were not only unclothed, but in debt for what they had purchased or borrowed in recent years; and "what never before has occurred, now is happening, the captains and the corporals of the army leave their posts, as they find themselves in the same misery as the soldiers . . . going to the rural estates to feed and clothe themselves . . . [destroying] order and military discipline."

In the first years of the eighteenth century, the Wars of the Spanish Succession in Europe intensified difficulties in the Spanish-American colonies. When in 1702 the new Chilean governor, Francisco Ibáñez de Peralta, received a payment of 292,000 pesos—against a debt of over 2 million pesos, he made sure that his own salary and certain other obligations were paid in full, leaving little for the garrison. (Ibáñez had already opened a butcher shop, sold a number of official positions, and collected payments for renewal of the encomiendas.) This situation provoked a military uprising that led to serious internal disorders. The governor ordered rebellious soldiers tried by military tribunals, and executed a number of the revolt's leaders, despite an earlier promise of pardon if they surrendered. In 1704 the military subsidy was eight years in arrears, and the army lacked armaments and munitions. In these conditions official policy sought to avoid provocation of the Araucanians by soldiers or missionaries.

By the last two decades of the seventeenth century, the effects of the 1655 uprising had been largely overcome north of the Bío Bío River. To the south the Araucanians remained in control. The degeneration of Spanish military capabilities from the Homeric exploits of the sixteenth century to the professional rabble-garrisons sent from Lima in the seventeenth left the conquest incomplete. Corruption, war-profiteering, and insufficient troops combined with the fierce resistance of the Araucanian and allied Indian armies to prevent Spanish control of the regions most coveted by Pedro de Valdivia and his followers.

In the first decades of the eighteenth century, tentative initiatives to renew the conquest and establish settlements in Araucania met with another general uprising (1723). In response, Governor Gabriel Cano y Aponte (1717-33) ordered the dismantling of the forts of Colcura, Arauco, and Tucapel and the erection in their stead of forts with similar names north of the Bío Bío River. Apparently the Indians did not share Francisco Encina's judgment that "contrary to the fantasies and neurotic mysticism of the Jesuits and the nineteenth century historians, the Indians' condition when left to themselves was much worse than the harshest servitude imposed by the Spanish." A new agreement, celebrated at Negrete in 1726, established the usual obligations of the Indians to receive Christian missions and to ally themselves against enemies of the king; it restored "peace" temporarily, until the next major conflict later in the century (1766).

In 1700 some 100,000 to 150,000 Spanish, mestizos, Indians, mulattoes, and Negroes lived in Spanish Chile. From 1541 until 1664, 20,000 to 30,000 Chilean soldiers and settlers had died fighting the Mapuche at an official cost of 17 million pesos—though the Jesuit Rosales estimates the toll from 1545 to 1674 at 42,000 Spaniards, including deaths from accidents and epidemics, and a military subsidy of 40 million pesos from the Peruvian and Spanish treasuries. This does not include the vast personal fortunes expended in sixteenth-century enterprises of conquest. Estimates of Indian losses are too varied to be relied upon, but there can be no doubt they amounted to many times those of the European invaders, especially taking into account death through epidemic diseases. The material losses of the indigenous peoples of Chile likewise cannot be accurately measured— for they had no great stores of wealth but rather lost their autonomy, their land, and ultimately their cultural integrity.

The uncompleted military conquest would be resolved only late in the nineteenth century, but the authoritarian politics of conquest had already created in Chile the foundations of a highly stratified class society in which labor was denigrated and laborers were exploited. The politics of conquest also institutionalized political corruption, arbitrary use of government authority, disrespect for and evasion of law, and the social and economic institutions of Hispanic capitalism that would condition the development of a more complex social and economic system in Chile in the nineteenth and twentieth centuries.

These latter characteristics Chile shared with most of the Spanish colonies. Unlike the principal colonial centers, however, relative geographical isolation, poverty, and lack of significant gold and silver mines contributed to the development of an agrarian-based economy in Chile. Relative ease of communication and concentration of population in the central valley, along with the constant threat and chal-

lenge of the Indian frontier, forged a colonial elite with strong lo-
calistic orientations, a fortress mentality, and a significant military
tradition. An impressive ability to coopt royal officials through business
or marital ties and to absorb new wealth and successful immigrants
created an integrated political, economic, and social elite with interests in agriculture, commerce, and mining. Intermarriage, shared social values, and dependence for economic well-being upon the exploitation of the rural labor force unified the Chilean upper classes and
helped forge a unique variant of Hispanic capitalism on the periphery
of the Spanish Empire.

Chapter 3 • Hispanic Capitalism

The colonial experience in Chile drastically reduced the indigenous population of the territory between Copiapó and the Strait of Magellan and resulted in a deterioration in the quality of life for the overwhelming majority of the territory's population. Disease, warfare, and exploitation destroyed the fabric of Indian life. At the same time miscegenation gave rise to a new people descended from the conquistadors and their Indian or Negro slaves and servants, or from Indians and their Spanish captives. Accustomed to polygamy, Indian women adapted to Iberian promiscuity if they were not forcefully subjected to it, and bore increasing numbers of "Spanish" children. To a lesser extent Spanish women gave birth to the children of their Indian captors or lovers. Though by 1810 the entire population of Chile had probably not reached the size of the indigenous population at the time of conquest, its character testified to the profound ethnic transformation that accompanied the social and economic evolution of colonial Chile.

If, in retrospect, the most important product of colonialism in Chile is the mestizo, the Spanish had not come to Chile with that intention. They came to take mineral wealth and the booty from Indian empires—as they had done previously in Mexico, Central America, and Peru. Shortly after the founding of Santiago in 1541, gold

TABLE 4. ESTIMATED POPULATION OF CHILE, 1540-1620

	Spanish and European Creoles	"White" Mestizos	Negros and "Non-white" Mestizos	Encomienda and Peaceful Indians	Unpacified Indians	Total
1540	154		10		1,000,000	1,000,164
1570	7000	10,000	7000	450,000	150,000	624,000
1590	9000	17,000	16,000	420,000	120,000	582,000
1600	10,000	20,000	19,000	230,000	270,000	549,000
1620	15,000	40,000	22,000	230,000	250,000	557,000

(After Rolando Mellafe, *La introducción de la esclavitud negra en Chile*, 1959, p. 226.)

from the mines at Marga Marga and other gold washings in the northern and southern districts seemed to justify the prospect of a profitable extractive economy based upon the forced labor of subjugated indigenous peoples. But by 1600 the relative poverty of easily worked gold mines in Chile became evident, and when the Spanish lost all the southern settlements (1598-1604), the products of the countryside came to dominate the colonial economy. Rapid proliferation of livestock soon made tallow and hides Chile's most important exports.

Both in the export of gold and tallow, Chile's Spanish settlers operated from the outset in the intercolonial and international market. The essentially commercial motivation of the Chilean conquest and the distinctly export orientation of the colony's leaders contradict the common characterization of the early colonial economy as feudal, autarkic, or merely subsistence. Yet caution must be exercised in labeling this colonial economy capitalist merely because of its participation in international commerce. The colonial economy functioned within a Hispanic, absolutist juridical order that had more in common with a bastardized Iberian feudalism than with nineteenth-century liberal capitalism. Spanish imperial theory, property institutions, and commercial policy, as well as the economic enterprises of the religious orders and the Araucanian war, combined to give a distinctive character to colonial economy and society. If it was capitalist, then it was a special sort of capitalism, modified by the unique milieu of colonial Chile—a miserably poor backwater of the Spanish Empire. The colonial economy of Chile produced a surplus for export, but it did not do so under the fundamental conditions of capitalist production—the sale by free workers of their labor to the possessors of money and the means of production. Private enterprise and private profit depended upon coerced labor and the protection of royal authority for commercial monopolies, price-fixing, and severe limitations upon economic competition. Thus, while Hispanic capitalism in Chile certainly entailed commodity production for local, regional, and international markets, it did not depend upon a significant wage-labor force until the nineteenth century.

In principle, every economic enterprise in colonial Chile operated only with the permission of the royal authorities or the cabildo, which fixed by decree the price for commodities, labor, and services. Spanish imperial policy sought to limit trade among the colonies to approved channels and to direct the economic surplus to Spain. In turn the colonies were expected to import goods carried from Spain in Spanish vessels. The high cost of transport made many colonial agricultural products noncompetitive when moved great distances from the point of production, but the necessities of frontier life often led local artisans and landlords to ignore prohibitions on local industries or limitations on the cultivation of particular crops such as grapes. Almost from the outset smuggling played an important role in commerce both among the colonies and between the colonies and non-Spanish merchants. Chile could trade legally with Spain only via the merchant fleet that came to Panama once a year or, sometimes, less often. After sailing to Panama via Peru, Chilean merchants had to cross the isthmus on mules to obtain merchandise from the annual fairs where Spanish merchants dictated the prices. The Spanish merchants greatly overvalued their own merchandise. While they sought profit margins that often reached over 500 percent, they paid poorly for colonial commodities. The rigors of travel, the rigged markets, and the capital required severely limited the access of Chileans to this commerce, and left most legal Chilean commerce in Peruvian hands.

Resource allocation within the colonial economy did not occur as a result of the functioning of a capitalist market. Official policy discouraged economic competition, established publicly authorized monopolies, and, by the seventeenth century, created a number of publicly owned haciendas and industries intended to supply food, clothing, shoes, and materiel to the Chilean frontier garrison. For all these economic activities, the labor force consisted largely of slaves, subjugated or tributary Indians, fixed-term "indentured" laborers (*asientos de trabajo*), and agricultural tenants until well into the eighteenth century. Even then the development of a wage proletariat came slowly as class relations in the countryside moved toward tenant labor.

Three primary bases of wealth initially underlay the colonial economy: land, Indian or Negro labor, and the authority to exploit them. To these were added commerce and artisanship and, after 1600, the military *situado*. Always, however, the most important "commodity" remained political authority: from government concessions, licenses, grants, or official positions stemmed all economic opportunity, including land grants (*mercedes*), mining concessions, and the right to exact tribute or exploit Indian labor.

In the early years of the colony, gold mining took first place in the incipient economy. The most fortunate of the conquistadors appropriated the mines and washings worked by the Indians prior to the arrival of the Spanish, and obtained respectable quantities of the yellow metal. At Marga Marga, near Valparaíso, mines that had supplied the natives with the tribute for the Incas now passed into the hands of Pedro de Valdivia and several of his companions. With the relatively simple techniques employed, gold production required large numbers of laborers. Estimates of the number of Indians forced to work in the mines and gold washings are neither systematic nor reliable, but the contemporary chronicler Pedro Mariño de Lobera claimed that in 1553 more than 20,000 Indians worked the mines of Quilacoya alone. While this figure is probably exaggerated, there can be no doubt that thousands of Indians were forced to extract gold for the Spanish from La Serena in the north to the southern mines in Osorno and Valdivia.

Work in the mines was strenuous. The Indian labor force detested their virtual enslavement, the separation from their families, and the harsh working conditions. As disease and overwork killed off Indian laborers, the Spaniards sought to replenish the labor supply from the encomienda Indians (Huarpes) transported across the Andes and with the captives from the war to the south.

In the mining process itself, groups of Indians dug the earth and put the excavated material into tubs, or *bateas*. Other Indians then carried the dirt-filled tubs to the water's edge. Still other laborers, usually Indian women or Negro slaves, spent almost entire days in water up to their knees washing the dirt in a procession of *bateas* until only gold remained at the bottom. Along the streams and rivers the laborers also employed techniques similar to the gold-panning methods of the California gold rush. Thanks to Indian and Negro labor, a few of the earliest conquistadors managed to turn the dream of gold into reality in the Chilean colony.

Owing to the frontier conditions on the Chilean periphery of the Spanish Empire, it is impossible to make accurate estimates of the quantity or the value of the gold extracted in the sixteenth century. As 20 percent of all gold mined (the *quinto*) belonged legally to the royal treasury, there was, of course, no incentive for precise accounting by the conquistadors. During the first few months following the settlement of Santiago, the Spanish obtained some 7000 pesos' worth of gold at Marga Marga, and in 1547 Pedro de Valdivia sent a large gold shipment to Peru. Royal officials estimated that to that time the *quintos* equaled approximately 40,000 gold pesos. Taking into account the inevitable losses to corruption and unreported gold, the Indians produced well over 200,000 gold pesos for the Spaniards at the mines from 1541 to 1547. While this was not an inconsiderable sum, the Chilean mines could not compare with the incredible wealth of the silver mines at Potosí in what is now Bolivia or with the mines of Mexico later in the sixteenth and seventeenth centuries.

In 1552 the most important mines were located at Quilacoya near the Bío Bío River. The defeat at Tucapel (1553), where Valdivia died, took these riches from the Spaniards, but new mines were discovered shortly thereafter at Osorno and Valdivia. The Jesuit chronicler Diego de Rosales tells us, with obvious exaggeration, that in 1561 the Indians' labor produced some 1.2 million pesos at the Madre de Dios mines near Valdivia and in the mines at Choapa in Coquimbo. About Osorno, Father Rosales reported that "the land has gold and silver mines, and it is taken in such abundance that with one or two days' work the Indians mine enough to fill their quota for the week; mining stones so large that they break them into pieces and give them to the encomenderos [to pay off their obligations]." A less poetic account by Juan López de Velasco suggests that from 1542 to 1560 gold output in Chile reached more than 7 million pesos.

As the sixteenth century progressed, gold production dramatically declined. The royal *quintos* went from 35,000-40,000 pesos in 1568 to 32,000 pesos in 1571 and 22,000 in 1583. By way of contrast, Potosí produced 170,000 pesos in *quintos* in 1570. Chronic warfare in the southern territories limited output, and at the height of the Indian uprising in 1600 total royal income from Chile, including the *quintos*, amounted to only 3000 pesos. A royal official reported that "this is all the royal income there is here for now, because the whole territory is so afflicted with war that the pacified Indians cannot mine gold, because they are all employed in making supplies for the war." Even before the uprising another report to the king (1594) had noted that "the Indians serving in the cities of La Serena, Santiago, Concepción, and the others have so diminished in number that gold is hardly mined in all the kingdom and their number [the Indians'] is barely sufficient to sustain the cultivation of the haciendas and tend to the cattle of the encomenderos." Thus, with the possible exception of the mines at Andacollo, gold mining had dropped off sharply by the last decade of the sixteenth century.

In spite of this decline, the location of the mines had influenced substantially the sites the Spaniards chose for the towns that were to become the cradles of European culture in Chile. Though all of the first settlements were destroyed at least once by Indian attack or by pirates and several times by earthquakes, tidal waves, or floods, each was refounded. Their names can be found on modern maps of Chile: La Serena, Santiago, Concepción, Imperial (now Carahue, to the west of Nueva Imperial), Villarrica, and Valdivia. In each town the settlers looked to the municipal council, or cabildo, to order urban economic activity and also, initially, to establish regulations governing exploitation of the mines, agricultural lands, and the cottage industries created in the towns and encomiendas. These towns, however, remained little more than struggling villages with one-story adobe or wooden houses roofed with tiles or straw. Only an occasional two-story building or the larger constructions of the religious orders even hinted at the skyscrapers of later years. In Santiago most of the houses were built around patios—many planted in gardens or fruit trees. Through the middle of the cobbled or dirt streets of the town ran open sewers. The other towns were much smaller and even less prosperous.

In these towns soldiers with seigniorial aspirations formed households with Indian women and servants. As the colony grew, the number of domestic servants increased; the more held by a household, the higher its social status. As few skilled artisans came to Chile in the early years, these households developed a sort of pioneer self-sufficiency, until increased population permitted more economic specialization. For those artisans who did set up shop in Santiago, the cabildo attempted, with little success, to replicate the guild system of Spain. The cabildo regulated the quality and price of almost all manufacturing services, and commodities, including such items as bread, tools, clothing, and fish. As soon as brickmaking took on a commercial character, the cabildo decreed official prices and established a fine of ten pesos in addition to forfeiture of goods sold in excess of these prices. To establish a brickyard required an official permit, and at times a permit was denied if the proposed location posed environmental hazards to the town. As early as 1548 the cabildo approved official prices for different types of clothing made by tailors and for the products of armorers, smiths, and carpenters. Adjustments took place as business interests or consumers pressured the municipal officers. Public policy in colonial Chile left no room for the "free competitive marketplace," and the tradition of government responsibility for regulating industry and ensuring availability of basic commodities at reasonable prices survived even the superficial imposition of liberal capitalist ideology in the nineteenth century. In at least one case the cabildo even prevented a settler from leaving town lest Santiago lose its only blacksmith.

The earliest colonial manufacturers met demands for food, shelter, clothing, and armaments. The first recorded flour mills were established at the foot of Santa Lucía by Rodrigo de Araya and Bartolomé Flores (Blumenthal). Other early enterprises included shoemakers, smiths, armorers, tanners, and saddle makers. Pottery, textiles, and cordage became important cottage industries. In the manufacture of textiles the Spanish took advantage of the developed Indian traditions in weaving. Boatbuilding also gained importance around Valdivia, Osorno, Concepción, and Valparaíso-Concón.

Some of the early manufactures testify to the entrepreneurial skill of the conquistadors. For example, Antonio Nuñez arrived in Chile shortly after Pedro de Valdivia and acquired large rural estates near Santiago and Valparaíso. Nuñez built the first warehouses at Valparaíso, engaged in commerce between Peru and Santiago in his own ships captained by his sons-in-law, established the boatbuilding works at Concón, and negotiated a fishing concession with the cabildo at Santiago (1579). In a business transaction that could be understood by any modern Chilean capitalist, Nuñez offered to bring fish to Santiago *if the cabildo would fix a convenient price for a period of three years*. The cabildo agreed, but Nuñez recalculated his costs and, before delivering a single fish, petitioned for an increase in price "due to the high costs of boats and nets, which will be at least 500 pesos, and since seven or eight workers will be required to cast the nets, in addition to three or four Indians. . . ." Colonial entrepreneurs, like their modern counterparts, sought monopoly market positions, guaranteed prices, captive markets, and cheap labor in collusion with government officials. This tradition of Hispanic capitalist enterprise car-

ried over from the conquest to become the prevailing spirit of the
colonial economy.

Whereas Spanish colonial towns were the centers of political authority and the beginnings of urban culture and industry, most of the
population lived in the countryside, and the agricultural encomiendas,
mines, and rural industries produced the bulk of colonial commodities. The encomenderos and hacendados created textile sweatshops,
oil presses, wineries, tanneries, mills, rope and tool manufacturers
and even, briefly, sugar mills in Copiapó and Aconcagua, to process
the produce of the land. At the end of the sixteenth century Chile
paid for its imports of European and Peruvian merchandise with exports of tallow, hides and leather goods, sheepskins, wine, wood, apples, hemp, salted meat, olives and olive oil, and copper. Despite
recurrent warfare, the Chilean economy produced a considerable
surplus of food and agrarian products. Excellent yields in the territory's virgin soil converted the river valleys into gardens, while the
proliferation of livestock made meat available to all classes. In 1565
shippers charged 46 gold pesos a head to transport cattle from Callao
to Valparaíso. The success of the Chilean livestock industry meant
that thirty years later 300 head of cattle sold for 450 pesos (1.50 pesos
per head) in Santiago. Due to the unending Araucanian war, however, the encomenderos preferred to raise mules for trans-Andean
transport, which the royal governors would not requisition as they
would horses. At the end of the century a horse brought 150 pesos or
more as compared with 1.50 pesos for a cow. A shortage of horses led
Governor García Ramón to prohibit further mule breeding (1607);
and when this measure failed, Governor Jaraquemada (1611) ordered the gelding of all jackasses within twenty days, subject to a
fine of 100 gold pesos per animal for noncompliance. The extensive-
ness of the Chilean countryside and the value of mules for transport
and as export commodities to Potosí made this measure as unsuccessful as the one decreed by García Ramón.

With the loss of all the southern towns and mines at the end of
the sixteenth century, the Chilean economy was reduced to several
regional economies centered upon the small towns of La Serena (46
houses), Santiago (200 houses), Concepción (66 houses), and Chillán (52 houses). Gradually the trans-Andean settlements of Cuyo
were incorporated de facto into the economy of Río de la Plata,
though Santiago continued to import Huarpe Indian laborers from
the encomiendas across the Andes. Though the foundation of wealth
and power throughout the colony remained control of land, labor and
commercial opportunities subject to the discretion of government de-

cision makers, the varied natural ecologies of these regions, and their location with respect to the battlefields contested by Spanish and Araucanians, led to distinctive patterns of social and economic development. Thus an accurate portrayal of socio-economic evolution in colonial Chile requires focusing some attention on the diversity of regional development from the northern provinces to the central valley and then to the southern frontier.

In 1544 Pedro de Valdivia ordered Juan Bohon to found a city somewhere in the valley of Elqui or Coquimbo as a way station between Peru and Santiago. After four years as little more than an encampment, an Indian attack destroyed the settlement entirely. With the arrival of reinforcements at Santiago from Peru, Valdivia sent Francisco de Aguirre to refound La Serena. Aguirre chose the modern site some 2000 meters from the sea. Valdivia gave all the land and Indians from the valley of Choapa to the valley of Copiapó to only eight *vecinos*.* Unlike the rapid turnover among most of the Chilean encomiendas and land grants in the early years, the northern encomienda grants often remained in the same family for many generations. No better example of this could be found than the Aguirre family whose descendants retained the encomiendas of Copiapó and Coquimbo until the abolition of all encomiendas in Chile in the late eighteenth century (1791), and remained important landowners in the region into the twentieth century.

The town of La Serena grew slowly. By 1610 nine square blocks contained a church, Augustinian and Franciscan convents, and government buildings, surrounded by fields and orchards. No more than one hundred Spaniards and mestizos and some eight hundred tributary Indians resided in or about the town. Growth continued slowly until 1680 when pirates led by Bartholomew Sharp sacked and burned the settlement. Many of the principal *vecinos* abandoned the town and fled to their rural estates. After another pirate attack in 1686 the cabildo attempted to prevent total abandonment of the city by decreeing heavy fines for those leaving without permission. Increased wheat exports and mining activity in the last decade of the seventeenth century brought renewed vitality to La Serena, while its port at Coquimbo became an important point of transshipment of copper to Peru. Copper smelters near Coquimbo sent the elaborated red metal to Callao, and artisans sent their copper wares south to

---

* A *vecino* was a principal citizen in an urban center, a tax-paying property owner with a "voice" in the cabildo; he was also often an encomendero.

Santiago as well as north to Lima. Nonetheless, in the first decades of the eighteenth century the French engineer Frezier still remarked on the "scarcity of population, the rudeness of the streets without pavement, the poverty of the houses built of mud and roofed with straw, which gives La Serena the aspect of a country village [*campo*]."

In the first decades of the seventeenth century the major export commodities from the *norte chico* included, along with copper, the livestock products of tallow, hides, lard, and sheepskins. Small amounts of wheat also went from the northern valleys to Peru or Potosí. Although data on agricultural production and exports for the seventeenth century are incomplete, recent studies suggest that between 1620 and 1690 agriculture gained in importance relative to livestock, and the *norte chico* became an important source of hemp, cordage, aguardiente, pisco, wine, and wheat for the Peruvian market. By the beginning of the eighteenth century the present-day agriculture-livestock-mining triad had already emerged, along with the accompanying cycles of mining booms and depressions.

The regional economies of the *norte chico* between Copiapó and Quillota, furthest removed from the Araucanian wars and closest to Peru, developed within a far more stable environment than did the regions south of Santiago. Indians imported from across the cordillera along with Araucanian captives worked the gold mines, planted, tended, and harvested crops, and labored in the limited number of artisan industries, or *obrajes*, and mills. But the limited grain exports to Peru belied the delicate balance between population, agricultural potential, and food supply throughout the region. As population increased in the late seventeenth century, hints of future regional grain deficits were evident. In 1695, in response to expanded Chilean wheat exports to Peru and the accompanying rise in local prices, the cabildo in La Serena ordered producers to sell one-tenth of their output at a fixed price to the town's bakers in order to ensure availability of flour and bread below market prices. By 1724 more drastic measures prohibited export of grain or flour outside the region, even to Copiapó or Illapel. These measures, adopted also in modified form in central Chile, sought to guarantee local consumption at reasonable prices. The need for those measures and others like them from 1692 to 1750 pointed to a basic conflict between participation in the international economy and the provisioning of local markets at regulated prices. This conflict, which reappeared frequently in the history of Chilean agriculture, inspired the age-old responses of smuggling, black market trading, and hoarding of commodities until more favorable prices could be obtained. Thus, in 1747 the cabildo in Copiapó authorized the corregidor to regulate producers in order to assure adequate supplies. Later it noted that a number of *vecinos* had violated the decree, which established a maximum price for wheat and flour, and had hidden away the wheat. As late as 1798 the cabildo complained about "manipulation of grain prices by a small number of persons in times of scarcity."

In the middle of the eighteenth century the region around Copiapó still was essentially a mining district, producing silver, gold, and copper. The region imported foodstuffs, such as wheat, jerked beef, lard, and livestock products, to support the mining population, though it exported wine to Peru. This situation changed little in the rest of the century. La Serena also experienced a renaissance of mining after 1735-40 but barely produced enough wheat to supply its own needs. Like Copiapó, the La Serena district imported tallow, lard, flour, and livestock, in contrast to its relative self-sufficiency in these products earlier in the century.

These economic changes in the *norte chico* were accompanied by an alteration in the composition of the population and the work force. The decline of encomienda Indians throughout the seventeenth century coincided with an increase in mestizos, mulattoes, and other ethnic mixtures, or *castas*, as the offspring of conquistadors, Indians, and Negroes made the population more heterogeneous. Miscegenation and the urban population increased more in the *norte chico* than further south—in large part because the north avoided the costs and scars of the Araucanian wars which devastated the Concepción-Bío Bío region. By the mid-eighteenth century the attraction of work in the mines contributed to the growth of urban centers in the *norte chico*; between 1755 and 1778 Copiapó expanded from a settlement of 2900 to a small city of 5300, with a rate of increase in excess of 3.5 percent per year.

Both natural increase and migration to the mineral districts added population to the *norte chico*. Still, the encomenderos resisted employing mestizo, Indian, or *casta* free laborers, preferring to rely on traditional labor arrangements with "their" encomienda Indians. The mestizos, free Indians, and *castas* thus became a sort of underclass, prohibited from occupying official posts, joining the priesthood, or obtaining the status of master artisan. As the encomienda system declined, this underclass found its way into the mines and haciendas as labor-rent tenants, renters, sharecroppers, or peons. Others took up the life of a vagabond or a criminal. Cattle rustling was so serious by the middle of the eighteenth century that the hacendados received judicial authority within their estates, which often covered entire re-

gions; and punishments for robbery increased in severity from flog-
gings or banishment to prison sentences or, when a theft involved
more than five cows, death. In addition, the authorities attempted to
force transients into productive work. Local registers kept track of all
those living within a district and required "all *vecinos* to report vagabonds and all those entering or leaving the district to present themselves to the corregidor." Those who could not prove they had jobs
were assigned to public works.

The existence of a growing and mobile proletariat did not suit the
needs and expectations of colonial elites and threatened to "corrupt" the sedentary labor force. The concentration of agricultural
lands into vast estates along with the political limitations on creation
of private enterprises prevented absorption of this underclass into the
economy as small farmers, artisans, or merchants. Many could find
no employment or could do so only seasonally in the mines or at harvest time. In a report on the state of Chilean agriculture, industry,
and commerce at the end of the eighteenth century, a royal official
commented that "this lack of employment makes common the lamentable use of certain modes of forgetting their plight, of removing
the weight of such a sad, languid existence; of those beverages with
which the unfortunate, with the pretext of enjoying their afflictions,
seek a cure for living." In the same report Manuel de Salas noted the
tendency of these vagabonds to remain single, to be promiscuous,
and to avoid the responsibilities of a family, thereby "becoming the
fathers of a new generation of the underclass [*miserables*], vagabonds
like their fathers, without homes and with little more possessions
than those sufficient to cover their bodies." By the end of the colonial period, the conditions leading to intergenerational "inheritance"
of misery had already taken shape in the *norte chico*.

From these transients or drifters sprang also in the period 1690-
1750 an incipient wage-labor force of peons, or *gañanes*, in the mines
of the northern district. Often, however, an advance loan of food,
clothing, or tools reduced the peon to a sort of debt-servitude, even
though decrees at the end of the century prohibited advance payment
of more than one month's salary to single workers or two months' to
married workers. To obtain employment in the mines, workers had
to have a paper, or *boleta*, in which the last employer confirmed that
the worker owed no further debt. This system of internal passports
served to monitor the movements of thieves or other "undesirables"
as well as of indebted laborers who sought entry into a new mining
camp. If an Indian, a mulatto, or a Negro fled from the mines while
he owed money, he could be punished by a fine and by flogging "to

serve as an example to the others." Even the worker with a *boleta* could not legally leave the mine without giving notice to his employer. In this manner debt-peonage and mining on shares replaced the encomienda. In both cases Hispanic capitalism depended still upon an exploited but essentially pre-proletarian labor force, though by the middle of the eighteenth century a true wage proletariat was beginning to emerge in the mining districts of the north. Gradually this mestizo and *casta* labor force replaced the dwindling numbers of encomienda Indians.

The miner worked from sunup to sundown with a noonday meal and rest period of two hours. He received jerked beef and bread as food rations. With his earnings and perhaps some minerals "stolen" from the mine owners, the miner could enjoy Sundays or holidays at the combination store-saloons, or *pulperías* and *bodegones*, of the nearby camps or villages. These *pulperías* served as social centers, gambling dens, dance halls, and houses of prostitution. In 1781 fifty-two such *pulperías* could be found in Copiapó and ten at the small settlement at Huasco.

Despite the increase in population in the *norte chico*, until the end of the seventeenth century not a single new major city was founded— only a large number of mining camps, trading centers, and small settlements. Indeed, at the end of the colonial period La Serena with 5000 to 6000 residents still ranked as the largest urban center in the north. Throughout the region the population was concentrated in the river valleys—Elqui, Sotaqui, Salsipuedes, Andacollo, Limarí, Quillota, Aconcagua—and the mining camps, as it is to this day. At the end of the colonial period the *norte chico* remained a sparsely settled, agro-mining region which sent copper, silver, gold, and livestock products, especially goatskins, to international and intercolonial markets.

In the early years Santiago and the central region served as a base camp for the enterprise of conquest. Rebuilt after an Indian attack that left the town in ashes a mere seven months after its foundation, Santiago grew slowly during the first half-century of its existence. It suffered, nevertheless, from some problems common to most urban places. In 1551, taking note of the frequent disorders and robberies at night, Lieutenant Governor Rodrigo de Quiroga and the cabildo decreed that no one could go out of his house at night after curfew under penalty—for Spaniards, of losing their weapons and being arrested, and for the Indians or Negroes, of 100 lashes.

In addition to dealing with law and order, the cabildo had to provide essential public works. The Mapocho River periodically inun-
dated the town. Residents needed a safe supply of potable water.
Lack of bridges across the river impeded communications and commerce. Dusty or muddy streets required cobbling. During the sixteenth
century the cabildo began to deal with the physical needs of the
city. For example, in 1578 water was brought from the cordillera to
the central plaza, but the service could not be maintained, and in
1588 Santiago residents again turned to water from the Mapocho. In
1578 the cabildo also cobbled a number of streets. By the first decade
of the seventeenth century, after a flood had destroyed the Hermitage
of Saturnino and part of the lower sections of the town, construction
began on the flood-control works. Notwithstanding these improvements, the town continued to have a rural flavor: the cabildo prohibited pigs from slogging around the water in the plaza and,
while the public waterworks underwent rehabilitation (1613), prohibited washing of clothes at certain points on the river bank, under
penalty of 200 lashes.

At the turn of the century 500 to 700 Spanish and mestizos and
several thousand Indians resided in this village capital. Despite the
frontier simplicity of the physical environment, the wealthiest residents imported luxury goods from Europe and China via Peru. Merchants brought velvet, silk, and damask to a colony that often lacked
munitions, horses, and military supplies and whose very existence remained in jeopardy: In the midst of frontier warfare a would-be
aristocracy clung to its pretensions. According to one chronicler,
"every Spanish woman wanted thirty Indian servants to do her washing and sewing as if she were a princess." Even in the face of the loss
of the most prosperous colonial towns (those south of the Bío Bío
River) after 1598 and the threat to Santiago itself, the conquistadors
and their successors maintained the superficial forms of a European
nobility they wished to emulate.

The elite of the new-society-in-formation consisted of encomenderos, public officials, including religious functionaries, and merchants. After Pedro de Valdivia's initial generosity, the relative scarcity of sedentary Indians in Chile forced the first governor to reduce
the number of encomiendas granted to the *vecinos* of Santiago from
sixty to approximately thirty between Copiapó and Maule. When
Valdivia died in 1553, a very small number of encomenderos, including his mistress, Inés de Suarez, had been granted the natives in

most of the territory of Chile. These grants served as the basis of wealth and power over generations for certain of Chile's colonial elite.

The abbreviated case history of the encomienda of the German-born conquistador Bartolomé Flores is illustrative. To Flores, Valdivia commended "all the caciques and principals, with their Indians, named below, to wit, Talagante, Mavellangai, Codamolcalebi, Upiro, Lebalo, Guarcamilla, Acai, Nabalquivi, Conquemangui and Namarongo, with all their Indians and subjects in the valley of Mapocho." Flores consolidated these grants into the two estates of Talagante and Putugan (Linares), where he raised horses, chickens, and pigs and cultivated wheat, barley, beans, and corn. On these estates Flores built the first oxcarts in Chile and taught the Indians certain manual skills. Flores married the daughter of the cacique Talagante, and his heir from this union, Doña Argueda, married another German-born conquistador, Pedro de Lisperguer, who had arrived in Chile with Governor García Hurtado de Mendoza (1557). Two other children born in Peru also came to Chile and obtained encomienda grants through marriage. These lands, and others conceded throughout the seventeenth century, remained in the hands of Flores' descendants until 1721-24. Many of the Indians from the southern grant were transferred to the Santiago region, but as was typical of the encomiendas during this period, decimation or flight reduced radically the number of tributary peoples. In 1721 the Talagante grant had a mere fourteen tributary Indians. Nevertheless, these estates and those of the other encomenderos played a significant role in the economic development of the central region during the colonial period. At least twenty of the original grants persisted intact until the final abolition of the encomienda in Chile in 1791.

In Santiago and central Chile there was a rapid growth of livestock and agricultural production, centered in the vast estates of the encomenderos and the hacendados. By 1571-74, according to a nineteenth-century historian, the Santiago regional economy produced "a great quantity of wheat and barley, much wine, and all the other commodities, fruits, and livestock of Spain; there are also many orchards and gardens within and without the city. . . ." Commerce with Peru developed immediately, with the arrival in 1543 of reinforcements for Valdivia and goods sent in exchange for the gold dust collected by the settlers. The extent of this trade can be judged by the loot taken by Sir Francis Drake when he sacked Valparaíso in 1578: 2500 to 3000 jugs of wine, salted meat, flour, agricultural and livestock products ready for shipment to Lima and Potosí.

In the first years a sea trip from Callao to Chile could take over a month. Maritime communication, therefore, was irregular; only 24 ships arrived from Peru between 1543 and 1556; and seventeen sailed from Valparaíso to Callao-Lima, a trip that took three to four months due to the southerly winds and the Humboldt Current. Six others were lost at sea. A trip from Santiago to Madrid could easily take a year. Despite the difficulties and perils of communication, the export economy developed steadily, and Valparaíso, with only a handful of residents, began to serve as a port of commerce.

While the countryside produced most of the colony's wealth, the principal beneficiaries were colonial administrators and merchants in the towns. The colonial merchants, who took great risks to bring goods to Chile and to send them from Chile to Lima or Spain, charged prices that yielded enormous profits. A study of the wealthy residents in Santiago and La Serena from 1567 to 1577 shows that only 15 to 25 years after the conquest, merchants paid almost as much into the royal treasury on the gold registered for payment of the *quintos* as did the encomenderos. The amount of smuggled or unregistered gold acquired by merchants in urban shops or through trade with the Indians cannot be estimated. Some encomenderos also invested the gold "their" Indians mined in commodities or merchant ventures; from the outset, merchant capital and encomendero interests formed an interrelated elite, rather than two distinct social groups. Thus, trade and commerce took their place as integral elements in the colonial economy even under the harsh conditions of sixteenth-century conquest.

Unlike the La Serena region, however, the *vecinos* of Santiago bore a heavy burden in the Araucanian war. The military disasters of the sixteenth century threatened the very existence of the regional economy as well as the maintenance of the Chilean colony itself. The development and character of the economy of the central region at that time depended substantially, therefore, upon the vicissitudes of warfare.

The monarchy's response to the colony's distress after the fiasco at Curalaba at the turn of the century created a new source of wealth, which relieved the colonials of much of the economic burden of warfare and also allowed them to pay greater attention to their economic enterprises. By decree of March 21, 1600, the Spanish monarch authorized a yearly subsidy, or *situado*, of 60,000 ducats, or 82,500 pesos, from the royal treasury in Peru for three years to assist the Chilean colony in its struggle to survive. The new Chilean governor, Alonso de Ribera, received most of this subsidy in the form of clothing and supplies for the troops en route to Chile. Ribera's reports to the king on the desperate conditions of the Chilean garrisons—"so poorly disciplined that their style of warfare seems more like confusion and barbarism than like Spanish militia"—persuaded the crown to create a permanent military establishment of 1500 soldiers whose salary would be paid by the viceroy of Peru. Later this number was increased to 2000. In 1603 the crown raised the military budget to 140,000 ducats; and in 1606, to 212,000 ducats, or 293,000 pesos.

Thus to secure its Chilean outpost, the Spanish state took over the administration and the financing of conquest, for which it utilized the wealth of the mines at Potosí and the income of Peru. Ribera added to this subsidy the revenues obtained through taxes on the sale of captive Indians, and also organized royal estates to provision the troops with grain, beef, and livestock products. At Melipilla the governor established royal textile workshops to supply clothing, blankets, and other goods to the garrisons. These estates—Loyola, between Chillán and Concepción; Catentoa, between Maule and Chillán; and Quillota—harvested 7,410 fanegas of wheat, 500 of barley, and 200 of potatoes in 1604. Large herds of sheep and cattle as well as hemp plantations at Quillota provided part of the basic necessities for the army. In 1607 the Loyola estate earned slightly more than 53,000 pesos, and the Catentoa estate, some 75,000 pesos. Ribera also created a tannery in Santiago and a number of artisan industries in Concepción. Following Ribera's example, his successor established a cordage industry at Quillota and constructed a large number of oxcarts as baggage wagons for the military.

The military subsidy stimulated the colonial economy by increasing demand for supplies and by largely freeing the settlers from the obligations of annual military campaigns. It also brought a continual flow of Spaniards and mestizos as troops, especially to the Concepción region. But the purchase of many supplies for the army in Lima limited the beneficial effects on the Chilean economy; and owing to the institutionalized corruption at Lima, the Chilean army received silk stockings, damask, and honey as well as a number of commodities available in Chile such as soap and oil. The luxury items profited Chilean officials and merchants but did little to help the war effort. The Peruvian viceroys insisted that the major share of the subsidy be spent in Peru, which benefited Peruvian producers and merchants much more than the Chileans. Not until 1685 did Governor José de Garro get authorization to have the subsidy sent in money from Potosí. But, as noted in Chapter 2, at the end of the seventeenth century the subsidy arrived late or not at all.

Throughout this century the royal *situado* and warfare against the Indians reinforced the agro-commercial economy of the Santiago-central region. Loss of the agricultural and livestock output between the Itata and Maule rivers after the uprising of 1655 forced the central district to supply most of the needs of the entire colony; and as the century progressed, it had to respond to demands for grain from Peru, though the quantities of grain sent to Lima remained paltry (9000 to 12,000 fanegas per year) until late in the seventeenth century.

The Santiago-central region provided most of the wheat needed by the colony until the 1680s without pushing prices over three pesos per fanega. Except under the extreme conditions of warfare or siege, even the poorest Chilean produced enough to eat or could purchase food at reasonably low prices, while animal products in particular were available in abundance. Existing external markets did not permit a significant expansion of commercial agricultural production. In contrast, livestock products, such as tallow, salted beef, lard, hides, and sheepskins, as well as wine could compete favorably in the Lima-Potosí markets. At midcentury (1647) Martín de Mugica wrote to the king that Chile exported 20,000 quintals of tallow to Peru (and internal consumption amounted to about the same).

The livestock economy fitted nicely with the social attitudes of the encomenderos and hacendados who preferred the prestige of horses, cattle, or sheep to the plebeian tasks of farming. As the livestock economy also required considerably less labor than cereal production, there was also less need for Indian laborers whose numbers were declining in the encomiendas.

The perilous state of the Chilean colony at the end of the sixteenth century had induced the viceroy to exempt Chilean products from the traditional import duties, or *almojarifazgo*. From this time the number of land grants, or *mercedes de tierra*, around Santiago greatly increased in number; by 1604 most of the territory of modern Valparaíso and Santiago provinces had been legally granted to Spanish owners. Important factors in the rush for *land*, in contrast to the earlier desire for grants of Indians, included the Peruvian demand for Chilean livestock products, the need for sheepskins used to transport quicksilver from Huancavelica to Potosí, and the needs of the army to the south.

Land grants varied considerably in size, but some exceeded 5000 hectares. Sometimes grantees sold portions of the land in order to obtain capital to purchase livestock and initiate an agrarian enterprise; or the land grants emerged indirectly from previous encomienda grants. In either case the land became valuable as the livestock-export economy opened up business opportunities. Most of the large land-owners or encomenderos were *vecinos* of Santiago, even when they held rural estates located in Cuyo, La Serena, or Chillán. According to the *audiencia* in 1647, Santiago had 516 established households with a total of almost 5000 residents. At least one-third of the *vecinos* held encomiendas. Of a list of 164 encomenderos called upon by the governor for aid in putting down the Indian rebellion of 1655, over one-third (59) were royal officials or descendants of sixteenth-century encomenderos. The remaining two-thirds (105) came from families that arrived in Chile in the seventeenth century or that had not earlier obtained encomiendas. Increased land values, participation in commerce, and the casualties of war made entry into the small Chil-ean elite relatively open for the able or for those with "good" family connections.

In 1604, to safeguard their investments, and supposedly to protect the remaining Indian villages, the cabildo of Santiago commissioned a land survey and boundary markings by Ginés de Lillo. Lillo's survey became the basis for the boundaries of many of the Santiago region's most important estates in the following centuries. From 1604 to 1620 *merced* holders attempted to acquire unclaimed lands near their properties through grants of *demasía* which added "leftover" land to existing estates. By the middle of the seventeenth century the legal basis for the Santiago region's vast haciendas was firmly established. Concentration of landownership peaked in the period from 1670 to 1680. The extensive seigniorial estates precluded formation of a large class of small independent farmers.

An earthquake at Lima in 1687 produced a crisis in the agricultural valleys that supplied wheat to the Lima market. Destruction of irri-gation systems left the lands "infertile" for a number of years. Prices for wheat soared as high as 25 to 30 pesos per fanega, ten times the normal price. Chilean and Peruvian merchants took advantage of the catastrophe and Chilean wheat was shipped to Lima. In the *norte chico* the Peruvian crisis intensified already existing patterns of trade; for the Santiago region the opening of the Lima market offered the chance for a radical transformation of its pastoral economy. At first, the limited grain surplus produced in the region permitted only a weak response; soon thereafter the valleys of Aconcagua, Mapocho, and regions to the south were planted in wheat, and 150,000 to 200,-000 fanegas were exported annually. In 1712, though prices had re-turned to 2 to 3 pesos per fanega, the Santiago-central region sent some 180,000 fanegas of wheat to the Peruvian market.

Land values increased with the expanding demand for wheat. Wheat cultivation also required greater labor input than the livestock enterprise. In order to attract tenants, the landowners offered rentals, or *préstamos*—land "loaned" with only a token rent. As the encomienda Indians died off or fled, mestizo, *casta*, or even poor Spanish workers replaced them as peons or tenants. Indians, slaves, indentured labor, "free" laborers, and tenants all played a role in the expanding agrarian economy. Even the indentured or "free" laborer rarely obtained a money wage but rather received the equivalent of 5 to 7 pesos a month (1685-1707) in food, clothing, and other payments in kind. As these arrangements excluded from the money economy the great mass of Chileans who worked in the countryside, the internal markets for manufactures were exceedingly small.

As the eighteenth century progressed, the role of the encomienda Indians drastically declined, while coincidentally tenancies and the system of *inquilinaje* became more important. The origin of the *inquilino* laborer, who became the backbone of the rural labor force in Chile, still stirs controversy among Chilean historians. A traditional interpretation has the encomienda Indian as the forerunner of the *inquilino*. More recent studies of several regions in the central valley point to the *arrendatario* and the worker receiving *préstamos de tierra* from the early eighteenth century onward. Of course, as wheat cultivation expanded, many of the remaining encomienda Indians fled to other farms and/or took on mestizo culture and were incorporated as peons or *arrendatarios* in the rural economy. Thus, the institutions of tenancy, as they evolved, allowed for absorption of the Indian laborer, as well as the rural *casta* and mestizo, as *inquilinos*, while encomenderos continued to exploit tributary Indians as long as possible.

In the large estates more tenants could be absorbed without seriously disrupting the livestock economy, and the tenants produced an increasingly larger share of the wheat of the central region. The *préstamos de tierra*, or rentals, consisted of variously sized parcels, but as land increased in value, the token rental fees and commodity rents often became labor rents, or the landlords required labor services in addition to commodity rents. As land became scarcer and its value increased, the hacendados required more service from the tenants. Soon the landlords required individual *inquilinos* to provide a worker year round for the agricultural labors of the *estancia* or hacienda. They also demanded additional labor at peak agricultural periods, such as planting, round up, or harvest. In the later years of the eighteenth century, the term *arrendatario* was less used and thereafter replaced by *inquilino*—the service tenant who predominated until the mid-1960s in Chilean agriculture.

Lack of land outside the large estates made possible establishment of a service tenantry, and labor-rent obligations multiplied as internal and external demand for wheat increased. However, if *inquilinaje* in Chile bore some resemblance to *colono* or service-tenant labor systems in other Latin American nations, its origins and the predominantly mestizo composition of its work force distinguished it from the harsher arrangements involving Indian labor in Peru, Bolivia, and Ecuador. Even when economic conditions worsened, Chilean *inquilinos* as a class did not experience systematic cultural and ethnic repression on the scale of the rural labor force in the Andes, nor did debt-peonage typically restrict their mobility.

Neither external nor internal markets placed great demands on the Chilean landlords in relation to the territory's agricultural potential. By mid-eighteenth century Chile produced perhaps 400,000 quintals* of wheat on less than 50,000 hectares. Even the largest rural estates rarely cultivated more than 100 hectares of wheat. Commercial expansion of agriculture enriched a number of landowners and provided considerable opportunities for improvement to a relatively small portion of the rural labor force who succeeded at crop farming or stock raising as tenants. But even the "boom" after 1687 and continued expansion in the eighteenth century did not absorb the growing numbers of floating population which squatted on "vacant" land, took up banditry, or served the landlords as a pool of seasonal laborers. Labor surpluses made debt-peonage unnecessary and, therefore, relatively rare.

The sharp increase in demand and massive exports of wheat to Peru (1687-1700) not only influenced rural land-tenure and labor systems but also created serious problems for local consumers. The Santiago cabildo first attempted to monitor the harvests and retain a fixed proportion in the region in order to avoid scarcity or excessive increases in price. Landowners registered only a fraction of the harvested grain to circumvent the cabildo's regulations. In response the cabildo in 1695 urged the governor to prohibit wheat exports. With the *audiencia's* approval the governor revoked all licenses for export of wheat. Opposition from landowners and merchants included the clever request by the Jesuits—who owned many of the most important rural estates in Chile—for permission to "transfer" 1000 fanegas of wheat from their storehouses in Chile to their college in Lima.

---

* One metric quintal equals 100 kilograms.

The governor rejected this request and even forced a merchant ship at Valparaíso to unload wheat already in the ship's hold.

In the following years the tension continued between the need to provision the local market at reasonable prices and the economic opportunities of the Peruvian market. Dual pricing schemes attempted to limit the price of wheat sold locally, but the rapid expansion of commerce made effective regulation practically impossible. Increased production, however, lowered prices substantially. In 1713 over 140,-000 fanegas of wheat left Chile for Peru in thirty ships; two-thirds of these embarked from Valparaíso with wheat from the central region, seven from Penco-Concepción, and two or three from Coquimbo.

The wheat trade also promoted the commercial and physical growth of Valparaíso. A small group of merchants and warehouse owners soon controlled the wheat market in the port. Despite the efforts of the cabildo to limit commercial corruption, this group often defrauded producers with discounts for spoilage. As the years went by, the Lima shippers also conspired to depress the price paid to Chilean wheat producers. The wheat trade epitomized commerce in the context of Hispanic capitalism: a monopoly or a small clique of suppliers colluded with government officials to fix prices and restrict supplies of basic commodities in order to guarantee "reasonable" profits.

The end of the seventeenth century saw not only the transformation of agriculture in the Santiago-central region but also a significant increase in contraband trade with European powers. The succession to the Spanish throne of the French Duke of Anjou, who governed Spain as Philip V, placed Spain alongside France in a long war against England, Austria, Portugal, Savoy, and Holland. Unable to defend or supply its overseas empire, Spain authorized French vessels to maintain communications with its colonies. Contraband trade mushroomed, and Chilean governors profited enormously from new commercial ventures. When the French engineer Frezier arrived in Valparaíso in 1713, he commented on "the abundance of merchandise in the country when we arrived and the low prices." The limited market for European goods in Chile ruined many merchants in Lima who could not compete with French manufacturers. The contraband trade also brought a reversal in trade patterns as merchandise arrived in Concepción and Valparaíso from Europe and then was shipped to Lima. On a lesser scale, merchandise also arrived via Buenos Aires and the base for contraband at the Portuguese settlement of Colônia do Sacramento. In 1712 the Spanish crown worked out an arrangement with the French King, Louis XIV, to halt the contraband trade.

However, it had become so excessive that the Spanish waited seven years to re-establish the fleets bringing merchandise to the "annual" fairs at Portobello (Panama) in order to allow the surpluses from contraband merchandise to be absorbed. In 1724 the French expeditions temporarily ended, but British merchants had by then replaced them.

The Treaty of Utrecht (1713), ending the War of the Spanish Succession, gave the English a thirty-year monopoly on the slave trade with the Spanish American colonies; during this time the English were to bring 144,000 Negroes to the Atlantic ports. Of this quantity, 400 could come yearly to Peru and Chile. Queen Anne of England granted the slave monopoly to the South Seas Company, which established itself in Buenos Aires. From 1715 to 1739, sixty-one ships brought over to Buenos Aires 18,000 Negroes, nearly 4000 of whom were shipped on to Chile and Peru. Since they were not as successful at slaving as they had anticipated, the English turned to smuggling. On the pretext of transporting necessities for the Negroes, all sorts of merchandise came into Buenos Aires and from there via Mendoza to Chile. In return, the English took silver or gold in payment. Traders loaded merchandise into oxcarts for the trip across the pampas and in Mendoza transferred their goods to mules for the Andes crossing. Mendoza's merchants and cabildo identified so closely with the contraband trade that they banished the new corregidor who had been sent from Santiago to stifle it.

By 1722 commercial reform allowed greater shipping activity through the so-called "registered ships," or *navíos de registro*. Direct trade between Europe and Buenos Aires was extended overland to Chile. Protesting Lima merchants urged an end to this link, but the Spanish fleets could no longer compete with the French and the English. In 1735 the merchants of Cádiz and Peru requested that no further fleets come to Panama until they could dispose of the merchandise on hand. Nevertheless, a fleet arrived in 1739, only to be rerouted to Cartagena due to the destruction of Portobello by an English squadron under Edward Vernon. This marked the end of the fleet system and forced the crown to open a new Pacific route for the *navíos de registro*.

After two hundred years as a colony Chile could finally trade with Spain by sea, although Callao remained an intermediary port of call. Due to the war with England, however, French vessels contracted by merchants at Cádiz, carried out the first legal trade between Chile and Spain. In the following three decades the Chilean market never lacked for European manufactures; indeed the market was so glutted that prices declined considerably for most imported merchandise, and many merchants, unable to sell their goods, went bankrupt.

In the last quarter of the eighteenth century, new reforms further reduced commercial restrictions. Prohibitions on much intercolonial trade disappeared in 1774; and with the creation in 1776 of a new viceroyalty centered in Buenos Aires, trade restrictions were eliminated between Chile and Río de la Plata. Despite protests regarding the coincident separation of the western Argentine province of Cuyo from Chile, the creation of the Río de la Plata viceroyalty benefited the Chilean economy. The initial measures of the viceroy, Ceballos, encouraged Chilean commerce by opening the ports to European goods destined for Cuyo. Lastly, the crown also removed Callao as a mandatory stop. Between them these measures eroded Peruvian domination of Chile's commerce.

Yet with all the commercial restrictions of the colonial period, it is difficult to point to any that fundamentally impeded development of Chile's agrarian economy. Inconveniences for merchants or small groups of elite consumers resulted from prohibitions on bringing sugar from Mexico or trading directly with Buenos Aires and Potosí. But Lima was the logical market for most Chilean products. In 1650, and even by 1800, there was little European or North American demand for the commodities of Chile's agrarian economy, as there came to be in the middle of the nineteenth century. In 1788 the value of all (official) Chilean exports (676,222.50 pesos) did not pay for Chilean imports of sugar and yerba mate (684,617.04 pesos); total imports exceeded 2 million pesos.

Efforts by Ambrosio O'Higgins (1788-96) to stimulate expansion of production, in part through import substitution, and to open new markets for Chilean commodities met with little success. Sugar, cotton, and other tropical products, even when the crops survived in Chile, could not compete with Peru or Mexico. Likewise, Chilean industries could not compete with European or North American manufactures. Imports of luxury goods—fine textiles, furniture, jewels— could only be paid for by minting coins from the gold, silver, and copper taken from the earth and exporting money to maintain the pretensions of the colonial aristocracy. European merchants brought manufactured goods to the Chilean market and took gold, silver, or livestock products in return, but offered no great prospect, at the time, of absorbing significant amounts of rural Chile's products. Chile's economic development, given its agro-mineral output, depended upon fluctuations in the international economy's demand for a range of primary or semi-elaborated products. This remained the case long after the end of Spanish colonial domination. Mining booms in the *norte chico* in the eighteenth century increased import capacity, but the concentration of wealth and the inability to compete with imported manufactures stifled internal industrial development.

European manufactures entered Chilean markets throughout the late seventeenth and the eighteenth centuries. At the end of the eighteenth century import duties amounted to one-third those charged by the first national government after 1810. The textile "factories" in Chile declined after 1650, as did the sugar mills. The only surviving industries were shipbuilding, cordage, foundries, and those processing products of the agrarian economy such as tanneries, wineries, and flour mills. Perhaps more extensive commerce in mineral products with British and French merchants might have allowed even greater imports of European manufactures, but this could not have benefited colonial industrial development or altered the institutional structure of the agrarian economy. Unlike the Spanish prohibitions on direct trade with Buenos Aires prior to 1778 and the demands for "free trade" which inspired Argentine independence, freer trade offered little benefit to overall Chilean economic development in the seventeenth and eighteenth centuries.

If Spanish commercial policy did less to shape Chilean development than is often supposed, the internal dynamics and customs of Hispanic capitalism left an indelible mark on Chilean society. It molded economic and social practices and expectations so as to create numerous institutional obstacles to political and economic advancement for the colony and the future Chilean nation. Much more important than the often-evaded commercial regulations, the factors that impeded social and economic development were the authoritarian, arbitrary processes of policy making, the bureaucratic modes of implementation or circumvention, the use of public resources for private profit, the mingling of public and "private" enterprise, the denigration of labor, and the exploitation of the labor force. More important than any Spanish mercantile restrictions as impediments to Chilean development were the institutions of enterprise which condemned the vast majority of laborers to a subsistence existence outside the money economy. The encomienda system in Chile practically made slaves of the Indians. Extreme concentration of land in the large estates condemned the mestizo rural laborers to generations of exploitation. State-supported monopolies on commerce and the artisan trades limited opportunities for the evolution of a prosperous middle class. The royal bureaucracy's comprehensive regulation of prices and economic activity ensured that private enterprise was never really a private matter—that public policy inhibited operation of anything like a market economy. The combination of Spanish seigniorial institutions, neofeudal labor systems, and monopolistic commercial enterprises created a highly stratified society in the Santiago–central region, and the lack of effective internal demand inhibited the development of domestic industry. Chilean elites maintained much of this legacy of colonialism long after they had rejected Spanish imperial domination.

At the end of the eighteenth century the Santiago–central region was still an essentially rural society. Only Santiago, of all the urban places, looked like a city. With a population of 25,000 in 1780, Santiago grew to an urban center of 34,000 to 40,000 in the first decade of the nineteenth century. In a territory with between 500,000 and 750,000 inhabitants outside of Indian territory, the urban centers contained barely 10 percent of the population. While this was similar to general trends of urbanization in the Western world, it meant that the daily existence of most Chileans consisted of toil from sunup to sundown in the countryside or mines.

Between 1740 and 1754 governors Manso de Velasco and Ortiz de Rozas organized and partially financed the foundation of new towns in the central region: San Felipe, Los Angeles, Cauquenes, Talca, San Fernando, Melipilla, Rancagua, Curicó, Copiapó, Florida, Casablanca, Petorca, Ligua. These towns, which would later become important urban centers in the region, were still, in the words of Amunátegui Solar, "miserable villages" at the end of the eighteenth century. Valparaíso, despite its importance as the major port for the commerce of the central region, had a population of only 4500 as late as 1808.

The relative smallness of the urban population belied the overriding concentration of political and economic power in Santiago and Valparaíso. In the capital the cabildo and royal officials determined the regulations that would affect the economic interests of the colonial elites and granted the concessions, monopolies, and privileges that were the source of economic opportunity. Hispanic capitalism linked urban elites to the landowners, miners, and merchants when they were not one and the same. Despite the rural base of economic production, family connections, business partnerships, and the politics of colonial society knit together the economic life of the colony in the major urban centers. Unlike the dispersion of economic power and decision making characteristic of European feudalism, Hispanic capitalism in Chile concentrated wealth and decision making in urban centers even while feudal-like production generated the economic surplus.

In the last quarter of the eighteenth century important public works enhanced the city of Santiago. Under direction of the architect Joaquín Toesca, the city rebuilt the dikes destroyed by the floods of 1783, and work on the new mint, La Moneda, was intensified. In 1795 George Vancouver admiringly called the Santiago mint the "best building in all the Spanish colonies." Roads between Santiago and Valparaíso also received attention made necessary by the expansion of commerce. Sidewalks on major streets and beautification projects testified to the fact that the town had become a city. Here lived the colonial aristocracy, a mixture of landowners, merchants, and the growing number of royal officials brought to the colony as a result of administrative and commercial reforms implemented by the Bourbons in the late eighteenth century. A number of elite *criollo* families intermarried with the colonial administrators and the new arrivals from Spain. Between 1701 and 1810 some 24,000 immigrants came to Chile from Spain, including numerous Basques. Arrival of these Basques at a time of commercial expansion altered the composition of the Chilean elite. The Basques succeeded in commerce, bought rural estates (including some of the estates confiscated from the Jesuits expelled from Chile in 1767), and soon occupied official positions in the colonial administration.

Marriage of royal officials with the daughters of *criollo* elites, a violation of royal policy, created significant conflicts of interest. These led frequently to complaints by those negatively affected as well as to injury to the public interest: "By their [the *oidores*] marriages here, infinite [numbers of] relatives, the connections and haciendas that they have, and by their maximum opposition to that which is . . . advantageous to royal finances, all is reduced to becoming a [victim] of their passions." Not only intermarriage but also expanding opportunity for *criollos* in the royal service created problems for the crown. In 1759 six of the eight members of the *audiencia* were *criollos* and in 1776 all the *oidores* had been born in the colonies. This contrasted markedly with general patterns of peninsular dominance of high administrative and judicial offices throughout the Spanish Empire. Though decrees in 1776 purged *criollos* and their peninsular relations from the *audiencia* to overcome their supposed opposition to fiscal reforms, in the last decade of the eighteenth century *criollos* and *peninsulares* related to Chileans reassumed influence in the *audiencia* and in other official positions. Jacques Barbier's study of colonial elites in Chile confirms that from 1796 to 1810 there were always at least two Chilean *oidores* in the audiencia. Still, tension existed between the aspirations of the colonial aristocracy for control of the local society and the efforts of the crown to limit the corrupting influence of family ties and local loyalties. Above all, however, the efforts by the Chilean elites to influence or control royal officials merely point again to their own awareness that in the context of Hispanic capitalism all wealth, economic opportunity, and status were ultimately linked to politics.

By the beginning of the nineteenth century the institutions of Hispanic capitalism had shaped the Santiago–central region into a highly stratified socio-economic system. A small elite lived well—if not as splendidly as the upper classes in Peru or Mexico—from the returns on colonial commerce, the salaries of official position, and the corruption linking politics and business. Landowners reaped profits from agriculture and livestock. Rural workers and tenants suffered from hunger and lived in misery. The economy grew, and the living conditions of much of the rural population and the emergent proletariat *worsened*. Economic growth within the context of Hispanic capitalism led to the development of a society in which, as one royal official said, "nothing was more common in the countryside, where harvests had recently been taken in and sold for the lowest of prices, than to see the hands that had recently harvested the crops extended for alms." In Santiago the same official reported that he continually saw "similar conditions in regard to the public works of the capital, where numbers of the unfortunate present themselves seeking jobs, begging for admittance to work."

The internal contradictions of Hispanic capitalism already constrained Chilean development. In the words of Manuel de Salas, "the decadence of this kingdom was a necessary result of its economic structure."

Of all the Chilean territory, the Concepción–southern region offered the brightest prospects to the conquistadors with Valdivia in the first years of conquest. Here could be found gold mines, good land for livestock and agriculture, and large numbers of Indians for a potential work force. Some of the conquistadors gave up encomiendas in the Santiago region in exchange for grants south of the Bío Bío River. But the defeat at Tucapel (1553) marked the first of many military disasters that thwarted Spanish dreams of enrichment in what appeared to be the most attractive region of Chile. For the entire colonial period this southern region was an open wound—an insecure frontier where Spanish economic enterprise and urban culture barely managed to survive against the Indians and the calamities of nature.

Valdivia's forces first established the city of Concepción in 1550 near the site of present-day Penco. The town was destroyed in 1554, symbolically refounded in 1555 and abandoned, then re-established again in 1558 when Hurtado de Mendoza arrived with reinforcements from Peru. In recognition of the town's role as the principal fort on the Indian frontier, the crown created Chile's first *audiencia* at Concepción in 1565. But in the words of Carvallo y Goyeneche, "This had no purpose: all were military men and a *consejo de guerra* would have been more appropriate than a legislature; pens were as useless then as swords were necessary." When an earthquake and tidal wave destroyed the town again in 1570, a chronicler tells us that the residents "didn't know what to do, believing that the world was coming to an end, because they saw black water gush up from the cracks in the earth, and a smell of sulphur that seemed like the inferno. . . ." To the end of the sixteenth century Concepción remained a small military camp; only after 1603 did it begin to take shape as a permanent city with the stationing there of the large permanent military garrison.

The other settlements founded south of the Bío Bío River in the sixteenth century constituted no more than small fortified encampments. Mining activity around Imperial (present-day Carahue), Osorno, and Valdivia made them relatively prosperous, though they were always menaced by the threat of Indian attack. In 1575 an earthquake damaged all the southern settlements, but the settlers rebuilt them; and in 1580 Governor Martín Ruiz de Gamboa founded the city of Chillán during the annual military campaign. These southern settlements developed around the prosperous livestock and agricultural estates of the encomenderos as well as around gold mines.

The dispersion of the Spanish forces among so many small settlements left each town extremely vulnerable to any large-scale Indian attack. Had enmity not existed among various Indian groups, these southern outposts could not have survived at all. For most of the last decade of the sixteenth century the Spanish lived as prisoners in their own forts.

Despite its insecurity, the southern territory developed important agrarian enterprises and sent large quantities of gold north to Santiago and Peru. The rural estates produced wheat, barley, oats, vegetables, and great quantities of apples, which in later years became a major Chilean export. Abundance kept prices low. Livestock multiplied rapidly among the Spanish and also the Indians, who soon had large herds of sheep and horses as well as lesser amounts of cattle. Southern industries included the well-known textile workshops, or *obrajes*, at Osorno as well as mills, tanneries, crafts, and the mines. The Osorno *obrajes*, utilizing local Indian labor, produced cloth that the chronicler Mariño de Lobera compared favorably with the textiles of Flanders. Much of this production found its way to Santiago, Lima, and even Europe. Indeed, Osorno, Valdivia, and Imperial were the most prosperous settlements in Chile—until the military disasters after 1598. In 1598 the town of Valdivia had 600 Spanish and mestizo residents, and over 60 percent of all Spanish and mestizo settlers in Chile lived south of the Bío Bío River. By 1600, 90 percent of all Chilean Indians also lived south of the Bío Bío, as disease, enslavement, and warfare radically reduced their population in the north.

In the years 1598 to 1604 the Araucanians erased all Spanish settlements south of the Bío Bío River. Chile thus lost all the wealth of its southern economy. Unsuccessful military campaigns (1603-12) followed by a policy of "defensive warfare" (1612-26) left this territory in the hands of the Indians. After 1626 the crown ordered a return to active efforts to reconquer the lands south of Concepción, but these efforts degenerated into periodic pillage and slave hunts and proved ineffective. The only "products" harvested by the Spanish in these years were Indian slaves and concubines. Though able to send military expeditions through Indian territory, the Spanish could not guarantee the safety of permanent settlements. After years of raids, pillage, and occasional battles the Chilean governor ordered resettlement of Angol in 1637. A fire reduced the fort to ashes in 1638, and in the peace of Quillín (1641) the Spanish agreed to abandon Angol and to establish the Bío Bío River as a frontier between the sovereign Indian people and the Chilean colony.

In order to defend the Chilean colony against Indian and European adversaries, the viceroy of Peru committed a large expeditionary force (12 ships, 1800 men, 188 artillery pieces, as well as artisans) to the resettlement of Valdivia in 1645-46. For some years to come Valdivia depended directly upon the viceroyalty instead of on the Chilean authorities. It served as an isolated outpost in Indian territory, strongly defended and communicating only by sea with Peru or Santiago.

North of the Bío Bío River, between the Maule and Itata rivers, the Spanish maintained ongoing rural enterprises even after the loss of the southern towns. This district became the granary for the limited Concepción region; its wheat and livestock products fed the frontier garrisons and even provided a surplus for export. But the Spanish slave raids and pillaging finally provoked the Indians into another large-scale uprising in 1655 in which the Spanish lost the forts and fort towns of Arauco, San Pedro, Colcura, Buena Esperanza, Nacimiento, Talcamávida, San Rosendo, Boroa, and Chillán. As a measure of the impressive economic growth that had occurred in this region, Carvallo y Goyeneche estimated that in sacking 396 rural estates, the Indians took 400,000 head of livestock and occasioned losses amounting to over 8 million pesos—in addition to capturing some 1300 Spaniards and over half the colony's armaments. Also destroyed were the entire farm infrastructure and small manufacturing enterprises such as mills and tanneries, which had been established between 1603 and 1654, along with crops in the cultivated fields and vineyards. The Spanish army lost some 900 men—over half its effective strength—and the surviving settlers retreated to Concepción or dispersed across the Maule River.

Two years later (March 15, 1657), with the Indian rebellion uncontained, an earthquake and tidal wave again utterly destroyed Concepción, the only remaining town in the southern region. Casualties amounted to forty dead; the survivors faced a winter without supplies or shelter. This tragedy, combined with the Indian threat, prompted an official of the *audiencia* at Santiago to propose moving the frontier north to the Maule River. Instead, the new governor, Pórter Casanate, led a successful campaign against the advancing Indians, pushing them back across the Bío Bío. Slowly the Spanish rebuilt Concepción, and by the 1670s the Maule-Concepción triangle regained self-sufficiency in basic foodstuffs. By the end of the century both wheat and wine production had recovered to pre-1655 levels, and the region again sent livestock products, wine, and wheat to Lima. The opening of the Lima market to Chilean wheat in the 1680s stimulated the rural economy of the Concepción region as it had the central valley, but the direct export trade remained relatively small; an average of only two to three ships a year trafficked between Concepción and Callao during the last two decades of the seventeenth century.

Delays in the arrival of the military subsidy between 1700 and 1717 seriously injured the southern economy and debilitated the frontier garrisons. The crown reduced the annual *situado* to 100,000 pesos after 1705; it actually arrived only in 1706 and 1717. By the early 1720s the effective garrison consisted of about 700 soldiers instead of the authorized 1500 to 2000. The reduced garrison found itself dis-

persed in a number of small forts, including some south of the Bío
Bío River. These served as centers of trade with the Indians, but the
abuses of soldiers and traders also provoked the Indians' anger.

The Indians took advantage of the decline in colonial military capabilities and in a general uprising in 1723 besieged and forced abandonment of the southern forts at Tucapel, Arauco, Colcura, and
Purén. Raiding the haciendas between Laja and Chillán the Araucanians took thousands of cattle (40,000 according to one estimate)
and again disrupted the rural economy. In a midcentury report to
the king, a Jesuit urged a new frontier policy. He also conveyed an idea
of the character of the forts destroyed in the 1723-26 uprisings: "If
the forts don't defend us nor scare the enemy, what good are they?
They serve merely to conserve a few 'ranchos' covered with straw,
for—with the exception of Arauco, that is all they amounted to, in
an area with few Spanish families. . . . To defend so little did not
justify provoking the Indians' hostility." An indication of the economic effects of this uprising was that the tithes, or *diezmos*, collected by the Bishopric of Concepción declined from 18,000 pesos in
1717 to 7000 pesos in 1724. The same report tells us "in the year of
1738, the *diezmos* did not exceed 11,000 [pesos] because the Indians
took over 100,000 head of cattle and again as much of smaller livestock from 1724."

Despite the intermittent warfare, cattle rustling, and minor incidents, the pastoral-agricultural economy in the Maule-Concepción
region survived. Some settlers, called *conchabistas*, even carried out
a good amount of trade with the Indians, exchanging wine, hardware,
and trinkets for Indian ponchos, textiles, and livestock.

Just as Concepción was recovering from military disasters and natural calamities, still another earthquake and tidal wave (July 8, 1730)
leveled most of the city. The bishop wrote to the king that two-thirds
of the principal buildings and houses of the city, along with granaries,
storehouses, and shops, had been destroyed. Emergency relief and
military supplies arrived from Santiago to avoid a military disaster
while the city recovered from the earthquake. The viceroy at Lima
advanced 50 percent of the next year's subsidy, and the governor in
Santiago contributed over 10,000 pesos to the churches and residents.
Twenty-one years later (1751) an even worse earthquake entirely destroyed the settlement again; after struggles between the bishop and
those wishing to relocate the town, Concepción was officially refounded in 1764 in the valley of Mocha, between the Andalién and
Bío Bío rivers.

Apart from Concepción, a city of perhaps 6000 residents by 1800, few significant urban centers grew up in the southern district. At the end of the eighteenth century Carvallo y Goyeneche reported 449 families at Chillán (also destroyed by the earthquake of 1751) living in small adobe houses. The plaza "which is 150 *varas* square lacks the adornment of impressive buildings, with the exception of the house of the priest . . . built in the style of the capital." Other towns of the region, founded in the 1740s and 1750s by administrative order of the governor, included Quirihue (1741) which "merits not even the name of village with its five families"; Gaulqui, in the district of Puchacai, where 14 families resided; San Luis Gonzaga (1766), in the district of Rere, with 40 *vecinos* and a total population of 201; Los Ángeles (1741), the most important town in Rere with 159 *vecinos* (less than 800 total residents). In a number of small forts handfuls of soldiers also formed "urban" nuclei on the frontier. Farther south the colonial authorities in Lima and Santiago financed the refounding of Osorno, in the last decade of the century, with expenditures of over 30,000 pesos; in 1796 some 1,012 settlers (170 families) had established themselves in a region lost to the Spanish for many years. In all, however, if we accept the estimates of Marcello Carmagnani, fewer than 8 percent of the population in the southern region lived in "urban" situations near the end of the eighteenth century, and most of these resided in Concepción.

Social structure and land-tenure patterns in this region differed from those in the central valley and to the north of Santiago. Lack of security made maintenance of large estates extremely difficult. Most of the Spanish and mestizos who wanted to farm had access to parcels and could provide for their own sustenance. With a population composed largely of soldiers, ex-soldiers, and the familes of soldiers, racial and social stratification was much less rigid than in other parts of the Chilean colony. Most of the inhabitants led a life of subsistence scratched from the soil, or from the low military pay, small mines, trade with the Indians, livestock and related manufactures, or pillage. In the last decade of the eighteenth century Carvallo y Goyeneche accurately described the region's pathetic state:

> Almost all of its inhabitants are laborers, the only work available. With this they do not want for food but they live a miserable life. Those who do not want to believe this need merely enter the houses (or I should say, huts) and observe the rustic clothing, food, and manners of the men, the weariness of the women

> and the nudity of the children. . . . It is a cause for tears that
> a region so potentially rich, does not produce for itself or for the
> peninsula Spain the immense wealth [which it could].

In the last half of the eighteenth century the rural economy of the region grew—but not dramatically. From 1750 to 1778 no more than seven ships a year departed from Concepción harbor with the tallow, hides, sheepskins, fruits, and wine from the rural estates. In the last decades of that century and the first decade of the nineteenth, commerce and contraband increased with the appearance of whaling ships and smugglers from the United States, Great Britain, and elsewhere. Nevertheless, the southern region remained a real frontier, with the unconquered Indians south of the Bío Bío still outside effective jurisdiction of colonial political authorities. Not until the 1880s did an independent Chilean nation definitively incorporate this southern zone.

With regional variations Hispanic capitalism shaped colonial Chile into a highly stratified caste-class society whose political and economic institutions survived long after imperial rule. The sparsely settled northern agro-mining district, the dominant Santiago–central region, and the Concepción frontier territory had impressed upon them a common juridical mold, altered in practice by local conditions, but uniform in its formalism and its flexibility of application—at the discretion of government officials. Overt deference to authority combined with systematic evasion of the law became the norm. Intermingling of private and public business blurred the distinctions between corruption, "conflict of interest," and routine public administration. The war against the Araucanians conditioned economic development while offering royal officials, soldiers, and merchants enormous opportunities for profit, promotions, and patronage. Centralized, authoritarian, and often arbitrary policymaking became the expected, accepted pattern of government. Concentration of wealth, status, and real estate in the hands of a privileged few, denigration of work, and exploitation of labor were all essential ingredients in the socio-economic structure of the colony.

As long as the legitimating symbol of empire—the monarchy—remained intact, there was only minor resistance to the institutions and processes of Hispanic capitalism in Chile. Colonial elites made no significant attack on the legitimacy or fundamental character of Spanish rule prior to 1810. And even when events in Europe precipitated independence movements in Spanish America, Chilean leaders ultimately re-established political order by reaffirming the basic assumptions and institutions of the colonial era, with the exception of submission to Spain and European monarchism. The Spanish crown might lose its dominions in America, but Chile would retain the indelible markings of Hispanic capitalism.

Chapter 4 • Independence and the Autocratic Republic

In the last decades of the eighteenth century administrative reorganization of the Spanish Empire left Chile an autonomous captaincy-general, no longer subject directly to the viceroy of Peru. Until 1808 the colony was governed by a succession of capable, professional administrators; its gradual material progress and the public sentiment of the leading *criollos* gave little premonition of the violent movement for political independence that occurred after 1810. Perhaps overstating the case, Manuel de Salas, the well-known colonial administrator and intellectual precursor of independence, claimed that Chileans "desired only to be good Catholics and good Spaniards, which they regarded as the two inseparable conditions of their happiness."

The last royal governors administered Chile with vigor and correctness. Ambrosio O'Higgins—whose illegitimate son, Bernardo O'Higgins, would become the George Washington of Chile—began his term of office (1787-96) with an extended tour on horseback of the northern regions, visiting the towns and mining districts. Intent on stimulating the Chilean economy and reducing its dependence upon imported commodities, O'Higgins attempted to introduce new crops and to reestablish colonial plantations such as sugar, cotton, and rice as well as to encourage increased exports of mineral products, hides, and wool to Spain. He also sought to establish direct trade between Chile, Guayaquil, Central America, and Mexico. To revive old trade patterns between Chile and Charcas, O'Higgins helped form a commercial enterprise with an eight-year monopoly to promote exports of copper, aguardiente, wine, and other products of the northern districts.

Though well-intentioned, this economic program (which anticipated to some extent the policy of import-substitution by Chilean governments after 1930) brought very limited results. The tropical and plantation crops failed to survive in the difficult conditions of northern Chile; the colony continued to import large amounts of sugar, cotton, and rice from Peru or elsewhere in the empire. Exports expanded slowly, and local industry did not develop to provision local markets with substitutes for the luxury goods imported from Europe, Lima, and Buenos Aires. Many of the structural constraints on economic development that plague Chile today were already evident in the obstacles facing Ambrosio O'Higgins' economic program during the last decade of the eighteenth century.

In the last days of O'Higgins' administration the crown established a *tribunal de consulado* in Chile. This was both a commercial court and an agency to promote economic development. The royal decree creating the *consulado* assigned it responsibility for "protection and stimulation of commerce . . . the advancement of agriculture, improvement in crops and commercialization of the fruits of the land, introduction of beneficial machinery and implements. . . ." Whatever the limitations imposed by colonial status, the establishment of the *consulado* indicated that Spain was not entirely ignoring the problems or the needs of the Chilean economy.

O'Higgins' achievements and his rectitude as governor of Chile earned him promotion to the Viceroyalty at Lima. His successor, Gabriel de Aviles y del Fierro, had lengthy experience in the colonial bureaucracy and military establishment. Aviles continued in the footsteps of O'Higgins and supported public projects such as dikes, cobbling of streets, and beautification of Santiago. In cooperation with Manuel de Salas, the syndic of the *consulado*, Aviles provided competent administration of the Chilean colony during his short tenure (in 1799 he was promoted to the Viceroyalty at Buenos Aires).

As the eighteenth century ended, Chile received a new governor with all the pomp and ceremony that it could marshal, including bullfights, feasts, theatrical presentations, and other public festivities. Far from hinting at any desire for independence from Spain, Santiago society welcomed the new governor with subservient splendor.

When the last of the royal governors assumed office in 1802, the colony remained loyal to Spanish authority. A long-standing dream came to fruition with initiation of work on the canal from the Maipo River to irrigate the land in the valley and augment the water in the Mapocho. Public works in Santiago continued with the completion of dikes and, also, after fifteen years, of the future presidential palace, La Moneda. When the governor died at the age of seventy-three in February 1808, few Chileans could have anticipated the juntas that would soon spring up throughout Spanish America to cut the bonds linking it to Spain. Notwithstanding Bourbon efforts to implement administrative reforms, no great change in internal administration or unusual abuses occurred to anger the colonials; there was in Chile nothing like the Stamp Act or the tea tax that incited the North American colonies to rebellion.

Though the colonials remained loyal to Spain, certain persistent complaints or dissatisfactions did exist. The *criollos* resented the preference given to native-born Spaniards in royal appointments and also the condescending treatment they themselves frequently received from Spanish officials or merchants. They also disliked certain of the commercial regulations and taxes that burdened Chilean commerce, and the lack of educational opportunities in Chile which necessitated travel to Lima or Spain for professional training. A belief of many Chileans that Peru maintained a privileged position vis-à-vis Chile—despite the favorable impact on Chile of certain of the Bourbon reforms—contributed to a resentment of royal policy. Geographical isolation and the evolution of a distinctive Chilean culture had also eroded the allegiance of some colonial elites to Spain. Finally, a very small minority of intellectuals, attracted by liberal, republican ideology and propaganda, had come to blame Chile's backwardness on Spanish imperial rule.

Even taken all together, however, these criticisms of the imperial system proved mild in comparison with those in Buenos Aires, Guayaquil, and Mexico City. In the words of Chile's well-known nineteenth-century historian, Barros Arana, "the most advanced men were persuaded that the reform of a few laws, the growth of population, and the diffusion of useful knowledge would make Chile a region privileged by her products and by the virile and enterprising character of her people." Most elites opposed Protestant or liberal doctrines imported from Europe, Britain, and the United States in the increasing number of foreign ships in Chilean ports after 1790 (when the Convention of San Lorenzo opened the South Pacific to European and North American shipping). Deliberate ideological subversion of Spanish rule was clearly the goal of a small number of North American merchants and seamen. Some of the 257 North

American ships that plied Chilean coastal waters between 1788 and 1810 carried copies of the Declaration of Independence and the Federal Constitution. Nevertheless, while most Latin American republics can point to at least one or two pre-revolutionary conspiracies of some import, no serious anti-Spanish conspiracies occurred in Chile prior to 1810.

Just as the conquest of Chile was an extension of the Pizarro-Almagro venture in Peru, so the Chilean independence movement depended on events in Europe and other parts of Spanish America. The movement for Chilean independence, like that of most other Spanish American republics, originated in European politics and warfare. Napoleon Bonaparte, in an effort to impose French hegemony in Europe, took his armies into Portugal and Spain in 1807. Charles IV and his son, Ferdinard VII, yielded the Spanish throne to Joseph Bonaparte. Spanish insurgents resisted his usurpation of the Spanish crown: in the name of Ferdinand VII, a junta at Seville directed the struggle against the Napoleonic armies; and in the Spanish American colonies, local juntas organized to defend the legitimate king of Spain.

News of Napoleon's invasion of Spain arrived in Santiago via Buenos Aires in mid-1808. The French usurpation of the Spanish crown raised the issue of how best to administer the colony on behalf of the legitimate monarch and what to do if the French occupation should become permanent. For a small minority of Chilean leaders this political dilemma provided an ideal context for pursuing complete independence from colonial rule. The majority of Chileans, however, saw the events in Europe as a temporary interruption of legitimate Spanish domination. Nevertheless, confrontations occurred between those professing to favor the temporary "nationalization" of authority in a local junta and those favoring continued submissiveness to French authorities in Spain. The former group found its principal leadership in the cabildo of Santiago, and the latter in the governor, Francisco Antonio García Carrasco and the *audiencia*.

Unlike the seasoned colonial administrators who had governed Chile ably in the late eighteenth and early nineteenth centuries, García Carrasco lacked administrative experience and political skills. He had assumed the governorship due to a reform that left the office in the hands of the highest military official above the rank of colonel in the case of the incumbent's death. With the continual arrival of disturbing news from Buenos Aires—especially reports of the revolt of May 22-25, 1810—the governor decided to take repressive measures.

His inept actions, including the arrest and deportation to Lima of three prominent *criollos* on charges of subversion, increased the tensions in Santiago. The *audiencia* attempted to restore calm by announcing García Carrasco's resignation and his replacement by the aged Conde de la Conquista, Mateo de Toro Zambrano, whose rank as brigadier of the royal armies gave him rightful claim to the office. But this desperate effort to maintain legitimacy failed; and on September 18, 1810, a *cabildo abierto*, or "town meeting," convened in the *tribunal de consulado* in Santiago, accepted the resignation of the governor, and proclaimed the creation of a national junta.

For the next two decades a dizzy succession of juntas, assemblies, congresses, military dictatorships, and supreme directors sought to impose their authority in Chile—with a three-year interlude (1814-17) when Spanish royal authority reasserted itself. At first the contending factions all proclaimed their loyalty to King Ferdinand VII or to Spain. The national junta set up September 18, 1810, swore "to govern and to protect the rights of the king during his captivity." A leader of the Chilean independence movement, José Miguel Infante, even justified establishment of the junta by citing Spanish legislation in the principal preconquest codification of Spanish law, the venerable *Siete Partidas*. If, as was probably the case, a minority of Chileans who were bent upon independence from the outset hid their motives behind the mask of loyalty to the king, this mask was enough to gain recognition for the junta from the council of the regency in Spain, making the Chilean junta the only one ever recognized by that body.

The political history of these two decades (1810-30) is conveniently divided into four main periods: (1) four years of civil war and uncertain advance toward independence, 1810-14 (called the *patria vieja*, or "old fatherland"); (2) reimposition of Spanish authority by the viceroy at Lima through force of arms, 1814-17 (called the *reconquista*, or "reconquest"); (3) dictatorship of Bernardo O'Higgins, 1817-23; (4) a chaotic succession of governments proclaiming liberalism, federalism, and republicanism, 1823-30.

After 1830 the internal strife was ended by a coalition of conservative business interests, the clergy, and the landowner class—led by a businessman named Diego Portales—which installed a unique political regime. Republican in form and authoritarian in practice (thus the epithet "autocratic republic" some Chilean historians have given to this regime), the new political order reconsolidated the Hispanic ideal of a strong, centralized executive who imposed order through decrees and the necessary coercion to ensure their implementation. A man who openly claimed he would have shot his father if it were necessary for public order, Portales wrote bluntly: "Democracy, which self-deceived men proclaim so much, is an absurdity in countries like those of America. . . ." Agreeing with the *criollo* intellectual Mariano Egaña that liberal principles were "the greatest enemies of America and would eventually bring her down to total ruin," Portales and his colleagues brooked no opposition to their programs and spared no effort to save Chile from the perils of imported liberal ideology. A great irony of Chilean independence was that the political order devised by Portales, Egaña, and the three presidents who served from 1831 to 1861 exhibited more than a passing similarity to the autocratic tradition of colonial rule.

Independence liberated elite *criollos* from the restraints of Spanish authority and left them free to exploit rural labor, miners, and urban shanty dwellers. It also opened Chile to British, North American, and European merchants along with a few European settlers. It did not mean political, social, or economic improvement for the vast majority of Chileans.

In the process of establishing the postcolonial order, political and constitutional conflicts developed which would recur often during the nineteenth and twentieth centuries. These included disputes over the basic character of the constitution, especially the balance of power between executive and legislature; over the relationship between Church and State; over the inclusiveness of citizenship and civic participation, at first limited to a small minority of wealthy Chileans; and over the scope of the state's authority to confiscate or expropriate private property in the public interest. This latter issue emerged with particular intensity in political maneuvering over abolition of slavery (1811-24) and elimination of titles of nobility and entailed estates (*mayorazgos*).

In the social and economic realm, the chaos of the years 1810-30 also raised critical policy issues that would endure in Chilean national life. Domination of mining output and commerce by foreign (mostly British) merchants and the Chilean government's dependence upon foreign loans, ships, armaments, and technicians to pursue the internal war of liberation against the royalists and carry out the naval expedition to Peru, made clear that shedding the colonialism of Spain would bring a more subtle economic exploitation by the stronger European nations and by North Americans. Lack of efficient internal taxing mechanisms and reliance upon revenues from foreign trade, particularly import-export duties, made public finance highly vulnerable to fluctuations in international trade and to the extensive smuggling and corruption at the ports. Attempts to raise revenues through authorizations of exclusive commercial monopolies and special concessions continued colonial practices and set precedents for policies that later surrendered Chile's most important economic resources, especially mineral wealth, to foreigners. Opening the ports to international shipping—but with significant import duties—generated debates between free trade advocates and early proponents of protection for Chilean industries. These debates set the tone for a persistent conflict over this issue which carried over into the twentieth century—and dramatically re-emerged in the 1970s.

The independence decades also saw an initial statement by a handful of Chilean elites of the need to attract immigrants from Europe in order to populate the country with peoples they considered racially superior to the predominantly mestizo and *casta* work force in the mines, countryside, and towns. The tendency for the most radical *criollo* leaders to blame Spain for Chile's backwardness added to the desire for Europeanization (especially immigrants from England, Ireland, and northern Europe) of the Chilean ethnic stock as well as for the Anglicization of Chilean institutions. This propensity to disparage the mental and technical capabilities of the working classes endured into the twentieth century; it reached its maximum expression in Francisco Encina's twenty-volume *History of Chile to 1891*. Over and over again Encina bemoaned the debilitating effects of miscegenation. Critical of the economic effects of free trade, Encina nevertheless emphasized the "precious gift of European blood" which the resident foreign merchants contributed to the "Chilean race."

The independence movement used Negro and *casta* troops to expel the Spanish, and decreed emancipation of the *offspring* of the approximately four thousand remaining slaves as a wartime expedient; but it ended by reinforcing the tremendous social gap between Chilean elites and the common folk. These class divisions would be the basis for bitter confrontations later in the nineteenth century, even as the newly formed Sociedad de Fomento Fabril (Society for Industrial Development, 1883) repeatedly called for European immigrants to replace the "lazy, shiftless, mongrel" Chilean laborers.

Independence brought a change in political form but not in social structure. While the English and French displacement of Spanish or Peruvian merchants in Valparaíso and Santiago after 1817 influenced furniture and architectural styles in the homes of the wealthy, the dwellings of the rural tenant laborers typically remained little more than straw-covered huts or, at best, small adobe *ranchos*. In the towns

and cities, lower-class residents could spend their leisure hours in the
chinganas (these were a combination of bar, dance hall, and brothel),
which were increasing in number, or at horse races, but they continued to live in "suburban" huts ringing the solid homes and commercial centers spreading out from the central plazas. As the towns
and cities grew and became more affluent in the later part of the nineteenth century, the fusion of liberal political ideology with social
Darwinism would both recall the racist sentiments of the early proponents of European immigration in the independence decades and
"justify" the misery that modernization and "progress" brought to a
growing proletariat after 1850.

From 1810 to 1814—a period labeled *patria vieja*, or "old fatherland"—by Chilean historians, the personalities and ambitions of
those later enshrined in the pantheon of the independence movement's heroes determined the politics of Santiago and Concepción.
The national junta formed on September 18, 1810, largely dominated
by Juan Martínez de Rozas, was followed by experiments with a national congress and then gave way to the dictatorship of José Miguel
Carrera and his two brothers. Feuds between Carrera, the prominent
Larraín family, and Bernardo O'Higgins created an environment of
intrigue and uncertainty. Jealousies between Santiago and the provincial junta at Concepción further confused and debilitated political
authority. In the meantime the United States consul, Joel Poinsett,
allied himself with the Carreras and promoted Chilean independence.

Mindful that, despite protestations of loyalty, the Chilean situation was developing into a full-blown separatist movement (as had
already occurred in Venezuela in 1811 and in New Granada and
Mexico shortly thereafter), the viceroy of Peru sent a military expedition to restore order in Chile. The military force disembarked at
the island of Chiloé, which was still directly dependent upon the
viceroyalty, and, after gathering new recruits, proceeded to Valdivia,
where royalists had already gained control. From there the expedition
went by sea to Talcahuano and captured Concepción, where a great
part of the garrison also took up the royalist cause. These events induced the major southern cities to swear again their allegiance to
Ferdinand VII.

Early in 1814 a second royalist expedition commanded by General
Gavino Gainza entered Chile. After a number of encounters with
the military forces led by Carrera, O'Higgins, and Juan Mackenna,
the royalist armies captured Chillán and Talca in the southern part

of the central valley. Thereafter a stalemate occurred between the opposing movements. In 1814 British commodore James Hillyar mediated a treaty agreement (Treaty of Lircay) that ended hostilities with Chile's recognition of Ferdinand VII, an exchange of prisoners, suppression of the Chilean national flag introduced in 1812, and a promise by the Spanish-Peruvian forces to leave Chile within a month.

This treaty proved unacceptable to both the viceroy and prominent *criollo* leaders in Chile. Carrera carried out still another coup in Santiago, banished his personal enemies, and determined to carry on the war against the royalists. O'Higgins refused to recognize Carrera's authority. To complicate matters, the Peruvian viceroy sent a new military expedition to Chile commanded by General Mariano Osorio. Osorio's advance from Talcahuano to Chillán brought Carrera and O'Higgins together again to meet the royalist threat. At the battle of Rancagua (October 1-2, 1814), Carrera failed to reinforce the besieged patriot army, and Osorio defeated O'Higgins. This ended the *patria vieja*. The remnants of O'Higgins' army as well as Carrera's forces fled to Mendoza, accompanied by a mass exodus of prominent *criollos* from Santiago. In Mendoza, José de San Martín, leader of the Argentine independence movement, welcomed O'Higgins; and plotting began for the campaign that would liberate Chile and Peru from Spanish rule (1817-25).

For three years Spanish officials sought to purge Chilean society of separatist sentiments. Secret police, courts-martial, and imprisonment of leading citizens alienated even moderate *criollos* previously uncommitted to independence. Instead of ameliorating *criollo* resentment, the Spanish "reconquest" (1814-17) greatly intensified discrimination against native-born Chileans. Spanish army personnel received salaries up to five times larger than those of *criollos* of the same rank; Chileans were denied government appointments and were refused the economic concessions that stemmed from official largesse. When Chileans complained of these conditions, the governor was reputed to have told his entourage: "I shall not leave to the Chileans even tears with which to weep."

Polarization of sentiment in Chile coincided with San Martín's planning of an expedition to oust the Spanish from all of the southern cone of South America and Peru. While San Martín's agents collected intelligence, and the general prepared his forces in Cuyo, Manuel Rodríguez, former secretary to Carrera, carried out the guerrilla activities against the royalists which made him the hero of the

independence movement most acclaimed by leftists and revolutionaries in Chile in the 1960s and 1970s. In the mid-1980s, the most
prominent guerrilla opposition to General Pinochet called itself the
Manuel Rodríguez Patriotic Front.

Crossing the Andes in early 1817, San Martín defeated the royalist
army at Chacabuco to the north of Santiago. Mobs in Santiago ransacked the houses and property of royal officials and wealthy royalists;
they also destroyed the portraits of royal governors (back to Pedro de
Valdivia) hanging in the government palace. No longer did those
bent on independence mask their intentions. On February 14, 1817,
San Martín and O'Higgins entered Santiago at the head of the victorious army. After San Martín declined the cabildo's offer to become
dictator of Chile, O'Higgins accepted the "supreme directorship" of
the colony.

During the ensuing year Spanish victories in the central valley
again threatened Santiago until San Martín won the decisive battle
on the plains of Maipo (April 5, 1818). By mid-1818, therefore, despite continued royalist resistance in the south, Chilean territory
from Copiapó to Concepción was free of Spanish authority. In 1820
the British Lord Cochrane, lending his services to the rebels' cause,
returned from an unsuccessful strike at Callao and captured Valdivia
in a daring amphibious assault. Attention then turned to the liberation of Peru—though not until 1826 did Chilean soldiers commanded
by Ramón Freire wrest control of the island of Chiloé from the
Spaniards.

Notwithstanding these military victories, the political chaos and
economic costs of more than a decade of civil war, together with continued instability, made political independence cause for less than
unconditional jubilation even to the separatists. And like many revolutions, the personal and ideological struggle within the circle of
separatist leadership took its toll among most of those later included
in the pantheon of revolutionary heroes: José Miguel Carrera, like
his brothers earlier, executed in Mendoza; Manuel Rodríguez, assassinated, seemingly with O'Higgins' knowledge; O'Higgins, exiled to
Peru (1823), whence he would never return to his native land.

Bernardo O'Higgins, though born in Chile, spent much of his
youth in England and Europe. Despite a number of efforts to gain
the approval of his father, the former governor of Chile and viceroy
of Peru, the latter seems never to have responded to the desire of his
illegitimate offspring for formal recognition. In Europe, O'Higgins

met Francisco de Miranda, the leading Venezuelan proponent of Latin American independence, and was influenced by Miranda's zeal for liberation of the colonies from Spain. O'Higgin's returned to Chile as one of a small minority of *criollos* committed to independence even prior to the Napoleonic invasion of Spain.

After leading separatist troops from 1813 to 1814 and fleeing to Mendoza when defeated by the royalists at Rancagua (1814), O'Higgins returned to Chile as a subordinate of General San Martín in an army aspiring to liberate Chile and Peru from Spanish rule. O'Higgins also belonged to the secret revolutionary group called *logia lautarina*. This lodge, dedicated to independence for the Spanish American colonies, swore its members to secrecy on pain of death and required that members who gained high position in any of the liberated colonies submit for prior approval the names of those they would appoint to military, government, or other positions in the new regimes. The lodge also sought to control government policy. Critics of the lodge saw it as a group of anticlerical, masonic subversives bent on destruction of the old order. A modern biographer of O'Higgins even suggested, with obvious hyperbole, that "the lodge controlled the new Chilean administration as completely as the Party controls the government in a Communist state." Due to his association with the lodge, a segment of Chilean opinion came to see O'Higgins as somewhat less than a truly national leader and blamed him and the lodge for the executions of the three Carrera brothers as well as for the assassination of Manuel Rodríguez.

O'Higgins believed that it was necessary, with a people like the Chileans, "to confer good upon them by force" when other means failed. He promulgated a new constitution in 1818. The document called for a five-man senate with members elected from the provinces. O'Higgins essentially handpicked the membership, as he also did later the delegates to the constitutional convention of 1822.

Despite manipulation of government appointments, the O'Higgins government lacked firm institutional supports. Conflicts with Church leaders over a variety of issues—expulsion of a priest who asked the wife of an O'Higgins supporter to leave a church because she was wearing an inappropriate low-cut dress; establishment of Protestant cemeteries; and introduction of Protestant teachers to develop an anticlerical educational system—weakened O'Higgins' position. Confrontations with certain aristocrats over elimination of titles of nobility, and efforts to abolish the entailed estates, as well as strife with his "own" senate also created problems for O'Higgins. Finally, the implacable resistance of friends and supporters of the Carrera brothers, who never forgave O'Higgins for the Carreras' death, undermined his administration.

Financial difficulties associated with the war effort and corruption also contributed to O'Higgins' failure. Describing the situation in Chile in 1820, a sea captain wrote in his journal:

> No permanent System of Finance had yet been established whereby the Expenses of the Government & of the War might be defrayed and on every emergency Recourse was had to temporary loans and forced contributions. Nothing like a regular appraisement of Land & other Permanent Property had yet been attempted, or any one Species of Regular Taxation resorted to, and when arbitrary contributions were levied the quotas were evidently determined by favoritism or Caprice.

In attempting to raise revenues, O'Higgins re-established the colonial tobacco monopoly, or *estanco*, only to suspend it for two years after protests by foreign merchants. At the same time the Supreme Director's confidant and finance minister and a prominent merchant were apparently speculating in tobacco and other commodities. Furthermore the finance minister, although a Chilean by birth, had sided with the royalists and even accompanied one of the early Spanish expeditions from Peru which sought to reconquer Chile. These circumstances—in addition to the general amnesty for most former royalists who had sworn loyalty to Chile, and the government's attempts to return to the royalists some property confiscated from them—provided effective ammunition for those who wished to discredit O'Higgins. Resistance by merchants to new commercial regulations, political intrigues surrounding a new constitution (1822), a debate concerning a loan secured in London, failure to pay the fleet in Valparaíso, and a threat to replace Ramón Freire, commander of the army at Concepción, all contributed to O'Higgins' downfall.

In 1822 two of the country's five senators left on diplomatic missions. Another expressed a desire to leave public office. O'Higgins then suggested that the senate temporarily suspend its sessions and transfer legislative authority to himself as Supreme Director. The senators met this breach of the principles of liberalism with categorical opposition. Ramón Freire led his forces at Concepción against Talca and threatened to march northward. The city of La Serena followed Concepción's lead, and O'Higgins' opponents in Santiago adhered to the movement to oust him from office. With an emotional farewell speech, O'Higgins surrendered the presidential sash and left for Peruvian exile, never to return to Chile.

Political uncertainty followed O'Higgins' abdication. A barrage of political slogans, ideologies, and personalities accompanied a confusing succession of congresses, assemblies, interim supreme directors, presidents, and military rebellions. Ramón Freire, who had led the Concepción forces, attempted to govern the country from 1823 to 1826 and returned to office several times between 1826 and 1829. Freire later attempted an invasion of Chile from Peru (1836), after being forcibly exiled to the former viceroyalty.

Freire's term in office and his interventions between 1826 and 1830 were associated with superficial experiments with liberalism and federalism in Chilean politics. Exponents of European or North American liberalism sought to impose republican institutions and practices on Chile's traditional administrative, economic, and social structure. To many, liberalism also meant religious toleration or anticlericalism. Implementation of liberal principles implied confrontation with perhaps the most significant social institution and symbol of Hispanic society: the Catholic Church. This alone assured bitter resistance to liberalism by some prominent *criollo* families.

A small number of influential intellectuals and political leaders also proposed a federalist regime, with considerable regional autonomy, for a new nation lacking strong traditions with local government. The schemes for decentralizing political authority or copying North American federalism appealed to certain regional interests seeking to cast off the economic and political domination of Santiago and Valparaíso as well as to those intellectuals who equated progress and freedom with emulation of the institutions of the United States. But neither liberalism, nor liberal principles and a federalist constitution, corresponded to the socio-economic reality of Hispanic capitalism in Chile after independence.

In 1824 the Freire government confiscated the possessions of the regular clergy. This ruptured Church-State relations, including dismissal of the ex-royalist bishop, Rodríguez Zorilla, whom O'Higgins had re-established in his office in an effort to negotiate diplomatic relations with the Pope. Regional uprisings and Freire's inability to organize effectively the national public administration resulted in continued intrigues, polarization of sentiments by opposing forces, and ruin of the public finances. By 1825, in the words of Chilean author Augustín Edwards, "Freire . . . distracted and impotent, saw his authority being set at naught. Santiago alone recognized the Governing Junta. . . . Meanwhile neither Concepción nor Coquimbo recognized either Freire or the junta. The anarchy into which the country had fallen was reaching a climax; it was under the rule of four governments." Totally frustrated, Freire resigned from office. Personal ambitions combined with rabid commitments to misunderstood slogans threatened to dismember the new nation.

After an enthusiastic speech by federalism's most avid supporter, José Miguel Infante, in July of 1826, Congress formally approved a federal system for Chile. The legislature then embarked upon a piecemeal program designed to define the nature of Chilean federalism. Congress divided Chile into eight provinces, each of which would have a provincial assembly and its own constitution. In addition, local government would continue to exercise a broad range of authority in the *municipios*. In a country lacking provincial political and administrative machinery, let alone provincial constitutions, federalist ideology did not correspond to political reality, but it did intensify regional conflicts that made effective national government illusory.

Meanwhile the army went unpaid, the public treasury remained empty, and president succeeded president. Civil strife reached such a level that Congress requested Freire to reassume the presidency and impose order. After winning several battles against opposing forces, Freire again resigned, to be followed in office by the vice-president, Francisco Antonio Pinto. In August 1827 the country reverted to a unitary form of government, ending its imitation of North American federalist principles.

Pinto's administration adopted a new liberal constitution in 1828 that pleased neither ardent federalists nor important liberal factions. Conservatives viewed the constitution as an unrealistic document inspired by imported utopian ideology. By abolishing the *mayorazgos*, the constitution generated opposition in the old aristocracy, while President Pinto's anticlericalism disturbed a broader segment of "public opinion." Conflict degenerated again into civil war.

Led by the personalities who would dominate Chilean politics for the next two decades—Diego Portales, Manuel Rengifo, Joaquín Prieto, and Manuel Bulnes—conservative forces defeated the remnants of the liberal army, commanded by Ramón Freire, at the battle of Lircay in April 1830. The new government banished Freire to Peru—just as Freire had earlier done to Bernardo O'Higgins.

Political activity in the post-independence decades took place within very restricted social circles. Intellectuals wrote constitutions and liberal legislation for a country unfamiliar with the practical meaning of federalism, inalienable rights, or effective limits on government authority. Chileans understood the idea of benevolent despotism and the practice of pragmatic despotism. Royal officials had implemented well-intentioned decrees as their consciences, local interests, "reality," or corruption determined. Involvement of "the people" in legislation or administration conformed neither to the theory nor to the practice of Hispanic politics. It proved no surprise, therefore, that after independence the emergence within elite circles of overlapping ideological factions and personalist movements, such as those of O'Higgins, the Carreras, and Freire, anticipated the multiparty politics of later years without involving the masses except as cannon fodder. Those who supported liberal and/or federalist principles were known as *pipiolos* ("upstarts" or "novices"), and those defending more traditional principles, including the existing privileges of the Church, as *pelucones* ("bigwigs"). But within these two camps, factional disputes and personal loyalties prevented the development of unified political movements, let alone political parties in the modern sense. The highly partisan tabloid newspapers slandered the opposition at will. Political factions and various governments stretched freedom of the press to its limits. No end seemed in sight to the quick succession of presidents and constitutions which accompanied the movement of armies, rebellions, and bandits across the country.

In these conditions public finance fell into a dreadful state. Tax farming on the colonial model continued with respect to the tithes (*diezmos*) and the tolls paid by muleteers and carters on the principal roads. Lack of respect for shifting government authorities and knowledge that the tax farmers retained 30 to 40 percent of the taxes levied increased still further the propensity to evade payment. This held true especially in the case of the *diezmos* paid in kind by the peasantry. Corrupt administration of the customs houses also kept needed revenues from the government. The observations of John Miers, an English businessman more than disenchanted with Chile, summarize the deplorable state of affairs:

> I have elsewhere alluded to the mode in which the duties upon the custom-house were paid, and to the great extent of the contraband introduction of foreign goods. It now remains to say a few words upon the mode of levying the customs. The duties are always, after the Spanish system, estimated and levied at so much percent upon a valuation, not determined by the market price of the articles, but by the arbitrary valuation of the vistas, or custom-house searchers: it is, therefore, impossible for a merchant to calculate upon the actual cost of introduction of foreign goods; but, as the government of Chile does not allow their officers a sufficient salary, they are obliged to connive with the

merchants, both in smuggling and in fixing undervaluations, receiving from the latter a proportionate bribe. Similar parcels of goods may at one time be valued in the custom-house at 1000 dollars, at another 100 dollars, and the usual tariff duties paid thereon accordingly; the difference is a robbery to the state, no advantage whatever results to the foreign manufactures, but goes entirely into the pockets of the custom-house officers, merchants, and agents.

Miers concluded that "the foreign trade of Chile, like all matters in state, justice and police, is maintained by empino [sic] influence, intrigue and bribery."

Ironically, however, it was the chaos of public finance that brought to the fore the businessmen and military leaders who ended two decades of near anarchy with a conservative restoration. Led by Diego Portales, a merchant who had remained aloof from the independence struggle, an alliance of the Concepción military elite, merchants, prominent *pelucón* families, and the Church hierarchy established—at bayonet point—a unique political regime in Chile. This regime set it apart from its sister republics as a model of political stability and economic growth in the nineteenth century.

Diego Portales was born in 1793 in Santiago, the son of an influential royal official who served as superintendent of the mint. Distantly related to two colonial governors, his ancestry linked him to Chile's Basque-Castilian aristocracy. After giving up his own position at the mint, Portales formed a commercial partnership with Manuel Cea in the export-import trade, and moved to Lima. Failure of the joint enterprise brought both partners back to Chile where in mid-1824 they contracted with the Freire government to take over the state monopoly (*estanco*) on tobacco and certain other commodities in exchange for servicing the loan contracted by Chilean agents in London in 1822.

The Portales-Cea Company obtained the *estanco* contract amidst rumors of improprieties in the bidding process, including an allegation that a rival firm lost the contract despite its higher bid. If these allegations were true, it proved fortunate for those who lost the contract. Contraband imports of goods subject to the *estanco*, illegal tobacco plantations, and the high price paid for the contract contributed to the enterprise's commercial failure. Portales and his partner attempted to enforce their monopoly rights by destroying illegal tobacco plantations and seeking stronger intervention by government authorities to stop the contraband trade. While personal enemies of the partners and opponents of the government accused the firm of fraud and bribery, it struggled unsuccessfully to meet its obligations on the British loan. In September 1826 Congress voted to liquidate the *estanco* concession and return the monopoly to the government. Though Portales bitterly resented the government's failure to negotiate new terms or even to allow his firm to administer the government monopoly on a fee basis, the equitable manner in which Manuel Rengifo liquidated the *estanco* contract formed the basis for the future cooperation between those two hard-headed businessmen who would dominate Chilean political economy after 1830.

Many people believed Portales' participation in politics stemmed from a desire for revenge against those who had deprived him of the *estanco* contract. Others saw Portales' motivation in his distaste for liberalism and the continual disorder following independence. Whatever the motivation, Portales' solution for political disorder, imposed in cooperation with conservative interests, the higher clergy, and the military forces of Prieto and Bulnes, emphasized *restoration* of legitimacy, law and order, and fiscal integrity. Implementation of this program required a strong, centralized government which did not tolerate opposition or even criticism. Acting as President Prieto's chief minister and then as "informal" adviser, Portales cashiered the liberal officers of the army, many of them "heroes" of the independence period, persecuted the opposition press, and controlled elections to ensure the victory of government candidates. This was the beginning of the "autocratic republic" which one Chilean historian described as "the last and most beautiful chapter of Spanish colonial history." Less romantically, an English historian suggests that "the atmosphere in Chile after 1830 was one of fear and trembling."

Portales' style and beliefs left little room for constitutions or formal principles. He favored decisive, pragmatic action unconstrained by legal obstacles or constitutional limits. While Portales concerned himself with action, however, other conservative leaders and intellectuals felt the need for a constitution to define the nature of the new regime, to formalize its structure, and to legitimize its practices. Ironically, then, Portales played almost no official role in elaborating the Constitution of 1833 which institutionalized what historians have called the "Portalian state." Nevertheless, the centralized, authoritarian character of the constitution owed as much to Portales as to its principal author, Mariano Egaña.

Both Portales and Egaña sought restoration of legitimacy, law and order, and public morality. They recognized the critical need to build viable national political institutions as instruments through which to govern effectively and stimulate economic recovery. Above all, they sought to provide political stability. Both Portales and Egaña disdained democracy, popular suffrage, and liberalism. Egaña called for establishment of an authoritative centralized regime that did not allow "anarchy in the shadow or name of popular rule, liberal principles, republican government. . . ." Portales urged creation of a "strong, centralizing government, in order to set the citizens on the straight path of order and virtue." The Constitution of 1833 formalized these antidemocratic principles. The new constitution created a strong executive with authority to declare a state of siege in any part of the country when Congress was in recess. Declaration of a state of siege entailed suspension of all constitutional guarantees in the affected territory. In each province and administrative subdivision the president appointed intendants and governors as his direct agents. All pretense of provincial initiative, let alone federalism, disappeared. The power of Congress to approve annually the budget, taxes, and the size of the military provided the basis, later in the century, for bitter executive-legislative confrontations and even civil war (1891). But from 1831 to 1861 three strong presidents each served the two constitutional five-year terms and efficiently suppressed opposition forces.

The 1833 constitution also maintained the Roman Catholic apostolic religion as the state faith and excluded from "public exercise" all other religious doctrines. The founders of the autocratic republic thus sought to transfer the privilege of appointing Church officials, or *patronato*, from the Spanish crown to the new national regime—though the Church did not concede that the republican government had inherited the *patronato* from the empire. Summarizing the intent of the constitution, General Prieto called it "a means of putting an end to the revolutions and disturbances which arose from the confusion in which the triumph of independence left us. For this reason the system of government to which the republic was subjected . . . may be called autocratic in view of the great authority or power . . . concentrated in the hands of the citizen elected as president."

Executive control over distribution of certificates qualifying citizens to vote made effective challenges to the incumbent nearly impossible. This system of executive dominance of elections was adroitly described by Chilean historian Luis Galdames:

> The constitution permitted the re-election of the president to succeed himself for a second period of five years, and while this provision remained in force all the presidents availed themselves

of it to have themselves re-elected. This meant, then, ten-year presidential terms. Re-election was achieved without difficulty, owing to the irresistible power placed by the constitution itself in the hands of the chief of state, who named the mayors and members of the municipal councils, the governors, intendants, and judges. . . .

In practice, the intendants and governors controlled the elections of senators and representatives within their own jurisdiction. The chief of state and his ministers made lists of the people who were to make up each chamber for a constitutional period, and the elections were carried out according to these lists. It was rare that more than three or five opposition candidates succeeded in defeating the government candidates in the different departments. The orders of the minister of the interior to the agents of the executive were expressed more or less in these terms: "His Excellency instructs me to make known to you that Señor or Señores [here the names] should be chosen in your department for the post of [here the name of a senator or deputy]." If any candidate of the opposition attempted to electioneer at any point whatever in the country, the respective government agent would receive from the minister of the interior a communication like this: "Manage to prevent Don [name] from coming to your department by advising him to refrain from presenting himself in it. If he insists you can have him arrested as a disturber of the public peace.

Suffrage limitations restricted the vote through property or income qualifications and literacy requirements. But lax enforcement and deliberate delays in implementing the literacy requirement allowed landowners to enroll their tenants as voters and commanders of the militia to do likewise with their troops. After 1840 the Congress allowed those already registered to continue to vote despite efforts to impose the literacy requirement on *new* voters. In this way the votes of the rural work force became a valuable asset of the owners of large rural estates.

Along with electoral manipulation, the alliance of merchants, landowners, clergy, and military officers which restored law and order did not lose sight of Portales' admonition: "The stick and the cake, justly and opportunely administered, are the specifics with which any nation can be cured, however inveterate its bad habits may be." Thus, Chile would largely avoid the chaos and instability of the rest of Latin America, despite rebellions in 1851 and 1859, by imposing a modified version of "benevolent" despotism. Only later would incipient industrial groups and renewed anticlericalism among prominent elite families upset the mutuality of interests shared by members of the relatively small ruling class. The Constitution of 1833 provided a viable instrument for maintaining existing class relations, including restoration of the *mayorazgos* and consolidating the political position of prominent *criollo* families. It also helped create a business climate attractive to foreign capitalists and Chilean merchants alike.

At Portales' urging, Manuel Rengifo served as Minister of the Treasury from 1830 to 1835. Rengifo reorganized the system of public finance, transferred the customs houses to the ports, rationalized regulations and duties on the coastwise trade, and took a number of measures intended to increase fiscal revenues. Though some of Rengifo's tax policies drew criticism, the overall effect of his program was to establish a sound basis for Chilean public finance and to inspire the confidence of domestic and foreign capital. Unfortunately Rengifo's successes made him a likely presidential candidate for an alliance of dissatisfied conservative elements and certain liberal factions. In September 1835, Portales returned from his self-imposed "absence" from politics and assumed the ministries of War and the Interior. Joaquín Tocornal, President Prieto's firm supporter and perhaps the most proclerical member of the government coalition, replaced Rengifo as Minister of the Treasury. Despite Rengifo's successful economic policies, his spirit of political conciliation and his moderation on the politico-religious issues of the times lost out to the expediencies of the presidential election of 1835 and Portales' intolerance of any drift toward liberalism. Under Portales' leadership Prieto was re-elected—after the agitation and propaganda of the electoral campaign had led to reimposition of government through "state of siege." Notwithstanding the considerable economic progress and improvement in public finance, when Prieto began his second presidential term (1836-41), institutionalization of the political system detailed in the Constitution of 1833 seemed far from certain.

A new constitution has nowhere guaranteed political stability. This is especially the case in Latin America. It is important therefore to attempt to understand how the repressive policies of the Prieto administration, a fortunate stroke of international politics—that is, a successful war against the Peru-Bolivia confederation—the "martyrdom" of Portales, and the character of Prieto's successor, Manuel Bulnes, solidified the "autocratic republic."

In the wake of civil wars and clashes of personalist factions from

1810, numerous Chilean émigrés found themselves in Peru, while Peruvian exiles went to Chile. Shortly after Prieto's re-election (1836)
General Freire sailed from Peru with a military force, landed in Chiloé, and moved to the mainland. Internal dissidents also threatened
rebellion. Freire was captured and eventually exiled to Australia. But
in response the Prieto government broke relations with Peru.

Relations between Chile and Peru had been tense in any case, due
to Peru's failure to repay the loan extended for the San Martín expedition (1820-22) and to disputes over import duties that discriminated against Chilean merchandise as well as over goods deposited in
the warehouses at Valparaíso or ships landing in Chilean ports. General Andrés Santa Cruz's efforts to unify Peru and Bolivia and the
Peruvian government's support for Freire exacerbated this tension.

Portales saw Santa Cruz's policies and armies as a direct threat to
Chile. He sent two ships to Callao, which took the Peruvian navy,
such as it was, by surprise. Santa Cruz negotiated a settlement that
left the Peruvian ships in Chilean hands, but Portales remained un-
satisfied because Santa Cruz refused to apologize for the imprisonment of the Chilean chargé d'affaires. Bent upon war, Portales believed the judgments of the numerous Peruvian exiles in Chile that
large-scale rebellion against Santa Cruz would result if a Chilean
army merely appeared in Peru.

The Chilean Congress declared war and sent Mariano Egaña to
Peru at the head of a small squadron. The Chileans demanded (1) sat-
isfaction for the injuries done to their chargé d'affaires, (2) dissolution of the Peru-Bolivia confederation, (3) an indemnity for the
Freire expedition, (4) recognition of liability for the loan extended
for the San Martín liberation expedition, and (5) limitations on Peruvian naval forces. When Santa Cruz rejected these humiliating conditions, the Prieto government prepared for war by declaring a state
of siege in all of Chile. With Portales exercising extensive emergency
powers, those who "disturbed public order" or were "disrespectful toward the government" faced banishment or execution at the hands of
military tribunals.

Portales' regime of terror incited rebellion. In June 1837 mutinous
troops, led by Colonel José Antonio Vidaurre, assassinated Portales.
Government defeat of the rebellious troops was followed by the execution of the assassins. Now Portales became a martyr as the government tried to link his assassins and the rebellion to General Santa
Cruz's agents in Chile.

During 1837 Chilean forces under Admiral Blanco Encalada faced
defeat in Peru from Santa Cruz's armies. Surrounded and in despair,

Blanco Encalada recognized the Peru-Bolivia confederation and returned the ships earlier seized at Callao. The Chilean government rejected these concessions, blockaded Peruvian ports, and dispatched a new force commanded by General Manuel Bulnes, the victor at Lircay and Prieto's nephew. Accompanying this expedition were a number of Peruvian exiles, including ex-President Agustín Gamarra and the future Peruvian caudillo Ramón Castilla. Troop movements by both sides in and out of Lima and the interior culminated in early 1839 at Yungay, where Bulnes decisively defeated Santa Cruz and dissolved the Peru-Bolivia confederation. He returned to Santiago a military hero.

The war against the Peru-Bolivia confederation united Chilean political elites. While defeat, in Encina's words, might have sent "leaders, government and order tumbling to earth," victory contributed to a new national pride. According to Barros Arana, when Bulnes made his triumphal entrance into Santiago, "he was greeted by a fanfare unknown until then in the celebration of public festivities. . . ." For months after the victory, Chile celebrated its new-found "greatness" with public festivities and theater productions that re-enacted the military glories of the Chilean armies.

Bulnes' victory made him the perfect successor to Prieto and at precisely the right time in the five-year electoral cycle. In control of the army, and enjoying popular acclaim, Bulnes then married the daughter of ex-President Francisco Antonio Pinto, his principal opponent in the presidential race. For the first time in Chilean history a peaceful transition to the presidency took place with Bulnes' inauguration in 1841. During the next decade Bulnes' great popularity, his support for the development of legislative and judicial institutions, and his refusal to become a *caudillo* on the model of contemporary Latin American rulers, all served to solidify the "Portalian state." Thus the fortuitous outcome of Chilean bellicosity provided the basis of solidarity and legitimacy, as well as the leadership that spared Chile the political disorder and *caudillismo* common to Latin America in much of the nineteenth century. It also institutionalized a centralized autocratic regime that discouraged democratization of Chilean politics.

Consolidation of the autocratic republic also depended upon the improved state of public finance and of the economy in Chile after 1830. From 1810 to 1830 loss of perhaps 15 percent of the male population in the 20-to-40 age group, in the military campaigns in Chile, Río de la Plata, and Peru, caused a temporary scarcity of labor in the

TABLE 5. AVERAGE ANNUAL VALUE OF AGRICULTURAL AND
LIVESTOCK PRODUCTION (IN PESOS)

Years	La Serena	Santiago	Concepción
1750-59	44,377	427,084	181,615
1760-69	41,409	461,086	189,530
1770-79	40,055	621,086	262,961
1780-89	33,543	551,441	270,669
1790-99	45,198	556,046	244,242
1800-09	84,296	885,292	425,376
1810-19	80,766	623,877	271,357
1820-29	76,156	824,439	187,740

(Source: M. Carmagnani, *Les mecanismes de la vie économique dans une société coloniale, Le Chili*, pp. 213, 235, 249.)

northern mines and in the countryside. Marauding soldiers and bandits in the rural areas discouraged agricultural production. In addition, Peru's internal strife and financial crisis disrupted Chile's normal export trade in wheat, livestock products, and other agrarian commodities.

Recent estimates for the value of agricultural and livestock production, by region, illustrate the decline in output that accompanied the independence struggle.* Declines in the northern region and even in Santiago were relatively moderate, with recovery beginning after 1820. In the Concepción-southern region continued warfare and Indian problems contributed to a persistent decline in output until 1830; the absolute value of production in 1830 failed to regain the level attained in the decade 1760-69.

The most serious decline in economic activity occurred south of the Maule River where, in any case, Chilean agriculture was least secure due to the Indian frontier. Short-term local food shortages resulted from the seemingly unending civil wars. In 1822 the cabildo at Concepción reported that "eleven years of a ferocious, devastating struggle have reduced the province to the most extreme calamity in its history. Its residents . . . have consumed whatever work animals or beasts of burden, not taken by their enemies or their defenders, to keep themselves alive."

In the La Serena–northern region the independence movements little affected agricultural production. Free trade meant expanded

---

* Naturally, given the internal situation, these estimates are more suggestive than definitive—and the price inflation at the time probably leads to an underestimate of the decline in output.

demand for minerals and stimulation of the northern economy. But migration to the north, due to the war and to the hope for opportunities in the mines, placed increased pressure on the region's limited food-producing capabilities. In 1826 the provincial assembly of Coquimbo lamented that this city "must buy everything, for it produces little but metals. Smaller animals are brought from Chillán, more than six thousand animals come each year from the environs of Santiago; . . . tallow from Maule; flour and grain from Aconcagua, wood from Chiloé, Valdivia, and Concepción."

With the achievement of independence, the northern region's mines provided the primary source of the copper and silver that financed imports of European goods, paid for military supplies, and attracted foreign investment. In the 1820s, however, many foreigners who invested in mining enterprises lost their capital, as the cost of food, fuel, and supplies and the lack of adequate transport undermined these speculative ventures. Indeed, the prospectuses of some of these "mining" ventures seem to have deliberately misled British investors. For example, the Chilean Mining Association declared that "few countries are so well watered as Chile, affording means of conveyance by water to the ports of the Pacific. . . ." This was true, of course, but the prospectus failed to mention that there were no navigable rivers in the northern region, no coal, no lumber, and that provisions had to be brought over a considerable distance from the south. Despite the disappointments suffered by many speculative investments, new discoveries of copper and silver augured well for the development of mining in the northern region. Gold production declined, but the mint in Santiago maintained the level of silver coinage achieved in the period 1790-1809, despite increased contraband and the dislocation of war. In 1832 a silver strike at Chañarcillo created boom conditions in the northern territory and brought also some of the earliest significant labor conflicts in Chilean national history. Even at this early date the harsh conditions experienced by the peons spawned an incipient militancy among the growing mining proletariat. A rebellion at Chañarcillo in 1834 foreshadowed hundreds of future confrontations between miners and mine operators in the nineteenth and twentieth centuries.

Though the northern mining districts afforded the most glamorous economic potential and paid for the bulk of Chilean imports, agriculture and livestock remained the foundations of the Chilean economy. Based in the Santiago–central region—especially with the wartime dislocations in the south—agriculture continued to be extensive and backward. Wooden plows pulled by teams of oxen broke the ground for sowing the traditional colonial crops. Productivity declined with the spread of agricultural pests and the reduced fertility of the land. Threshing still depended on horses and was carried on during extended fiestas and accompanied by considerable consumption of wine, *chicha*,* or *aguardiente*. As in the rest of Latin America at this time, winnowing with wooden pitchforks evoked images of biblical harvests.

Livestock production also remained primitive. No new breeds were introduced before 1830; animals took five or six years to "fatten" on natural pastures before slaughter. Even then they yielded only 60 to 70 percent of what cattle provided in Europe. Nevertheless, hides and tallow contributed substantially to Chilean exports, as they had since early colonial days. But while the Chilean countryside was admirably suited to dairy production, the output of milk, cheese, and butter was quite low; to 1820, at least, butter cost more in the Concepción region than in the United States. Although the contesting armies of the independence decades provided markets for foodstuffs and drove up prices, they also created conditions of uncertainty or devastation in which Chilean agriculture barely held its own (in the central region) or retrogressed (in the Concepción–southern territory).

Through all the strife, however, the large rural estates continued to dominate in the countryside. Ironically, by 1827 the independent nations of Chile and Peru had re-established the basic structure of colonial trade. Chile exported over 500,000 pesos of wheat, flour, salted meat, tallow, barley, wood, and other argricultural commodities and minerals to Peru. In exchange, Peru sent back almost 350,-000 pesos of goods to Chile—approximately half in sugar. The blood spilled to win political independence consecrated the reconfirmation of colonial patterns of commerce as well as colonial economic institutions in the rural areas.

While internal productive activity stagnated, the arms trade, whaling and contraband of all sorts made Valparaíso an important Pacific way station to North America as well as to western Spanish America and to British colonies in Asia. The port's strategic location brought increasing numbers of British, North American, and other foreign merchants to Valparaíso, Santiago, and other principal towns. Some of these merchants settled permanently in Chile, founding businesses and families which became fixtures of Chilean high finance and Chilean society—including Waddington, Sewell, Walker, Chad-

---

* *Chicha* is a hard cider made from grapes or apples.

wick, Davies, Bunster, Clark, Gibbs, Lynch, and Eastman. Two future Chilean presidents would descend from an Italian immigrant-merchant, Pedro Alessandri, who arrived in Valparaíso in 1820.

Provisioning the army of liberation provided economic opportunities for colonial merchants and public officials, much as had the royal *situado* in the past. In contrast to Santiago, which changed little from 1810 to 1830, Valparaíso grew rapidly from a town of 5500 to a city of almost 20,000. A floating population of several thousand from the ships in the bay frequented the increasing number of shops, cafés, billiard parlors, bars, and brothels. An underworld of muggers, thieves, and murderers preyed upon drunken sailors and began to make Valparaíso the rough-and-tumble, bawdy Pacific port for which it became famous.

By 1822 foreigners represented nearly one-quarter of the residents of the port and virtually dominated commerce. Establishment of warehouses in which shippers could deposit merchandise for a set fee helped increase mercantile activity. Chile's merchant marine grew from three ships, owned by Spaniards, in 1810 to well over seventy by 1830. Foreigners owned many of these, but native Chileans and naturalized citizens also took part in the shipping trade. The dramatic growth of international trade also reinvigorated the shipbuilding industry. Despite the great increase in shipping, however, port facilities remained exceedingly inadequate. No docks existed. Peons, up to their waists in water, carried ashore heavy bundles on their backs from small boats sent from the anchored wooden sailing vessels. From Valparaíso merchandise went overland on mules to Santiago or to the northern towns and mining districts. Not until several decades later would railroads and steamships dramatically alter colonial modes of transport and communication.

Expansion of commerce confronted Chile's leaders with numerous political issues related to domestic industrial development, public finance, and, in the short run, successful completion of the war against Spain and achievement of diplomatic recognition by England, the United States, the Holy See, and other European powers. Diplomatic efforts by the Chileans to maintain the neutrality of England and, more important of the British Pacific squadron, during the years of war against Spain made Chilean governments cautious in dealing with powerful English merchants. The need to pay for military supplies and to meet salaries of public personnel, along with the ascendancy of English, French, and North American "free trade" doctrines, pushed Chile away from protective tariffs and toward a commercial policy that emphasized revenue-producing export and import duties.*

Chile had opened its major ports to trade with all friendly or neutral nations in 1811. The decree authorized introduction of all commodities except rum, beer, wine, aguardiente, hats, and items subject to the government *estanco* (especially tobacco). Foreign merchants could engage legally only in the wholesale trade; retail trade and coastal navigation were supposedly reserved for Chilean citizens, but violations of these provisions were common. From 1810 to 1830 import duties averaged 35 percent or more *ad valorem*, but contraband or corruption in assessing the value of imported goods significantly reduced government revenues. Export duties varied considerably from product to product, ranging from 6 to nearly 20 percent.

Government policies allowed low-priced imports to eliminate almost entirely the remaining Chilean manufactures save for some household production, food processing, mining and livestock-related artisan activities such as soap- and candle-making and tanneries. These developments conflicted directly with the commitment of elites like Manuel de Salas or Rodríguez Aldea to stimulate industrial growth through some form of protection for Chilean enterprises. Efforts to combine limited protective tariffs with revenue-producing duties, and the repression of contraband, which probably accounted for over half of Chile's imports, displeased the merchant community and contributed to O'Higgins' ouster.

The penetration of the economy by foreign interests in the period between 1810 and 1830 paved the way for a much more serious domination of Chile's economic development by British and North American enterprises later in the nineteenth century. By 1849 some fifty British firms controlled most Chilean exports: nearly 50 percent of the value of these exports went to England, and English goods accounted for 30 to 40 percent of the value of Chilean imports. Reacting to these trends more than a century later, historian Francisco Encina declared:

> What resulted in these years was not, as usually suggested, an intensification of international trade. Rather what occurred was an exploitation of the Chilean economy by foreign interests. They traded 60 percent of their goods, at least, for silver, gold,

* "Free trade" in this context meant opening ports to international commerce—not the elimination of import duties.

or copper . . . avoiding the customs house. . . . Luxury goods
went down in price while the price of articles of primary necessity which the country did not produce went up. . . . Between
1823 and 1830 some three or four thousand foreigners . . .
sucked the blood from the Chilean economy . . . while 95 percent of the Chilean people had retrogressed to the life style of
the last third of the seventeenth century.

This view perhaps exaggerates the effects on Chile of the replacement of Spanish influence by that of England and North America.
Chilean miners, landowners, small manufacturers and merchants,
sometimes in partnership with foreign investors, also participated in
the import-export trade. Likewise, Chilean policymakers and minor
officials exerted their influence over (or exacted their price from)
foreign businessmen and merchant houses. However, lacking the
basic financial infrastructure and economic clout to compete in international markets, the Chilean economic elites, practically of necessity, allowed themselves to be incorporated into the web of international commerce which the British spun throughout Latin America
and elsewhere in the nineteenth century. Nevertheless, the tightening
noose of foreign control over the Chilean economy and the vulnerability of that economy to fluctuations in the international market in
the nineteenth century give credence to both Marxist and Hispani-
cist analyses of economic policy in the early independence era.

When installation of the "Portalian state" brought an end to the
political chaos of the independence movements, the Prieto government faced the enormous tasks of reorganizing public finance,
rationalizing commercial policy, and determining the direction of
economic development. The government fulfilled these tasks by
adopting strict internal economies and by accepting Chile's role as
a supplier of raw materials to the more developed capitalist economies and importers of manufactured goods. Public personnel were
dismissed, government expenditures on frills were reduced, and a
good climate was created for business. Emphasis was placed on hon-
esty and efficiency. This meant two things. First, law and order were
re-established, and harsh penalties were meted out to common criminals. Second, government sought to encourage private enterprise. As
Minister Rengifo put it in his report to Congress in 1835:

The measures which favorably affect the economy of a State
may be reduced to two types: First, . . . laws that remove obstacles to industry, that protect property and its use, that reduce

the costs of production, and that open free channels for the export [*salida*] of national products; second, . . . laws which regulate taxes with moderation and discernment . . . and prevent expenditures from the public treasury for purposes other than those of strict administrative necessity.

To attract foreign trade and shipping, a decree of 1832 established warehouses of deposit (*almacenes francos de depósito*) in Valparaíso; by 1835 the government was operating sixteen such warehouses and renting out another twenty-seven. Administrative reforms put the public treasury in order and established confidence in public credit. Gradually the government attempted to pay off the public debt.

More than anything else, the political economy of the "Portalian state" aimed at stimulating production of traditional colonial commodities and incorporating Chile into the world capitalist economy. Summarizing this strategy, Chilean author Miguel Cruchaga tells us that "They believed the country was not ready . . . for the development of manufactures, and desiring to give it easy access to articles of consumption and easy export opportunities for what was produced, they sought to facilitate commerce with the foreign countries who could provision us at least cost." This strategy suited the interests of the major economic groups in Chile, landowners, mine owners, exporters-importers, and domestic as well as foreign merchants. It allowed the upper classes to import luxury goods from Europe, live the good life, modernize the cities, and maintain traditional social relationships and property institutions in the countryside. But it also contained serious internal contradictions which would become ever more evident as modernization of transport and communication, along with economic growth in the nineteenth century, created industrial and working class-interests for whom liberal political economy meant ruin or deprivation. In the short run, however, the autocratic republic proved a highly pragmatic reconciliation of the economic interests of the upper classes with both the demands of foreign capitalists and the need for internal order. It preserved the essentials of Hispanic capitalism, restored centralized political authority, and maintained the social stratification of the colony, while allowing "free trade" to cater to the tastes of the upper classes. This was the fruit of Chilean independence.

Chapter 5 • Modernization and Misery

Consolidation of authoritarian government after 1839 gave Chile a truly national political system with administrative capabilities that paved the way for impressive economic growth during the next three decades. Attracted by the relative political stability, foreign investors brought the wonders of modern technology to Chile. The first railroad, built between 1849 and 1851, connected the mining regions of Copiapó to the port of Caldera; by 1863 another line linked Valparaíso to Santiago and was extended south to San Fernando. The American entrepreneur William Wheelwright, who had introduced steam navigation to Chile in the 1840s, directed construction of the telegraph line between the capital and Valparaíso in 1851-52; twenty-five years later the telegraph provided communication to forty-eight Chilean towns as well as connections to Peru and Argentina. Steamships and railroads permitted increased movement of products from the northern mines and the agricultural hinterlands of the central valley and the Concepción region to the port cities and the exterior. From Talcahuano, Valparaíso, La Serena, Caldera, and other legal and illegal points of departure, Chilean commodities left for North America, Australia, Asia, and Europe. An apparent economic miracle quadrupled the value of Chilean exports between 1845 and 1875, while the number of ships entering Chilean ports more than doubled in the decade of the 1860s alone.

Beginning with the discovery of silver at Chañarcillo in 1832, followed by strikes at Tres Puntas to the north of Copiapó and at other mines in the mid-1840s, silver production increased dramatically. After reaching an official level of 100,000 to 200,000 kilos annually between 1851 and 1856, recorded output hovered in the neighborhood of 10,000 kilos a year until the 1870s, when the Caracoles mine came into production. Copper production likewise expanded from a level of 8,000 to 10,000 metric tons a year in the period 1844-50 to almost 35,000 metric tons in 1860. In that year the value of copper exports exceeded 14 million pesos—double the national budget and approximately 56 percent by value of all Chilean exports. During the next decade annual average copper production more than doubled again, with the principal center of production remaining at José Tomás Urmeneta's mine at Tamaya (see Map 8). To the south, in the Concepción region, coal production also dramatically expanded from some 7800 metric tons in 1852 to more than 186,000 metric tons in 1876.

Agricultural production also grew significantly in the middle years of the nineteenth century. Cereal, livestock, and vineyard output increased to meet the demands of the transitory foreign markets opened with the discovery of gold in California and Australia. The growth of the northern mining economy, and the commercial expansion of the principal towns and cities, further encouraged the agricultural economy. Between 1844 and 1860 the value of agricultural exports—led by wheat, flour, and barley—quintupled; between 1871 and 1876 the value of agricultural exports exceeded by fifteenfold the levels attained in the mid-1840s. In the 1850s, complementing expanded cereal cultivation, North American and British entrepreneurs sparked development of a new flour-milling industry, which soon took second place only to copper as the major industry in the Chilean economy.

Shortly thereafter the first Chilean joint stock companies, banks, and credit institutions took shape, and the *Caja de Crédito Hipotecario*, established in 1855, soon became the most important mortgage bank in South America. The first joint stock companies in commercial banking, which emerged in the early 1850s, allied Chilean, British, and North American capital in insurance and railroad enterprises. Landowners, merchants, and mining interests came together to capitalize new economic activities through the modern financial institutions of Western capitalism—the corporation, or *sociedad anónima*. Significantly, the Chilean government also participated in the financing of railroads, setting an important precedent for "mixed" public-private economic ventures linking an ever more integrated economic elite to the apparatus of the state.

Accompanying these trends came diversification of retail trade and an incredible rise in imports of tropical commodities and manufactured goods by the wealthy residents of Valparaíso, Santiago, Tomé-Concepción, and the northern mining districts. In a study published in 1874, entitled *Our Enemy, Luxury!*, a Chilean author captured both the glitter of a superficial prosperity and the dangers of the preference by national elites and foreigners for imported luxury goods.

Economic expansion created new economic interests, made social stratification somewhat more complex, and exacerbated regional animosities as both the southern and northern provinces sought to keep pace with the progress of Santiago, Valparaíso, and the central valley. With some 115,000 residents, Santiago no longer seemed merely a colonial administrative center. Connected by rail in 1863 to the port of Valparaíso, which was itself a bustling commercial center of over 60,000 people, Santiago was becoming more and more a real urban capital in a growing new nation.

As the towns became cities, there developed an impressive liberal intellectual movement. Made possible, in part, by the policies of President Bulnes and his minister, Manuel Montt, favoring intellectual activities and expansion of the educational system, the movement gave rise to the "Generation of 1842" led by Victorino Lastarria and to the creation of the University of Chile. The new university began to function in 1843 under the direction of Andrés Bello, eminent Venezuelan philosopher, jurist, and statesman, who dedicated his life to public service in Chile until his death in 1865. Soon after a normal school was established, and in subsequent decades, the system of primary instruction expanded: the 1850s witnessed the creation of more than 500 public schools. The Montt government (1851-61) also stimulated construction of libraries, technical schools, and even special institutions for the deaf. By 1861 some 45,000 children attended public and private institutions of learning, and several thousand were enrolled in secondary schools. Nevertheless, the vast majority of the population—especially those living in the countryside—still could not obtain even a minimal education for their children. Like the superficial prosperity of the nation, the educational system remained accessible primarily to the privileged few in the principal urban centers.

The intellectual movement of the 1840s combined the talents of Chileans with those of expatriates from Argentina, Venezuela, and Colombia, who found refuge from *caudillismo* and tyranny in an orderly Chile, whose authoritarian regime spared it from the widespread anarchy characteristic of Latin America at the time. Although the movement was made possible by Chile's stability, it soon proved subversive to the incumbent regime. Typifying the anti-Hispanic spirit of this movement was an article by Francisco Bilbao that appeared in 1844 in a periodical called *El Crepúsculo* (*"The Twilight"*). This article, entitled "Chilean Society," harshly criticized the colonial past, the Church, and most of the country's political institutions. The government ordered the burning of all copies of the periodical in which the article appeared. In September of the same year José Victorino Lastarria delivered the first annual paper on Chilean history at the national university. Lastarría's paper, called "Investigation into the Social Influence of the Conquest and the Spanish Colonial System upon Chile," blamed the Hispanic heritage and the Church for most of the nation's problems. The government that funded the National Institute at which Bilbao studied and created the University that gave Lastarría a public forum could not tolerate a direct confrontation with the Church or so bombastic a challenge to the social order. Government leaders viewed the University as a training ground for political and professional elites; the emergence of political opposition and challenges to the foundations of the Chilean society within the University community set the stage for an ongoing drama of intellectual and political ferment in Chile's institutions of higher education. For the next two decades the intellectuals of the "Generation of 1842" could be found at the forefront of social and political movements that opposed the leadership and policies of the autocratic regime.

Despite criticisms by liberal intellectuals, Chile's apparently impressive economic growth and political stability temporarily overshadowed both the vulnerability of its economic system and political frailties. Because it depended upon duties from international trade for most of its revenues, the government tended to centralize power and resources at Santiago and Valparaíso. Even though the northern mining districts and the southern cereal-flour complex produced a disproportionate share of the nation's exports, Chile's political leaders made only marginal budgetary allocations to the northern and southern provinces. As a result, considerable regional opposition arose against the autocratic regime. Reflecting this provincial resentment, an editorial in *El Curicano* in December 1858 decried the fact that

> while the capital absorbs all the income, receives all the material improvements, concentrates all the benefits, the provinces . . . languish in misery and backwardness. . . . Under the Spanish regime the provinces were exploited and paid heavy taxes to

support the Spanish court. Now, there is little difference. We
pay heavy taxes and are exploited in a thousand ways to beautify
the court of Santiago. In our jurisdiction [department] the government does not invest a tenth of the funds we contribute to
the national treasury.

The growing ideological, political, and regional fragmentation of the
Chilean elite would lead to civil wars in 1851 and 1859 and to a gradual, but fundamental, transformation of the autocratic republic into
the quasi-parliamentary, oligarchical system that predominated from
the 1890s to the 1920s.

Just as the apparent stability of the political system masked its
gradual transformation, so, too, did favorable international economic
trends disguise the fragility of the Chilean economy. Temporary markets in California and Australia had stimulated agricultural production, processing industries, and shipping from 1849 until almost 1860.
Soon, however, California wheat and flour competed favorably with
the Chilean products even at Valparaíso.

Foreign and immigrant-owned commercial firms in Valparaíso
controlled much of the country's credit system. Operating under a
flexible option-buying scheme, these merchant lenders loaned capital
to mining and agricultural interests against future production. They
reserved the option to pay for agricultural commodities or minerals
at the market price current when credit was extended or at the
market price at the time of delivery. Under this system producers
bore all the risks of price changes, while lenders benefited from
either a decline or a rise in market prices. Foreign investors also
gained control over much of Chile's flour-milling industry, mining,
shipping, and commerce. Fluctuations in demand and prices for
Chilean minerals and agricultural commodities in the international
marketplace produced periodic economic crises with serious political
implications.

Above all else, the mid-nineteenth-century Chilean economy continued to depend upon mineral exports. Periodic discoveries in
Chile's northern provinces stimulated the rise of mining towns and
their accompanying ports throughout the *norte chico* from 1832 until
the late 1870s. Export duties from the mineral sector provided the
national government with over 50 percent of public revenues during
the entire period. Continuing essentially colonial politico-economic
relations, the central government siphoned off most of the tax reve-

nues from the mines without investing substantial resources in the northern provinces.

The independence period commenced in 1811 with the opening of the Agua Amarga silver mine south of Vallenar (see Map 8). This and other mines helped pay the costs of the war for independence. Establishing a pattern later followed by other northern regions, the area around Vallenar experienced rapid growth in population along with increased cultivation of nearby agricultural land. Then, with exhaustion of the silver veins, population in the zone decreased to perhaps 3500 by the early 1850s. Following the Agua Amarga strike in 1825, the rich Arqueros discovery located inland from Coquimbo seemed so important that the Chilean government established a new mint at La Serena. After Arqueros the next big silver strike occurred at Chañarcillo in 1832. Chañarcillo reportedly yielded more than 12 million pesos' worth of silver in less than a decade, and the surrounding region, especially Copiapó, enjoyed boom conditions. New discoveries in the late 1840s, in particular at Tres Puntas between Copiapó and the "port" of Flamenco to the northwest, prolonged the silver fever. In 1843 the government officially proclaimed Copiapó a city; and, graced by this blessing, population in the department of Copiapó mushroomed from 11,300 in 1843 to almost 65,000 in 1865.

Tres Puntas exemplified the difficulties facing the mining industry in Chile's northern provinces: poor roads, lack of water, and scarcity of almost all basic necessities including food, fuel, and implements. Yet within five years a settlement of some 4000 residents had sprung up around the mines. Despite the high cost of everything needed for survival, Tres Puntas, like the other mining towns, grew and prospered as long as the ore held out. As late as the mid-1860s mining activity persisted at Tres Puntas, and miners still sent ore by mule and wagon to Flamenco over what a contemporary writer called a "tolerable road."

Other less significant silver discoveries kept the miners' hopes alive until the next big strike in 1870 at Caracoles (legally in Bolivia), located on the road between Antofagasta and San Pedro de Atacama. Again the pattern of rapid urbanization occurred; by 1873 Caracoles had become a growing, prosperous town with more than 2500 residents. Commercial houses from the coast established branches, hotels opened, and the usual proliferation of cantinas, houses of prostitution, billiard parlors, and retail shops proclaimed the importance of the new northern mining district. This development took place despite the total lack of nearby water sources, fuel, and local agricul-

MAP 8: Major Mining Discoveries 1811-1870, Atacama and Coquimbo

ture. Everything had to be brought in from the coast or across the Andes. Carters and muleteers charged twice as much to carry goods between Antofagasta and Caracoles than did shipping companies to bring freight to Antofagasta from Europe. Nonetheless, miners dug out the ore; more than 1200 carters and thousands of mules carried it to Antofagasta—now, due to Caracoles, a growing Bolivian port city.

Located in a region disputed by Chile and Bolivia, the Caracoles minerals renewed a conflict only partially resolved in a treaty of 1866 in which the two nations set Chile's northern boundary at latitude 24° South and specified that the two countries would divide equally revenues from guano and mineral deposits within the territory located between latitudes 23° and 25° South. Bolivia agreed to finance construction of a port at Mejillones and to maintain a customs house with a monopoly for exacting export duties on the minerals of the region. The 1866 treaty also promised Chile one-half the revenue collected at Mejillones from export taxes on guano or other minerals. This stipulation gave Chilean agents the right to audit the accounts of the customs house, a provision the Bolivians bitterly resented as insulting to national sovereignty. In time Bolivia ignored the terms of the treaty by exporting minerals extracted from the shared territory through the more northerly port of Cobija, and refused to pay Chile its share of the custom receipts. In 1871, shortly after the Caracoles silver strike, a new Bolivian government disavowed all international agreements made by the previous administration. Subsequent negotiations and a new treaty in 1874 failed to resolve the fundamental issues. Less than a decade later Bolivia would lose all the territory and riches under dispute, along with its access to the Pacific, when it was defeated by Chile in the War of the Pacific (see Chapter 6).

Despite the great importance of silver to Chile's northern provinces, copper mining proved even more significant. Since colonial times Chilean copper had found its way to Europe, Asia, and North America. In the 1830s British vessels carried the red metal from Chile to India. British capitalists made significant investments in Chilean copper mining from the mid-1830s and early 1840s when Joshua Waddington exploited mines at Chañaral Alto in the department of Combarbalá. By the mid-1860s British interests had invested more than 4.5 million pesos in the Caldera area alone, almost all of which involved copper.

Although British and other foreign interests made substantial investments in the copper industry, a small number of daring, persistent Chilean capitalists and adventurers played a key role in the northern copper business. Suggestive, if untypical, was the eighteen-year quest of José Tomás Urmeneta at Tamaya, northwest of Ovalle (see Map 7): in 1852 he finally hit an incredibly rich vein. During the next eleven years the Tamaya mine reportedly produced copper valued at 5 million pesos. Urmeneta subsequently established foundries at Guayacán and Tongoy on the coast and also contracted with Henry Meiggs to build a rail line from the port at Tongoy to the mines. Urmeneta expanded his investments to coal and railroads in the southern region, a fleet of steamships purchased in Europe and public works in Santiago. He also acquired the important Hacienda Limache near Valparaíso. An unsuccessful candidate for president in 1871, Urmeneta was an extreme example of how the mineral wealth of the northern regions filtered south to Santiago, Valparaíso, and beyond, incorporating a new commercial and mining element into the Chilean agrarian elite. His career epitomized the opportunities available to a favored few in the years from 1835 until the outbreak of the War of the Pacific in 1879.

Copper mines also provided the rationale for the first railroads in Chile, built by William Wheelwright between the copper-rich Copiapó littoral and the port of Caldera to the northwest. Arrival of the railroad converted Caldera from a small settlement of perhaps fifty residents in 1850 into a port town of 2,000 by 1853. The number of ships putting in at the port increased from 160 a year in 1850 to more than 600 five years later. In contrast, the previously favored point for copper shipment at Puerto Viejo, to the southwest, was practically abandoned. Writing in the late 1850s, Vicente Pérez Rosales noted that "the railroad to Copiapó brought gas, beautiful buildings, theater, conveniences, luxury, abundance of fuel and food, along with a spirit of enterprise, attracting thereby numerous foreigners and Chileans to the city and the surrounding regions." Extension of the line to the mines near Púquios and around an irregular semicircle to the northern Bay of Chañaral stimulated economic activity throughout the departments of both Chañaral and Copiapó. The region's physical and economic subsistence soon came to depend more upon steamships, steel rails, and locomotives than upon mules, wagons, and the precarious river-valley agriculture of southern Coquimbo.

While copper deposits encouraged investments in modern transportation, the copper mines themselves generally remained technologically backward and almost entirely dependent upon imported fuel. As in the case of silver, Chilean copper miners relied upon technology essentially unchanged from colonial times until the introduction of the reverberatory furnace in the 1860s and 1870s. They ex-

tracted only the richest ore and sold the slag to traders for delivery
to more modern refineries in Germany, France, and England. The
mining industry utilized British coal along with domestic supplies
shipped from the Concepción region. Higher-quality British coal
made the Chilean coal industry around Lota, Coronel, and Lebu in
southern Chile vulnerable to British oversupply of the copper districts. As late as 1862 a large importation of British coal resulted in
serious production cutbacks at Lota and Coronel. Fortunately for
Chilean producers, a combination of British and Chilean coal proved
technically most desirable; and consequently the foundries at Caldera tended to use a 50-50 mixture of Swansea and Chilean coal. The
overall share of the coal market in the copper districts going to the
British varied year to year from 25 to 50 percent.

In addition to silver and copper, a number of less significant mining activities, along with extraction of guano and nitrates, hinted at
Chile's economic future by the end of the 1870s. Like the silver
mines and copper discoveries, exploitation of other mineral resources
encouraged related agricultural and commercial ventures. In the favored river valleys of Coquimbo and Atacama provinces, crop cultivation and livestock husbandry increased production to meet a part
of the growing demand for food and animal products. Towns rose,
stagnated, or declined with the fate of the mineral discoveries that
had created them.

The sequence of mineral discoveries from the 1830s to the early
1870s brought waves of fortune hunters to the provinces of Atacama
and Coquimbo. The former province tripled its population between
1843 and 1875, while the population of Coquimbo province doubled.
This contrasted markedly with the relatively stable population of the
predominantly rural departments of the middle central valley. By
the mid-1870s most of the population of the northern provinces lived
in "urban" settlements of more than 2000 people, though overall
population density of these provinces was much sparser than those
of the less urbanized middle central valley. The overwhelming influence of mining and the lack of large areas of cultivable land concentrated the population of the north into ports, administrative centers, and mining districts.

The obvious physical and economic contrasts between the northern provinces and the central valley lent a distinctive character to
life in the north. Higher salaries, higher costs of living, and the concentration of wage workers in isolated production centers gradually
forged a militant proletarian labor force. The great power of the
mine owners in association with government officials, also often on

the payroll of the mining enterprises, and the dramatic ups and downs of the mining ventures encouraged the evolution of a volatile political culture among northern workers. The agricultural export boom of the 1850s, which so greatly benefited Valparaíso merchants and Chilean landowners, meant higher food prices for the northern miners. Demands for higher wages led to strikes, violence, and looting by miners during the civil war of 1851. Miners, artisans, dockworkers, and muleteers in the *norte chico*, especially the region around Copiapó, played an even more significant role in the subsequent civil war of 1859. In the railroad machine shops and foundries of Caldera, workers cast cannon to use against government forces; in Chañarcillo, Copiapó, and other mining centers workers formed battalions that helped make the *norte chico* a temporarily "liberated zone." If the motivation of the mining entrepreneurs for rebellion could be detected in the decrees promulgated during this temporary "liberation"—for example, reduction by 50 percent of export duties on minerals—the experience of armed revolt by thousands of northern workers made the northern labor force more aware that government authority and the interests of the propertied classes conflicted with their own. With the War of the Pacific (1879-83) and the Chileanization of the nitrate fields, the northern work force would expand even more dramatically, class consciousness would become more acute, and class struggle would intensify. Soon thereafter the reality of the "social question" and industrial conflict would sweep southward from the northern provinces into Chile's heartland.

Modernization and material progress in the middle decades of the nineteenth century brought hard times to many of Chile's people in the central valley. While acreage under grain cultivation and production more than tripled between 1850 and 1875, thousands of rural families migrated to Santiago, Valparaíso, or the northern mining districts or looked for work in railway construction and public works projects. Whereas the population for the entire country increased from about 1,000,000 in 1835 to 2,100,000 (outside of Indian territory) in 1875 and to over 2,700,000 in 1895, that of rural central Chile had by 1895 barely changed from its 1865 level of 950,000.

Santiago, Valparaíso, and provincial capitals drew substantial population from the rural areas (see Table 5). Between 1865 and 1875 alone, Santiago's population increased from 115,000 to more than 150,000, while Valparaíso grew from 70,000 to almost 100,000 (42%). Favored central valley towns such as Curicó also experienced dramatic growth in the decade 1865-75; this provincial town almost

TABLE 6. COMPARISON OF URBAN AND RURAL POPULATION IN SELECTED
NORTHERN AND CENTRAL VALLEY DEPARTMENTS, 1875

Department, Northern Provinces	Total Population	"Urban" Population as % of Total
Copiapó	31,877	68
Caldera	10,511	78
Vallenar	13,569	51
Freirina	15,541	53
Serena	29,057	67
Coquimbo	12,650	73
Elqui	12,147	52
Ovalle	39,567	32
Combarbalá	14,002	17
Illapel	32,011	41

Department, Middle Central Valley Provinces	Total Population	"Urban" Population as % of Total
Melipilla	32,253	23
Rancagua	98,092	13
Caupolicán	75,186	15
San Fernando	72,668	15
Curicó	57,312	24
Vichuquen	35,546	8
Lontué	19,791	16
Talca	90,597	30
Loncomilla	31,689	21
Linares	53,420	14
Parral	33,652	16

doubled its population, growing from 5900 to 10,000, while the population of Curicó province remained almost stable at 90,000.

Although immigrants played a relatively minor numerical role in the urbanization process, at Valparaíso and in the northern mining towns a foreign presence was ever more apparent. For the country as a whole, immigrants composed less than 2 percent of the population in 1875; but in the province of Atacama they accounted for 11 percent, and in the department of Copiapó, approximately 20 percent. More important than their numbers was the financial and commercial power wielded by these groups.

The prosperity of foreign merchants at Valparaíso or in the mining districts contrasted sharply with the plight of the mass of rural laborers in the central valley. After 1860 wages in the countryside fell further and further behind the rising cost of food and basic necessities. The conditions of the *inquilinos* worsened as landlords required the service tenants to work more days, provide more family labor, or pay additional peons to fulfill the family's labor obligations. The tenants received ever smaller land allotments and faced restrictions on pasture rights for their animals. By 1858 a Chilean writer told his countrymen to "open your eyes and every day you see families leaving their homes. . . . Their single purpose is to leave the place where they cannot earn a living. . . . Travel our roads and you will see numerous families with all their belongings on their backs moving toward the capital to increase the existing pauperism."

Between 1849 and 1855 Chileans went in search of gold in California or to work on the railway under construction in Panama. The California census of 1852, which probably underestimates the Chilean presence, enumerates over 5500 in California at that date. Railroad gangs constructing the Santiago-Valparaíso line occupied a work force of 9000 to 10,000 a year; railroad projects in Peru (1868-72), directed by American entrepreneur Henry Meiggs, recruited 25,000 to 30,000 Chilean workers. Extension of the Chilean line to San Fernando (1862), Curicó (1868), and Talca (1874) employed thousands more. The Chillán-Talcahuano line (1869-74) provided jobs for over 9000 peons—and yet the army of rural unemployed increased.

Despite complaints by hacendados that construction projects and Meiggs' Peruvian venture created a shortage of hands, Chilean agriculture in the central valley experienced peak performance between 1868 and 1872. More important, except in critical periods of the agricultural cycle such as harvest, wages for rural labor failed to climb above the typical 10 to 25 centavos a day plus meager food rations. Upset at the inconvenience of competing for harvest labor with railroad crews, landowners filled the country's newspapers with exaggerated reports of the awful conditions and epidemics suffered by Chileans in Peru. Meanwhile the tide of migration carried thousands out of the rural districts as the rural poor sought better opportunities elsewhere.

The fact that a promise of a wage of 62 centavos a day plus food rations could move 30,000 Chileans to Peru indicates the plight of the Chilean rural lower classes. Thousands of families endured precarious lives in squatters' huts on marginal land along the coast; thousands more lived an ambulatory existence following the crops from Aconcagua south. Still others turned to banditry and cattle rustling, making some of the rural districts unsafe for travel. Official reports of the 1840s and 1850s contain many references to the large "vagrant" population of the central valley. Under these conditions hacendados in some areas could attract harvest labor by sponsoring a type of harvest fiesta called *mingaco*, thereby "paying" the workers only with food and drink.

With the sweat and blood of these workers and that of their families, a small wealthy elite initiated the physical modernization of Chile in the middle decades of the nineteenth century. Railroads built to carry minerals of the north to Caldera or the cereals of the central valley to Valparaíso permitted Chilean and foreign entrepreneurs to live an extravagant existence in the principal urban areas. Wealth accumulated in mining and commerce bought land and social status. To the list of traditional landed families like the Aguirre, Larraín, or Errázuriz, mining and commercial fortunes added British, French, and German surnames along with those of newly enriched Chileans. The economically integrated upper class that emerged treated the Chilean masses with contempt. Railroad and mining interests bewailed the drunken orgies of their workers, while landowners defended the practice of paying workers in company scrip on the grounds that it spared them the temptation of "foolish" consumption outside the haciendas.

Sumptuous houses and importation of luxurious European furnishings absorbed many of the windfall profits associated with wheat and flour exports, commerce, and mining. Santiago, Valparaíso, and even lesser central valley towns boasted new, lavishly decorated edifices. Upper-class gentlemen emulated the life styles of European capitalists and aristocrats. Prestigious social clubs and the National Agricultural Society (1869) brought together sociopolitical elites to decide matters of state and economy outside the public halls of the Congress. The best-endowed maintained haciendas near Santiago or Valparaíso as recreational retreats with ornamental gardens and well-furnished residences, or *casas de fundo*. With the extension of the railroad south to Talca, lesser properties, located farther from the capital, increased in value and, subsequently, in the ornamentation of the landowner's "big house."

No less impressive than the sumptuous buildings in the cities, the gracious country residences stood in stark contrast to the rude huts of the campesinos whose pitiful wages barely provided subsistence. Low labor costs inhibited the same landowners, so fond of modern urban convenience in their townhouses, from modernizing farm technology. Chilean landowners preferred labor-intensive, sickle-and-scythe harvesting of cereals long after most of North America and Australia had mechanized the wheat harvest. A minority of Chilean landowners adopted machinery, new crops, and new breeds of animals and pastures or began construction of irrigation canals; but the economics of Chilean agriculture—cheap labor and vast rural estates with uncultivated land—did not invite large-scale mechanization prior to the 1880s. The poverty of the Chilean masses limited internal demand for agricultural products; and by the early 1870s Chile's inability to compete with North American and Australian producers restricted expansion of its output despite the importance of the British market. Under these conditions, even without substantial mechanization, Chilean agriculture based upon the large haciendas could not provide year-round employment to the growing number of rootless rural laborers.

Industry offered no solution to the employment problem. Modernization and commercial expansion brought little industry to Chile. An American naval officer visiting the country at midcentury noted that Chile was "almost without factories of any description . . . dependent on foreign nations for every supply except food." This description ignored the numerous small-scale producers of household goods, cordage, rigging, tanneries, and the like, but it accurately portrayed the lack of any significant manufacturing establishment, apart from flour mills and breweries established by German immigrants in the south and the mining enterprises in the north. Major economic interest groups such as landowners, merchants, and mine owners generally opposed protective tariffs to encourage local industry. Dependent upon the export trade, albeit in different ways, landowners did not wish to pay taxes on imported European goods; mine interests, closely linked to British firms, commercial houses, and shippers, supported "free trade"; merchants, like merchants everywhere, defended the right of the consumer to buy quality goods at low prices. Occasional editorials in Santiago or regional newspapers in the 1860s and 1870s supported, without notable success, some form of protective tariff to encourage domestic manufacturers. Debates in the legislature resulted in new tariff laws in 1872 and 1878, but conflict existed between the primary goal of increasing government revenues from custom duties and any effective tariff barrier to encourage Chilean industry. Protectionist sentiments existed but, with some notable exceptions such as special duties on imported sugar and beer, did not make significant gains until the tariff reforms in 1897. Even then, protectionism remained controversial. In response to economic crises, labor conflicts, and urban riots in the period 1903-07, President Pedro Montt led a movement to reduce tariffs on manufactured consumer goods and meat products. Not until the tariff reforms of 1928 would industrialization through protectionism become a dominant economic policy in Chile.

In the mid-1870s the overwhelming majority of Chilean manufacturing establishments were quite small, typically artisan producers of consumer goods or more durable items such as carriages and wagons. Rarely did firms employ large numbers of workers or operate anything like an industrial assembly process, although by 1874 some of the Talca flour mills were utilizing imported steam-powered machinery. Even shipbuilding, a likely enterprise given Chilean participation in the Pacific grain trade and the country's extensive mineral exports, experienced no significant growth. Of 259 Chilean-registered ships in 1865, only twenty-six were constructed in Chile, and all but six of these came from boatworks in the southern region. A brief war with Spain between 1864 and 1866 over supposed insults to Spanish honor resulted in the loss of a number of these ships and a change in the registry of others. The Spanish blockaded Chile's main ports of entry, but lacked sufficient ships and troops to make the blockade effective along Chile's entire coast. Frustrated by the stalemate and Chile's refusal to provide the proper salute to the Spanish flag, the Spanish fleet bombarded Valparaíso, seriously damaging warehouses and port-works. Although the blockade caused temporary disruptions of commerce, it did nothing to stimulate Chilean shipbuilding even in the face of the obvious lesson of the nation's vulnerability to one of Europe's third-rate powers.

With no significant industry to occupy a growing population, the central valley sent its surplus labor into construction projects, the northern mines, or to foreign lands in search of employment. Mining depressions, reduction of public works, or decline in demand for the products of Chilean agriculture meant immediate crisis for the mass of the population, just as it meant bankruptcy for overextended entrepreneurs, landowners, or merchants. According to the census of 1875, more than 60 percent of the enumerated male labor force worked as unskilled laborers (gañanes) or "farmers" (agricultores). Of the more than 300,000 women reported in the census, approximately 85 percent worked as cooks, servants, washerwomen, seamstresses, or weavers. These figures obviously understate the contribution of women to the economy, especially in agriculture, but do provide a revealing glimpse into the economic opportunities open to most of Chile's female population during these years. Women achieved access to Chilean universities only after 1877, and as late as 1907, according to a group of Chilean historians reporting on the rise of the middle class in the country, there were only "3[women] lawyers, 7 doctors, 10 dentists, 10 pharmacists and 3980 school teachers." More generally, including the data for unskilled and semi-skilled laborers in the countryside, construction crews, ports, and railroads, together with miners and various artisans (for example, 14,000 shoemakers, 250 candle and soap makers, etc.), the census suggests that 85 to 90 percent of all actively employed Chilean males corresponded to these working-class categories. Even with the most ample interpretation of *comerciantes*, or "merchants," of the professions, of industrialists of various sorts, of white-collar and public employees, and of miscellaneous non-"working-class" categories, substantially less than 10 percent of the enumerated actively employed corresponded to an emerging "middle" stratum or to the numerically tiny economic elite.

Thus the economic progress of the middle decades of the nineteenth century quite narrowly restricted wealth to an upper crust of society and allowed a thin veneer of ornamentation and physical modernization to cover the major urban centers. This veneer cracked with each economic recession or decline in prices for Chile's principal exports. Loss of the California and Australian markets after 1856, declines in copper prices, and the switch to a gold standard by European nations in 1873 shortly after the rich silver strike at Caracoles (1870), all drastically affected Chile's prosperity.

The economic recession of 1857-58 brought widespread unemployment and bankruptcies, followed by civil war in 1859. The worldwide economic depression of 1873 set in motion a train of events that looked even more disastrous for Chile. The shift to a gold standard by European powers was followed by a 50 percent drop in copper prices. Bad weather ruined the Chilean wheat crop of 1876-77. Famine followed. The economic depression seemed to climax forty years of economic "development." Government revenues, still dependent upon the devastated export sector, drastically declined. Budget reductions exacerbated employment problems with a cutback on public works and government personnel. Government borrowing to meet the crisis increased the fiscal deficit; in desperation President Pinto proposed direct taxation of income, real estate, and capital. Finally, as a last resort, the government shifted to paper currency—while the country now imported wheat to feed itself. Despite a favorable upturn in the balance of trade in 1878, the bubble seemed about to burst. The limits of the export-oriented economy had apparently been reached.

But then, much as the victory in the early nineteenth-century war against the Peru-Bolivia confederation had helped to consolidate the Chilean polity, another war against the same adversaries would now provide Chile with a new "golden goose"—the nitrate fields of the Atacama desert. The nitrate boom would allow the hard economic realities of export-dependent development to be put off for another four decades. As occurred with export booms throughout Latin America in the late nineteenth century—whether they were based upon coffee, sugar, wheat, minerals, or other primary commodities—exploitation of the nitrate fields provided Chile with extensive export revenues which financed public works and modernization without coming to terms with the internal contradictions of the economy or the structural inequalities of Chilean society. At Santiago, Valparaíso, and other central valley cities and in the central valley countryside, landowners could patch the cracked veneer of prosperity and continue the beautification of their urban mansions and country estates while they postponed confrontation with the reality of the country's growing population of urban and rural poor.

The agro-commercial expansion of the mid-nineteenth century took on a special meaning for the population of the Concepción–southern region and the Araucanians to the south. In the southern area traders, farmers, and speculators maintained contact with local chieftains, but farms and settlements in the frontier territory remained subject to periodic raids or even relatively large-scale uprisings that wrought considerable destruction of property and loss of life. Araucania remained outside the Chilean nation.

External demand for wheat, flour, and animal products made southern lands potentially more valuable. Expanded cereal cultivation accompanied by the growth of a prosperous flour-milling industry in the environs of Tomé put renewed pressure on the Indian lands. Partly in response to these pressures, an Indian insurrection from 1859 to 1860 coincided with the civil war that pitted Concepción forces against the central government, and caused much destruction in the areas of Negrete, Nacimiento, and Los Angeles. In April 1859 the periodical *El Correo del Sur* called in no uncertain terms for violent repression and blamed the Indians and "Indian territory" for numerous real and imagined evils:

> The necessity, not only to punish the Araucanian race, but also to make it impotent to harm us, is so well recognized that almost everyone desires that such measures be taken as the only

way to rid the country of a million evils. It is well understood that they are odious and prejudicial guests in Chile. . . . The thousands of families that today find themselves in misery; the innumerable robberies committed by these savages . . . are clamoring for prompt and extreme measures, since conciliatory measures have accomplished nothing with this stupid race—the infamy and disgrace of the Chilean nation.

Once again the lure of quick profits and Indian land pitted the Araucanians in a struggle for survival against the superior firepower of "civilization." Now "odious guests" in their own land, the Indians faced a last desperate attempt to maintain their land and their autonomy against the encroaching outsiders.

The land rush occasioned by expansion of cereal cultivation—accompanied by government colonization schemes, legal chicanery, and corruption—necessitated troops to enforce the "property rights" of Chilean landowners. A new Indian uprising, led by a Frenchman who proclaimed himself King Aurélie Antoine I and swore to free the Indians from Chilean tyranny, spurred the government to renewed repression. Reminiscent of the military tactics of many colonial governors, the Chilean leaders established forts at Mulchén and Angol in 1863 and then "defense lines" near Malleco (1867-68) and Traiguén (1878-79), as troops drove the Indians further south and east. The official frontier shifted to the Malleco River in 1866, and in 1875 Bío Bío became a new Chilean province (see Map 9).

Chilean squatters, speculators, and would-be hacendados rushed to gain control of "empty" frontier lands. From 1852 to 1866 the national government attempted unsuccessfully to regulate land transactions in the southern territories. A ban on land deals with Indians in 1858 failed to stem the tide. Legislation defining as "public" all frontier lands that had not been "continually and effectively occupied for at least one year," set in motion thousands of legal conflicts between the government, Indians, squatters, and land speculators. Many of the conflicts were resolved outside the courts by force; others were decided by bribes or by influence exercised by powerful economic interests.

Finally in the mid-1870s Congress enacted a law that required public auctioning of all contested lands in a region bounded by the Renaico River to the north, the Malleco to the south, and the Vergara to the west (see Map 9). The down payments required were so high that they practically excluded peasants, workers, and artisans from acquiring these lands; incentives for private colonization companies

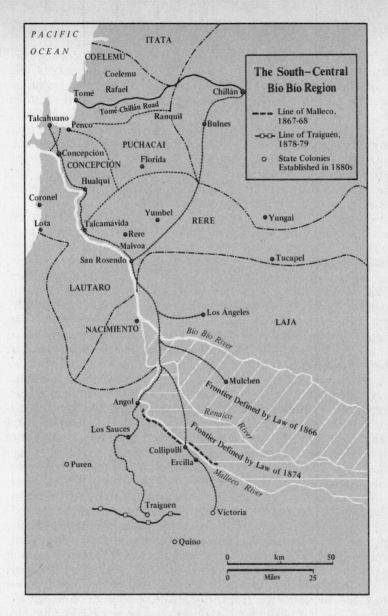

MAP 9: The South-Central Bío Bío Region

(Source: John Whaley, "Transportation in Chile's Bío Bío Region 1850-1915," Ph.D. dissertation, Indiana University, 1974.)

to bring in "high quality"—that is, northern European—colonists discriminated against Chilean settlers. The government seldom sold properties of less than the legal maximum of 500 hectares. Instead of creating a frontier yeomanry, government policy allowed the frontier territory to become another domain of the large hacienda. In imitation of the central valley model, political and economic elites carved out new manorial possessions upon which ex-squatters, landless peasants, and Indians became *inquilinos* or peons. Between 1850 and 1875 ex-presidents and future presidents of Chile, along with such well-known entrepreneurs as Waddington, Bunster, Cousiño, and Smitmans, acquired large rural estates in the southern provinces.

Passage of the 1874 public lands legislation coincided with the maiden journey of the southern region's new railroad from Concepción to Chillán. Since the 1850s local elites in the frontier territory had struggled to obtain government support for a southern railway. At midcentury the region contained only two important urban centers: Concepción and Chillán. Agriculture and livestock entirely dominated the regional economy, though an incipient coal industry and a few fishing villages along the coast provided a hint of things to come. The gold strikes in California and Australia that stimulated demand for Chilean wheat and flour encouraged the export trade at Concepción-Talcahuano and brought dramatic growth to Tomé. Developing as the center of the milling industry and recipient of foreign investment and technology, Tomé accounted for more than 90 percent of the provinces' reported 842,000 quintals of flour by 1855. Expanded production and commerce also benefited Concepción and Talcahuano, which was the only legal port of entry for the entire southern region. But until railroads began to operate after 1874, high freight rates and the constraints of transport by oxcart seriously disadvantaged the southern region in relation to the central valley.

Loss of the California and Australia markets, economic depression in 1857, the havoc of civil war, and Indian uprisings (1859-63, 1868), all represented setbacks for the frontier provinces. With virtual completion of the Santiago-Valparaíso railroad in the early 1860s and its connection to San Fernando, southern agriculture faced the prospect of being unable to compete with the central valley. Until the early 1860s the southern mill industry supplied most of the flour exported by Chile; thereafter the southern share dropped off to somewhat less than 50 percent of the total, and what had been a modern industry in the 1850s failed to keep pace with rapid technological innovations in flour milling in the United States and Europe. By the late 1870s Chilean millers could not compete effectively in the international market, though trade with Peru, Ecuador, Argentina, and Brazil continued, along with less significant shipments to Europe or North America. Moreover, the share of the export market accounted for by shipments through Valparaíso rose from less than 25 percent between 1846 and 1850 to over 90 percent in 1880. Fortunately, after bumper crops in 1862-63 and a short-term decline in prices, increased Peruvian demand for Chilean wheat and the growing British market rescued the economy of the region from disaster. Over the next ten years British purchases of Chilean wheat increased from approximately 340,000 pesos in 1863 to more than 2 million pesos in 1874—when the railroad connected Talcahuano to Chillán and the wheatlands of the interior.

Southern agriculture expanded by putting more and more land under cultivation by means of slash-and-burn technology. With large tracts of land available, high yields on virgin soil, and relatively cheap labor, southern agriculture could expand output with small amounts of capital investment. Agricultural workers received low wages along with food rations consisting of beans, potatoes, corn, and unleavened bread, or *galleta*. Peons rarely ate meat. Agricultural implements generally remained primitive: wooden plows, and weighted bramble-bush harrows. While labor supply remained plentiful and secure, no need to mechanize existed. Into the 1870s most hacendados of the south employed labor crews for the harvest, and paid temporary wages double or triple those paid to the resident labor force. Significant mechanization would come only later in the nineteenth century, when the supply of harvest laborers became less secure and workers less compliant due to the possibility of other employment in railroad and public construction projects or in the nitrate fields taken from Peru and Bolivia in the War of the Pacific.

Foreign markets for southern agriculture and the demand for coal by northern mines also stimulated the growth of some of the cities and towns of the region. Near Concepción the coal-mining enterprise of Matías Cousiño changed Lota from a rustic village into a mining town of some 5000 by the mid-1860s. Shortly thereafter the government extended telegraph service to Lota and from there to Nacimiento on the Araucanian frontier. Copper foundries, a brick factory, and other associated commercial establishments contributed to Lota's expansion. Coal mining also stimulated commercial development around Lebu and Coronel between 1862 and 1874. From 1865 to 1875 the population of Coronel increased from 2,132 to 5,568; by 1875 Lebu's population exceeded 5700.

The mining proletariat created in the 1860s and 1870s would even-

tually make the coal-mining region one of the most explosive areas of
class conflict and union struggle in Chile. In the short run, development of the Chilean coal industry meant that despite the low quality
of Chilean coal, the country could supply more than 50 percent of
domestic consumption. Perhaps even more significant, the coal trade
along with lumber and food exports expanded contacts between the
two regions most hostile to policy emanating from Santiago and between workers in the most dynamic sectors of the Chilean economy.

By 1851 flour-milling and shipping activities at Tomé had transformed a tiny settlement of a dozen shacks into a mushrooming town
with some 2000 residents. Favored by nearby sources of water power
and an oxcart road connecting it to the wheat fields of the interior,
the population of Tomé more than doubled in the next decade,
reaching some 5300 in 1865. In contrast, Talcahuano's population declined from 2500 to 2000, and Concepción remained more or less
stagnant, as Tomé took the fore in the cereal and flour-based commercial boom. After 1877 this situation would reverse itself as the
favorable freight rates on the rail line between Talcahuano and
Chillán killed off the oxcart traffic between Tomé and the interior.

Intraregional rivalries between Tomé interests and those at Concepción made even more discouraging the central government's neglect of the southern region. Limited economic progress, including the
temporary booms of the early 1850s, did not fully incorporate the
Concepción–southern region into the incipient process of modernization experienced by the central valley. The Indian frontier continued
to limit southern expansion, while Santiago politicians and speculators treated the region as a vast opportunity for economic exploitation. Complicating this situation, some foreign interests even
suggested that Chile had no effective control of or legal claim to
Araucania. For example, a report by a British representative in Santiago to the Foreign Office in 1875 stated this position explicitly: "It
seems to me that the Chilean government cannot claim any legal
title to Araucania. It certainly has not had success in the conquest of
this territory nor has it acquired rights to this territory through any
treaty. . . ."

Only with the War of the Pacific and the nitrate boom of succeeding decades would the full importance of southern agriculture become apparent to the national government. Only then were the
Araucanians finally subjugated—though not fully incorporated—into
Chilean national life. For the Araucanians and for numerous Chilean
landless peasants and squatters, the agro-commercial growth of the

south in the mid-nineteenth century meant still another confrontation, and eventual defeat, by the economic and political forces associated with the expansion of Western European and North American capitalism. For the Araucanians it meant a final death struggle to maintain their land and autonomy. For most of the poor mestizo peasants and squatters it meant loss of the last opportunity to escape the poverty and lack of mobility inherent in the social structure of the central valley latifundia.

What most distinguished Chilean political development after 1830 from events in the other Spanish American republics was a remarkable constitutional continuity. Four elected presidents each served two consecutive five-year terms between 1831 and 1871. Congressional elections occurred on schedule with the repeated return of representatives of Chile's elite families to the Senate and Chamber of Deputies. Presidents and legislators of all political persuasions came overwhelmingly from a small number of intermarried, extended kinship groups with well-known surnames.

Oligarchy buttressed by endogamy and *compadrazgo** preserved the basic solidarity of a ruling elite whose economic interests extended from agriculture to mining, commerce, banking, and, later, industry. The geographical compactness of Chile's central valley—unlike the fragmentation or the greater size of Colombia, Mexico, Peru, or Brazil—facilitated national unity and elite consensus on fundamental social and economic institutions—even when philosophical disagreements or the clash of personalistic factions led to political conflict. To illustrate, a doctoral dissertation by Gabriel Marcella completed in 1973 found that one extended family—the Errázuriz—contributed four presidents and 59 parliamentarians from 1831 to 1927. On occasion as many as six served in the same legislature. Overall, Marcella reported that among 599 deputies and senators (out of 782 for whom some quantity of kinship data was available) there appeared 98 sets of brothers, 61 sets of father and son, 57 sets of uncle and nephew, 20 of cousins, 12 of father and son-in-law, and 32 of brothers-in-law. Moreover, the influence of kinship in the legislature *increased* rather than decreased between 1834 and 1888. Chilean political stability from 1831 to 1891 depended more than a little upon restricted suf-

---

* *Compadrazgo* is a common form of fictive kinship prevalent throughout Spain and Latin America; literally "godmother" and "godfather" for baptism, marriage, etc.

frage, low levels of political participation, and maintenance of government positions in the hands of a small, intermarried, social, and economic oligarchy.

Notwithstanding these oligarchical features and the relative political stability of nineteenth-century Chile when compared with the rest of Latin America, there existed underlying tensions between economic interests in the outlying provinces and Santiago as well as between autocratic and oligarchic tendencies within the Chilean political system. These tensions, along with conflicts over the relationship between Church and State, fragmented the ruling elite. The Hispanic tradition of an authoritarian executive conflicted with the evolving desires of the leading families to rule Chile in their collective interest and to protect themselves from an overzealous president or an administration that took political debate outside the confines of salon, parliament, or the prestigious Club de la Unión.

Application of certain provisions of the 1833 constitution—in particular those requiring annual legislative action on the national budget, periodic approval of tax rates and tax collection, authorizations to maintain military personnel and to station troops within ten leagues of where Congress was in session—led gradually to an erosion of presidential dominance between 1841 and 1891—when a bloody civil war would confirm the victory of Congress over the executive.

The autocratic interpretation and implementation of the 1833 constitution by President Prieto (1831-41) could not eliminate entirely the influence of imported liberalism or the desire of certain Chilean elites to emulate British and Continental parliamentarism. Nevertheless, the presidential regime provided no formal mechanism for changing executive leadership through parliamentary elections or votes of no confidence. Instead, gradually but insistently—using the leverage of Congress' budgetary and tax authority—the foes of presidential dominance imposed constraints upon executive action and established the principle of ministerial responsibility to Congress.

As early as November 1841, Congress agreed to suspend consideration of legislation authorizing tax collection as well as the budget bill until the executive submitted an expanded legislative agenda—including legislation aimed at extending congressional oversight of public expenditures. Executive agreement to these demands meant de facto abrogation of an exclusive constitutional prerogative of the executive: designation of matters to be considered in the extraordinary sessions of the legislature. More important, President Bulnes' acceptance of the congressional demands was an implicit recognition of the legitimacy of legislative checks on government policy.

Influenced by Belgian procedures, legislators intent on asserting congressional authority also introduced the practice of "interpellation"—a questioning period to hold ministers accountable for their acts. Under this procedure individual deputies could request particular ministers to appear in the chamber to explain or justify government policy. Combined with delays on critical legislation, the practice of interpellation moved Chilean politics in the direction of quasi-parliamentarism. Liberal intellectuals such as José Victorino Lastarria argued that interpellation and censure of ministers were rights inherent in the supervisory authority of Congress and served as guarantees against executive irregularities and abuses.

After bitterly contested congressional elections in 1849, during which the Bulnes government mounted a campaign of repression against the liberal forces, dissident conservatives, and the opposition political groups based on family ties or personal friendships, Lastarria submitted reform proposals to the new Congress. These proposals aimed to limit further presidential authority as well as to guarantee freedom of the press and the right of assembly. Though Congress did not approve these reforms, the attacks on executive dominance continued.

In 1850 a new political movement emerged called the Society of Equality. Headed by Francisco Bilbao and a number of personalities like Santiago Arcos and the Matta brothers who would play important roles as political reformers, the society held numerous public meetings and demonstrations against the government. In response, the intendant of Santiago prohibited further meetings and declared the society "dissolved"; all similar organizations were outlawed. Government officials closed opposition newspapers, and many of the leaders of the reform movement fled into exile.

Toward the end of President Bulnes' second term in office (1851), conflict intensified. The government election machine, based upon control of the votes of the militia, provided more than sufficient votes to make Bulnes' chosen successor, Manual Montt, the next president—despite support by liberals and regional interests in Concepción and La Serena for Bulnes' cousin, José María de la Cruz. Since the president appointed militia officers, and the officers handled distribution of the "certificates of qualification" that allowed the militiamen to vote, presidential intervention in elections generally spelled defeat for the opposition. Officers could also withhold certificates from unreliable militiamen and give them to more "trustworthy" citizens. Although this practice had become more or less expected, the increasing resistance to presidential dominance and the frustration of important economic interests in the provinces made it impossible for Bulnes' opponents to swallow the election results.

Opponents of the regime contested the legitimacy of the rigged elections and broke into armed revolt in Concepción and La Serena. Rebel forces in Coquimbo requisitioned the British ship *Firefly* and extorted contributions from wealthy government supporters. Before the intervention of the British squadron—encouraged by the Montt government—the northern rebel forces occupied the towns of Elqui, Huasco, Ovalle, Combarbalá, and Illapel. Miners from the important El Tamaya mine marched on Ovalle, and other groups occupied haciendas around Illapel. Miners, construction workers, and peasants mobilized to the rebel cause in other northern towns—an event in which some Marxist historians have discerned elements of an armed popular insurrection. Although this interpretation is not entirely inaccurate, the basic struggle in the 1851 revolt pitted the incumbent political machine against regional and liberal forces protesting the outcome of the elections and the more fundamental subordination of the southern and northern provinces to Santiago. Indicative of this underlying source of conflict was the leadership of the Concepción rebel forces in 1851 by would-be railroad entrepreneur, landowner, and liberal politico, Pedro Félix Vicuña. Vicuña's proposal for government subsidies of his project for a southern railroad had fallen upon deaf ears in Santiago shortly before he led the Concepción forces in support of the defeated liberal candidate. Vicuña also owned a major newspaper in the region and had himself named intendant of the province by the rebel forces. Thus the desire for political reform and frustrated economic interest, as well as personal ambition, motivated the rebel leadership in the civil conflict of 1851.

As in the north, the Montt government availed itself of British support to help quell the southern rebellion. In the words of the exiled Argentine Domingo Sarmiento, in a pamphlet he wrote supporting the Montt government, "British capital needs the guarantee of peace . . . to invest millions in the interior and to stimulate the export of cereals. . . . Montt is public tranquility, authority, good faith, and efficient administration." Within three months the Montt government reasserted control in both the northern and southern provinces.

Victory in the civil war in 1851, however, did not end the movement to put legislative checks on the presidency. By 1857 not only government policy but also the very composition of the president's cabinet became hostage to congressional approval. In August 1857 Congress approved an opposition senator's motion to postpone consideration of the budget until the president announced who would be appointed to the new cabinet. President Manuel Montt reluctantly acquiesced and, at congressional insistence, even named members of the liberal opposition to the cabinet. In effect this development put the Congress in control of the cabinet, making the Chilean political system a curious mixture of parliamentary and presidential government. The threat of congressional refusal to approve budget legislation or other critical government programs gradually transformed the autocratic presidential regime envisioned by Portales into a delicately balanced system of negotiation between government and opposition forces. On any particular issue, government supporters could defect and form an opposition majority to complicate further the life of the incumbent executive. Thus, by 1861 the institutional foundations of the multiparty "parliamentarism," for which Chile became well known after 1891, had substantially modified the autocratic regime installed by Portales and Prieto.

Erosion of presidentalism could not have occurred without a coincident ideological and political fragmentation of the Chilean elite. Introduction of liberalism as a political ideology in early nineteenth-century Chile threatened in two essential ways the hegemony of Iberian autocracy re-established by Portales: (1) rejection of Catholicism as the exclusive moral underpinning of the state and (2) acceptance of social pluralism, including freedom of association, freedom of the press, and the gamut of civil liberties associated with the British liberal tradition.

In the 1840s the "Generation of 1842" had arisen, as previously mentioned, from the new (1842) University of Chile. This liberal movement, headed by José Victorino Lastarria, brought an immediate response from the Church, which opposed any hint of religious toleration. Among the partisans of the national coalition surrounding President Bulnes (1841-51) as well as his successor, Manuel Montt (1851-61), were a number of personalities who favored a dilution of the Church's influence or at least a firmer exercise of the *patronato* by the State over the Church. Their efforts, together with liberal attacks on the Church and the intervention of foreign governments—especially the British—on behalf of foreign nationals resident in Chile, resulted in a series of laws offensive to the Church and to devout Catholic politicians. Among other provisions, these laws expanded the power of civil authorities to supervise the activities of parish priests, and allowed non-Catholics to marry without conforming to Catholic ritual.

This politico-religious conflict divided the government coalition.

Continued disputes between the Bulnes and Montt governments and the Church gave rise, in 1857, to the Conservative party, which gradually became the political voice of the Catholic Church. This meant that an integral part of future electoral battles and parliamentary debates would consist of issues related to the privileges and role of the Church in Chilean society. In addition, the Conservative party, finding itself in opposition to the incumbent executive, now supported the movement to shift the balance of power from the president to party coalitions in the Congress—albeit for different reasons than the liberals.

Approval of certain anticlerical measures by the Bulnes and Montt governments did not mean acceptance of the secular implications of liberalism. In the short run, the secular conservatives now known as the "Montt-Varistas," or the National party, continued to oppose social pluralism, unrestricted civil liberties, freedom of the press, and elections uncontrolled by the national executive machine. The Montt government, in particular, repressed opposition elements after facing civil war in 1851 and 1859.

Despite the outcome of the 1851 civil war, the formation of the Conservative party in 1857 seriously weakened the antiliberal government coalition. Now both Catholics and liberals favored further restriction upon presidential authority and institutionalization of "parliamentary" government. The Catholics desired a stronger Church role in government and society; the liberal program included expansion of the suffrage, prohibition of presidential re-election, and reform of the restrictive press laws. To complicate matters further, many liberals did not share the violently anticlerical positions of Bilbao or Lastarria. Indeed many Conservatives and Liberals came to take a common political stance against the incumbent regime.

Montt's apparent intention to impose the forceful minister of interior, Antonio Varas, as his successor, along with the government's hesitancy in granting a complete amnesty to those involved in the insurrection of 1851, pushed the Conservatives and the majority of Liberals into a "fusion" that sought to prevent Varas' election. A group of intransigent liberal anticlericals rejected this fusion, but nevertheless joined the opposition. Led by the future founders of the Radical party (1863), men like Guillermo Matta and Justo and Domingo Arteaga Alemparte, as well as other opposition forces, launched an antigovernment propaganda campaign across the nation.

The government response—declaration of a state of siege, arrests of prominent opposition leaders, closure of opposition periodicals—moved Pedro León Gallo, a rich miner and leader of the opposition in Copiapó, to send a private army against the government. As in 1851, the rebellion centered in the *norte chico* and spread to Concepción, but outbreaks also occurred in Valparaíso and the central valley. While the government eventually crushed the rebellion after both sides had sustained numerous casualties, Varas withdrew his candidacy, and Montt named José Joaquín Pérez as the government-supported candidate. Neither the moderate liberals nor the clericals in the Conservative party had any serious objections to Pérez as Montt's successor.

By 1861, therefore, the ruling elite had fragmented into at least four major groups: National party, Conservative party, Liberals, and militant liberals, who eventually formed the Radical party in 1863. The new President formed a cabinet composed of Nationals, Liberals, and Conservatives. Soon after taking office he approved an amnesty law for all political exiles. Despite Pérez' effort to conciliate long-standing animosities, personal and political differences made the coalition ineffective. Pérez then turned the cabinet over to the Liberal-Conservative "fusion" which gained a congressional majority through the expected executive intervention in the 1864 congressional elections. The National party (the party of Montt) and the Radicals now formed the opposition. Pérez governed for ten years without declaring a state of siege; at the end of his term in 1871 a constitutional amendment prohibited immediate presidential re-election.

During the next presidential term (1871-76) further legislative reforms consolidated the congressional-oligarchic system. Control of elections passed to juntas, or committees of wealthy taxpayers—a reform that assured significant minority representation in Congress, as well as the predominance of the landed elite in the central valley. It did not, however, settle the ongoing "religious question" including controversies over secularizing cemeteries, civil marriage, public education, and, more generally, separation of Church and State. This "religious question" remained the most prominent political schism in Chile until 1891, nearly a decade after the War of the Pacific (1879-83), when efforts by President Manuel Balmaceda (1886-91) to reverse the course of over half a century of political evolution by reasserting executive dominance, led to a bloody civil war. Indeed, the oligarchic "parliamentary" regime that had evolved between 1841 and 1876 and entrenched itself after 1891, would continue to wrangle over the "religious question" into the twentieth century, long after the social and economic issues of industrialization, class conflict, and democratization seemed to portend more profound and radical changes in Chilean politics and society.

In 1876 newly elected President Aníbal Pinto faced not only the "religious question" but also the economic depression that had begun in 1873. Policies suggested to combat the economic situation, such as working on Sundays and fiesta days, antagonized the Church. Government attempts to exert control over public education and proposals to secularize the cemeteries added fuel to the fire. The economic crisis heightened tempers. Clericals promised rebellion if the religious reforms passed; anticlericals accused priests of hoarding food while others starved. The death in 1878 of the conservative archbishop Ramón Valdivieso further divided opposition forces when the president refused to consult with the Church hierarchy before choosing Valdivieso's successor. When President Pinto selected a priest notorious for his illegitimate birth and liberal politics, clerical forces successfully petitioned the Pope to oppose his appointment. The issue remained unresolved for years.

Confronted by the mounting difficulties of the economic situation and the hostility of the ultramontane opposition, Pinto's situation seemed ever more impossible. While prosperity could provide the grease to make the delicately balanced political machine function, an end to the windfalls of the export economy and foreign investment typical since the 1840s spelled disaster. Fortunately for Chile's elites, Bolivia shortly provided the Pinto government with a pretext for declaring war and for the subsequent annexation of the nitrate fields of the Atacama desert. The nitrate fields would provide the means to lubricate the Chilean economy and political apparatus for some years to come. They would also spawn a militant proletariat that would force Chile to confront directly the "social question" and the politics of industrial class conflict.

Chapter 6 • Nitrate

Plagued by economic difficulties and internal political dissensions, Chile faced the possibility of war with Argentina, Bolivia, and Peru. Owing to poorly demarcated boundaries in Patagonia, a territorial dispute with Argentina had simmered since Chile's creation of the Punta Arenas colony in the early 1840s. A flare up of this dispute in the late 1870s menaced peaceful relations between the two nations. To the north, investments of Chilean capital and the migration of thousands of Chilean workers to extract guano, nitrates, copper, and silver from the Bolivian desert of Antofagasta created increasingly tense relations between Bolivia and Chile.

Skillful negotiations avoided war with Argentina, but the vast economic stakes in the north made a peaceful settlement with Bolivia impossible. A new Bolivian government contravened the provisions of the 1874 treaty prohibiting Bolivia from increasing export taxes on the Chilean nitrate operations for a period of twenty-five years, and imposed a surtax on nitrate shipments of ten centavos per metric quintal (100 kg). The Chilean government's support of the Anglo-Chilean owned Antofagasta Railroad and Nitrate Company (whose stockholders included Chilean congressmen and cabinet members) in its refusal to pay the tax led ultimately to war.

In the course of the Chile-Bolivia dispute in the 1870s, Peru entered into a secret alliance with Bolivia in February 1873. The alliance provided for mutual guarantees of independence and territory against aggression by a third party. According to the terms of the alliance, neither nation could conclude a peace, a truce, or an armistice without prior approval of the other; nor could either cede territory or privileges that would reduce or limit independence or sovereignty. Peru's interest in such a treaty stemmed from its almost total economic dependence upon the export of guano and nitrates to Europe. The expansion of European agriculture led to a spectacular increase in demand for fertilizer, which, in turn, stimulated intensive economic activity in Peru's southern provinces, particularly Tarapacá, and in Antofagasta in Bolivia. This activity, on top of the silver strike at Caracoles and the extensive copper mining in the 1870s, made the Peruvian and Bolivian deserts suddenly highly prized economic assets.

Depletion of the guano deposits that had provided Peruvian governments with most of their revenues between 1830 and 1870 led to increased emphasis on nitrates. In contrast to the Peruvian government's monopoly on guano, however, the nitrate industry developed under the control of private capital. Prior to the War of the Pacific (1879-83) foreign interests (Chilean, British, German, and French) acquired almost 50 percent of the productive capacity of the Tarapacá nitrate fields. Perhaps just as important, more than half the population of the province of Tarapacá consisted of foreigners (57%); further south in the district of Iquique this figure reached almost 70 percent. In the municipality of Antofagasta, Chileans constituted 85 percent of the population. Thus, in the nitrate fields, Peru's principal economic resource, both much of the ownership and the labor force owed their principal allegiance to other nations.

Responding to financial difficulties, the Peruvian government in 1875 decreed "nationalization" of many of the nitrate plants, or *oficinas*, issuing payment certificates redeemable in two years and bearing 8 percent interest. In reality this "nationalization" was a mixed venture associating the Peruvian government and international finance capital in an effort to create a nitrate monopoly. Unable to float bonds to finance payments, the Peruvian government failed to redeem the certificates. Eventually many of the certificates changed hands as speculators in Lima paid from 10 to 60 percent of face value. Mismanagement by the Peruvian government, poor coordination between government and those operating the nitrate plants, coupled with a devastating earthquake in 1877 that destroyed numerous coastal loading platforms, brought a 25 to 30 percent decline in nitrate exports. Peruvian certificate holders and guano creditors put great pressure upon Chile to annex Tarapacá, but the Chilean gov-

ernment made no effort to contest Peru's sovereign right to nationalize property within its territory.

New Bolivian taxes on nitrate exported from the province of Antofagasta proved to be a different matter. Here a treaty protected Chilean economic interests, and most of the population was Chilean. In
Antofagasta a Chilean company produced all of the nitrate, and of
the port's 8000 inhabitants more than 75 percent were Chilean.
When Bolivia ordered enforcement of the new nitrate tax in December 1878, and the Antofagasta Company refused to comply, Bolivian
officials ordered the arrest of the company's manager and seizure of
company property sufficient to cover the debt owed for the new tax.
The manager took asylum with Chilean authorities. Relations between the two countries deteriorated rapidly. In February, Bolivian
officials notified the company that its confiscated property would be
auctioned to pay the nitrate tax; in the meantime the captain of the
port prohibited further nitrate exports, causing suspension of operation and unemployment for more than 2000 workers. In response to
Chilean protests, Bolivia revoked the company's nitrate concession—
putting the company out of business—and then eliminated the nitrate tax.

After Bolivia rejected arbitration, a Chilean military expedition
landed at Antofagasta and took control of the city. Chilean forces
also occupied Caracoles and Solar del Carmen, while a warship went
to Cobija to protect Chilean interests. Bolivia shortly declared war
upon Chile, decreed confiscation of all Chilean property, and gave
Chilean citizens ten days to leave the country. Peruvian diplomats
hurried to Santiago in a final attempt to prevent full-scale war, but
public revelation of Peru's secret alliance with Bolivia undermined
the Peruvian role as mediator. In early April, Chile declared war upon
Bolivia and Peru.

None of the belligerent nations were prepared to go to war. The
Chilean army, quite small throughout the middle decades of the
nineteenth century, numbered less than 2500 men, most of whom
were stationed on the Indian frontier. Though somewhat better
equipped and provisioned than Bolivia's or Peru's forces, the Chilean
army lacked training in modern warfare, had no experience with
large-unit maneuvers, and was practically without auxiliary services.
The national guard, even more so than the army, had been seriously
affected by the government's recent economy moves. Never a well-
trained military organization, even the national guard's significant
political role seemed threatened when the government in 1878 re-

duced it to approximately 7000 men—a 70 percent decline. Chilean naval forces, depleted by the sale of a transport and a corvette for economic reasons, consisted of six ships—only two of which the director of arsenals considered seaworthy. Although the addition of the merchant marine and vessels purchased during the war would allow Chile to move troops by sea to the war zone, at the outbreak of hostilities Chile's naval posture was dismaying. Having closed the Naval Academy and School for Mariners in 1876, the Chilean government had to hire foreigners to man its tiny armada.

Peruvian and Bolivian forces, though they outnumbered the Chileans, suffered from the effects of a half-century of political disorganization and internal strife. Neither Bolivia nor Peru were equipped to fight a modern war or to provision a large army over any considerable period of time. Peru's navy, relying upon two sound ironclads and a number of far less seaworthy wooden and iron vessels, appeared to be a worthy match for Chile's anemic fleet. Foreigners also manned the Peruvian navy, though their quality as described by a contemporary—"the offscouring of the foreign merchant and naval services"—left something to be desired.

Notwithstanding their lack of preparedness, both the Chileans and their adversaries mobilized relatively large armies, reaching in Chile's case over 45,000 men by the end of the war. In the first months of the war Chilean forces successfully occupied most of the Bolivian desert. Rugged terrain made it extremely difficult for Bolivia to send troops across the Andes to Antofagasta. Following a series of Chilean-Peruvian naval encounters, Chile dominated the seas by the end of 1879. When its armies took Pisagua and Iquique, the resultant political disorders in Peru and Bolivia ousted the presidents of both these nations. In early 1880 Chilean forces moved into Arica and Tacna. A bloody battle, during which the opposing forces left 5000 casualties on the field, gave Chile control of Tacna in May 1880. Twelve days later the port of Arica also fell to the Chilean invaders.

After efforts by United States diplomats to mediate the conflict in late 1880 failed, Chile sent an army of 25,000 men to Lima. Chilean soldiers crushed the Peruvian defenders in mid-January 1881, and Lima became an occupied city. Though a guerrilla campaign continued until 1883, Chile controlled Lima and Callao, confiscated considerable Peruvian property, and levied taxes to support the army of occupation. The Chileans also imposed port duties and encouraged increased production by the nitrate industry.

The victorious Chileans dictated a harsh settlement to Peru and Bolivia. By virtue of the Treaty of Ancón (October 23, 1883), signed

MAP 10: Chilean Expansion Northward

A. Original Chile-Bolivian boundary. B. Claimed by Chile in 1842. a. Established by treaty in 1866, but in A-B nitrate revenues were divided equally. C. Original Peru-Bolivian boundary. D. Boundary of Chile as a result of the War of the Pacific, 1883, with D-E to be occupied by Chile ten years. d. Chile-Peruvian boundary by settlement of 1929.

Source: W. J. Dennis, *Tacna and Arica*, New Haven: Yale University Press, 1931.

by a president imposed upon Peru by the Chileans, Peru ceded Tarapacá to Chile and agreed to a ten-year Chilean administration of the provinces of Tacna and Arica. A plebiscite, which was never held, was to decide which nation ultimately retained these territories. Of the fourteen articles in the peace treaty, nine referred in some way to guano or nitrates—a clear indication of the underlying issues of the "fertilizer war." Bolivia, though not a party to the treaty, eventually signed a truce with Chile in March 1884; it stipulated that confiscated property be returned to Chilean citizens. Antofagasta passed into Chilean hands, and Bolivia acquired access to the then Chilean-administered port of Arica. Chile conceded to Bolivia 35 percent of the import duties on goods passing through Arica destined for Bolivia. No peace treaty was signed between Bolivia and Chile for twenty years, when Bolivia recognized Chile's absolute and perpetual dominion of Antofagasta.

The terms of the Treaty of Ancón greatly benefited Chile. The victor in the war that was ostensibly fought over a ten-centavo surtax on nitrate exports, took as spoils the single most important source of Peruvian and Bolivian national wealth—the mineral-rich Atacama desert—along with Bolivia's access to the Pacific. For the next century this desert wealth would be the single most important factor in Chilean socio-economic and political development. The manner of its acquisition remains a source of bitter resentment. Neither Peru nor Bolivia has forgotten their loss; they remain unresigned to Chile's "absolute and perpetual dominion" over the conquered territories. Numerous Peruvian generals still desire to recapture the battle monument at the Morro de Arica and redeem Peru's national honor. Similar sentiments in Bolivia have led the three nations to continue one of the most costly arms races in Latin America.

The War of the Pacific enlarged Chilean territory by more than one-third. It also had immediate and profound effects on Chilean national life. The war itself significantly increased demand for foodstuffs and wine, thereby stimulating agriculture and livestock production in the south, the central valley, and the *norte chico*. Coastal shipping dramatically expanded as merchants contracted to supply the army in the north. Industry also responded positively to the war, particularly those firms producing foodstuffs, beverages, tobacco, footwear and leather goods, and other materiel for the military. According to a report of the National Manufacturer's Society (*Sociedad de Fomento Fabril*), founded in 1883, more factories were founded between 1880 and 1889 than had existed in Chile prior to the war. The enormous quantity of capital investment in the nitrate sector and the gush of tax revenues flowing to the national government from the nitrate companies helped to pull Chile out of the prewar economic stagnation. The merchant marine quintupled in size between 1880 and 1883, and coastal shipping, or *cabotaje*, expanded dramatically, since shipments to Antofagasta or Tarapacá had become domestic commerce.

The Chilean victory not only provided an economic bonanza but added to the pantheon of national heroes military leaders such as Baquedano and Prat. The war also reinforced the prevailing Chilean belief in the nation's racial and cultural superiority over its northern neighbors. Chile *was* special in Latin America, and after the War of the Pacific, Chileans of all classes believed more than ever in their national destiny.

With the end of the war a new spirit of nationalism contributed to renewed concern for Chile's lack of significant industry. In the first issue of its *Boletín*, the Sociedad de Fomento Fabril proclaimed that "Chile can and should be an Industrial Nation." The same proclamation went on to say that "only by dedicating its energies to industrialization will Chile achieve the stable base of political and economic equilibrium of the most advanced nations. . . . To contribute to this great objective, to make Chile an industrial nation, the Sociedad de Fomento Fabril has been founded under the protection of the government." Committed to encouragement of Chilean industry through moderate protective tariffs and government subsidies, the SFF represented a potential threat to the economic policies favored by the integrated elite triumvirate of landowners, merchants, and miners. In the short run, however, the fact that the act of foundation of the SFF occurred in the principal salon of the National Agricultural Society, at the behest of a minister of the national government, suggested that the new industrialists would not be far removed from the traditional holders of power. The list of the officers and members of the executive committee of the new industrial society revealed also the disproportionate influence of immigrants and their offspring in Chile's economic elite and its industrial life. Only three Spanish surnames accompanied those of the other members of the directorate: Edwards, Subercasseaux, Hillman, Tupper, Tiffou, Mitchell, Gabler, Lanz, Klein, Muzard, Lyon, Bernstein Crichton, Osthaus, Stuven.

In addition to stimulating industry, the War of the Pacific also affected labor supply throughout the republic. Military recruitment with appeals to patriotism, bounties, or through impressment depleted the work force in the nitrate fields, the northern mines, and the countryside. As the Chilean army moved north, desertions helped repopulate the nitrate fields, and demobilization after the war let loose thousands of potential laborers for employment in the desert, the *norte chico*, or public works. Mobilization of thousands of Chilean miners, campesinos, and laborers not only disrupted the labor supply but also changed the world view and long-term aspirations of the war veterans. Most had little inclination to return to the subordination of the central valley haciendas. Some acquired land in the southern frontier regions, but those who did not increase the ranks of vagabonds, beggars, and criminals sought their fortunes in the nitrate fields and the booming towns of the conquered territory, or went south to Coquimbo, Valparaíso, and Santiago. Wartime experiences and the opening of the northern desert as a *Chilean* mining region portended a radical transformation in the character of the Chilean work force and the beginnings of a truly industrial wage proletariat.

Rapid military victories against Bolivia and Peru also made available a large army capable of subjugating the people of Araucania. At the onset of the war some Indian groups took advantage of troop movements to the north and carried off a small-scale uprising in the region around Traiguén. In response President Pinto ordered the conquest of the Araucanians and the establishment of a new frontier line at the Cautín River. Closing off the Andean passes that linked the Araucanians to their brethren in Argentina, Chilean troops gained control of Indian territory in a concerted offensive. Simultaneous campaigns against the Indians by Argentine troops, modern weapons, and troop mobility resulting from the newly constructed southern railroad finally integrated the frontier territory into the Chilean nation. Roads, bridges, telegraph lines, and the army brought Carahue, Villarrica and Temuco—regions lost since the days of Pedro de Valdivia—into the national patrimony. Reduced to wards of the Chilean state on shrinking tribal lands, the Araucanians faced cultural and economic destruction at the hands of corrupt government officials, traders, speculators, and Chilean settlers seeking land to farm.

The national government tried to ensure orderly and rapid development of the frontier territory by claiming the right to dispose of all the *terrenos baldíos*, or "vacant lands." Influenced by theories of racial superiority, some Chilean authorities looked to northern Europe for colonists to populate the newly opened frontier territories. More than 10,000 colonists from Germany, France, and Switzerland settled at Victoria, Ercilla, Quillén, Temuco, Traiguén, Galvarino, Contulmo, and other frontier outposts in the 1880s. Instead of setting an example of European yeomanry, however, the colonists took quick advantage of Chilean and Indian sharecroppers and rural laborers, adapting thereby to the convenience of Chile's exploitive rural labor systems. The immigrant colonists who prospered in agriculture found *inquilinaje* a useful device to promote their interests, just as did the Chilean landowners in the central valley. Some colonists also contributed greatly by establishing artisan manufactures and even some industry, but most preferred towns or cities to the hardships of peasant pioneer farming in the Chilean south.

In any case, the government was unable to compete with Argentina, Brazil, or Uruguay in attracting the numbers of Europeans it desired to "upgrade" the Chilean race. Instead, it fell back on public auctions to deliver the frontier lands into private hands. Spontaneous colonization, squatting, and speculation continued as the major instruments of settlement in the southern region.

Conquest of the Araucanians ended the most important pre-1879 rationale for maintenance of a standing army in Chile. The frontier had provided a genuine military mission for Chilean armed forces since the time of independence, making them a necessary and valued element of national life. Acquisition through war of the northern territories and the persistent Argentine border dispute now gave a new mission to the Chilean military. The threat of conflict with Peru and Bolivia or with Argentina made military preparedness a national concern. In 1885 the Chilean government contracted the German lieutenant colonel Emil Körner to become subdirector of the Escuela Militar and to direct the modernization of Chilean military education. In the same year a military periodical first appeared, and shortly thereafter a military club, the Círculo Militar, was established in Santiago. Both periodical and club received government subsidies.

Under Körner's leadership Chile founded the Academia de Guerra, or War College, in 1886 with the stated purpose of improving the technical and scientific education of army officers. The Academia de Guerra nurtured a new Chilean junior officer military elite; critical of outdated methods, political patronage, and government inefficiency, it would eventually (in the 1920s) challenge the traditional political parties for control of the Chilean state. In the short run, only five years after establishment of the Academia de Guerra, Körner and his small core of followers would play a key role in the Chilean civil war of 1891. From the outset, therefore, the professionalization and modernization of the Chilean military on the Prussian model entailed serious consequences for Chilean politics—just as similar Prussian or French military missions soon affected civil-military relations in Ar-

gentina, Bolivia, Peru, and other Latin American nations. The War
of the Pacific proved a turning point in Chile's civil-military relations
as well as being the most important economic watershed in its history.

A mere seven years after termination of the War of the Pacific,
Chile faced its most serious and bloody civil war of the nineteenth
century. Chilean historians still debate the causes of this civil war,
with explanations ranging from narrow political interpretations to
those that attribute it to President Balmaceda's (1886-91) tragic confrontation with British imperialism and its Chilean lackeys. Events in
Chile between 1970 and 1973 led many people to draw analogies between Balmaceda and President Salvador Allende as nationalists and
reformers who met defeat at the hands of foreign interests and the
Chilean oligarchy. As with most such historical controversies, there is
evidence to support all versions of the conflict. No understanding of
the civil war of 1891, however, can ignore the complex relationships
between the changes in Chile's political economy wrought by the
War of the Pacific and the persistence of long-standing political issues, such as the "religious question" and the constant tension between the Congress and the executive.

The nitrate fields of the Atacama desert added an entirely new factor to Chilean political economy. Basic questions had to be answered
about how to integrate the wealth of the desert into the economy.
Should the state operate the fields as a national industry, as the Peruvians had attempted? Should private capital be allowed to exploit the
nitrate deposits and control the transportation networks, especially
railroads, that shipped the nitrates to the ports? To what extent
should foreign capital be permitted to invest in the nitrate industry?

Imbued with a fundamental commitment to liberal economic ideology, the government of President Pinto set the direction for the
next four decades of nitrate policy by imposing an export tax of 40
centavos per metric quintal upon the nitrate company at Antofagasta.
After Chilean troops seized Tarapacá, thereby bringing the richest deposits of nitrate also within Chilean control, the government increased the tax to $1.50 pesos. Considering that the original dispute
between the Antofagasta Company and the Bolivian government—
the dispute that precipitated war between Chile, Bolivia, and Peru—
had arisen over an additional 10-centavo levy by Bolivia on nitrate
exports, President Pinto's policy hardly made the nitrate producers
happy.

Meanwhile President Pinto created a commission to consider long-range nitrate policy. This commission recommended return of the nitrate concessions to the holders of the Peruvian certificates, along with an export tax of $2.20 pesos per metric quintal. This recommendation established the basis for Chilean political economy for the next four decades. Private enterprise, foreign and national, would exploit the nitrate fields, and export taxes on nitrate would constitute more than 50 percent of all Chilean government revenue.

The Chilean government's decision to allow substantial foreign participation in the nitrate industry and the sale of certain Chilean-held certificates to foreigners soon placed thousands of Chilean workers in large nitrate complexes, or *oficinas*, controlled by foreign administrators. By 1883 the work force in Tarapacá alone had increased to 7000, with similar increments in the ranks of dock workers, construction and railroad crews, prostitutes, merchants, and industry related to nitrate production. Investments in public services in Iquique and Antofagasta provided jobs for still more, as demobilized troops returned from Peru. Nitrate mining depended upon pick and shovel; as the industry expanded in the last decades of the nineteenth century, it required more and more workers in the *oficinas*.

Caliche, the ore of the nitrate industry, consists of sodium nitrate and varying amounts of potassium nitrate, trace metals, iodine, and insolubles. Variation in nitrate content made some deposits more valuable, but the basic refining process was relatively uniform. Found in deposits up to two meters thick, the ore was blasted from the desert crust, crushed, and boiled in caldrons or dissolving tanks until it formed a solution and precipitated out impurities. When cooled, the evaporation formed *salitre*, or nitrate crystals. In the 1850s and 1860s coal-fueled furnaces that piped steam to dissolving tanks began to replace the fire-heated caldrons, thereby increasing the efficiency and scale of the *oficinas*. Mechanical ore crushers also made their appearance, but the industry remained highly labor-intensive. Laborers blasted the desert crust, crushed the *caliche*, loaded the ore for hauling, manned the catwalks over the open tanks, cleaned the pipes and machinery, and performed numerous specialized jobs in the production process. Women sewed the bags of fertilizer and served as cooks, laundresses, and seamstresses. Nitrate companies took few safety precautions; workers frequently suffered burns or mutilations by machinery. Amputees and otherwise disabled nitrate workers became a common sight in Iquique, Antofagasta, and other nitrate towns where displaced laborers drifted in search of subsistence.

Though the nitrate industry employed a large number of unskilled workers, the market for nitrates proved extremely volatile. Producers responded to short-term contractions in sales or declines in price by reducing output or laying off workers. Consequently the labor force of the nitrate fields periodically faced unemployment, and the Chilean government's revenues, increasingly dependent on nitrate export duties, could decline or increase precipitately over very short periods of time. In good times the nitrate companies could not always count upon sufficient workers to meet demands; in bad times thousands of displaced workers departed from the nitrate pampa to the northern cities and south to Coquimbo, Valparaíso, and Santiago. Fluctuations in international demand for nitrates, therefore, caused periodic political crises as Chile struggled to manage the consequences of large-scale movements of unemployed workers out of the nitrate fields into the ports, the *norte chico*, and the central valley.

The War of the Pacific also marked the onset of long-term price inflation. Paper money issued to finance the war, and the usual rise in prices associated with the artificial demand of a wartime economy, introduced serious inflation as a permanent facet of Chilean economic life. In the nitrate regions the companies controlled both the workers' income, usually paid in company scrip called *vales* or *fichas*, and the price of consumer goods at the company store, or *pulpería*. Thus, inflation pitted workers against the nitrate capitalists at the most basic level of subsistence. When labor was relatively scarce, the companies could use "low prices" at the *pulpería* to attract workers; when labor was more abundant or demand for nitrate slackened, the workers received less favorable treatment by the companies. Payment in company scrip limited the workers' ability to purchase consumption goods from independent merchants or peddlers. In order to maintain the workers as captive clients of the *pulpería*, the nitrate companies attempted to restrict independent traders from entering the nitrate *oficinas*. If a worker wished to use the company scrip in the "outside" world, storeowners typically discounted the scrip 10 to 30 percent. Under these conditions there emerged among the workers a sense of exploitation and a list of quite concrete demands for improvement of their situation. The militant expression of these demands in a strike in 1890 would play a key role in the civil war of 1891 when nitrate workers joined congressional forces to defeat President Balmaceda.

In the decade after the War of the Pacific these internal contradictions of the nitrate industry and the industry's sensitivity to the international market made themselves felt quite strongly. By 1885 nitrate prices declined from their wartime high of 12 shillings to 5s. 4d. In an effort to control the decline in prices, the major nitrate companies formed a "combination," or cartel, assigning quotas according to installed capacity. This first of several "combinations" (1884-86) over the next thirty years had some success in reversing the price trend; but as conditions improved, the more efficient producers relied on their technological advantage or the richness of the deposits they exploited, and the "combination" disappeared. Rapid increases in output and in exports—1886, 451,000 metric tons; 1887, 713,000 metric tons; 1890, over 1,000,000 metric tons—unaccompanied by a corresponding increase in demand again placed pressure on the companies to control the level of supply. Given the bulky nature of the "ore," storage could quickly become a problem if exports slackened off, leaving production shutdowns as the most obvious instrument for dealing with the fickle market.

Limiting production or exports favored neither the Chilean government nor the labor force. Government revenues were tied to the total tonnage exported—not to price. Production cutbacks or shutdowns meant unemployment for the workers. Complicating this picture further, enterprising British capitalists who had made a financial killing by acquiring the Peruvian nitrate certificates, sought to consolidate control over the industry, including the railroad networks that linked the pampa with the coastal cities. The most ambitious, like John Thomas North, who became known as the "Nitrate King," also invested in related commercial ventures. In North's case investments included a company that controlled the water supply at Antofagasta and the region's principal bank. Competition among foreign capitalists for control of the nitrate railroads, for workers, for nitrate concessions, and for other favors from the Chilean government further enmeshed the evolution of the nitrate industry in Chilean politics. Meanwhile a growing nationalist sentiment in Chile publicly condemned the increasing foreign influence over the nation's new economic resources.

Revenues from the nitrate fields permitted the Chilean government to embark on a most ambitious program of public works, including impressive extension of the rail and telegraph network as well as significant expansion of the educational system. In 1888 a newly created Ministry of Industry and Public Works absorbed more than 20 percent of the national budget, and investments in education accounted for another 15 percent of government expenditures. With increased expenditures came new public jobs, and new opportunities for the national government to distribute patronage positions to its supporters. Control over government contracts and over large deposits of government funds in private banks gave the president increased leverage in national politics. More generally, as public resources expanded, the role and perceived importance of the State grew immensely both in relationship to the economy and in regard to social and political opportunities within Chilean society. Personal and party feuds over the spoils of the new wealth, job opportunities, and government contracts made nitrate prosperity almost as much a political liability as an asset for the incumbent administration. At the same time, both the administration and the Chilean economy faced extraordinary vulnerability to international markets and prices for nitrates. Chilean politics and economy depended critically upon foreign demand for fertilizer, upon foreign bond-markets, and upon decisions made by foreign investors and commercial interests.

Nor did economic expansion eliminate fundamental conflicts within the Chilean polity. President Domingo Santa María's (1881-86) Liberal government steamrollered anticlerical legislation through a Liberal-dominated Congress. Engineered through the legislature by Minister of Interior José Manuel Balmaceda, laws establishing secular cemeteries, civil marriage, and civil registry of births profoundly offended Conservative interests, now in a decided though still influential minority. The latter, losers in the congressional debates, would not lose the opportunity to avenge themselves when Balmaceda took office as president and faced Chile's worst political crisis of the nineteenth century. Santa María's government also extended the suffrage to all literate, adult males—and then intervened in congressional elections in the most overt fashion to secure a compliant legislature. In power, liberals like Santa María proved just as enamoured of presidential discretion and just as likely to abuse presidential power as any of the Conservative or National party presidents of the mid-nineteenth century. Such inconsistency between action and previously proclaimed principles divided the Liberals into numerous factions and personalist cliques based upon animosity toward Santa María, Balmaceda, or other government ministers, the desire for a public post, or ideological commitment to particular reforms.

Santa María's choice of Balmaceda as his successor—and the knowledge that through presidential intervention in the elections Santa María could impose his choice—totally disrupted the Congress. An alliance of independent Liberals, or *sueltos*, Conservatives, and Radicals tried to obstruct passage of the tax bill that permitted the government to collect revenues to carry out its program. The opposition sought in this way to persuade Santa María to withdraw his support for Balmaceda. Though they failed to carry the day, this action set the tone for Balmaceda's difficulties in his next five years as Chile's president. If Santa María's own authoritarian bent as president seemed to conflict with his liberal record in Congress, Balmaceda's confrontation with Congress would be even more ironic inasmuch as throughout his long and distinguished public career he had been a champion of the parliamentary system and especially of congressional checks on the executive.

President Balmaceda took office at a time when public revenues were increasing dramatically as a result of the nitrate duties. Between 1886 and 1890 government revenues rose from 37 million pesos to over 58 million. Although Conservatives criticized the government for its failure to re-establish the convertibility of the Chilean currency, Balmaceda's policy of investing the windfall nitrate revenues in social and transport infrastructure, public works, and education produced quite positive results. Despite a general prosperity and visible evidences of the government's progress in realizing its program, personal rancor and political infighting over ministries and patronage weakened Balmaceda's coalition. At the same time the President faced a number of issues concerning the financial manipulations of John T. North and other entrepreneurs in the northern provinces.

From 1888 on Balmaceda delivered a number of ominous speeches hinting at an increased state role in the nitrate industry or, at the least, at an effort to enlarge the role of national producers in the nitrate regions. In March 1889, Balmaceda traveled to the northern provinces. At Iquique the president publicly blamed foreign monopolists in control of the nitrate railroad and nitrate production for difficulties in the industry. He also stated that the state ought not to create an industrial monopoly but should prevent private monopolies from controlling production or restricting output. In short, Balmaceda sought to defend the government's stake in the revenues of the nitrate industry and to encourage further national investment without injuring the rights of foreign investors. In addition, he sought to balance the conflicting pressures from a variety of British firms and their Chilean supporters and retainers, including congressmen and cabinet members seeking new nitrate, railroad, and commercial concessions.

Other voices in Chile called for more radical measures, including complete nationalization of the nitrate industry. But Balmaceda himself never made this proposal or supported it. In his annual address to Congress in June 1889, Balmaceda proposed public auctions of certain state-owned nitrate fields limited to Chilean bidders. The president further recommended that foreign purchase of nitrate properties be limited to one-half of new concessions. Though certainly national-

istic in orientation, this policy proposal—never adopted by Congress—
hardly constituted an attack on existing foreign investment in nitrates
or exclusion of further foreign participation in the nitrate industry.
And though certain historians see in Balmaceda a "decided anti-
imperialist," Balmaceda never took actions considered universally
hostile to foreign investment in Chile. Indeed, in a manner of questionable propriety, he supported the associations of certain of his congressional adherents with foreign interests. On the other hand, Balmaceda's commitment to a program of internal modernization and
national development depended upon a continuous flow of nitrate
revenues, and he certainly opposed any private program that might
artificially restrict nitrate production and hence decrease the government's ability to finance public programs. In this sense the interests
of the large British investors directly conflicted with those of the Chilean state and the policies of the incumbent government. Despite Balmaceda's careful *actions* in regard to foreign investment, his public
statements made British interests wary, thereby creating powerful potential allies for the president's domestic adversaries.

Toward the end of 1889 the nitrate industry again faced a situation
of surplus; stockpiling began, and prices declined. It looked as though
another producers' "combination" would form to withhold production until the adverse market reversed itself. Balmaceda's government
not only sought to avert this development and prevent layoffs, but
also moved against John North's Nitrate Railway Company which
monopolized nitrate hauling in Tarapacá. The government correctly
recognized the burden on the industry of the monopoly prices charged
by the Nitrate Railway, and therefore entered into negotiation with
other entrepreneurs for the construction of other nitrate lines. Significantly, the greatest threat to North's railway came from the potential
competition of other British investors, including the long-established
commercial house of Gibbs and Sons.

When the government canceled the Nitrate Railway's monopoly
concession, and entered into negotiations with Campbell, Outram
and Company to construct a railroad from the *oficina* of Agua Santa
to Caleta Buena, the Nitrate Railway interests appealed the decision
in an effort to preserve their economic dominance in the region. President Balmaceda's Council of State ruled against the Nitrate Railway.
North's company claimed that the executive had exceeded his constitutional authority, in that appeal of the monopoly concession was
a matter for the courts. Influential domestic political opponents of
Balmaceda supported North's constitutional arguments as further ammunition in the struggle against the president, though this did not

necessarily mean support for the Nitrate Railway's monopoly. Nitrate Railway interests, playing on the executive-legislative tensions to press their claims, sent a memorandum to the Senate calling upon that body to hold Balmaceda accountable for violations of the constitution. Not only did this controversy intensify internal political dissension, but North's allies persuaded the British Foreign Office to raise the matter with the Chilean foreign minister despite objections by competing British companies within Chile. British diplomatic pressure added to Balmaceda's woes.

The complexity of the situation increased still further with the upcoming presidential elections of 1891, the spread of labor conflicts across the nitrate fields, and the deteriorating economic situation. Balmaceda, despite public disclaimers, seemed to favor as his successor a personal friend and wealthy landowner, Enrique Salvador Sanfuentes. Despite election reforms in the 1870s, the overriding influence of the president, in congressional elections as well as presidential elections, continued unabated. This meant that presidential blessing and mobilization of the presidential electoral apparatus generally guaranteed victories at the polls. Illustrative is a letter to Balmaceda in 1890 from a would-be congressional candidate, cited by Harold Blakemore in his brilliant study *British Nitrates and Chilean Politics 1886-1896*:

> I recollect that Your Excellency told me to write to you when I thought it was time for my re-election to the Deputies, and since I think that time has now come, I take the liberty of writing to Your Excellency to say that I wish to continue in my post as Deputy for the next period, with the sole aim of serving Your Excellency's policies at all times and with the same loyalty as always and with the unshakeable resolve of not missing a single day of the sessions.

Once elected, of course, the president could neither control the deputy's actions nor guarantee his loyalty—as Balmaceda discovered. Nevertheless, the president's control over elections through the cabinet, the intendants, and the governors, made selection of ministers and administrative officials prior to elections of primordial political significance. Since Sanfuentes counted numerous personal enemies among his Liberal colleagues, Balmaceda's ministerial appointments from 1889 on were subjected to ever more intense congressional scrutiny.

Partisan politics couched in the rhetoric of fundamental constitutional issues concerning presidential authority polarized the opposing forces. Policy regarding the volatile nitrate economy pushed the opposing factions toward violent confrontation. The president came to view interpellation or censure of his ministers—a practice well-established by this time and strongly supported by Balmaceda during his legislative career—as antipatriotic or "political" attacks on his program for national development. Gradually Balmaceda hardened his position against congressional manipulation, acting ever less diplomatically toward the growing number of congressional critics. In January 1890 the president closed the special session of Congress and appointed a new cabinet without reference to party alignments in the legislature. Contrary to custom, he refused to reconvene the Congress upon the appropriate request by the *Comisión Conservadora* of the legislature. When the next ordinary session of Congress convened in June 1890, Balmaceda's message to it focused mainly upon the need to reverse the trend toward weakening of the executive authority by a "bastard parliamentary system" that led to "the dictatorship of Congress." These remarks and the particulars of the president's reform proposals represented a direct attack upon the very principles liberal politicians, including Balmaceda, had fought for since the 1830s.

Three days later the Senate overwhelmingly censured Balmaceda's cabinet, headed by Enrique Sanfuentes; the Chamber of Deputies took similar action on June 7, 1890. In a move totally without precedent, Balmaceda refused to accept the resignation of his ministers, and Congress countered with the now traditional device of refusing to discuss the law authorizing tax collection until the president had appointed ministers acceptable to the legislature. Balmaceda persisted in his refusal, and tensions mounted. Only mediation by the archbishop of Santiago brought a temporary compromise in August, with the appointment of a Supreme Court judge to head the cabinet.

Precisely as the political crisis heightened, a cyclical downturn in the nitrate industry fueled discontent among workers in the northern provinces. Continued monetary inflation reduced the workers' real income as prices rose, and unemployment even threatened subsistence. Isolated incidents of violence and work stoppages had reflected growing dissatisfaction among the workers between 1884 and 1889. In early July 1890 a strike by dockworkers in Iquique spread to rail and foundry workers, the mines at Huantajaya, throughout the nitrate pampa, north to Pisagua and south to Antofagasta. The workers' petitions varied from one work site to another, but typically they demanded an end to payment in company scrip, monthly cash settlements in silver or the equivalent in currency, freedom of commerce in the nitrate fields and mining camps (an end to monopolies by the company store), and elimination of the arbitrary fines or discounts from their wages which the companies imposed. For the first time in Chilean history workers carried off a "general strike" that threatened production from Tarapacá to the coal fields of Concepción.

Balmaceda received urgent appeals from employers in Tarapacá to use troops to restore order. Initially hesitant to intervene and seemingly supportive of the workers' demands in his public pronouncements, Balmaceda nevertheless dispatched warships with troops to the north. Violence, looting, and repression by company police or soldiers in some *oficinas* left dozens of casualties; at other locations the strike evolved more or less peacefully. Within ten days employers agreed to most of the workers' demands, thereby ending the strike—though in most of the *oficinas* and the cities employers failed to live up to their promises. Having temporarily squelched the strike by agreeing to meet the workers' terms, the employers gained time for the troops to arrive and deploy themselves. The presence of military units discouraged the workers' further efforts to revive the conflict, though it spread as far north as Arica and south to Valparaíso.

In the port of Valparaíso rioting and extensive looting brought harsh reprisals from police and military units sent from Santiago. Other military units arriving from Concepción stifled militancy in the coal mines, but lesser movements or isolated incidents of violence occurred at Quillota, Los Andes, Santiago, and Talca. With the restoration of order employers across the nation fired leaders of the strike movement and reinstituted the traditional practices on the work sites against which the workers had protested. A glut of nitrate stocks in relation to world demand allowed employers to rid themselves of "undesirable" laborers at the same time as negotiations continued to establish another "combination" to depress output until market conditions improved.

The timing of the labor crisis—Chile's first experience with a truly national, if spontaneous, labor movement—coincided exactly with the political crisis between Balmaceda and Congress. According to the 1833 constitution, Congress had to authorize tax collection every eighteen months. Refusal to authorize tax collections left the government, in theory, without revenues to carry on its daily operations. Instead, Balmaceda responded by notifying banks with government deposits held at thirty days' notice of intended withdrawal, to consider these accounts henceforth as "deposit accounts on call." This measure startled the financial community and escalated further the conflict with Congress. Feelings were so polarized that it became difficult to remember that the supposed issue at stake remained Balmaceda's refusal to accept congressional demands that he appoint a new cabinet.

By this time the opposition attacked Balmaceda's increasingly "dictatorial" and unconstitutional behavior, while Balmaceda reacted with insults in kind concerning the opposition's lack of patriotism and their political motivation. Seeking to create a personalist political machine apart from the old Liberal party upon which he could no longer rely, Balmaceda entangled himself in the jealousies and intrigues of local politics and patronage. Naturally the single most important issue continued to be designation of his successor, and this gave added importance to the distribution of patronage around the country and the appointment of "reliable" administrators in the provinces.

Balmaceda proved unable to negotiate an acceptable compromise with the opposition. Progressively bitter charges of antinationalist, unpatriotic activities punctuated the running battle with the growing legislative opposition. Throughout the entire year of 1890, Congress refused to pass the budget bill or to authorize force levels for the military. Undaunted, the president illegally decreed that the 1890 legislation would remain in effect. In quick response to this overtly unconstitutional act, Congress called upon *capitán de navío* Jorge Montt and the navy to support it against the president's usurpation of power. The fleet sailed north to occupy Iquique and gain control of the nitrate revenues for the congressional insurrectionists. Balmaceda, who had the loyalty of most of the regular army, imposed a state of siege, instituted highly repressive policies against the press, and suspended civil liberties in an effort to suffocate the rebellion.

Civil war continued for seven months with severe losses on both sides. Ultimately, control of the nitrate revenues, financial and material support by British and other foreign interests, and the skillful leadership of Emil Körner left congressional forces victorious. Congressional agents successfully delayed arrival of two new ironclads the government had ordered from France, and obtained Mannlicher repeating rifles which helped carry the day for the congressional army. Ironically, the nitrate revenues Balmaceda had counted on to carry out his development program bought arms and equipment abroad for his enemies. The congressional army, recruited largely among the nitrate workers, received training under the direction of the Prussian officer contracted by presidents Santa María and Balmaceda to modernize Chile's army and defend the newly acquired nitrate regions. Since railroad construction in the north had been dominated by private interests, the civil war found Santiago unconnected to the north

by a longitudinal rail line. Defection of most of the navy, which had
received large amounts of money from the Balmaceda government
for modernization, prevented Balmaceda from transporting sufficient
forces north to overcome the insurgents. After his army was defeated
at Concon and Placilla by an amphibious assault directed by Körner
and a number of Chile's new professional, Prussian-trained officers,
Balmaceda took refuge in the Argentine embassy. He left in charge
in Santiago General Baquedano, the hero of the War of the Pacific,
who had remained neutral in the civil war. The day after his presidential term ended—September 19, 1891—Balmaceda shot himself.
In October, Jorge Montt was elected Balmaceda's successor, and Chilean politics entered a new era of congressional dominance.

The outcome of the civil war shifted the balance of Chilean politics from the executive to the Congress but did little to change the
nation's dependence on nitrates. Population in the northern provinces more than doubled between 1885 and 1907; workers traveled
from the *norte chico*, the central valley, and even further south to
seek their fortune in the nitrate fields. Average levels of employment
in the nitrate fields jumped impressively from nearly 6500 in the
1880s to almost 50,000 between 1910 and 1920. Cyclic downturns
continued to inflict periodic depression, shutdowns, attempts to form
production cartels, and massive unemployment. Economic depression
between 1896 and 1897 saw nitrate production reduced to 40 percent
of capacity. Large-scale unemployment followed. Financial panic associated with the government's unsuccessful experiment with a return
to convertible currency (1895-98) and increased defense expenditures—
25 percent of the budget—exacerbated the crisis, but still only provided a relatively mild hint of the more severe crises that would occur
during the next three decades of nitrate dependence. As the labor
force increased, the misery inflicted by the downturns of the economy
became more severe. Instead of 5000 jobless workers, the nation now
periodically faced the desperation of tens of thousands of laborers
temporarily without work, means of subsistence, or domicile. The
workers retained by the companies experienced wage cuts.

The linkage of the nitrate economy to the agriculture of the central valley and the Concepción–frontier region further integrated the
regional economies into a national economy. Downturns in nitrate
affected agriculture, coal mines, commerce, and a slowly growing industrial sector. Led by food and primary product-processing firms—
canneries, flour mills, breweries, match factories, sugar refineries—

along with foundries, cement, and even a nascent locomotive works, Chilean industry expanded during the last decade of the nineteenth century and into the first years of the twentieth. Forty percent of Chilean factories in 1895 dated from no earlier than 1890—almost 60 percent of these were located in Santiago or Valparaíso. Imported technologies made some of Chile's new industries—for example, cement, modernized flour mills, and wineries as efficient, by the first decades of the twentieth century, as any in the world. Increasingly integrated in their economic relationships, domestic firms produced input—alcohol, wood, paper, containers—for other national industries as well as consumer articles for the growing cities and nitrate districts. Moderate protective tariffs adopted in the 1890s reflected the effective lobbying by industrial interests like the SFF and the growing concern of certain Chileans to make Chile an industrial country. The Errázuriz Echaurren administration (1896-1901) also directed its ministries to give preference to Chilean manufactures in public projects, so long as domestic manufacturers charged no more than 10 to 15 percent more than foreign competitors.

Urbanization in the years after 1885 increased Valparaíso's population to over 120,000 and that of Santiago to more than 250,000 by the turn of the century. Iquique grew into a bustling nitrate port of 33,000 inhabitants, and Antofagasta's population rose to 14,000. Housing, sanitation, and public-health conditions in the growing urban concentrations remained sorely inadequate. Feeble government responses to smallpox epidemics in the early 1880s and to a catastrophic cholera epidemic in 1888, which according to official estimates took over 30,000 lives, reflected both the sorry state of public-health programs and the incapacity of the Chilean state to respond effectively to the problems of an urbanizing, modernizing society.

To the south, rural migrants continued their exodus out of the countryside to Concepción, Talcahuano, and Talca. By 1907 the Chilean census classified 43 percent of the population as urban. Though the crude definition of "urban"—as concentrations over 1000—gives a somewhat misleading impression, it cannot be denied that ever more Chileans were potential customers for Chilean agriculture and manufacturers as they left the rural estates and settled in towns, mining camps, or nitrate fields. And it was to this internal market that Chilean manufacturers largely dedicated their attentions. Of the total value of exports in 1900 (162 million pesos), only 3.3 million corresponded to manufactures—less than wealthy Chileans spent on imported perfume, jewelry, liquor, and fine textiles.

If nitrates brought uncertainty to the Chilean economy and much of the labor force, it also brought great wealth to a small number of capitalists and stock speculators. It allowed Chilean governments to avoid serious examination of the internal tax structure and to eliminate taxes on wealth or income. Balmaceda himself proposed abolition of the income and inheritance taxes introduced in the late 1870s. Nitrate financed public works, railroad construction, private mansions, and construction of irrigation canals for Chile's agricultural heartland. The nitrate industry's expansion generated secondary and support industries in the north and in the central valley and also provided a market for Chilean agriculture and coal mines while stimulating coastal shipping. More than anything else, however, the nitrate industry altered the character of the Chilean labor force. The conditions in the nitrate fields spawned an increasingly militant labor movement which carried its struggle against exploitation south to the countryside and the cities. The plight of the northern work force became a platform for political reformers and a school of leadership for a new generation of labor leaders.

A select group of Chilean intellectuals joined the battle with short stories, novels, and plays depicting the misery of Chile's masses in contrast to the decadence and pedantry of the nation's political elite and the splendor of the manor house on the hacienda or the urban mansion of the northern mining magnates. Publication of *Casa Grande* in 1908—by a member of Chile's oligarchy who scathingly attacked the character of his brethren—and of *Sinceridad: Chile íntimo en 1910*—by a schoolteacher writing under the pseudonym Dr. Julio Valdés Cange—focused attention in Chile upon the reality of what became known as the "social question."

The "social question" or "workers' question" by any other name still meant industrial class conflict combined with serious concern by some Chilean leaders with mass poverty, educational backwardness, and the whole range of issues associated with social and economic development. The War of the Pacific and the nitrate economy had ushered Chile into the industrial age. Unfortunately the civil war of 1891 reaffirmed the oligarchic tradition of Chilean politics, even reinvigorated the power of central valley landowners with legislation granting municipal autonomy and extending responsibility to local government for administration of congressional and presidential elections. The contradiction between the politics of parliamentary stalemate, and the evolution of an industrial labor movement influenced by imported socialist and Marxist ideology, would destroy the nation's commitment to the 1833 constitution and radically alter class relations. Finally, in the 1920s this process would culminate in a military coup d'état when Chilean parliamentary government would prove unable to confront head on the reality of twentieth-century industrial society.

Chapter 7 • Politics, Labor, and the Social Question

In 1927, thirty-six years after congressional forces imposed parliamentary government upon Chile, José Manuel Balmaceda's son presented the presidential sash worn by his martyred father to an ambitious military officer named Carlos Ibáñez. Balmaceda's son delivered an emotional speech, claiming that Ibáñez represented the "perfect incarnation" of *Balmacedismo*—the principles for which his father had died.

Whether or not Ibáñez rightfully belonged to the tradition of Balmaceda or sympathized beyond convenient political rhetoric with Balmaceda's programs of the late 1880s, he explicitly rejected the interminable, parliamentary squabbles and the restrictions on executive authority that had frustrated his predecessors. More than had any Chilean president since the era of Portales, Ibáñez returned to Hispanic authoritarianism and condemned the imported liberalism that dominated Chilean political life in the late nineteenth and early twentieth century.

A prominent military officer trained in the Prussian tradition established in Chile by Emil Körner, Ibáñez led a new generation of Chilean military officers who despised parliamentary practices, politicians, and, above all else, politics. They blamed politics for Chile's economic problems, for the increasing class conflict, for the corruption and venality of public life, and for all else that ailed the nation. These views were epitomized in 1924 by a Chilean officer writing to a civilian government minister:

Even though you, at this time and place, represent for us the most disgusting element in our country—politicians—that is, all that is corrupt, the dismal factional disputes, depravities and immoralities, in other words, the causes of our national degeneration, we recognize that you, despite the fact that you must defend sinecures, hand out public posts, and support avaricious ambitions, that you are one of the few honest politicians.

If the sentence was long, the sentiments it expressed reflected the frustration of the professional military with more than three decades of congressional neglect of Chile's most pressing problems. It also expressed the utter contempt for politics and politicians held by the military and by Chile's growing class of technicians and professional people. The professional military nurtured by Balmaceda's successors through the first decade of the twentieth century (and then neglected, to the Congress's ultimate regret) would no longer tolerate the sterile politics of salon, intrigue, and immobility that had both weakened the military institution and made the armed forces shock troops for oligarchical repression.

Whatever the objections to Ibáñez' dictatorial regime, it is easy to understand the disdain of a moralistic professional soldier for the type of political system that functioned in Chile after 1891. Even apart from the immediate issues of 1924 prior to the September 5 coup that brought the military into the government—Congress's decision to pay its representatives a salary contrary to constitutional prohibitions, while salaries due civil servants and military personnel were in arrears; its constant meddling in military personnel matters; its failure to pass social legislation in the midst of growing labor conflict—Ibáñez and his followers could no longer brook the political charade called parliamentary government in Chile.

Manuel Rivas Vicuña, one of the country's most respected politicians—and eventual political enemy of Ibáñez—captured the fundamental character of the Chilean political process during the post-1891 years. He described his "Election Memories of 1918":

Would I again have a seat in Congress? We could hardly wait for the train to arrive in Curicó.

What happened here?—I asked the first person I encountered in the station.

The same as usual, *patrón*, the bosses [*futres*] got together and stole the money sent by the government for the elections.

Afterward I found out from my friends that an agreement had been reached. My name and that of the Conservative candidate had triumphed without opposition; they had made no use of the blank check that I left in the event of an electoral struggle, and they had made only small payments to the voters.

The bosses had stolen the money sent by the government for the elections.

I've been lucky to avoid the necessity of buying votes for my campaigns. I've had no competition the four times I was elected deputy, and my friends generously took care of my electoral expenses.

The general rule, I've been assured, is the opposite and reveals that from the worker to the great proprietors, all believe that elections are a business that provide those elected not just with honor but also with [material] benefit.

Vote buying [cohecho] is a habit so deeply rooted it will be very difficult to eradicate.

The men who acquired offices in the Congress through vote buying debated interminably while Chilean society underwent profound socio-economic changes. In 1915 an ex-president of the Federation of Chilean University Students gave a funeral oration for the nation's political leaders—at the end of a presidential term in which President Ramón Barros Luco told his compatriots that "there are only two types of problem: those without solution and those that solve themselves." The military intervention of 1924 and Ibáñez' authoritarian regime (1927-31) were reactions to this type of political thinking and to the politics of parliamentary stalemate.

Ibáñez' usurpation of presidential authority and subordination of Congress also temporarily halted more positive trends during the parliamentary period—institutionalization of respect for civil liberties and political liberalization in the Chilean polity. Whatever the defects of the parliamentary period, however, it had allowed for the evolution of freedom of the press, for a growing, if not complete, recognition of the legitimacy of opposition movements and parties, and for a formal respect for the procedures of liberal democracy. Despite electoral corruption and empty political rhetoric, along with Congress's failure to deal with pressing social issues, the country's political institutions permitted expanded suffrage and a more open pattern of recruitment to public office. The military intervention of 1924 and the subsequent Ibáñez administration not only ended, temporarily, this trend toward political liberalization, but it represented a resurgence of the traditional Hispanic intolerance for liberalism, intensified by a military ideology of national regeneration.

In 1887 the recently organized Partido Demócrata brought a new political ideology and style into Chilean politics. Led by Malaquías Concha, the party proclaimed as its objectives "political, economic, and social liberation of the people [*pueblo*]" and proposed numerous reforms, including direct election of the president, municipal administration of the departments (eliminating the presidentially appointed governors), taxes on land and capital, compulsory public education, and support for industrialization through protective tariffs. Appealing especially to artisans and the lower middle class, the party also promoted policies designed to improve the lot of the urban poor.

The Partido Demócrata evolved as Chile's first populist political party, electing its first deputy to Congress in 1894. By 1903, it had obtained representation from Valparaíso, Santiago, and Concepción. The most progressive elements within the Partido Demócrata later emerged as leaders of the ever more militant labor organizations of the cities, the nitrate and mining camps, and the southern coal mines, as well as of the Socialist Workers Party (POS) formed in 1912. The party sponsored mass rallies, supported the workers' press and cultural centers, and generally provided a legitimate voice of political opposition on behalf of the working classes. Though it never became a truly proletarian-based organization and continued to recruit its leadership from artisans and the middle class, the Partido Demócrata nevertheless challenged the assumptions and policies of the landowning, commercial, and industrial interests that dominated Chilean politics.

The hypocrisy and the contradictions of the parliamentary era permitted greater latitude for political and social organization by workers and the urban poor than could have occurred under a more authoritarian civilian regime or a military government. Chilean elites believed themselves to be progressive. With the exception of the Conservatives who insisted still on the prerogatives of the Church or opposed universal education, they identified with the civil libertarian tradition of Britain. After all, Congress had only recently won a victory for liberty against the threat of executive tyranny! The constant changeovers of cabinets, punctuated by acrimonious debates in the legislature and the press, provided a milieu in which the political system could usually tolerate the worker press and even moderate representatives of the working class. This did not mean acceptance of all elected representatives of the working class. The Congress refused to seat Luis Emilio Recabarren, the most important labor leader in the country, after his electoral victory in 1906, on the pretext that he refused to swear the customary oath. One deputy commented that "even if it were not strictly in accord with justice to expel Mr. Recabarren from the Chamber, it would be necessary to do so for social morality . . . since it is not tolerable that the ideas of social dissolution sustained by Mr. Recabarren be represented in the Chamber." Nevertheless, the parliamentary system did allow increased political influence for middle-class and provincial interests. Before the parliamentary era ended (1924), Recabarren and other self-declared revolutionaries had also gained seats in the Congress.

Parliamentary politics tended to diffuse and weaken governmental authority. The multiplicity of political parties and factions and the electoral reforms that placed supervision of elections and registration in the hands of 267 "autonomous" municipal administrations, decentralized national politics. The Congress became a creature of local political machines which were frequently dominated by landowners, mining interests, or industrialists in accord with the economy of each congressional district. Executive intervention through use of the police or military could still influence electoral outcomes, but generally money to buy votes became much more important than naked force. In these respects the Chilean political system shared the corruption that accompanied expansion of the suffrage and democratization throughout most of the Western world, though expansion of the suffrage came much more slowly in Chile than in the United States or Argentina. As late as 1920, only 5 percent of the population cast ballots despite electoral reforms in 1874 and 1888 that removed property qualifications and extended the vote to adult, literate males. Still, dishonesty in public life and patronage as a principal instrument of assembling and maintaining local political machines reached no more distressing levels in Chile than it did in the United States or Argentina during the same period.

Unlike the United States, in Chile no wave of immigrants served the elite as urban "voting cattle"; government remained largely in the hands of a small clique of "political families" with aristocratic pretensions and a political base in the countryside—in an increasingly complex urbanizing society. Overt military intervention in Chilean politics in 1924 and the subsequent Ibáñez dictatorship (1927-31) meant, above all else, an end of an era in Chilean national life when socio-economic changes moved the country rapidly into the twentieth century, yet political leaders clung to a bastardized version of imported nineteenth-century liberalism.

No other problem so dominated Chilean development after 1891

—and received so little meaningful attention by Chilean political leaders—than the continued growth of the urban and industrial proletariat and the intensified struggle between labor and capital called the "social question." Modest but persistent industrial growth in Chile from the 1890s until the world depression of the 1930s gradually increased the number of workers employed in factories, workshops, construction industries, and other urban manual jobs. This urban working class remained unprotected by social legislation or a strong labor movement.

Liberal philosophical and economic doctrine current in Europe and transplanted to Chile condemned associations of workingmen that attempted to negotiate collective agreements with employers as contrary to "liberty" and the "right to work." In England, where the Industrial Revolution first made itself felt and gave rise to the social question, laws against workers' "combinations" and repression of labor organizations were the common reaction by government and employers to labor activism. Only after years of organized struggle, protests, violence, and the resultant political reform did the English working classes obtain legislation that limited the duration of the work day, protected child labor, set minimum wages, or guaranteed the right of organization.

As the industrial age advanced, the same type of struggle eventually developed in the rest of Europe, the United States, and Latin America. Thus the social question in Chile, as in the rest of the Western world, consisted of political, social, and economic issues derived from the technological and demographic effects of industrialization during the nineteenth and early twentieth centuries.

Prior to 1924 Chilean laws provided no institutionalized procedure for dealing with conflicts between worker and employer. In theory a worker sought employment from an individual employer and came to an agreement concerning wages, conditions of work, and length of employment. Each worker had to reach his or her own agreement with the employer. No collective agreement or written contract existed, and prevailing custom defined as subversive strikes or work stoppages. According to this classic liberal interpretation of the worker-employer relation, the worker could freely come and go as he or she pleased, and could work or not work, depending upon the attractiveness of the employment offered. Likewise employers, competing for workers in the free labor market, would offer conditions of work and sufficient pay to attract and retain workers.

In reality, of course, this highly idealized conception of the labor market—imbued with the legitimacy of prevailing law and enforced as necessary by the police or the military from country to country—

ignored the tendency for industrial ownership to become gradually more concentrated, for owners of factories to cooperate in holding down wages, and for the threat of unemployment in the cities to pose a life-and-death dilemma for the growing proletariat.

This liberal formulation also failed to recognize that the extensive political influence of the propertied classes had shaped the laws restricting labor organization but allowing employers' associations that effectively lobbied legislatures and administrators in their own behalf. For example, the Sociedad de Fomento Fabril (SFF) in Chile, which opposed labor organizations and collective labor agreements, attempted to protect its own interests with constant lobbying for protective tariffs. Its members also were sent to Congress, staffed government bureaucracies, or acted as ministers of state. Between 1883 and 1930, 36 percent of the association's executive council members served as congressmen, senators, or ministers of state. During the same period the monopolistic or oligopolistic structure characteristic of Chilean industry in the 1980s had begun to emerge. By 1918, 3.3 percent of all manufacturing firms employed 43.2 percent of manual workers in industry. A small number of firms dominated most of the important manufacturing sectors, including textiles, sugar, breweries, wineries, foundries, tobacco, cement, paper, glass and bottles, chemicals, vegetable oils, and coal. Collusive marketing and supply agreements reinforced the lack of competition as the larger firms attempted to freeze potential competitors out of the market. In a fashion compatible with both Hispanic and the liberal capitalism of the late nineteenth century, Chilean entrepreneurs sought to eliminate competition throughout the economy except in the labor market. Here they enthusiastically accepted the principles of British liberalism long after the advent of labor legislation and the recognition of the legitimacy of labor organizations in Britain. Although the industrialists strongly supported protective tariffs, government subsidies, monopoly profits, and influential industrial associations working closely with the government, they staunchly opposed organized collective action on the part of workers to improve their living conditions or to demand higher wages.

Likewise, Chile's wealthiest landowners, organized in the National Agricultural Society (SNA) since 1869, actively lobbied to restrict the negative effects of "free trade" on cattle interests. Highly influential in Chilean politics—from 1873 to 1901, 25 to 33 percent of the members of Congress belonged to the SNA—the landowners sponsored legislation in 1888 to establish a protective tariff on imported cattle. Landowners thus hoped to insulate Chilean cattle producers against the more modern cattle industry of Argentina. The proposed legislation indirectly provided incentives for landowners to revert land to pasture, even as the country proved unable to supply sufficient foodstuffs at reasonable prices to feed the growing cities and northern mining districts.

The cattle tax issue infuriated the leadership of the newly formed Partido Demócrata and became a symbolic rallying point for lower-class protests against the general inflation which was eroding an already precarious standard of living. Landowners responded that the lower classes ate little meat anyway and that in any case beans were healthier. A wave of protests and strikes in Santiago and the provinces, along with the other issues facing the Balmaceda government in 1888-89, led to withdrawal of the proposed cattle tax by its sponsors. A decade later, however, the landowners successfully put through legislation that imposed a duty on imported cattle in conjunction with the protective tariffs supported by the SFF for manufactured goods. Meat prices rose considerably from 1897 to 1902 amidst continual political conflict over a "tax on poor people's stomachs." Finally, in late October 1905, urban unrest related to the spiraling inflation culminated in two days of mob violence, looting, and destruction. This period, known since then as the "Red Week," found the army out of Santiago on maneuvers. To put down the violence the government and private groups distributed arms to members of Chile's most prestigious social club, the Club de la Unión, and to youths from elite families. These white guards massacred hundreds of people in the streets of Santiago. The SNA and other social leaders blamed the riots on agitators "stirring up class hatred." In reality, as the movement developed, usurious merchants, retail shops, and other symbols of the exploitation and deprivation of the poor, all felt the spontaneous wrath of the urban underclass.

Despite the events of October 1905, the cattle tax remained in effect until the economic crisis of 1907, when the government "suspended" its operation for two years. Congress reinstituted the cattle tax in December 1909, and it remained in effect until 1918—when almost 50 percent of all congressmen owned large haciendas. Whatever the real contribution of the cattle tax to increasing food prices and the widespread nutritional deficiencies among the urban poor, its survival until the end of World War I reflected the influence of the SNA and the ambiguity of the Chilean elite's commitment to the "free market" of liberal doctrine. Though seasonal competition between agriculture, public works, and the nitrate producers sometimes forced employers to sweeten the pot, only the labor force was truly expected to compete in the "free" market—for jobs!

By 1920 more Chileans worked in manufacturing than in the mining sector. Other urban employment, in construction, commerce, services, on the docks, and in transport, further enlarged the non-rural work force. It also added to the number of Chileans out of the immediate influence of the owners of large rural estates. Manufacturing itself had achieved moderate diversification, although it still lacked heavy industry and a significant capital goods sector. Diversification meant specialization of the work force and a growing pool of skilled laborers. Urban life for these workers pitted them against the continual inflation and periodic recessions generated in great part by the country's vulnerability to fluctuations in the nitrate market. These business cycles subjected much of the labor force to a grinding poverty that contrasted markedly with the prosperity and economic modernization that surrounded them.

Workers saw the palatial mansions of Santiago politicians and their extended families, along with the evident affluence of the new industrial elites. Technological innovations brought streetcars, automobiles, electric lights—even airplanes—to a nation where the best urban transport only a decade earlier consisted of elegant horse-drawn carriages. Workers could also not fail to notice the overwhelming influence of immigrants and their offspring in the nation's new factories, for by the outbreak of World War I foreign-born industrialists owned slightly more than half of all the country's manufacturing establishments, and foreigners filled more than half of the technical positions in industry.

Unlike the situation in neighboring Argentina, European immigrants did not swell the ranks of Chile's working classes. Whereas by 1914, some 40 percent of Argentina's agricultural labor force and 60 percent of the urban proletariat had been born abroad, in 1907 only 1 percent of Chile's rural labor force and fewer than 4 percent of industrial workers were foreigners. This means that before World War I the labor movement in Chile was influenced far less by immigrant leadership and imported ideology than its counterpart across the Andes. Chilean authorities and political leaders did sometimes blame the labor agitation prior to the 1920s upon "waves of human scum thrown upon our beaches by other countries," but such hyperbole could not deceive government officials and employers who knew that the flow of immigrants to Chile hardly reached "wave" proportions. Only after the Russian Revolution of 1917 did Chile pass a Residence Law allowing the government to forbid entry into the country or to deport "foreigners who preached violent change in the social or political order." In contrast, Argentina passed much harsher legislation in 1902 in response to a more serious participation by immigrants in a growing labor movement. Even in 1918, however, Chilean leaders, who wanted to use the immigrants as scapegoats for mounting social tensions, had to admit that the leadership and the rank and file of the Chilean labor movement, as well as of the socialist-oriented political movements, consisted overwhelmingly of Chileans.

Historical treatments of the origins, character, and evolution of the Chilean labor movement in the early nineteenth century remain extremely fragmentary. Lack of source material means that efforts to identify the first strike by Chilean workers face insurmountable obstacles. Chilean historians often cite the rebellion of miners at Chañarcillo in 1834 as a starting point in the story of the Chilean labor movement, but this rebellion certainly had antecedents in the northern mining camps of colonial times and the early national period. Whatever the specific chronology of significant events in labor history, the sporadic, spontaneous protests, rebellions, or strikes prior to the 1880s clearly preceded the more integrated, politically significant movements of the parliamentary era. A study published in 1971 by Manuel Barrera documented 299 strikes in Chile's first century (1810-1910) in addition to numerous other "movements, rebellions and incidents." Of the 299 strikes, only 42 occurred before 1890, while the remainder took place between 1901 and 1910. Even if this study underestimates the number of strikes before 1890, the Chilean labor movement as an organized, militant, *national* socio-political force dates essentially from the last decade of the nineteenth century.

Beginning with the general strike of 1890, described in Chapter 6, the Chilean labor movement developed impressively, if unevenly, until World War I. A heterogeneous collection of mutual aid societies, cooperatives, anarchist-oriented resistance societies, and brotherhoods, or *mancomunales*, of the nitrate regions brought together thousands of workers in a struggle to better living conditions, to provide minimal levels of security, or to petition Congress for legislation improving their lot. Tactics and objectives varied from one organization to another. Many of the mutual aid societies limited their attention to self-help efforts, such as burial expenses, and temporary relief in time of unemployment, sickness, or disability. Sometimes, however, an organization that began as a mutual aid society or a cultural group evolved into a more militant labor organization or engaged in explicitly political activities. In this sense, workers' organizations constituted an extremely diversified agglomeration conforming to no unified ideological, political, or social pattern. Paternalistic Conservative politicians, following in the steps of the earlier Catholic workers' circles of the 1870s, patronized the formation of Catholic workers' clubs while anarchists, socialists, and Democrats spread contradictory reformist and revolutionary propaganda among the workers.

The disunity of the workers' organizations and their geographical separation did not prevent the evolution of an increasingly hostile attitude among laborers toward capitalists and landowners. Shortly after the civil war of 1891, with the general strike of 1890 still fresh in mind, the leader of congressional forces and new Chilean president, Vice Admiral Jorge Montt proposed legislation outlawing strikes and other disruptions of economic activity. In justifying the legislation to Congress, its authors noted that "strikes promoted in the name of freedom to work are often the pretext adopted by demagogues to disturb order, cause injury or ruin to industry and misery to the workers." Significantly, the Congress did not pass this legislation, perhaps indicating an authentic commitment to freedom of association by certain parliamentary leaders, despite their abhorrence of movements menacing the flow of nitrate revenues or public order.

More important than legislative proposals, the Montt government moved to enlarge the army and intensify the German-oriented modernization begun before the civil war. In 1895 General Körner contracted thirty-six foreign officers (33 Germans, 2 Swedes, and 1 Dane) to serve as instructors in the Chilean army. Supported by calls from the most influential newspapers to expand the armed forces in the nitrate districts to convince the capitalists that the government would defend their property, as well as by the still more reactionary attacks on the very legitimacy of any political party representing lower-class interests, the Montt government acquired modern military hardware and made clear its commitment to law and order. If border disputes with Argentina or threats of renewed conflict with Peru and Bolivia were the main stimulus for modernizing the armed forces, in practice the Chilean labor movement became the principal target of military operations.

Successive governments through the first decade of the twentieth century maintained this commitment; by 1902 the permanent army had grown to 17,500, compared with its theoretical size of 2500 in 1879. The combination of a rapidly developing labor movement, the resistance by the government and ruling classes to acknowledge the legitimacy of such a movement, and a larger, modernizing military set the stage for a series of well-remembered tragedies that became symbols of struggle and forged a heritage of martyrdom for the modern Chilean labor movement. These include the maritime strike in Valparaíso in 1903, the dockworkers' strike in Antofagasta in 1906, and the massacre of workers at Santa María de Iquique in 1907. Both the army and the navy became instruments of repression of the labor movement.

Labor conflict and political crisis followed trends in the nitrate economy. Following the general strike of 1890 and the subsequent civil war, the cyclic depressions of the nitrate industry, upon which the Chilean state increasingly depended for revenues, led to the periodic unemployment of thousands of workers in the northern deserts. In turn, the nitrate recessions caused economic downturns throughout the Chilean economy. As the size of the nitrate work force and the level of production increased from decade to decade, so did the human misery occasioned by recessions. Table 6 illustrates the cycles of boom and bust in the nitrate fields as reflected in the variations in the numbers of workers employed in the *oficinas*.

Until the disastrous depression of the 1930s, the nitrate industry

TABLE 7. WORKERS IN THE NITRATE INDUSTRY

Year	Workers Employed	Year	Workers Employed
1895	22,485	1923	41,099
1896	19,345	1924	59,649
1897	16,727	1925	60,785
1898	15,955	1926	38,118
		1927	35,788
1907	39,653		
1908	40,825	1928	59,963
1909	37,792	1929	58,493
1912	47,800	1930	44,464
1913	53,161	1931*	
1914	43,979	1932	8,535
1915	45,506	1933	8,486
1916	53,470	1934	14,133
1917	56,378		
1918	56,981		
1919	44,498		
1920	23,542		
1921	33,876		
1922	25,462		

* No data for 1931.

(Source: Laurence Stickell, "Migration and Mining: Labor in Northern Chile in the Nitrate Era, 1880-1930," unpublished Ph.D. dissertation, Indiana University, 1978.)

TABLE 8. STRIKES IN CHILE, 1911-20

Year	Strikes	Workers Involved
1911	10	4,762
1912	18	11,154
1913	17	10,490
1914	5	829
1915*		
1916	16	18,523
1917	26	11,408
1918	30	24,392
1919	66	23,529
1920	105	50,439

* No data reported for 1915.
(Source: *Boletín de la Oficina del Trabajo*, No. 18, 1922, p. 263.)

expanded continually, with periodic depressions (1896-98, 1907, 1909, 1914-15, 1919-20, 1922, 1926-27) which inflicted unemployment upon the northern workers and forced them to migrate out of the nitrate camps to the ports and toward the central valley. Government commissions routinely documented the plight of the workers and urged reforms, but official action before 1924 consisted of minor social legislation—a workers' housing bill in 1906, a law establishing Sunday as a day of rest in 1907, and a law establishing a mandatory scheme for insuring against industrial accidents in 1917. Meanwhile the level of conflict, the strength of organized labor, and the spread of working-class militancy throughout the country turned the "social question" from the paternalistic concern of a select number of benevolent intellectuals into the most critical political issue confronting the country. Table 7 indicates the mounting participation of workers in strikes between 1911 and 1920, though official statistics clearly underestimate the size of the organized labor force and the number of strikes that occurred.

Not only the northern mining districts and urban centers experienced the effects of labor conflict. In 1911 the *Boletín de la Oficina del Trabajo*—the official organ of the Labor Office created in the first decade of the century to collect and publish labor statistics—recorded for the first time a strike in the countryside by forty rural workers. Earlier labor conflicts between landowners and rural workers had certainly occurred in the nineteenth century, but now an official government publication noted the emergence of class conflict in the rural sector. By 1921 the SNA was so concerned by the possibility of the organization of rural workers and *inquilinos* that it sent a letter to the Chilean president, Arturo Alessandri, urging him to take vigorous action to prevent further labor disturbances in the countryside and to protect private property.

In great part the extension of class conflict to the countryside responded to the efforts of the Chilean Workers' Federation, or Federación Obrera de Chile (FOCH). Indeed, the history of the Chilean labor movement to this day is heavily influenced by the origins, development, political alliances, and ideological orientation of FOCH prior to 1927. Founded in 1909 among the railway workers of Santiago under the aegis of a Conservative lawyer, FOCH gradually evolved into a radical, militantly anticapitalist, working-class organization. Under the influence of Luis Emilio Recabarren, who initially charged the organization with being an instrument of the bourgeoisie but helped to wrest it away from more moderate leadership, FOCH linked sympathizers of the Partido Demócrata and the Partido Obrero Socialista (POS), socialist, anarchists, and syndicalists.

Intra-organizational struggles for power eventually forced reformist elements to leave the movement; by 1921 FOCH had affiliated with the Red International of Labor Unions (RILU), and in 1922 the POS became the Chilean Communist Party. Overlapping membership and leadership between FOCH and the Communist party divided the labor movement as non-Communist Marxists, socialists, and reformers left both the POS and FOCH. Combined with the economic crisis of the early 1920s, these internal divisions reduced FOCH membership from 60,000 to perhaps 30,000 in 1922. Weaker in Santiago and Valparaíso than the anarchists, FOCH continued to be a major force among the nitrate, copper, and coal miners, as well as among the maritime workers, tram workers, and rural labor in certain regions.

In addition to FOCH, anarchists and anarcho-syndicalists played a highly significant role among the Chilean work force through the mid-1920s. Especially influential on the docks, among artisans, and in the construction trades, the anarchists also competed for workers' loyalty in the coal mines, the nitrate fields, and other industries. Rejecting all compromise with the capitalist state, the anarchists identified government, church, and capital as the principal enemies. Anarchists played a key role in the formation of "resistance societies" and fomented strikes with varying degrees of success in the first decades of the twentieth century. In 1913 anarchist-inspired labor organization and job actions led to a general strike involving railway workers, port workers, construction and metal workers, tram workers, foundrymen, and workers in the Viña del Mar sugar refinery and the Chilean Tobacco Company. From 1913 to 1921, anarchist unions, mutualist societies, and resistance societies participated in the ebb and flow of labor's efforts to improve working conditions and to challenge antilabor legislation and policies. In addition, they encouraged tenant organizations in their struggle against the rising cost of housing. In the period 1917-20 they also joined in a wave of strikes and, allied with FOCH and other working-class organizations, in the Workers Assembly on National Nutrition (AOAN). AOAN demanded that President Sanfuentes introduce property and income taxes, free meals for schoolchildren, minimum wage legislation, and government regulation of food prices. When AOAN pressed its demands and strike activity continued, the Congress first passed a residence law aimed at the anarchists and then granted the president emergency powers. The president declared a state of siege in Santiago and Valparaíso; as strike activity continued into 1920, President Sanfuentes resorted to police and military repression of labor.

Security forces attacked union headquarters, arrested labor leaders, and shut down worker newspapers such as *Verba Roja* and *Acción Directa*. Particular attention was focused on the IWW headquarters in Valparaíso, where police arrested some 200 people. Government-encouraged crowds also attacked the headquarters of the Chilean Federation of Students (FECH), known for its pro-labor stance. While other labor groups and working-class parties (FOCH, POS) also experienced the repression, the elite newspapers and the government highlighted the "antipatriotic" and "subversive" character of anarchism. Viewed as an even more serious threat to established order than FOCH, the anarchists suffered serious repression at the hands of government and were again a special target of the Ibáñez regime from 1927 to 1931.

The anarchists emphasized direct action and rejected alliances with politicians or political parties—in marked contrast to FOCH. They also violently opposed the alliance between FOCH and the Communist party, arguing that the labor movement should not be dependent on any political party or any government. The anarchists' militancy and competition with FOCH or workers' groups supporting the Partido Demócrata occasionally led to physical confrontations and even murder within the labor movement. The coal mines of Lota, in particular, were the scene of bitter conflicts among opposing labor factions.

Unrelated to any of the larger labor organizations, there also developed a "socialist" movement in the far southern province of Magallanes among the workers of the enormous cattle and sheep ranches and meat-processing plants dominated by British capital. Here migrants from Argentina played an important role in the battle against employers, making the Punta Arenas labor organizations in part an extension of the Argentine socialists. Nevertheless, both the Radical party and the Partido Demócrata exercised a certain influence in Magallanes, as did FOCH and to a lesser extent the anarchists. With time the unions in Magallanes ranked among the most aggressive in the Chilean labor movement and were brutally repressed by British firms and Chilean authorities on more than one occasion in the decade 1910-20.

The evolution of a militant labor movement in the context of a political system catering to the aristocratic tastes of Santiago high society had produced an intolerable situation by the early 1920s. Congress repeatedly refused to adopt labor legislation or even to enact piecemeal reforms to ameliorate the worst abuses of labor contractors and unscrupulous employers. Meanwhile, the Chilean economy continued to depend upon export and import duties, particularly revenues from nitrate. Inheritance taxes, as well as taxes on land and capital had practically ceased to exist. A study published in the *Revista Chilena* by Alberto Edwards in 1917 concluded that taxes on land, capital, or income had declined from 18 percent of government revenue in 1880 to almost nothing in 1913.

The economic crisis precipitated by the outbreak of World War I led to reintroduction of a small "temporary" income tax on public employees and to an inheritance tax. These measures raised the proportion of government revenue derived from internal taxes to almost 10 percent. As soon as new economic relations with the Allies, especially the United States, produced an economic upswing in 1916, property tax rates declined, and Congress deleted the income tax on public employees; only 4 percent of government revenues came from internal taxes, while 89 percent originated in export taxes (61.5%) and import duties (27.1%). Five years after publication of Edwards' study, Raul Simón, later an Ibáñez adviser, concluded in an article entitled "Our Financial Situation" that "the war of [1879] gave us a military victory that subsequent governments converted into a diplomatic and financial defeat." Noting the debilitating inflation that devalued Chilean currency by more than 70 percent between 1880 and 1922, Simón called for new taxes on imports and proportionate increases in other taxes to replace the disproportionate dependence on export duties. But the Congress had no more intention of taxing landowners, industrialists, and property owners to finance the nation's development than it did of dealing effectively with the social question.

With the exception of a small number of progressive churchmen, the leadership of the Catholic Church reinforced the prejudices of conservative interests. In the first decade of the century the Chilean archbishop even attacked popular education and universal suffrage, while senators blamed the tide of labor protests upon "the campaign for compulsory public education that represents the wave of socialism threatening to overwhelm us." These attitudes hardly portended great hope for the future in a country barely 38 percent literate and where, in the capital city, fewer than one-third of the population aged five to fifteen were enrolled in schools.

Despite the poverty and illiteracy of the masses, the physical modernization and beautification of Santiago, Valparaíso, and other leading cities allowed the well-to-do to immerse themselves in a charming, comfortable, even pretentious lifestyle. The modernity and elegance of certain parts of Santiago, Valparaíso, or Viña del Mar contrasted markedly with the continued backwardness of much of the country and the squalor of urban slums, or *conventillos*. Social life for the wealthy centered in the aristocratic social clubs, the racing season, the opera, weekly or biweekly strolls along the Alameda between Cochrane and Ejército streets, or outings in fancy carriages in the exclusive Parque Cousiño. In the words of one Chilean historian of the period, "These outings represented an imitation of the customs of the times of the Spanish nobility in El Retiro, the French in the Bois de Boulogne or the wealthy bourgeoisie in Buenos Aires in the wide Avenida Alvear." For a theatre-box (*palco*) at the *teatro municipal* the affluent paid 1000, 5000, even 20,000 pesos. These *palcos* served as meeting places of the political factions, for as much political activity went on at the theater, the opera, and the social clubs as in the Congress, which often simply formalized decisions made at social affairs.

The "good families" were few, and for them Santiago was a small world turning on the axis of the "high life." The society pages of the newspapers avidly reported the *vida social* of the elite and the goings and comings of the guests at the artistic or literary circles patronized by aristocratic women of the capital. Chile was governed by gentlemen who valued civility, tradition, and lineage—but who could also accept new blood and new money into their ranks when need be. Summer vacations at a country estate or near Valparaíso, trips to Europe where their sons and daughters were educated, and competition among the damsels to stay abreast of European fashions rounded

out the good life for the masters of Chile. For most Chileans another
reality prevailed. More than half of all deaths recorded in 1913
were of infants and children under five years of age. The infant mortality rate more than tripled that of the United States, or the United
Kingdom, and significantly exceeded the rates in Egypt, Mauritius,
Japan, Argentina, and even Mexico.

Notwithstanding an outpouring of literature on the social question
and more than three decades of intellectual introspection on the
causes of Chile's social and economic decline from the supposed
greatness of the post-1879 period, the political system produced no
solutions for the nation's ills. Social life for Santiago high society
continued its whirl of *salones, tertulias,* operas, theaters, and summer
vacations. But with the economic crisis following World War I,
worker protests proved so threatening that the government declared
a state of siege in the northern provinces in 1919; while in Magallanes, in mid-1920, troops shot down striking workers after first
setting fire to their union building. Exacerbated by a lengthy strike
in the coal fields, the political and economic situation seemed on the
verge of breakdown. Congress could ill afford to put off any longer
dealing with the social question.

The emergence of the social question as Chile's most pressing
national problem coincided with truly dramatic demographic, technological, and economic changes in Chilean society. Population
movements to the south and north and out of the rural areas into
the cities intensified the trends initiated in the middle decades of
the nineteenth century. From an essentially rural nation of 2 million
people in 1880, Chile became an increasingly urban country of over
3.7 million in 1920 and of 4.2 million ten years later. Santiago's population mushroomed from 275,000 residents in 1900 to 700,000 by
1930, while Valparaíso reached a population of 200,000 in the same
year. By 1930 almost one-fourth of Chile's population lived in Santiago or Valparaíso.

More important even than the advancing urbanization of the population, Chilean society and the economy became truly national with
the extension of rail lines, telegraph networks, and steamship service
and the evolution of a national labor market. Not only did the population of the provinces of Tarapacá and Antofagasta, which more
than doubled between 1885 and 1920, became increasingly Chilean,—
in 1885, 40 percent "foreign"; in 1920, 11 percent; in 1930, 8 percent—but the impressive mobility of labor also created a nationally
integrated labor market. The periodic ups and downs of the nitrate
industry, with the associated ebbs and flows of workers between the

northern deserts, coastal towns, and southern provinces, contributed to increasing articulation between the country's regional economies. In a sense, though the patterns of trade characteristic of the mid-nineteenth century still prevailed, regionalism itself declined as a meaningful political force. In search of relief or work, workers shifted from southern agriculture to the northern mines or nitrate districts, then with recessions in the north, migrated to the ports of the *norte chico*, Valparaíso, Santiago, or into the central valley and beyond.

The longitudinal railroad that by 1915 connected Puerto Montt to Coquimbo linked the urban markets and the northern mineral districts to the central valley and southern producers. Steamship lines and the transverse, privately owned railroads of the nitrate regions made Chile's most dynamic economic sectors, along with the urban centers, the most important markets for Chilean agriculture and industry. With the exception of the northern railroads and the trans-Andean line, the Chilean state controlled the railroad system and deliberately extended it north and south with strategic and developmental, rather than commercial, objectives in mind. Cheap freight rates subsidized Chilean agriculture. In particular the railroad's penetration south allowed greatly expanded shipments of cattle, wheat, wine, lumber, and processed goods from the southern provinces to Santiago, Valparaíso, and north by ship to the nitrate and mining districts. This encouraged increased cultivation and modernization of southern agriculture, even as the seasonal competition for labor and hints of labor activism motivated southern landowners to mechanize the harvest.

The government also used the railroad, in times of recession, as a safety valve to funnel unemployed workers south or, in good times, to siphon labor north to nitrate and copper production centers. Fearing the concentration of unemployed workers in the northern ports, authorities issued free rail passes so that the unemployed could seek work or temporary quarters with relatives in other parts of the country. This policy somewhat ameliorated the immediate danger of a large-scale uprising, but it also spread throughout the entire country, in extremely visible, human terms, the effects of each nitrate recession. Creation of the government employment service (*Servicio de Colocaciones*), in response to the recession at the outset of World War I, further nationalized the labor market. In its efforts to place unemployed nitrate workers in agriculture, public works, or industry, the Servicio de Colocaciones soon found that landowners often rejected nitrate hands who, in any case, resisted the low wages and poor working conditions on the haciendas. Labor Department officials became accustomed to seeing complaints by landowners that nitrate workers placed in agriculture "stirred up" the *inquilinos*, refused to eat the food provided by the farm's administrator, or simply ate a meal and left. Thus, integration of the labor market began to erode the extensive traditional authority of the hacendados.

Unlike a true economic enclave, the nitrate economy spurred national economic integration. Though foreign investors remitted many of the industry's profits abroad, operation of the industry created markets for Chilean agriculture and lumber, coal, and processing industries and induced development of service and support activities. In turn, Chilean industries developed product lines intended as inputs for other domestic manufacturers as well as supplying consumer demands. Coastal shipping greatly expanded to provision the northern districts, while tax revenues from exports and imports yielded resources for extensive public works, modernization of the military, public education, and other government expenses. In addition, after 1900 Chilean capital made steady gains in the nitrate industry, and by 1920 national capital controlled over 50 percent of the nitrate sector.

If an enclave could be said to exist in the Chilean economy in the mid-1920s—in a political and social sense, only agriculture would qualify. The extreme concentration of good agricultural land, especially in the central valley, kept 60 to 75 percent of the region's rural labor force culturally isolated on the vast haciendas that dominated the countryside. In 1924 only 2,650 rural estates (2.7% of all farms) contained almost 80 percent of the agricultural land in the central valley. On these large estates the resident labor force remained at the mercy of the landowners for access to land, housing, and daily sustenance. Their votes belonged to the landowners who used them to install themselves in the Congress and to maintain the prevailing system of rural land tenure as well as to exert their influence more generally on Chilean national life. Congressmen from the provinces depended for their election upon landowners who mobilized their peons to vote and controlled the counting of ballots in the municipality. Frequently the most important landowners of a district virtually "owned" its congressional seat. In the 1920s the initial penetration by FOCH or political agents into the rural areas challenged this arrangement, but not until the 1950s and 1960s would political reforms destroy the hacienda as a political enclave that separated tenant labor from the national community.

In economic terms, however, the Chilean haciendas did not constitute an enclave but had participated in international commerce ever since the colonial era. The economic evolution of Chile from the late nineteenth century through the depression of the 1930s more completely incorporated agriculture into the national economy. Domestic markets became the primary consumers of the countryside's wheat, livestock, dairy products, lumber, fruits, and processed foodstuffs. This meant that domestic economic conditions, rather than European, North American, or Australian markets, became the primary determinants of economic opportunities for Chile's agricultural interests. Rapid urbanization and the population growth in the northern provinces also pushed food prices upward. Higher food prices exacerbated the social question facing the country and created pressures for political regulation of the prices of food and basic necessities to mitigate the decline in real wages received by urban labor between 1890 and 1914. After 1932 efforts to retain the hacienda system and at the same time to pacify the urban labor force by regulating retail food prices would produce a curious "arrangement" (see Chapter 8), which ensured the continued exploitation of the rural labor force. Such efforts did nothing, however, to increase production and productivity in Chilean agriculture—the only real solution to feeding, at reasonable cost, a growing urban population.

National economic integration accompanied by political immobility and the intensifying social question concerned not only Chilean intellectuals but also leading Chilean military officers. The army's professionalization under Prussian leadership instilled in it a new sense of nationalism and a belief that its duty included regeneration of the country. Military writers like Carlos Soto Alvarez (1905) and Jorge Boonen Rivera (1917) emphasized the role of the armed forces in teaching patriotism and acting as agents of order and progress. Boonen Rivera went so far as to suggest that the army should be directly responsible for the revitalization of the nation. Two years later Captain Tobías Barros claimed that the army was the personification of the national ideal and that through active political intervention it must act to prevent further disintegration of the national situation. By 1921-22 some military leaders argued that the army should participate in all government policymaking. In 1922 an army captain published a speech delivered at the military club, in which he urged the army to exercise political influence to unify the diverse forces of the nation, to restore morality to public life, and to end the parliamentary chaos and immobility. According to this officer, the army alone of all Chilean institutions could rise above petty self-interest to save the nation.

The army had every reason to be concerned with Chile's social crisis. Political leaders had constantly called upon the armed forces to repress the mounting number of strikes and demonstrations during the first two decades of the twentieth century. A compulsory military service law (1900) brought large numbers of illiterate recruits to both army and navy, since the well-to-do generally managed to avoid the draft. Both services created primary schools to provide instruction to their personnel. Military service brought thousands of Chileans into a national institution, instructed them in the military's view of patriotism and national history, deployed them in regions far from their homes, and even provided training that could serve them when they left the service. Military schools for machinists, telegraphists, blacksmiths, construction workers, and miners as well as military participation in public works and disaster relief—for example, after the 1906 earthquake at Valparaíso—further engaged the army in "nonmilitary" projects.

Military dissatisfaction with the politics of the parliamentary period and with Chile's seeming economic decline manifested itself early in the twentieth century. In 1907 officers of the Santiago garrison established a "Liga Militar" as a lobby to secure better conditions and benefits for the army. Four years later leaders of the Liga Militar broached the subject of a military coup with Gonzalo Bulnes Pinto—son, grandson, and nephew of former presidents. Bulnes refused to go through with the plans for such a *golpe*, but not before the Liga Militar had expressed its opinions on matters ranging from government corruption, public education, crime, and economic policy to the need for increased benefits for the armed forces. Another abortive military movement in 1915, aimed at placing in power "a strong government able to end the political anarchy preventing the progress of the nation"; and in 1919 still another conspiracy among high-ranking officers to "avoid political chaos" and end the "dangers of communism" failed to end the parliamentary regime.

Especially disconcerting to the new generation of professional officers was the continual intervention by congressmen in the process of military promotions and assignments. Likewise, the apparent congressional favoritism of the more aristocratic, British-influenced navy over the middle-class officer corps of the army created interservice rivalries and frustrations. Gradually the military, and especially a group of professionally oriented army officers, resolved to end the

regime of *politiquería* which they believed was debasing the army
and weakening the fatherland.

World War I set in motion economic and political forces that
doomed the parliamentary regime in Chile and ushered in the revival
of copper as a principal source of foreign exchange and government
revenues. It also shifted Chile's international economic orientation
toward the United States and away from Britain and Germany. Between 1900 and 1914, American investments in Chile increased from
approximately $5 million to almost $200 million—almost two-thirds
the value of British investments in Chile. In particular, American
investors acquired nitrate and mining properties, especially copper
and iron. By the end of World War I (1918) American investors
controlled over 87 percent by value of Chilean copper production,
which increased fourfold from 31.4 million pesos to 132.8 million
pesos during the course of the war. Modern technology, which allowed economic mining of low-copper content ore at El Teniente in
Rancagua and the giant open-pit mine at Chuquicamata in Antofagasta province, along with other deposits in the environs of Copiapó
and near Santiago, resulted in good profits from the Chilean mines
for the Chile Exploration Company, American Smelting, Kennecott Copper, and Braden Copper Mining, among other companies.
United States Steel and Bethlehem Steel also established themselves
in Chile prior to World War I and expanded operations during the
war. For the first time commerce with the United States exceeded
50 percent by value of Chilean foreign trade; by 1930 United States
capital would account for some 70 percent of all foreign investment
in Chile.

This fundamental reorientation of the Chilean economy toward
the United States included large-scale introduction of American technicians, capital, machinery, and cultural influence into a country
where North Americans had previously exerted little influence. Indeed, support by American diplomats for President Balmaceda during the civil war of 1891 and, earlier, Secretary of State Blaine's
efforts to mediate the War of the Pacific had made Chile's relations
with the United States less than cordial. Now the rapid "Americani-
zation" of critical sectors of the economy, the intensified economic
relations with the United States, and the latter's role in the termination of World War I meant the gradual replacement of British
dominance of Chile's economy by that of the United States. It also
brought a pervasive influx of North American consumer goods, popular culture, and prejudices.

The outbreak of the European war brought disaster to the Chilean economy, as it pitted Chile's two leading trading partners, England and Germany, against each other. Disruption of shipping lanes and diversion of British and German shipping to wartime duties drastically reduced nitrate exports in 1914 and early 1915. Thousands of workers lost their jobs; subsequently nitrate companies and the railroads cut wages between 10 and 15 percent. Government subsidies to finance stockpiling allowed continued production at a reduced level, and thus avoided a complete collapse. Nevertheless, nitrate production declined by 60 percent, and in Tarapacá alone over half of the 23,500 nitrate workers lost their jobs. In the city of Antofagasta *ollas del pobre*, the equivalent of soup lines, fed more than 4,500 people a day. By late 1914 more than 48,000 people had left the nitrate region. Many Peruvians and Bolivians returned to Tacna or farther north to their native lands; Chileans dispersed southward. In the rest of Chile bankruptcies, runs on banks, and economic contraction resulted from the nitrate depression. In addition, the early war years led to shortages of consumer goods and raw materials for Chilean industries resulting in a reduction in economic activity and generalized price increases.

Quickly, however, Allied control of the seas permitted Chilean minerals to reach European and United States markets. Demand in the United States for Chilean nitrate and copper contributed to an economic upswing. American bankers followed United States investors. With official American entry into the war in 1917, demand for Chilean raw materials, especially nitrate, more than doubled from the 1915-16 levels. Though German development of synthetic nitrates during the war presaged even worse problems for Chile at the war's termination, a temporary boom permitted a renewed splurge of public works, road construction, port modernization, and the politics of patronage. Taking advantage of wartime demand, selected Chilean industries such as cement, textiles, and sugar refineries responded well to opportunities for import substitution. At the war's end, however, traditional industries still accounted for most of the value of industrial production, with food (44%), beverages (5.2%), textiles (4.7%), tobacco (4.7%), clothing and footwear (18.7%), and wood and wood products (6.5%) contributing over 80 percent by value of industrial output.

The temporary wartime boom ended almost as quickly as it began. German policymakers prohibited imports of Chilean nitrate to protect the manufacturers of synthetics. American and European markets found themselves with a temporary overstock—and a developing synthetic nitrate industry of their own. Though prices for copper remained high for another year, by 1919 the nitrate industry had entered another severe depression. For the second time in five years massive unemployment threatened the northern regions, and the economic side effects afflicted the rest of the country.

During the wartime prosperity Minister of Interior Eliodoro Yáñez decreed the creation of a *voluntary* conciliation and arbitration system to deal with labor conflict. With the authority of this decree the government intervened "informally" in several strikes to procure negotiated settlements between 1918 and 1920. The Yáñez decree represented an important recognition by the Chilean government of the necessity for establishing a system for managing industrial relations, but government authority remained quite limited due to the Congress' refusal to legislate in the field of industrial relations. As labor conflict intensified during 1919 and 1920, along with the postwar national depression, the social question became the major national issue before the presidential elections. With a paragon of the old elite opposing a self-declared reformer for the presidency, with strikes breaking out all over the country, and with electoral violence at a new peak, Chile appeared headed for another civil war—this time an explicit confrontation between the political and economic oligarchy and the supporters of reform. The events following the 1920 elections, however, made the frustrations and aspirations of the Chilean military, rather than the new President or the Congress, the real key to Chilean development in the next decade.

Amidst the post-World War I economic crisis, Chile faced a presidential election in which one of the candidates, Arturo Alessandri Palma, proclaimed "I want to be a threat to the reactionary spirits, a threat to those who resist all just and necessary reforms . . ."; and his opponent, Luis Barros Borgoño, represented the tradition of Santiago's political families. Alessandri, an upper-middle-class lawyer who had considerable political experience in the Congress and the Senate, carried his campaign to "the people." His incendiary speeches attacked the oligarchy and promised to alleviate the misery of the working classes. Accompanied by a high level of violence and intimidation, the election results proved so close that Congress turned the matter over to a "tribunal of honor" to sort out the charges of fraud and to verify the credentials of electors as well as vote totals. As Alessandri's supporters feared that Barros Borgoño might "steal" the election in Congress, they carried out demonstrations in Iquique, Antofagasta, Santiago, Valparaíso, and Concepción, despite Alessandri's agreement to accept the decision of the tribunal of honor.

Three weeks after the election the war minister, Ladislao Errázuriz, mobilized the armed forces and sent army and navy units north to meet a supposed threat from Bolivia. The mobilization itself proved to be a greater threat to the soldiers than the illusory Bolivian invasion. Disease spread among ill-fed troops who lacked munitions and other supplies. Rumor suggested that the war minister and his associates were profiteering in provisioning the troops. Others believed that the mobilization was a political move to attempt to divert national attention from the recent presidential elections or even to remove military officers who supported Alessandri from Santiago. Although the electoral tribunal gave the election and the presidency to Alessandri, anger over their role as political pawns further heightened the professional officers' discontent with parliamentary politics.

President Alessandri governed Chile from 1920 to 1924 in the face of hostility and obstructionism from the Congress. Ministerial changes, threats to delay budget and tax bills, and failures to authorize the military garrison to remain in Santiago—in short, all the now traditional parliamentary practices for the frustration of presidential programs—continued despite the economic crisis and the spread of labor conflicts. Congress refused to pass the paternalistic social laws sponsored by the Conservative party or those introduced by the Alessandri administration. And only forty days after assuming office, the president, notwithstanding his proclaimed commitment to reform and social justice, used troops brutally to repress workers' movements. At the nitrate *oficina* San Gregorio a massacre of workers in early 1921 added still another group of martyrs to the northern proletariat's struggle for decent treatment by the nitrate industry and recognition of labor rights by the Chilean state.

Even when the president managed to obtain a Liberal majority in the congressional elections of 1924, he could not unite his supposed supporters or persuade them to act on the critical legislation delayed for over four years. Alessandri's use of police and military at the polls to "maintain order" marred the legitimacy of the electoral victory in any case. At the same time it further involved the armed forces in immediate political questions. By mid-1924, with government salaries in arrears, a mounting budget deficit, rampant inflation, and failure to deliver on even the most modest of his campaign promises, Alessandri supported legislation to provide a salary for congressmen.

In August 1924 Congress dropped its consideration of urgent legislation for creation of a national bank, for social welfare laws, for military appropriations, and for other pressing matters, in order to deal with what many judged to be an unconstitutional proposal for it to vote its members a salary, or *dieta*. On an afternoon in early September when Congress appeared ready to approve the particulars of the salary measures, a group of more than fifty junior officers filed ominously into the gallery of the Congress. Newspapers in the capital the next day reported that the government intended to discipline the officers, though no regulation prohibited military personnel from attending congressional sessions. In support of their colleagues a larger group of officers attended an evening session of the Senate, where they heard legislators criticize their behavior and then were asked to leave the building by the minister of war.

Agitation within the army led high-ranking generals to inform President Alessandri that any disciplinary action taken against the junior officers might lead to a collective reaction by the army. Alessandri downplayed the incidents, draping them in the letter of the law that allowed military personnel to attend congressional sessions except when military matters were being debated. The matter could not be disposed of so easily. On September 4, 1924, some 400 lieutenants and captains gathered at the Club Militar, to "strengthen the unity and comradeship among the elements of the army in these difficult times the armed forces are experiencing. . . ." The officers roundly attacked the minister of war, present at the meeting, and applauded General Luis Altamirano's words of support for the junior officers.

The next day high-ranking military officers presented a list of "petitions" to President Alessandri. These included action on the budget, social security laws, income tax legislation, social laws, payment of back salaries to public employees, and reformed pension, salary, and promotion schedules for the military. In addition the officers demanded the ouster of three ministers who had insulted them publicly in the Congress. According to one account, Alessandri had met the night before with certain officers and told them: "Request in writing the dispatch of specific projects [*de tales y cuales proyectos*]; I will sponsor them in Congress and close the Congress if they do not approve them." Alessandri's brother subsequently denied this account; but whatever the precise details, President Alessandri knew in advance about the military movement and had met with representatives of the protesting officers during the evening of September 4. On September 7, Alessandri vetoed the congressional salary bill and invited General Altamirano to head the cabinet; one day later Congress passed all the laws contained in the military petition. The military junta, though its petitions had been approved, refused to disband. A week later Alessandri resigned and left for Italy.

Prior to September 5, 1924, senior officers of the Chilean army and opposition politicians had seriously considered a coup against Alessandri who, according to the conspirators, had unconstitutionally intervened in the March 1924 elections, usurped power by dictatorial means, and dishonored the army. This conspiracy, organized by a secret society called TEA (tenacity, enthusiasm, abnegation), involved certain conservative elements of the armed forces in alliance with the opposition to Alessandri. When the movement of September 5, 1924, occurred, however, junior officers precipitated an essentially leaderless protest that evolved into a military coup. The more conservative, high-ranking officers—such as Luis Altamirano and Juan Pablo Bennett, who ultimately appeared as the leaders of the government junta—supported the junior officers in their professional demands such as for an improved salary schedule, for broadening of promotion opportunities, and for less political meddling in internal army affairs. They did not, however, support entirely the rest of the petitions on the list the younger officers presented to President Alessandri.

President Alessandri's resignation left the junta with no constitutional authority; the officers decided to request that Alessandri ask Congress for permission to absent himself from the country, and to accord him full presidential honors on his departure. When the President sought asylum in the American embassy, the junta faced the dilemma of devising an interim instrument for governing the country. Congress refused to accept Alessandri's resignation but voted him permission to leave the country for six months. The military junta then closed Congress and accepted Alessandri's resignation with the expectation of forming a provisional government. Behind the scenes, divisions within the armed forces made consolidation of the military government an impossibility. The junta announced a return to civilian politics and seemed to support the candidacy of Ladislao Errázuriz, the ultraconservative minister who had sent the armed forces on a wild goose chase to the northern deserts in 1920; but a group of officers headed by Ibáñez and Marmaduque Grove led a coup to "show . . . that the oligarchs are not masters of Chile." The *golpistas* called upon Alessandri to return and reassume the presidency. As a condition for his return, Alessandri demanded a return to civilian government, creation of a constituent assembly to consider constitutional reform, and return of the armed forces to their normal duties.

Alessandri returned to Santiago in March 1925 and resumed the duties of the presidency. Bowing to the influence of the armed forces and especially his war minister, Carlos Ibáñez, he failed to reconvene the Congress. In April, Alessandri named a commission to develop procedures for selecting members to a constitutional convention. When no satisfactory solution emerged, Alessandri commissioned a subcommittee to write a draft constitution for subsequent approval by plebiscite. From late May to July 22, the subcommittee worked on the constitutional proposal; in August a national plebiscite approved the new constitution under which Chile would be governed until 1973.

The new constitution shifted the balance of power from Congress to the executive. Included among its reforms were direct popular election of the president, an independent electoral tribunal to review election results, and prohibitions against congressmen serving as ministers or government employees. The presidential term was extended to six years with no immediate re-election permitted. Congress retained important budgetary authority and could override vetos, but it lost the traditional instruments used during the parliamentary era to immobilize executive policymaking—such as control over the cabinet, authority to prevent collection of taxes, and refusal to enact an annual budget.

Notwithstanding a shift of authority toward the executive, the new constitution officially recognized the role of political parties in national politics. By providing that the president and members of the House of Deputies and the Senate had overlapping and different terms of office, the constitution practically assured that no president could come into office in control of the legislative branch of government. Another provision in the constitution assigned the Congress the responsibility to choose the president "from among the citizens who have received the two highest relative numbers of votes"—if no candidate received a majority of the popular vote. In Chile's multiparty system, this provision gave Congress considerable leverage in "preconfirmation" bargaining with the two candidates who got the most votes in presidential elections. This leverage would prove significant time and time again in constraining or compromising the action of in-coming Chilean presidents. Thus while the 1925 constitution did decrease congressional authority and remove some of the traditional instruments whereby the Congress had controlled executive initiatives, it did not emasculate the Congress or eliminate its critical role in Chilean politics.

Shortly after Alessandri returned to Santiago, he presided over still another massacre of northern workers. At La Coruña, in June 1925, soldiers machine-gunned more than 1200 workers, destroyed their living quarters with field artillery, and brutally murdered a number of prisoners and wounded. A leading socialist, historian, and politician, Alejandro Chelén Rojas, coldly notes that "San Gregorio in 1921 and Coruña in 1925 stamped with workers' blood the administration of the caudillo who [instead of] a 'threat to reactionary spirits' was [a threat] for the dispossessed that had so many hopes for his government." Other historians have noted that Alessandri attempted to prevent Ibáñez from using force against the workers, but Ibáñez ignored Alessandri's orders, just as he had rejected the president's order to resign his ministerial post before the presidential elections. When Ibáñez published a public letter to Alessandri on October 1, 1925, explaining his refusal to resign, including his role as "chief of the revolution," Alessandri resigned the presidency for the second time. Just before his resignation, he appointed Luis Barros Borgoño—his opponent in the presidential elections of 1920—minister of the interior, and thus Barros Borgoño was the vice president after Alessandri's departure.

In the face of Alessandri's resignation, Ibáñez declared he would renounce his own candidacy if the major parties could agree upon a compromise candidate and avoid the spectacle of a complete return to politics as usual. The labor movement and leftist parties refused to comply, fomenting strikes and supporting their own candidate for the presidency, José Santos Salas. The traditional parties selected Emiliano Figueroa Larraín, a nondescript politician from a good family.

Figueroa Larraín easily won the election but failed to implement the spirit or the letter of the new constitution. Sensing his inability to deal with the realities facing the country or to control the minister of interior, Carlos Ibáñez, Figueroa Larraín requested permission to take a leave of absence from the country. This left affairs of state in the hands of Ibáñez. In May 1927, Figueroa Larraín officially resigned, whereupon Ibáñez had himself elected president in a carefully controlled election. Ibáñez obtained more than 222,000 of the slightly more than 230,000 votes cast.

Ibáñez's assumption of the presidency was blessed with far more auspicious economic developments than those confronting Alessandri in 1920. By 1924-25 international demand for nitrate had again strengthened. An all-time employment record, with more than 60,000 workers in the nitrate fields, brought renewed prosperity to the Chilean economy. Despite a recession in 1926-27 that briefly interrupted recovery, the final years of the decade saw a major boom in Chilean nitrates. Indeed, Ibáñez and his chief economic adviser, Pablo Ramírez, could take credit for the economic recovery that put most of the 70,000 unemployed in mid-1926 back to work by 1928. In the meantime, police monitored political and union activity and reported to Ibáñez and his ministers on the speeches or meetings of congressmen, politicians, and union leaders who seemed to oppose the regime. Reorganization of the national police (*carabineros*) under the minister of defense provided Ibáñez with a new, direct instrument for control of the opposition and a counterpoise to would-be challengers within the army.

Expanded production of copper added to the government's sources of revenue and to the economic recovery. So, too, did a large-scale influx of foreign capital in the form of private investment and loans. Total foreign investment in the country increased from $723 million in 1925 to more than $1 billion in 1930—exceeding domestic investment in both mining and industry. Taking advantage of increasing government revenues and the inflows of private foreign capital, the Ibáñez government embarked upon the largest public works program in Chilean history. Docks and port works, roads, sewage systems, water systems, and irrigation projects dotted the landscape from north to south. Construction of public buildings and paving of urban streets altered the faces of the nation's principal cities and employed thousands of workers. Dramatic expansion and reform of the educational system meant that in a decade Chile's schools had doubled their capacity. In an effort to encourage industry, the government pushed protective tariffs through Congress and founded the Institute for Industrial Credit. Previously the emphasis upon real estate as collateral for loans had seriously restricted access by domestic industrialists to investment capital. Industry responded to the new incentives with increased output and even some diversification.

This flurry of economic activity distracted most Chileans from the political repression of the Ibáñez regime. Also obscured was the growing indebtedness as a result of the large loans the government had contracted to finance the expansion of public sector activity. After years of sterile parliamentary debate and indifference, Ibáñez even managed to squeeze legislation on agricultural colonization and "land reform" out of the Congress in 1928. Establishment of the Caja de Colonización Agrícola as an agency to administer land purchases and subdivision of large estates marked an important first step, at least symbolically, in dealing with the structural defects of the Chilean agrarian economy. Despite the Caja's limited activity, even this innovation was rabidly denounced by leading Chilean landowners.

In additional ways also the Ibáñez government represented a break with the parliamentary era. Explicit concern with a positive role of the state in encouraging industrialization, technological progress, and administrative reforms to consolidate and regularize procedures in the public administration evidenced the passage from a predominantly rural, oligarchical society to a modernizing urban polity. Educational reforms, including establishment of national standards for professional and technical degrees from the private and public universities, indicated the gradual emergence of nonaristocratic, universalistic norms in recruitment to an expanding civil service. Technicians and middle-class professionals staffed growing ministries and public agencies previously manned overwhelmingly through political patronage by the traditional parties. A growing middle class challenged the traditional "political class" for control of the state; the "social question" and a changing socio-economic structure made restoration of the parliamentary republic unlikely. In 1931 intellectuals and professional administrators in the Labor Department produced the Labor Code which incorporated the "social laws" of 1924 and created an elaborate framework for a modern industrial relations system. The Labor Code of 1931 served as the foundation for Chilean industrial relations for the next four decades.

Adoption of the "social laws" of 1924 regulating unionization, labor contracts, cooperatives, and social security had been followed by confusion. Following civil code tradition, all legislation required implementing provisions. These came slowly. Government officials and employers interpreted the laws pushed through Congress by the military coup quite differently from place to place. The Labor Code of 1931 consolidated existing legislation, including the "social laws" of 1924, and added regulations concerning agricultural workers and domestics, both of whom had been excluded from the earlier legislation. The code also established a national system of labor courts, as well as institutions to administer mandatory collective bargaining and arbitration (*juntas de conciliación*).

In general the Labor Code created a highly paternalistic and authoritarian system of government-worker relations. The code limited worker petitions and strikes to individual firms and restricted severely the activity of union federations. It gave authority to the government to order a "return to work" whenever a strike or lockout endangered public health or the economic or social life of the nation. Any labor conflict that failed to meet the rigorous requirements specified in the code could be declared illegal, and the unions were liable for any damages or losses under such circumstances. In practice these restrictive regulations meant that from 1932 on, illegal strikes outnumbered legal ones by a wide margin.

Notwithstanding the Labor Code's defects from the perspective of labor, it represented formal recognition by the Chilean state of the right of workers to organize, to petition employers for improved working conditions, to strike, and to have the work place regulated by an official agency—the Labor Department. Employers now had the obligation to enter into written contracts with workers, to bargain with unions, to obey labor legislation and social security laws and, more generally, to adopt a more limited view of the privileges of proprietorship. The Labor Code ended the classical liberal view of unrestricted property rights. The resistance of employer associations and landowners to the code's provisions testified to their awareness of its profound implications. Above all else, the Labor Code meant that the state recognized its role as an active agent in regulating class conflict and in institutionalizing procedures for managing the social question.

Ibáñez did not undertake these reforms out of benevolence or a desire to win the support of the labor movement. As with labor codes in Brazil under Vargas or later in Peronist Argentina, the Labor Code was seen as a means to control the labor movement, to subordinate it to the state, and to cleanse it of leftists and Marxists. Ibáñez used the police and army to persecute FOCH, the Communist party, and the anarchists. He also exiled leaders of the major political parties who objected to his restriction of civil liberties, to his intimidation of the press, his overt manipulation of Congress, and his disdain for the old politics. Many conservative Chileans, to whom the fascist-corporative governments of Primo de Rivera in Spain or Benito Mussolini in Italy seemed to offer a welcome relief from liberal democracy, fully supported Ibáñez's repression of popular movements and organizations. They applauded government officials who praised fascism in Italy and the ability of fascist regimes to direct economic growth and to curtail the corruption of liberal democracy. They also appreciated the regime's emphasis on work, order, and discipline. Ibáñez seemed to offer a version of the Portalian state adapted to the conditions of the twentieth century. Initially, many middle-class reformers also supported Ibáñez due to his emphasis on economic reforms, industrialization, agricultural colonization, and labor legislation.

An explicitly authoritarian, corporative orientation combined with

a commitment to reform the apparatus of the Chilean state led both
to significant policy innovations and lamentable abuses. Ibáñez transformed Congress into a captive, generally compliant assembly, thereby
eliminating the central axis of traditional politics. He also created a
government-controlled organization, the Republican Confederation
for Civic Action, or CRAC, to replace existing labor organizations
and the multiplicity of political parties of the pre-1927 period and
thus sought to eliminate the influence of traditional and reformist
political parties and to control the labor movement in an authoritarian style which later became common among the populist regimes in
Latin America. In this effort Ibáñez ultimately failed, but there can
be no question that his presidency represented a brief return to the
ideals and methods of Portales—a swing of the pendulum away from
liberalism and constitutional government. Eschewing "politics" and
concentrating upon "cleansing" Chile by "cauterization," in both
economic and political policies he established a precedent for another military dictatorship—much more brutal—in the mid-1970s.
Like his successors in the 1970s, Ibáñez rejected liberal democracy,
detested radicalism, and blamed politics for Chile's decadence.

If in many respects Ibáñez broke with the old order, the dependence of his government programs upon nitrate and copper revenues,
along with increased levels of foreign investment and loans, made the
regime as vulnerable to fluctuations in international markets as any
Chilean administration since 1879. The stock market crash of 1929
soon paralyzed Chile's finances and wreaked havoc on the economy.
Government efforts to form a new cartel called the Compañia de Salitre de Chile, or COSACH, in cooperation with the Guggenheim interests, brought criticism from economic nationalists and opponents
of the government. It also failed to stem the effects of the depression.
The value of copper and nitrate exports declined from over 200 million pesos in 1929 to 18.1 million in 1932; over 50,000 workers lost
their jobs in the nitrate fields alone. Imports declined by over 75 percent in the same period, making Chile in this respect the country
most seriously affected by the international depression. The government could not service outstanding loans or obtain new lines of
credit. In February 1931, Congress extended Ibáñez's emergency
powers to deal with the economic crisis; in May, Ibáñez declared he
would maintain order by force of arms. Wage cuts for government
personnel and the military followed, along with new income taxes, an
increase in inheritance taxes, a moratorium on public works, and dismissals of public employees. These economy moves simply worsened

the effects of the depression and added to unemployment. In July the government suspended service on the foreign debt in foreign currency—since the country's reserves were practically depleted. Poor harvests in 1921-32 added to the misery.

By late 1931 the government's program to disperse the northern unemployed in the agricultural regions or to shelter them in temporary barracks called *albergues* in the urban areas seemed a dreadful failure. The nation simply did not have the resources to provide relief for the thousands of unemployed and their families. Illustrative is the following excerpt from a report by the intendant of Talca to the minister of interior in January 1932:

> Apprised of government plans to begin shortly the distribution of 2000 families of unemployed workers throughout the central and southern provinces, I hasten, with all due respect, to make the following observations. . . .
>
> In Talca, without counting those unregistered by the Secretaria de Bienestar Social, there are more than 5000 unemployed, of which more than 700 along with their families are in the *albergues*; others are camped in emergency shelters along the roads and at the sites of public works, living off the small amount that good-hearted people can supply.
>
> In the countryside the poverty is much worse. The landowners have cut back their work to the minimum. . . . With the lack of capital, poor harvests, and drastic decline in prices, agriculture faces a total collapse. Many have no way to pay salaries, but they give their *inquilinos* milk in the morning and hot meals at noon, though they don't work.
>
> . . . I visited nearby zones some days ago and saw tragedies of hunger and misery that can't be described.
>
> . . . For this reason it seems unlikely to me that the efforts by the government to place the unemployed in agriculture will have any success.

By the end of 1931 the director of the Labor Department reported to the minister of social welfare that "The situation of the unemployed is simply terrible in Iquique, Coquimbo, Ovalle, Calera, Santiago, Talca, and Talcahuano. . . . The city of Santiago is so congested with unemployed—that, with all the efforts we have made, there are an enormous quantity of families that, as in the rest of the Republic, have been violently evicted from their dwellings and live in unhealthy makeshift shelters [*ranchos*]." In the same letter the director noted that the government's cutbacks in public works and railroad activity aggravated the crisis; the latter decision also negatively affected coal production in the Lota region.

The concentration of unemployed in urban areas not only stretched government relief efforts but also threatened public order. Intermittent attempts by the government to eradicate particular *albergues* and disperse more workers into the rural regions met stiff resistance. In turn, industrial and commercial interests in some cities petitioned the government for more protection against "ill-intentioned individuals [*maleantes*] who sought to subvert public order."

Civilian and military opposition to the regime became bolder with the government's apparent weakness. In late July 1931 a "general strike" by professional associations, white-collar workers, and students demanded a return to constitutional government. As the cabinet decided to close all banks to prevent conversion of money into foreign currency and to impose controls on foreign exchange, doctors in Santiago went out on strike and vowed not to resume practice until Ibáñez resigned. Violence in the streets, resurgence of political opposition in all sectors including the military, and the insoluble economic dilemma forced Ibáñez to resign from office on July 26, 1931.

For the seventeen months following Ibáñez' resignation, the country suffered through several civilian and military governments of varying political tendencies, including the famous "100 days" of a Chilean "Socialist Republic," under the alternating leadership of Marmaduque Grove, Carlos Dávila, and an alliance with the newly formed socialist movement called Nueva Acción Pública, or "New Public Action." International economic conditions put unmanageable strains on any national government, while lack of political consensus denied all the military and civilian-military coalitions sufficient support to impose order or to direct economic recovery. In September 1931 conservative civilian politicians and the commander of the Chilean armed forces requested military assistance from the United States in order to put down a naval mutiny supposedly inspired by "communistic" elements. In conversations with the American ambassador, the Chilean commander emphasized the serious nature of the "imminent danger of social war" and referred to the continental, rather than local, character of the communistic activities that he believed threatened the nation. Handcuffed by a 1922 treaty limiting transfer of naval armaments, the United States nevertheless expressed a willingness to supply other materiel should the Chilean government make a formal request. United States representatives also expressed their "appreciation of the desires of the Chilean government to maintain order and stable institutions and to protect American interests in Chile. . . ."

Using airpower to defeat the naval mutiny, the Chilean government withdrew its request for American military assistance but, according to the American ambassador, subsequently asked for "a specialist in communistic propaganda and activities in order to assist in ferreting out the ramifications and origins of the movement in Chile." The State Department replied that "this Government regrets that there is not available in the Government service a specialist whose services it could offer. . . ."

The confusion following Ibáñez's ouster ultimately produced a significant realignment of political forces on an explicitly Left-Right ideological continuum. Small socialist movements merged to form the Socialist party (1933); a split between Trotzkyists and Stalinists divided the Communist party; splinter groups from existing parties created the Radical Socialist party (ex-Radicals), the Democrat party, or, Partido Democrático (ex-members of the Partido Demócrata), and the center-right Agrarian party (ex-Liberals and Radicals). These divisions and realignments introduced new personalities and new energy into Chilean politics while setting the stage for political struggle during the next four decades.

In the short term, however, six different governments "controlled" the country within a 101-day period in 1932. Seeking to end the chaotic situation—and with much of the officer corps disillusioned with the military role in politics—General Bartolomé Blanche assumed provisional executive authority and scheduled the presidential election for October, 1932.

Contested among candidates representing the spectrum of political opinion, the presidential elections restored civilian government to Chile and returned Arturo Alessandri to the presidency. Alessandri obtained 184,754 of the 339,709 votes cast, while 20 percent of the electorate supported the socialist (Marmaduque Grove) or the Communist (Elías Lafertte) candidate. Subsequently the Left pressed Alessandri for social reforms, thereby restoring the social question to center stage in Chilean politics. In turn the Right sought restoration or reaffirmation of their status and privileges—which had been challenged by certain policies of the Ibáñez administration as well as by the "Socialist Republic."

At the depths of the depression and in the midst of political uncertainty, no one could have forecast that for the next forty years Chile would be the only Latin American nation without illegal changes of government and with a system for formal democracy. Neither could anyone have predicted, despite increasing American economic interest in Chile, the major role United States policy would play in Chile's internal political development over the next four decades.

Chapter 8 • Chilean Democracy

1932 —

Chile's political instability between 1920 and 1932 gave way to four decades of legally elected civilian governments. From 1932 until September 1973 Chile was the only Latin American nation in which competitive party politics, uninterrupted by coups, assassinations, or revolutions, determined the occupants of the presidency, Congress, and higher policymaking positions in the national bureaucracy. The same political parties competing at the national level also vied for control of local government institutions and for influence in national and regional student federations, labor unions, and other community or class organizations. Direct election of the president according to the provisions of the 1925 constitution made the selection of the chief executive a truly national event.

Incorporation of women (1949) and illiterates (1970) into the electoral registers increased by more than 30 percent the population eligible to vote. Improved literacy rates (50%, 1939; 75%, 1960), increased political awareness among working classes, and mandatory registration and voting did much to increase the number of voters in national elections. Important electoral reforms in 1958 and 1962 liberated the votes of rural workers from the control of landlords and reduced the possibility of vote buying and election fraud, thereby extending effective suffrage to practically the entire adult population.

The Chilean political system during these years combined multiparty politics with presidential government. Unlike a parliamentary system, governments did not "fall." Presidents served six-year terms, and during these six years cabinet shifts could reflect new party alliances or an executive decision to govern with a "nonpolitical" cabinet of technical experts or even a cabinet of personal loyalists. But the extreme fragmentation of the party system made it difficult for presidents to control legislative action or even to maintain the total support of their own party. Congressional and municipal elections which did not coincide in time with presidential elections added to legislative independence and to the unlikelihood that presidential electoral coalitions could be translated into majoritarian *governing* coalitions. Thus despite the increased authority of the president under the 1925 constitution, the old tensions between the legislature and the executive characteristic of the parliamentary period still played an important role in national politics.

Political tension between the president and the Congress did not mean total stalemate, but it did impose a certain constraint on the ability of presidents to implement the electoral platform upon which they campaigned. Since presidential electoral platforms generally contained more "Left" or populist planks than the Congress would accept, the growing frustration among leftist members of presidential coalitions meant their eventual collapse, and a gradual drift of policy toward the Right during each president's term of office. Thus Congress allowed Conservatives, Liberals, moderate and traditional Radicals, and certain middle-class business interests to limit the reformist projects of presidential coalitions.

Control over the votes of rural labor assured the Conservative and the Liberal parties, along with some Radicals, of enough congressional seats to retain important veto power over presidential programs. The "stability" of Chilean formal democracy, therefore, depended upon the continued dominance of the landowners over the votes and the political activity of their farm work force. This dominance, in turn, depended upon maintenance of the hacienda system through the prevention of rural unionization and the exclusion of outside political influences.

Recurrent challenges to the hacienda system after 1930 threatened to upset Chile's political stability. The urban labor movement and Marxist political parties made periodic efforts to encourage agricultural unionism and to wrest control of rural votes from the landowners. Every national administration, however, relied upon a complex system of economic and political subsidies to the landowners, including the repression of the rural labor movement, in order to install and preserve Chilean formal democracy. And, much to their later, self-confessed distress, Communists and Socialists colluded in elaborating an "arrangement" that made maintenance of the hacienda system and exploitation of rural labor the cornerstone in the edifice of Chilean formal democracy.

The world depression of the early 1930s marked the beginning of a period in Chilean history when more than ever before internal developments responded to international economic and political movements. Disruption of foreign trade radically reduced the nation's import capabilities. According to League of Nations' estimates, no other nation in the world suffered a more severe impact from the international economic collapse than Chile. By 1932, imports, in real terms, stood at only one-sixth their 1929 levels. The Chilean government declared a moratorium on debt repayments (June 1931) and adopted a series of policies intended to alleviate the consequences of the abrupt decline in government revenues from taxes on exports, an extreme balance of trade deficit, lack of foreign credits, and a deterioration in the terms of trade (36% from 1929 to 1932). With imports down in real terms by over 80 percent (1929-32) and gross domestic product reduced in real terms by almost 40 percent during the same period, Chilean manufacturers rejected liberal economic principles in regard to international trade and urged upon the government policies to encourage local production. Import quotas, licenses, tariff barriers, currency devaluation, and a complicated system of multiple exchange controls discriminated against foreign commodities.

These conditions accelerated greatly the uneven process of industrial development that had been under way since before World War I. Led by the textile sector, Chilean manufacturers of chemicals, metal products, machinery, furniture, paper, non-metallic minerals, along with current consumer goods, achieved a significant increase in output and, by 1940, had altered the *structure* as well as overall contribution of industry in the national economy. Import-substitution industrialization reduced manufactured goods from 50 percent of the value of Chilean imports in 1925 to only 16 percent in 1969—with imports in the later year largely capital goods and high technology items.

In the years after 1930, utilizing imported foreign technology, capital goods, and primary or semiprocessed inputs for industry, Chile created a significant industrial sector, whose structure and composition altered as the predominance of agricultural-based firms (60 percent of total manufacturing income and 47 percent of employment in 1938) ended. Growth of the textile, chemical and petrochemicals, cement, and metal sectors—among other non-agricultural-based manufacturers—reduced the employment share of the agricultural-based firms to 35 percent in 1961. Overall, though the employment share of industry rose only from 17 percent in 1940 to approximately 20 percent in 1970, the absolute number of workers in industry almost doubled. By 1970 more than 560,000 Chileans earned their living in industrial employment, and this industrial labor force was becoming more significant in Chile's political life.

Government measures to stimulate industrialization led also to a significant increase in the size of the state bureaucracy. New credit institutions, exchange control commissions, and boards to regulate agricultural exports and establish retail price controls, added a network of governmental intervention in the national economy. Creation of a national development corporation (CORFO) in 1939 and the subsequent establishment of public and mixed-venture enterprises, as well as semi-autonomous "decentralized" public agencies in housing, school construction, agricultural extension, and social security entailed an even more significant amplification of the role of the state in defining the direction and character of national economic development.*

Not only did new state institutions indicate the changing role of national government in Chilean society, but they also created new employment opportunities for a growing group of salaried professionals and white-collar workers. The political implications of thousands of attractive government jobs were not lost on the political parties in their efforts to capture legislative majorities or to form government coalitions. By the early 1940s the public sector accounted for more than 50 percent of all internal investment capital, and in the years 1930-49 public employment more than doubled—a rate of increase twice that in mining or agriculture and 32 percent above even industry and construction. These developments provided the basis for the consolidation of a bureaucratic "middle class" associated with an interventionist state. It would mean that a large proportion of the middle groups in Chilean society, both civilian and military, would support a further expansion of public activity in welfare, health care, education, and government-owned enterprises. If government activism meant marginal benefits for the working classes, it meant employment for the graduates of secondary schools, technical schools, and

---

* Between 1942 and 1952 these semi-autonomous, decentralized agencies gradually acquired their own legal identity and varying incomes derived from their own activities, apart from additional appropriations from the national budget.

TABLE 9. GROWTH OF VOTER PARTICIPATION IN
PRESIDENTIAL ELECTIONS, 1925-70

Year	Total Votes Cast	Voters Registered	Percent of Population Registered to Vote	Population Total
1925	260,895	302,212	7.4	4,073,000
1927	233,103	302,142	7.2	4,188,000
1931	285,810	388,959	8.8	4,429,000
1932	343,892	429,772	9.0	4,495,000
1938	443,898	503,871	10.2	4,914,000
1942	466,507	581,486	11.1	5,244,000
1946	479,019	631,527	11.2	5,643,000
1952	955,102	1,105,029	17.6*	6,303,000
1958	1,250,437	1,521,272	20.8	7,316,000
1964	2,530,697	2,915,121	34.3	8,503,000
1970	2,954,799	3,539,747	37.0	9,566,000

* Including women for the first time in a presidential election.

(Source: Instituto Nacional de Estadísticas, *Demografía*, Chile, 1969; and Fernando Silva Sánchez, *Los Partidos Políticos Chilenos*, Viña del Mar, Chile: Imprenta Lourdes, 1972. After Edward W. Glab, Jr., "Christian Democracy, Marxism and Revolution in Chile: The Election and Overthrow of Salvador Allende," unpublished doctoral dissertation, Northern Illinois University, 1975, p. 148.)

universities. Employment in the central administration more than tripled between 1925 and 1965, while national population barely doubled; this 300 percent increase in public employment did not include those holding positions in the semi-autonomous public enterprises such as the national airline (LAN) or national petroleum industry (ENAP).

In contrast to the aspirations and predictions of Chilean proponents of industrialization, however, significant industry did not mean increased economic independence. Wars in Europe, Korea, and Vietnam, international business cycles, and a complex, sophisticated network of multinational enterprises operating within a still more complicated international metals market limited Chilean economic performance. American, European, and multinational financial institutions determined the availability of credit and foreign investment for Chilean development.

Foreign corporations owned the principal enterprises that earned foreign exchange for the nation. Since intricate bargaining procedures among industrial consumers, the copper firms, and the United

TABLE 10. EMPLOYMENT IN PUBLIC SECTOR, CENTRAL ADMINISTRATION

Year	Number
1925	32,877
1935	41,266
1945	59,645
1955	75,542
1965	109,699

(Source: Germán Urzúa Valenzuela and Ana María García Barzelatto, *Diagnóstico de la burocracia Chilena 1818-1969*, Editorial Jurídica, Santiago, 1971.)

States government fixed the prices for these companies' copper output, production of increasing quantities of manufactured consumer goods did little to alter the historical reliance by Chile upon the export of one or several minerals. Indeed the combination of copper dependency and dependence upon foreign technology, capital goods, credit, investment funds, and technicians to carry out the process of industrialization made Chilean domestic development ever more vulnerable to external economic forces and to foreign manipulation.

Not only economic dependence increased in the period after 1930. International power struggles and ideological divisions conditioned Chilean politics. In the early 1930s a clear Left-Center-Right system of political cleavage replaced the old politics of factions, personalist cliques, and traditional party alignments. Marxism, liberalism, social Catholicism, and fascism all had supporters in Chile. The popular front, the Spanish Civil War, and nazism all influenced Chilean politics in the 1930s and 1940s. After World War II the so-called Cold War drew United States agents and diplomats directly into Chilean politics in efforts to influence elections, manipulate labor organizations, disseminate American policy perspectives, and defend American investments. Likewise, the Soviet Union and Eastern European nations contributed funds and ideological orientation and direction for the country's Marxist parties and labor organizations. Although Soviet expenditures and influence in Chile never approximated that of the United States, the effects of Cold War rhetoric and the global confrontation between capitalist "free world" nations and the Soviet bloc gradually permeated Chilean society at all levels.

If the process of industrialization between 1932 and 1964 did not free Chile from dependence upon copper exports, foreign investment, or the fluctuations in the international economy, it did accelerate the trends toward urbanization and rural stagnation evident in the first decades of the twentieth century. Employment opportunities in industry attracted migrants from the countryside to major manufacturing centers in Santiago, Valparaíso, Concepción-Talcahuano, and other provincial centers such as Temuco and Talca. Even more than expanded economic opportunity in industry, however, the worsening conditions of labor in Chilean agriculture motivated rural workers and youths to flee the countryside. Real wages for rural workers declined by approximately 18 percent between 1940 and 1952 and by another 38 percent between 1953 and 1960. Tenant agricultural laborers (*inquilinos*) suffered a decrease in quantity and/or quality of land allotments and other non-cash perquisites such as rights to pasture animals, firewood, and food rations. Landlords supplied a lesser share of seed, fertilizer, or other inputs. In the period 1940/44–1950/ 54 the real earnings of sharecroppers and tenants declined by 27 percent, while landowners achieved a real gain in earnings of 33 percent. Indeed, the price of labor in agriculture declined relative to all other inputs between 1940 and 1960. Combined with the declining real income of agricultural labor, the rising real wages of blue-collar workers in manufacturing during the same period (1940/44–1950/54) accelerated the exodus from the countryside. Whereas total population approximately doubled from 1920 to 1960 (see Table 10), rural population increased by less than 18 percent. By 1960 more than half of all Chileans lived in cities of 20,000 or more, well above the comparable figures for all major world areas except North America and Oceania.

Underlying these demographic and economic trends could be found a complex, contradictory set of political arrangements that permitted the most traditional social and economic institutions in the nation, the large rural estates, to survive intact through four decades of dramatic social change and economic modernization. To a great extent the survival of the hacienda system and its extensive subsidization by the state represented the trade-off between Marxists, reformers, and traditional political interests that permitted the establishment and maintenance of Chile's vaunted "stability" and "democracy." Whenever this trade-off was threatened, political toleration ended. When the large estates finally faced their demise in the period after 1964, so too did Chilean formal democracy.

Arturo Alessandri returned to the presidency in 1932 determined to implement the 1925 constitution, to establish the legitimate prerogatives of the presidency detailed in that document, and to carry out the main provisions of the Labor Code. In contrast to his earlier administration, Alessandri now eschewed incendiary rhetoric in favor

TABLE 11. DEMOGRAPHIC CHANGES IN CHILE, 1920-60

	1920	1930	1940	1950	1960
Total Population	3,785,000	4,365,000	5,063,000	6,295,000	7,628,136
Rural Population		2,185,800	2,421,300	2,530,400	2,650,500
Population in Cities, 20,000 plus, as percent of total population in Chile	28	32	35	43	51
Population in Cities, 20,000 plus, as percent of total population in Latin America	14	17	20	25	33

of appeals to national unity. He appointed ministers without the traditional overriding concern with party coalitions and managed to retain key ministers for four or five years of his six-year term—a feat almost unheard of in the days of parliamentary government. The emphasis on national unity, order, economic recovery, and constitutional rule gradually pushed the president into an ever more explicit alliance with the Right—the forces that had the most to gain from "law and order."

Faced with the depression-induced unemployment crisis, the continual threat of new military intervention, and the growing militance of socialist and communist movements, Alessandri allowed, even encouraged, the activity of white guards, called the "Republican Militia." According to the United States State Department files, in May 1933 President Alessandri personally reviewed a public parade of forty-two regiments of well-armed and equipped militiamen as it passed La Moneda, the presidential palace. As both a temporary counterbalance to the military and a threat to leftist movements, the militia played a significant role in polarizing Chilean politics until 1936 when the president ordered its dissolution. By then, the president's trusted military commander, General Oscar Novoa, had crushed an attempted coup in December 1933 and, through careful duty assignments and retirement of officers deemed too "political," had gradually brought the officer corps under presidential control.

Neutralizing the military threat eliminated one of the most difficult problems facing the administration. An upturn in the international economy and cautious domestic policy ameliorated the economic situation. Notwithstanding the government's extremely conservative fiscal policies, greater demand for copper and nitrates, the surge of industrial growth, and incentives to the private construction industry pulled the country out of the depths of the depression. Under the direction of arch-conservative Minister of Treasury Gustavo Ross, the administration reduced expenditures upon public works by almost 50 percent from 1932 to 1934; nevertheless official unemployment had practically disappeared by the end of 1935. In response to legislation passed at the end of 1933 allowing tax exemptions for a period of ten years on all buildings initiated before December 1935, construction increased by 40 percent in 1934 alone. This incentive not only balanced the deflationary effect of reduced public works but also renewed confidence in the private sector concerning the government's attitude toward private investment. Following on this legislation, a new public works program in 1936, focusing especially upon construction of roads, hospitals, and schools, accelerated economic recovery. Combined with construction in industry and the upturn in the export market, these projects alleviated most of the unemployment existing when Alessandri took office in 1932.

Inflation accompanied recovery. Price increases seemed to outpace salary gains, and a government freeze on salaries in the public sector alienated public employees. Failure of agriculture to provision adequately the urban centers and mining regions confronted the government with a dilemma that would underlie the contradictions in domestic political economy for the next forty years. With an ever more politicized and expanding urban labor movement, rising food prices spelled trouble for the incumbent government. Efforts to control food prices without a significant per capita increase in agricultural production required administrative controls on retail prices. Decree Law 520 of August 1932 created the General Commissariat of Subsistence and Prices, or Comisariato General de Subsistencia y Precios. Although this decree was promulgated during the brief reign of the "Socialist Republic," its major provisions remained in effect into the

TABLE 12. NUMBER OF UNEMPLOYED, DECEMBER 1932-DECEMBER 1937

1932	262,445
1933	132,642
1934	38,309
1935	13,601
1936	15,701
1937	15,829

(Source: *Legislación social y sindicatos legales en Chile*, Editorial Ginebra, Santiago n.d., CCCVI.)

TABLE 13. LEGAL AND ILLEGAL STRIKES IN CHILE, 1932-57

Year	Legal Strikes	Personnel/ Workers Involved	Illegal Strikes	Personnel/ Workers Involved
1932	3	500*	3	100*
1933	7	648	3	100
1934	2	100	11	3,000
1935	10	1,197	20	4,236
1936	4	4,781	16	2,977
1937	4	460	17	2,569
1938	6	7,954	9	3,419
1939	20	5,674	6	5,249
1940	20	8,235	25	10,576
1941	15	2,041	16	890
1942	7	671	12	2,062
1943	26	1,897	101	46,832
1944	38	14,039	53	17,249
1945	36	32,334	112	66,612
1946	27	18,262	169	76,475
1947	37	17,887	127	51,652
1948	20	7,172	6	1,203
1949†	23	6,533	24	8,711
1950	28	12,058	164	41,833
1951	30	12,718	150	47,443
1952	45	28,073	156	89,566
1953	60	54,628	148	68,480
1954	61	25,009	247	49,687
1955	62	23,062	212	104,370
1956	25	5,138	122	95,300
1957	12	8,722	68	17,616

* Approximate figure.
† Year after implementation of Law for Permanent Defense of Democracy.
(Source: Chilean Labor Department, Annual Report 1948, and yearly, 1949-1958.)

1970s. It gave the General Commissariat authority to set prices for a wide range of goods considered of "basic necessity." It also extended authority to the General Commissariat to take charge of distribution of basic commodities, to expropriate or intervene in the administration of firms that refused to cooperate with government economic policies, to requisition production under specified conditions, and otherwise to regulate the operation of private firms. The more drastic provisions of this decree rarely were utilized from 1932 until the 1970s—when the Unidad Popular government, headed by President Salvador Allende, resorted to the terms of the 1932 decree to accelerate a program to transform Chile into a socialist society. From 1932 on, however, the government's authority to regulate the price of basic necessities created an expectation among the population that incumbent regimes would control the rate of inflation.

Along with the General Commissariat, the Junta de Exportación Agrícola was created to promote agricultural exports and otherwise to benefit producers; it also soon came under pressure from urban political forces. In times of rising prices and "food shortages" the labor movement and leftist political parties demanded restrictions on exports of agricultural commodities. In addition, the Junta de Exportación Agrícola, theoretically taking into account changing production costs, set floor prices for wheat. Inevitably, decisions on wheat prices were reflected in the price of bread—the basic food of the Chilean working classes. This made every price decision by the junta critical politically: it angered either producers or consumers.

Meanwhile, the increasing strength of the Socialist, Communist, and Radical parties and the growth of the labor movement during the second Alessandri administration made it politically impossible to ignore entirely pressures for price controls in urban areas. President Alessandri strongly favored the development of the *legal* union movement under the terms of the Labor Code, since he saw the code as a major result of his own zeal in the 1920s. Accordingly the administration supported efforts by the Labor Department to encourage the organization of legal unions. The unions in turn pressed for lower food prices. This meant a clash with agricultural interests.

Successful implementation of price controls and a restrictive agricultural export policy depended upon artificial depression of producer prices for agricultural commodities. Only gradually did succeeding administrations elaborate a complex array of direct and indirect subsidies to the landowners—including negative interest rates on credit, low freight rates on state railroads, exemption from import duties on farm machinery, export bounties, and exceedingly low tax rates on land and income. However, the most important trade-off in the arrangement that came to reconcile the conflicting interests of industrialists, urban workers, salaried middle-class groups, and landowners emerged quite soon after Alessandri assumed office. Discrimination against the rural labor movement and repression of agricultural unionism would allow a superficial reconciliation of the contradictory interests of urban labor, reformist political movements, and the traditional landed elite.

From the end of 1932 until December 1938 the number of legal unions in Chile more than doubled, and membership rose from

54,000 to more than 125,000. At the same time, industrial relations gradually conformed to the provisions of the Labor Code as the technocrats of the Labor Department successfully channeled class conflict within the institutions established by the code. An exception to this trend, the predominance of illegal strikes over legal strikes, reflected the overly restrictive nature of the legislation regulating work stoppages; this exception did not prevent effective institutionalization of the procedures for labor disputes. Whereas prior to 1924 labor disputes represented a revolutionary challenge to the parliamentary system, the Alessandri administration (1932-38) most effectively established administrative capabilities for *routine* handling of worker-employer collective bargaining. The underlying revolutionary issues of the social question seemed to evaporate as unions and their political allies accepted the legitimacy of the *juntas de conciliación* and the labor courts.

Only in agriculture did employers *en masse* refuse to recognize the legitimacy of unionization and the very applicability of the Labor Code. In sharp contrast to his generalized commitment to implement the Labor Code, President Alessandri also discouraged agricultural unionization. Unfortunately for Alessandri, leading officials within the Labor Department, among them some who had helped to write the Labor Code, attempted to fulfill their duty by applying the terms of the code in the countryside. This included efforts to force landowners to introduce written contracts with all their workers, to pay social security taxes as the law required, and, most significant, to unionize agricultural labor.

The implications of a unionized agricultural labor force associated with reformist and Marxist political parties threatened not only the economic basis of Chilean agriculture but also the control of landowners over the votes of their agricultural tenants, sharecroppers, and resident laborers—votes that guaranteed the presence of rightist forces in the Congress.

The response to this threat by the Alessandri administration and the National Agricultural Society (SNA) provided the foundation for the political "solution" to the problems posed by rapid urbanization, industrialization, growth of the urban labor movement, and inflation. If rural labor could be forced to bear most of the costs of price controls discriminating against agriculture, and if landowners could be spared the inconvenience and cost of compliance with labor laws—while maintaining political control over the rural work force—then political "stability" could be maintained and the threat of discontent or violence in the cities could be reduced.

In response to initial unionization efforts in vineyards in Talca province and a small number of farms near Santiago in 1932 and 1933, the SNA protested to the Labor Department and to President Alessandri that the unionization provisions of the Labor Code did not apply to agriculture. Significantly, both the Labor Department and the Consejo de Defensa Fiscal, a kind of administrative supreme court, ruled against the landowners. The Labor Department concluded that "there is no doubt that the agricultural worker has the complete right to unionize." Taking its case directly to President Alessandri, however, the SNA secured a reversal of the Labor Department's decision in the form of an ambiguously worded telegram sent to all the department's offices:

> This Department, in conjunction with the government, is studying activities related to the unionization of workers in rural properties. Since there exist complex difficulties in carrying out these legal provisions, this Department orders you to refrain from assisting in the constitution of organizations of this type until you receive definite and precise instructions.

Since formation of a legal union required the presence of a labor inspector, this telegram effectively prevented organization of legal agricultural unions. No "definitive and precise" (or any other) instructions were forthcoming. True to the declarations made in his first presidential term (1920-24, 1925) when he noted the disadvantages of agricultural unionization, Alessandri's decision launched four decades of administrative, legislative, and physical repression of rural labor by successive national administrations. This repression served as the foundation of the political economy of Chilean formal democracy.

In June 1934—as if an omen of the future—*carabineros* massacred more than one hundred peasants protesting their eviction from their land in the frontier region of the upper Bío Bío. Rising in armed rebellion, the peasants of Ranquíl looted stores and threatened landowners before the national police murdered the movement's leaders and restored order. Shortly thereafter the Alessandri administration urgently requested Congress to approve new legislation on agricultural colonization, but the events at Ranquíl and the earlier action on rural unionization made clear the government's commitment to maintenance of the existing order in the countryside.

With the shift of the Alessandri government toward the Right, the most important reformist, middle-class party in Chile, the Radicals sought alliances with the Socialists and the Communists. At the urging of an agent of the Comintern, sent to Chile by the Soviets to influence the ideological orientation of the Chilean Communist party, the Chilean Communists adopted a popular front strategy. Comintern's new policy, enunciated in August 1935, told communist movements around the world that "the formation of a joint People's Front, providing for joint action with Social Democratic parties is a necessity. . . . Comrades, you will remember the ancient tale of the capture of Troy. The attacking army was unable to achieve victory until, with the aid of the Trojan Horse, it penetrated to the very heart of the enemy camp. We, revolutionary workers, should not be shy of using the same tactics."

In line with this new tactic Chilean Communists sought contacts with the ideologically divided Radical party, made efforts to reduce tension between themselves and the Socialists, and worked to form a united front against the Alessandri government. In December 1936, the Communists supported the formation of a unified national labor organization, the Confederación de Trabajadores de Chile (CTCH), headed by a Socialist secretary general, with a Communist serving as assistant secretary general. According to the agent sent by Moscow to Chile to direct the formation of the popular front movement, small favors and promises of support to selected leaders of the Radical party gradually created a nucleus of Radicals willing to include the Communists in a coalition aimed at capturing the presidency in 1938.

President Alessandri's hardening line toward the Left, his harsh repression of a railroad strike in 1936, and a growing willingness among leftist elements in the splintered Partido Demócrata, among Trotskyists, and other leftist fragments to oppose the government, produced a skeletal popular front executive committee in March 1936. Ideological diversity and the underlying distrust by Socialists and Radicals of the Communists dictated a mild declaration of objectives: restoration of democratic liberties, economic nationalism, socio-economic justice for the middle and working classes. Nevertheless, the alliance of organized labor with the popular front parties seriously threatened the political position of the Alessandri administration. One month later, by-elections for a vacant Senate seat from the provinces of Bío Bío, Malleco, and Cautín gave a surprising victory to the candidate of the Radical party.

Although the new senator was one of the wealthiest landowners in the region, national political analysts interpreted his victory as an initial indication of the viability of the popular front strategy. Despite continued reservations by more traditional leaders of the Radical party, including the party's eventual presidential candidate of 1938, Pedro Aguirre Cerda, most of the party's regional leaders sought to strengthen the popular front coalition. With upcoming congressional elections in March 1937, majority elements in the Radical party hoped through the popular front tactic to increase Radical influence. However, an intervening by-election in the northern provinces of Atacama and Coquimbo gave an unexpected victory to the Alessandrista candidate after a campaign that depicted the popular front as "a consortium organized by Moscow-bought Communists." Shortly thereafter, Radicals opposed to the popular front accepted ministerial posts in the Alessandri government.

The congressional elections of 1937 maintained rightist control in the legislature, though certain electoral trends encouraged supporters of the popular front. Both the Conservatives and the Liberals obtained higher vote totals than the Radicals, who again obtained approximately 19 percent of the ballots cast. The Communists polled only slightly more votes than the Chilean Nazi party. However, while the hold of the rightist parties over the rural districts combined with vote buying and coercion guaranteed their continued dominance in Congress, significant gains by the Socialist party helped persuade many Radicals to maintain the popular front for the up-coming presidential elections of 1938.

As the presidential election of 1938 approached, the Right chose as its standard bearer Alessandri's ex-treasury minister, Gustavo Ross Santa María. No doubts existed concerning Ross's ideological or po-

TABLE 14. ELECTIONS, CHAMBER OF DEPUTIES, 1937

Party	Deputies Elected	Votes	Percent of Total Vote
Conservador	35	87,845	21.3
Liberal	35	85,515	20.8
Demócrata	7	20,026	4.9
Agrario	3	9,721	2.3
Socialista	19	46,050	11.2
Radical	29	76,941	18.7
Nacista	3	14,564	3.5
Democrático	5	18,676	4.5
Independientes	3	17,040	4.0
Acción Rep.	2	9,802	2.3
Comunista	6	17,162	4.2
Sin representación	—	9,217	2.3
Totals	147	412,812	100.0

(Source: Germán Urzúa Valenzuela, Los Partidos Políticos Chilenos, Editorial Jurídica, Santiago, 1968, p. 81.)

litical orientation; he represented the interests of the propertied classes. He was reputed to have answered an appeal for legislation to benefit the middle class with "for me there are but two classes, upper and lower. To the first belong those who have gotten ahead in life; to the latter, those who, for whatever reason, have been failures." Ross's candidacy made clear the issues at stake in the 1938 election. An editorial in a leftist paper, *Claridad,* declared: "No one hates the people as he [Ross] does; no one is more likely to implement a 'strong' government, a government of hunger and the lash. . . . In choosing Ross, the Right has declared war on the Chilean masses. "Not unexpectedly Ross's supporters compared him to Portales; the candidate's campaign slogan "Order and work" supported the historical parallel.

Divisions within the popular-front parties appeared to preclude their choosing a single candidate to contest the election against Ross. The Radical party claimed the "best right" to select a popular-front candidate; Socialists asked the front to support Marmaduque Grove, one of the leaders of the short-lived "Socialist Republic" of 1932. In a convention arranged through tough bargaining, each party nominated its candidate: Radicals, Pedro Aguirre Cerda; Socialists, Marmaduque Grove; Communists, Elías Lafferte; Demócratas, Juan Pradenas Muñoz. Six ballots later the convention appeared deadlocked. The next days, April 16, 1938, the Demócratas shifted their support to the Radical candidate; and early on April 17 the Socialists withdrew Grove, and the convention unanimously nominated Pedro Aguirre Cerda. A leader of the Radical party's anti-popular-front faction, ex-minister of interior under Alessandri in the 1920s, wealthy landowner, experienced politician—Aguirre Cerda now found himself the presidential candidate of the antifascist, popular-front movement he had originally opposed. His reluctance to accept Communist support consoled the moderate elements of the Radical party who hoped that his victory would allow them to increase their share of congressional representation and would give them access to public employment.

A bitter, violent, shrill electoral contest gave the popular-front candidate a narrow victory. Only when key military leaders informed Ross that he could not count on their support in preventing Aguirre Cerda's inauguration did the rightist candidate concede victory. The distribution of votes in the election revealed the basic sources of rightist political and economic power, as well as the critical role that continuation by the supposedly leftist government of the repression of rural labor would play in maintaining "social peace" during the next ten years. The rightist candidate defeated Aguirre Cerda over-

TABLE 15. PRESIDENTIAL ELECTION, 1938

Province	Aguirre Cerda	Ross Santa María
Tarapacá	6,164	4,162
Antofagasta	11,339	4,984
Atacama	4,834	2,580
Coquimbo	10,748	7,874
Aconcagua	4,001	7,474
Valparaíso	22,667	19,105
Santiago	64,297	50,998
O'Higgins	7,091	11,095
Colchagua	2,542	9,789
Curicó	1,950	4,805
Talca	5,717	8,485
Maule	1,934	4,817
Linares	3,592	8,764
Nuble	7,813	13,853
Concepción	17,417	9,734
Arauco	2,481	2,318
Bío Bío	6,054	6,797
Malleco	5,978	7,929
Cautín	13,125	12,228
Valdivia	12,982	10,811
Llanquihue	2,854	5,784
Aisén	412	440
Chiloé	2,513	3,257
Magallanes	4,215	526
Total	222,720	218,609

(Source: Germán Urzúa Valenzuela, *Los partidos políticos Chilenos*, Editorial Jurídica, Santiago, 1968, p. 83.)

whelmingly throughout the agricultural heartland of the central valley. Importantly, however, Communist and Socialist agents in the countryside broke enough votes away from the landlords to reduce the Right's expected margin of victory in Talca from 10,000 votes to less than 3000 and to achieve victory in Cautín. In the major cities and mining districts the popular-front candidate emerged victorious with the support of middle- and working-class voters. Radical party and Demócrata votes in parts of the frontier provinces and the lake district provided a slim margin of victory for Aguirre Cerda or prevented a landslide for Ross. Significantly, the base of Radical power in the south consisted of landowners, industrialists, bureaucrats, and their clientele. Loss of these essentially conservative voters by the popular front, and others like them throughout the country, would have spelled defeat. To maintain their support the government would be forced to make important concessions in contradiction to its own populist rhetoric during the next three years.

Even more important, in the short run, the victory of Aguirre Cerda owed much to the unlikely last-minute support of Chilean Nazis and ex-dictator Carlos Ibáñez. In the 1938 presidential election Ibáñez again attempted to regain the presidency, railing against politicians and disorder. Supported by the Chilean Nazi party (*Movimiento Nacional Socialista de Chile*), Ibáñez never adopted Nazi rhetoric or uniform but could easily accept the Nazi vision of a strong state that ruled a disciplined people for the "common good." Among the Radicals and the Socialists, minority factions still remembered the Ibáñez presidency fondly. This meant that the popular-front candidate could lose enough votes to Ibáñez to permit the election of Ross.

Events leading up to the election produced an unlikely, indeed unique, alliance between the Nazis and the popular front. Disorders at the Congress when Alessandri read his last state of the union message were punctuated by shots fired toward the president by Nazi leader and deputy González von Marées. When the government applied an internal security law against the Nazis and other demonstrators, the Ibáñez forces and the leftists united in attacking Alessandri and the Ross candidacy. Meanwhile, Ibáñez attempted to secure popular-front support for his candidacy and the withdrawal of Aguirre Cerda.

Unable to undermine Aguirre Cerda's candidacy and equally unable to muster widespread popular support for the Ibáñez candidacy, the Nazis decided to overthrow the Alessandri government with a coup. Nazi plans called for occupation of key buildings in Santiago, support from sympathetic army units, and the assassination of both rightist politicians, including Alessandri and Ross, and leaders of the popular front. Facing imprisonment by September 8, 1938, on conviction for his role in the shooting incident in Congress, the Nazi leader set September 5 as the day for the coup. Nazi youths occupied the university and seized the Social Security building.

Now after six years of constitutional government, Alessandri faced still another threat to his overriding objective: institutionalizing the 1925 constitution and maintaining political order. He responded harshly, authorizing the use of artillery against the occupants of the university. Soon after, the Nazi youths in the Social Security building surrendered to *carabineros*—who opened fire with submachine guns and small arms. More than sixty Nazi bodies were later removed from the building. A week later Alessandri requested authority from Congress to impose a state of siege for the remainder of his term. Ibáñez, who apparently had not actively participated in the coup attempt, surrendered almost immediately to army units and was jailed.

A week later Congress authorized President Alessandri to impose a state of siege and newspaper censorship and to employ other "extraordinary powers" to maintain public order. Prevented from carrying on his campaign, and promised influence in a popular-front government by Aguirre Cerda, Ibáñez withdrew his candidacy two weeks before the election. From his jail cell González von Marées endorsed the candidate of the popular front. Thus a popular front proclaiming its antifascist inspiration received part of its margin of victory from supporters of ex-dictator Carlos Ibáñez and from Chile's Nazi party.

The heterogeneous electoral support that gave Aguirre Cerda the presidency, involved political contradictions incapable of resolution within the framework of formal democracy. Ibáñistas, Nazis, Communists, Socialists, and Radicals could not ultimately agree upon general policy or political methods.

President Aguirre Cerda faced several immediate crises shortly after assuming office. In January 1939 a disastrous earthquake in south-central Chile devastated Chillán, Concepción, and the neighboring provinces. Official reports counted over 50,000 deaths and many times that number of casualties. Aguirre Cerda reacted quickly, declaring martial law in the affected provinces and organizing relief efforts. International assistance from Europe, the United States, and neighboring countries permitted quick restoration of basic services and transport. A week later, taking advantage of the urgent need to provide for reconstruction, the president presented Congress with a six-year plan for national development and reconstruction.

The enormous amount of money Aguirre Cerda indicated would be necessary to carry out the popular-front program along with the costs of reconstruction after the earthquake frightened the rightist majority in Congress. Conservatives and Liberals recognized the need to provide for reconstruction, but the remainder of Aguirre Cerda's ambitious program for national development, including large sums for low-cost housing and stimulation of industrial development, portended accelerated inflation, higher taxes, and expansion of the state bureaucracy. Congressional rejection of the development program, despite support for a massive reconstruction appropriation, sent Aguirre Cerda on a speaking tour to the devastated provinces to rally popular support.

In an effort to achieve a compromise, the president's minister of finance, Roberto Wachholtz, devised a new package for Congress, which proposed two separate agencies—the Relief and Reconstruction Corporation to deal with the immediate problems occasioned by the earthquake, and the National Development Corporation (CORFO) to carry out the longer-term economic objectives. In addition, the new proposal called for heavy reliance upon foreign loans instead of internal financing of the development projects. To prevent the popular-front parties from using CORFO for political advantage, its board of directors would represent producer groups as well as government officials; a single representative of the Chilean Workers Confederation (CTCH) would be included to make known labor's views.

This new plan angered many of the government's leftist supporters, particularly Socialists, whom the President mollified with promises of more patronage. In March 1939, after overcoming the rightist opposition through pressure on selected congressmen from the devastated provinces, Aguirre Cerda won a narrow victory for his development and reconstruction legislation. After further jockeying between the president and Congress, Law 6334 went into effect in late April 1939. This victory for Aguirre Cerda and the popular front would provide the basis for greatly expanded state intervention in national development. It also subordinated Chilean economic policy to the main source of capital for CORFO—the United States Export-Import Bank (Exim Bank).

While Aguirre Cerda was fighting for approval of the reconstruction and development program, his popular-front allies, especially the Socialists and Communists, carried out a national campaign among urban and rural workers to mobilize support for the government. Labor conflicts, strikes, unionization efforts, and industrial violence created an atmosphere bordering on insurrection. For members of the President's own party, as well as for the Conservative-Liberal opposition, the most serious threat to maintenance of the fragile social order came from the massive wave of labor conflict and unionization in the countryside. An extension of the electoral campaign in the countryside directed by Communist functionaries, rural conflict and unionization in the first months of the popular front administration reached alarming levels. In 1939 the Labor Department officially registered 170 labor petitions from groups of rural laborers and *inquilinos*—compared to six the previous year. During the same period campesinos organized more than 200 agricultural unions.

The National Agricultural Society and local groups of landowners appealed directly to President Aguirre Cerda to halt rural unionization and labor conflict in agriculture. In the middle of March 1939 some of the country's most influential landowners informed the president that they confronted "the initial elements of a state of revolution . . . produced under the pretext of the right of rural workers to organize." In agreement with all the parties of the popular front and the CTCH, President Aguirre Cerda illegally ordered suspension of rural unionization, using the same administrative device employed by President Alessandri in 1933. Despite the supposedly "temporary" nature of this suspension, it remained in effect until 1946.

Taking advantage of the vulnerability of agricultural workers, and of the willingness of popular-front parties to trade the welfare of the campesinos for "social peace" and support of the government's reconstruction and development legislation, landowners carried out a purge of union leaders and evicted large numbers of "troublemakers" from their tenancies. By the time the CTCH and the Communist party had repudiated this sacrifice of the rural work force to political expediency, Aguirre Cerda's new minister of interior, Arturo Olavarría Bravo, had already devised his system of "judgment day," or *juicio final*, to deal with rural militancy. As described by Olavarría himself,

> . . . A group of carabineros [police] would arrive at a farm accompanied by a convoy of trucks. When the inquilinos were assembled in the area, the carabinero officer would order those who wished to continue the strike to stand on his left. The officer would then order that the strikers gather their families, cats, dogs, chickens, and belongings and get in the trucks to be evicted. . . . This tactic I converted into a system. General Oscar Reeves Leiva, Director General of Carabineros, called it *el juicio final*, as the good ones went to the right and the bad ones to the left, as it is hoped will occur one day in the valley of Jehosaphat. Of course, I did not have to use the *juicio final* many times. . . .

Only the Trotskyists rejected Aguirre Cerda's sacrifice of the rural work force. In particular, Emilio Zapata, the leader and organizer of Chile's first national peasant league, *Liga Nacional de Defensa de Campesinos Pobres* ("National Poor Peasants League"), protested the government's acquiescence to landowner demands. Zapata delivered an angry critique of the government in the Congress and gradually broke with the popular-front coalition. Recalling the situation of 1939, Zapata remarked in 1971:

What Aguirre Cerda had to do was tell the *patrones* that
they couldn't use lockouts or sabotage production, and that they
couldn't throw people off the land in political reprisal. . . .
Neither Aguirre Cerda nor his ministers were responsive. They
were walls without ears. . . . Although they possessed the legal
means to prevent it, they did nothing while the landowners
threw the campesinos "into the streets" for the crime of voting
for Aguirre Cerda or for joining *ligas* or unions.

Rural workers had no means to resist landowner reprisals. The popular-front government provided police to enforce court orders for evic-
tions, to break the newly formed unions, and to allow the landowners
to retain control of the countryside. This was the price Aguirre Cerda
was willing to pay to gain support for the rest of his program in Congress and to maintain "social peace." Socialists, Communists, and
the CTCH likewise agreed to the terms of the bargain. In exchange,
legislation outlawing the Communists was rejected, the industrialization program emerged from Congress, and the Socialists occupied
high-level administrative posts.

Aguirre Cerda's concession to the landowners did not end the
Right's campaign against the government. Neither did it prevent
Emilio Zapata's National Peasant League from carrying out its "First
National Congress of Chilean Peasants" in Santiago in April 1939.
Rejecting the popular front's policies, leaders of the Trotskyist-
oriented organization called for intensification of class struggle and
the end of the latifundia. Two months later the Communists sponsored a highly visible "First National Congress of Rural Unions,"
preceding the National Congress of the CTCH. In the meantime
(late April) Socialist leaders called for a purge of the bureaucracy of
all "traitors," so that the public administration could be put completely at the service of the masses.

Tensions increased as rumors circulated that Socialist leader Marmaduque Grove had prepared a May Day speech calling for dissolution of Congress, recognition of the Socialist militia as an official
arm of the government, and other revolutionary measures. The rightist press, in a fashion remarkably similar to the campaign that would
later precede the military coup of September 1973, emphasized the
precarious nature of Chilean democracy, the growing Communist
threat, and alluded to the military role in preventing leftist extrem-
ists from destroying constitutional government. Aguirre Cerda responded by applying the internal security law against a leading
rightist paper, *El Diario Illustrado*, thereby preventing the paper's

circulation outside of Santiago. Congress, in turn, censured the minister of the interior for violating freedom of the press in the *El Diario Illustrado* case.

In the annual military parade honoring Arturo Prat, Chile's naval hero of the War of the Pacific, the Right found its military sympathizer when, according to the rightist press, General Ariosto Herrera Ramírez jumped from his horse to order removal of a Communist banner from a balcony of the presidential palace. In early July *El Diario Ilustrado* published a supposedly confidential circular detailing plans by the Socialists for an internal coup, or *autogolpe*, including provisions for formation of a red army, elimination of opposition politicians, and infiltration of the armed forces. (Again, we have a striking parallel with the "white paper" and the so-called plan zeta denounced by the Chilean Right and the military in 1973.)

In turn, the government announced discovery of a plot to oust the President. The rightist press made light of the government's claims, but investigations led Aguirre Cerda to request General Ariosto Herrera to resign. Herrera refused, and his military colleagues elected him president of the Club Militar in August 1939. Emerging as a hero of the Right, Herrera also supported the officers punished by the government for their supposed participation in the plot of early July. Ignoring orders from the minister of defense, he overtly insulted Aguirre Cerda with a decision to reinstate the officers in question. Thereupon the government relieved him of his command and asked him to resign his commission. On August 25, 1939, instigated by comrades of the second division he commanded and by the rightist press, General Herrera led an abortive coup attempt, in which the ever present hand of Carlos Ibáñez again was apparent. With the movement's quick collapse, Ibáñez sought asylum in the Paraguayan embassy.

The abortive coup passed the initiative back to the popular-front government. Congress allotted the president state-of-siege authority for a period of twenty days, during which time Aguirre Cerda purged the military of conspiratorial officers. Now, however, the latent divisions within the popular front itself surfaced with vengeance. Competition between Socialists and Communists to gain control of student movements and the CTCH exacerbated the traditional hostility between the country's two major Marxist parties. Internal divisions within the Socialist party, between those favoring the moderate policies of Aguirre Cerda and the more militant *inconformistas* and ex-Trotskyists, led to a party split and formation of the Socialist Workers party (PST) in 1941. Aguirre Cerda's own party remained divided between the would-be populists and the more conservative advocates of middle-class-oriented reform.

By the end of 1939 Congress passed only two major pieces of legislation, including the reconstruction-CORFO package; by early 1940 Aguirre Cerda reorganized the cabinet, relying upon wealthy, respected, personally loyal appointees rather than designees of the popular-front parties. In July 1940 the president publicly announced that labor conflicts in the countryside could not be tolerated, because they diminished agricultural production. A month later the minister of the interior instructed the *carabineros* to repress the activity of "professional agitators who provoke problems in the countryside and industrial centers." The president's effort to conciliate the rightist parties coincided with mounting conflict between Socialists and Communists, as well as with the internal split in the Socialist party. Communist attacks upon the Socialist minister of development, who negotiated for loans in the United States, drastically increased the level of conflict and precipitated a rupture in the coalition.

In January 1941, Socialists demanded the ouster of the Communists from the popular front; refusal by the popular-front executive committee to expel the Communists led to Socialist withdrawal. The CTCH, divided between Communists and Socialists, also voted by a narrow margin to leave the popular-front government. Finally, after an impressive victory of popular-front parties and Socialists in the congressional elections of 1941, the president's own Radical party withdrew its support from him when he refused to accept party dictates in regard to ministerial appointments and patronage. To embarrass the president, his party colleagues now opposed legislation that he sent to the Congress. This opposition destroyed Aguirre Cerda's power, and he died, a broken man, in late 1941. In his own words, "the Chilean working classes were just as poor . . . and just as miserable as when I became President."

Two Radical presidents and one interim president followed Aguirre Cerda. Juan Antonio Ríos, who had been a critic of Aguirre Cerda's cooperation with the Communists, served from 1942 to 1946, when he, too, died in office. Ríos renewed Radical contacts with Conservatives and some Liberals as the Right recognized the benefits of state support for *private* industrial enterprise. They also appreciated Ríos' anticommunist position and his decision to sustain the administrative order against rural unionization. Rapprochement between moderate Radical party factions and the Right coincided with a growing middle-class conservatism; at the same time the Radicals were trying to reconcile their own internal cleavages with the shifting trends in national politics. Positioned in the center of the political spectrum, the Radicals opportunistically entered in alliances with the Left or the Right, as expediency required, in order to retain their hold on the presidency and the patronage of a growing bureaucracy.

A new, most unlikely, coalition of Radicals, Communists, and Liberals brought Radical leader Gabriel González Videla to office in 1946. The policies of industrialization through CORFO loans to private investors and heavy borrowing from the Exim Bank continued. Shortly after González Videla assumed office, the Communist party unleashed a campaign of labor conflict and strikes even more extensive than the movement of the first years of Aguirre Cerda's presidency. During the 1946-47 harvest, rural workers engaged in more than 650 labor conflicts and formed more than 300 agricultural unions. Again, organization of rural labor threatened to destroy the underlying trade-off reconciling the socio-economic consequences of urbanization and industrialization and the political power of the landowners.

Fulfilling a campaign promise, González Videla rescinded the order issued by Aguirre Cerda in 1939 to restrict rural unionization. Quickly, however, the new president also fulfilled a bargain made with his rightist supporters in the Liberal party, and supported new legislation (Law 8811) that made agricultural unionization practically impossible. In contrast to the Labor Code regulating the majority of Chilean workers, the new law outlawed agricultural strikes and severely limited the rights of rural workers to present labor petitions and to engage in collective bargaining. Now, instead of an illegal administrative order, congressional legislation sanctified the arrangement whereby rural labor bore a disproportionate share of the costs of Chilean industrialization and continued to serve as "voting cattle" for the owners of the large rural estates. This legislation remained in effect until 1967.

In contrast to their performance in 1939, Communist leaders in 1946 and 1947 persisted in their unionization efforts and in their leadership of industrial conflicts despite the opposition of the president. From their ministerial positions in González Videla's government, the Communists refused to acquiesce in the renewed repression of rural labor. They carried the struggle to the mines and the cities, and thus incited fierce rightist opposition while also alienating themselves from the president. As landowners and industrialists called for cooperation with the president, to "extirpate the Communist menace," Congress first extended González Videla's extraordinary powers to deal with subversion (Law 8837) and followed, in 1948, with the so-called Law for the Permanent Defense of Democracy (Law 8987). This legislation outlawed the Communist party, excluded its members from participation in the labor movement, and set up zones of banishment or "relegation" for subversives. This temporary elimination of the Communists from overt political activity and a "cleansing" of the labor movement restored political stability. It also reflected the integral relationship between the Cold War, American foreign policy, and Chilean domestic development.

American investment in Chile during the 1930s increased, as did Chilean awareness of the significant impact of foreign control over the copper and nitrates that provided most of the country's foreign exchange. Leftist political movements sought continually to undermine the position of United States firms, attacking the exploitation of Chilean resources by international monopolies and imperialism—already, by then, a synonym for the United States. The advent of a popular-front government with Marxist participation presented American interests with a delicate situation. To finance development projects the Chilean government needed resources; higher taxes on the copper industry appeared the most likely source of such capital. Further, the initial outline of the CORFO project, whether under Marxist or nationalist direction, threatened to expand significantly the state sector of the economy, to the detriment or even the elimination of American investments in oil, public utilities, mining, and basic industry.

The political compromise that had allowed the popular-front government to create CORFO shifted emphasis from internal to external financing for economic modernization and industrialization. Rather than greatly increased taxes on wealth and income in Chile, or taxes on the copper firms which would discourage further investment, moderate Radicals and industrial leaders opted for loans, credits, and foreign private investment as the source of risk capital. United States diplomats in Santiago and Washington, D.C., saw that it was possible to protect American interests through a careful lending policy and, at the same time, to support the anti-Marxist elements of the popular-front coalition; they developed a highly successful cooperative strategy for dealing with Aguirre Cerda's government. Despite Chile's hesitance to declare war against the Axis powers, the initial success of the policy American interests had elaborated gradually subordinated both Chilean economic policy and domestic political events to American needs during the Second World War and, in the aftermath, the Cold War.

Recognizing American credit policy's potential for influencing the popular front government, an embassy official made the following assessment of the alternatives open to United States policymakers:

> If we negotiate with Wachholtz [the moderate, Radical minister of finance in the first Aguirre Cerda cabinet] . . . . we will strengthen the moderate elements in the popular front here; whereas if we deferred the negotiations in the expectation that the dissensions in the popular front here would come to a head we would be taking a long chance.

By the end of 1940 the United States Export-Import Bank had arranged credits totaling $17 million for CORFO—to be used exclusively to pay for materials, machinery, technical assistance, or consultants from the United States. During the next eight years Exim Bank and other American-dominated financial institutions continued to bankroll CORFO's large-scale investment program in housing, industry, agriculture, and commerce. Whereas CORFO's policies directly threatened the position of selected American firms, its overall effect was to greatly expand the market for imports of United States capital goods, in addition to placing Chilean policymakers in a vulnerable position vis-à-vis decisions made in Washington, D.C.

World War II raised international prices for copper. Practically all of Chile's copper, however, was marketed through subsidiaries of United States copper firms established in Chile—for whom the Allied governments fixed a ceiling price upon copper products during the course of the war. Different Chilean sources estimate that the loss Chile sustained by its "contribution" to the Allied war effort was between $100 million and $500 million. Further, Chilean dollar reserves accumulated from exports to the United States during the war were unfrozen at a time when postwar inflation substantially reduced their purchasing power. Moreover, in the United States recession of 1949-50 production by American copper firms in Chile was reduced after four years of deterioration in the terms of trade. When the outbreak of the Korean War quickly snapped the United States out of the recession, the American government and the copper companies reimposed price controls on copper.

American control of Chile's principal economic resources accompanied intensified involvement in Chilean politics. Cold War intrigue made post-World War II Chilean politics a confrontation zone for "Communism" and the "Free World." American policy-makers considered the presence of Communist ministers in the González Videla government to be dangerous, and so allied with the Chilean Right in an active campaign to weaken, then destroy, Marxist political parties and the labor movement. Simultaneously the United States provided financial support for Socialist factions of the CTCH which opposed the rapidly increasing Communist influence. The United States gave badly needed financial assistance to the Chilean government on the condition that the Communist menace be eliminated. A split in the labor movement and the breakup of the CTCH were preliminary successes; a mounting anticommunist campaign by the rightist press and eventually by the González Videla government further heartened American diplomats and business interests.

Doubt still remained that González Videla would totally break his alliance with the Communists. Communist control of the labor movement, especially in copper and the coal mines, made any frontal offensive quite risky. Communist-inspired mobilization of rural labor and hundreds of agricultural labor conflicts in the 1946-47 harvest threatened the very foundation of the political arrangement elaborated by Aguirre Cerda and his Radical successors. Labor conflict in the northern provinces and a crippling coal strike panicked the Radical administration. In the meantime a representative of the Chilean government sought further economic assistance from the Exim Bank and the International Bank to bolster the Chilean economy. For, despite increased copper production, the declining terms of trade between Chile and the industrial nations significantly reduced the nation's import capabilities, even as the industrialization process necessitated greater quantities of capital goods, high technology, and raw materials.

Chile's suspension of foreign debt payments after the earthquake of 1939, complaints by American businessmen that Chile's request for loans to finance hydroelectric development threatened American private interests, and rumors of nationalization of American oil and power companies, all delayed approval of the requests for new assistance. Despite the secret assurances by González Videla's special emissary to the State Department that the Chilean president did not favor communism and would oppose Argentine President Juan Perón's efforts to undermine American influence in the southern cone, no quick commitment on financial assistance was forthcoming. To the contrary, the State Department officials involved in the negotiations made clear the department's concern that Chile "adjust its

TABLE 16. NET TERMS-OF-TRADE RELATIONS: PRICE INDEX FOR CHILE
(1938 = 100)

	Exports	Imports	Terms of Trade
1936	100.5	88.5	113.6
1937	129.7	96.9	133.8
1938	100.0	100.0	100.0
1939	107.5	94.7	113.5
1940	105.4	104.2	101.2
1941	109.2	113.1	96.6
1942	118.4	150.1	78.9
1943	120.9	168.7	71.7
1944	125.6	179.6	69.9
1945	129.7	183.2	70.8
1946	151.1	200.6	75.3
1947	201.1	245.4	81.9
1948	221.1	250.8	88.2
1949	220.3	246.1	89.5
1950	222.1	237.0	93.7
1951	279.4	276.9	100.9

(Source: Theodore H. Moran, *Multinational Corporations and the Politics of Dependence, Copper in Chile*, Princeton University Press, 1974, p. 71.)

debt situation" and improve the tax situation of the American copper companies.

Disappointed by the results of the economic mission to the United States, González Videla reportedly threatened the American ambassador with a deterioration in Chilean-American relations. In response, Ambassador Claude Bowers cabled a confidential message to the secretary of state, noting that "Chile is [a] key country in the struggle against Communism, and I feel that we should make every effort to overcome present impasse." As the Communist campaign of labor agitation mounted, so also did American concern with Chile as a Cold War battleground. Accounts of the rising Communist menace dominated correspondence from the American embassy in Santiago to Washington, D.C., from May 1947 on.

Anticipating a showdown with his ex-political allies, President González Videla requested an emergency shipment of coal from the United States in case of Communist shutdowns of the coal mines. Ambassador Bowers recommended to the secretary of state, "I suggest situation set forth above [reference to a general strike scheduled for late June 1947] be taken into consideration in connection with Chile's request for coal stockpile in its struggle to combat Communism." In September 1947, Bowers reported to Washington that González Videla was gradually eliminating Communists from the administration, and on October 6, 1947, the ambassador cabled that "González Videla declared war on Communism as a result of what he claims is a Communist plot to overthrow the Government and obtain control of the production (in order to deprive the United States of the use in an emergency) of strategic raw materials, namely copper and nitrates." Despite heavy commitments to Europe and other Latin American nations, the United States assured the Chilean president that emergency coal shipments would be available. Three days later Ambassador Bowers cabled: "Our war with Communists is on two fronts, Europe and South America." After another four days had passed, the ambassador added: "The issue is clear as crystal—Communism or democracy."

With American assurances of coal shipments to break the coal miners' strike, the government moved in police and military units to restore order and terminate the labor conflict. Subsequently Chile broke off diplomatic relations with the Soviet Union, Yugoslavia, and Czechoslovakia, nations that the Chilean president accused of engineering political chaos through their domestic agents, the Chilean Communist party. The Law for the Permanent Defense of Democracy, passed in 1948, outlawed the Communist party, eliminated almost 30,000 voters from the electoral registers, provided authority to purge the labor movement, and allowed the president to restore "democracy" to Chile. Implementation of Law 8811 on agricultural unionization, along with the Law for the Permanent Defense of Democracy, destroyed the impressive network of rural labor unions created from 1946 to 1947 and ended the threat to the hegemony of the political Right in the countryside. Thus the "arrangement" initiated by Alessendri and elaborated by the popular-front government could remain intact.

Appropriately, González Videla called upon Jorge Alessandri, the ex-president's son, to act as his finance minister. Anaconda announced plans for an additional $130 million investment in their copper properties at Chuquicamata. And despite the effects of the United States recession on a worsening Chilean economy, Exim Bank and the international lending agencies agreed to provide substantial economic assistance to the Chilean government. In the next four years Exim Bank not only financed the creation or expansion of a large number of Chilean industries, it also ensured, through its lending policies, that American machinery, technology, and patent holders participated in the process of industrialization. Exim Bank loans required the exclusive use of United States purchased capital goods for the Chilean industries receiving Bank credits and even that American carriers ship the goods to Chile. Further, whereas the Chilean government guaranteed the loans and even provided much of the capital, Exim Bank demanded that only private investors hold a majority of the industries' voting stock.

American influence in the development policies of the Chilean government benefited Chilean private investors as well as United States interests. Credit to agricultural and industrial interests from CORFO often entailed negative real interest rates; that is, inflation more than counterbalanced the interest rates, making credit a subsidy to debtors. Externally financed economic modernization was oriented toward importing capital goods for industry and labor-saving farm machinery and thereby strengthened the position of employers, especially in agriculture, vis-à-vis the labor force. Moreover, private investors achieved a dominant voice in the three major industrial complexes originating from CORFO initiative—the Pacific Steel Corporation (CAP), the National Petroleum Corporation (ENAP), and the National Electric Corporation (ENDESA). Key stockholders included Kennecott Copper Corporation and influential members of the National Society of Manufacturers. Even enterprises in which CORFO had a majority interest acted more like private firms than public enterprises, since entrepreneurs and bankers on the various government policymaking agencies assured a favorable attitude toward private business.

The growing economic, political, and cultural influence of the United States in Chile in the early post-World War II years did not eliminate certain basic contradictions between Chilean national interest and the interests of American companies or foreign policies dictated by the Cold War. Among some Chilean leaders and businessmen there developed a conscious awareness of the disadvantages of subordinating Chilean copper policy, industrialization, and domestic politics to changes in United States policy. Efforts to establish particular industries through CORFO brought Chilean officials and industrialists into direct conflict with U.S. corporations. Economic assistance conditioned with requirements to buy higher-priced American products or to ship in costlier United States carriers provided obvious examples of differences in American and Chilean national interests. Most of all, the disparity between what copper exports might bring the nation and what they actually provided in foreign exchange led groups on both the Right and the Left to resent, if not attack openly, the American copper firms.

Notwithstanding increased taxation of the copper industry in the early 1950s, pressures to exact greater benefits for Chile from the country's most valuable natural resource increased gradually in that decade and resulted, in the 1960s, in policies to nationalize the major United States copper companies. The Chilean Right gratefully accepted American support for an anticommunist campaign, credits for industrialization, cooperation in infiltrating the Chilean labor movement with "responsible" unionists, and educational exchanges, but they remained in their own way Chilean nationalists. This nationalism and their anger with American support for *agrarian reform* would ally them in the 1960s and early 1970s with middle-class and leftist political parties in efforts to eliminate American control over Chilean copper.

During three Radical administrations (1938-52), the combination of deficit-financing of industrialization, real salary gains for middle-class groups without proportional increases in internal taxation or government revenues, and the stagnation of agriculture heightened inflationary pressures. Despite government promises of progressive income redistribution and better educational opportunities, most urban workers along with the rural labor force actually lost ground in real income from 1938 to 1952, and more than one-third of the school-age children did not attend school. Worse, rather than gaining the "economic independence" promised by González Videla, the country had become increasingly dependent upon private foreign capital, loans, and marketing decisions made by the United States copper firms. Most strikingly, it had become more dependent upon imports of *food*. Domestic agricultural production did not keep pace with population growth and fell even further behind a rate of urbanization more than double that of population increase. Poor performance by agriculture necessitated a growing quantity of foreign exchange to feed Chile's people. It also meant further inflationary pressure added to currency emissions, deficit financing, and growth of the government bureaucracy.

Inflation meant frustration for the salaried middle classes and government employees even when periodic upward wage adjustments somewhat ameliorated the full impact of the price increases that caused suffering for most blue-collar workers and the rural labor force. By the 1952 presidential elections, with renewed labor agitation and González Videla's vacillating application of anticommunist and internal security legislation, Chile had a highly fragmented, weary, and frustrated electorate. Carlos Ibáñez took advantage of the population's exasperation with party politics and again emerged as an authoritarian, "above politics," antiparty candidate for president. Supported by a heterogeneous coalition of Socialists, middle-class groups, dissident Radicals and Conservatives, and the ascendant Agrarian Labor party (*Partido Agrario Laborista*), and also by a newly organized "Feminist Party," in the first presidential election after extension of suffrage to women in national elections in Chile, Ibàñez swept into office with a broom as a symbol of his intensions to "clean house." Promising electoral reforms, an end to corruption, and eventual elimination of the anticommunist legislation, the ex-dictator overwhelmingly defeated the divided opposition.

As in the 1927-31 period, Carlos Ibáñez' lack of commitment to formal democracy or to the Chilean party system made his second administration highly personalistic, authoritarian, repressive—and in some ways quite innovative. As in his earlier administration (1927-31), Ibáñez sought to utilize the state apparatus to encourage industrialization and to stimulate national development. Creation of the Banco Central, through consolidation of existing credit institutions, and support for public enterprise and semi-autonomous entities in various sectors of the economy, such as IANSA (sugar), CAP (steel), ENDESA (energy), and ENAP (petroleum), reaffirmed Ibáñez' activist, technocratic vision of the state. Loyal to neither party nor ideology, Ibáñez filled government posts with upwardly mobile politicians from splinter parties or ethnic minorities, such as Arab-Chileans. Indifferent to the long-term strength of the traditional parties, the president cooperated with the Falange (later Christian Democrat) deputy, Jorge Rogers Sotomayor, in adopting a far-reaching electoral reform (1958) that would drastically curtail the power of the landlords in Chilean politics. Further, after using Law 8811 and the anti-communist legislation to repress agricultural unionism and the urban labor movement throughout his term of office, Ibáñez fulfilled his campaign promise to eliminate the Law for the Permanent Defense of Democracy prior to leaving office. This paved the way for consolidation of a new electoral coalition between Socialists and Communists, the Popular Action Front (FRAP), which almost captured the presidency in the 1958 elections.

The electoral reform of 1958 introduced an Australian ballot (a single official ballot) and increased penalties for electoral fraud and bribery. A public ballot meant that landowners could no longer effectively control the votes of rural workers through distribution of party ballots and monitoring of the polls to assure that workers voted "correctly." In addition, the new election law made voting compul-

TABLE 17. PRESIDENTIAL ELECTION, 1952

Candidate	Vote Totals
Carlos Ibáñez	446,439
Arturo Matte (Liberals & Conservatives)	297,357
Pedro E. Alfonso (Radicals & Falange)	190,360
Salvador Allende (Socialists & Communists)	51,975
Total	954,131

sory and provided for jail terms or fines for nonvoters. This inducement to electoral participation combined with the official secret ballot ended the hegemony of the landowners in the rural districts. It also meant that the cornerstone of Chilean political stability, the hacienda system, would come under mounting pressure from 1958 on as the availability of rural votes sent Marxists, Christian Democrats, Radicals, and other smaller political parties into the countryside in search of rural votes.

If the eventual political consequences of the Ibáñez administration proved beneficial to rural workers and eroded the power of the Right, the immediate results of the administration's political and economic policies gravely affected the urban and rural poor throughout the nation. The end of the Korean War, and with it the plunging demand for Chilean copper, reduced Chile's import capabilities by almost 30 percent in 1953. At the same time, the country approached the limits of easy import-substitution industrialization. Investment as well as growth in economic output declined. In turn, government revenues decreased, but a system of automatic readjustment of salaries in response to inflation inhibited cutbacks in government expenditures. Stagflation that brought the annual inflation rate (86% in 1956) to the highest levels in Chilean history (before 1970-73) and international pressure on the government concerning debt payments moved the government to call in an American economic mission to design a program of stabilization. Hoping that the good relations between the Klein-Saks Mission and the International Monetary Fund would reopen international lines of support for the Chilean economy, the Ibáñez government attempted to implement the mission's recommendations.

The Klein-Saks recommendations conformed closely to what now is considered conventional, hard-line, antiflationary policies favored by the International Monetary Fund: elimination of "excess demand" through wage controls, restrictions on credit, cutbacks on government expenditures, elimination of subsidies by public services such as water and transport, reduced currency emissions, replacement of multiple exchange rates for a single "floating" rate, and removal of price controls except for "essential commodities." This program entailed suspension of automatic wage readjustments and efforts to ensure that wage increases did not exceed the rate of inflation. In addition, the administration adopted a generally favorable attitude toward development through incentives to private domestic investors and the American copper companies. So-called New Deal, or *nuevo trato*, legislation (1955), intended to attract further investment through "profit stimulus," reduced effective tax rates on Anaconda and Kennecott, as well as providing the companies with a number of commercial, accounting, and exchange control benefits.

The Copper Department created as part of this legislation eventually gave the Chilean government much-needed technical capabilities to monitor the copper industry; but the immediate effect of the *nuevo trato* was higher profits for Anaconda and Kennecott without the desired further investments by the companies in Chile. Worse still, from the Chilean perspective, Chile's share of the world market barely remained stable and the percentage of copper refined in Chile by the companies actually declined from a high of 89 percent in 1951 to merely 45 percent in 1958. In practice, the copper companies profited and private businesses adjusted to the inflationary situation, while salaried and wage-earning Chileans bore the brunt of the government's program. The administration imposed readjustments in remuneration substantially below the rate of inflation to "depress demand." Workers and salaried employees consequently found themselves with less money to spend on food, clothing, and shelter. To carry through on the program, the Ibáñez government was forced to deal harshly with the resultant labor agitation (1955-57) and rioting in Santiago (1957); among other measures labor leaders and "communists" were confined in detention camps under the terms of the Law for the Permanent Defense of Democracy.

Inflation rates declined; so did the standard of living of the majority of Chileans. When restrictions on credit and subsidies to industrialists and landowners also angered the groups who, with the middle classes, had helped bring Ibáñez to power, the government lost the base of support it had briefly captured in the years from 1952 to 1955. As the 1958 presidential elections approached, unification of the leftist parties and total rejection of Ibáñez' policies by the mass

TABLE 18. PRESIDENTIAL ELECTION, 1958

Province	J. Alessandri (supported by Liberals and Conservatives)	Bossay (Radical)	Zamorano ("leftist" priest)	Allende (FRAP)	Frei (Christian Democrat)
Tarapacá	3,558	3,859	529	8,299	4,922
Antofagasta	5,670	5,866	1,083	14,954	6,567
Atacama	2,533	5,423	247	6,167	3,621
Coquimbo	10,460	8,886	1,280	14,283	7,952
Aconcagua	10,018	4,233	1,530	7,290	5,953
Valparaíso	35,680	17,192	5,727	26,611	29,913
Santiago	151,797	51,984	11,194	121,452	91,305
O'Higgins	16,753	4,517	2,175	14,537	8,426
Colchagua	13,556	3,435	477	6,190	4,379
Curicó	6,509	2,458	704	6,067	3,107
Talca	9,763	4,163	7,206	8,584	6,377
Maule	5,823	4,551	830	2,749	3,375
Linares	10,674	4,044	4,156	7,927	5,912
Ñuble	11,988	11,164	811	10,947	11,290
Concepción	17,418	13,091	624	34,594	18,154
Arauco	1,932	3,125	61	6,258	1,616
Bío Bío	7,660	4,670	200	7,360	3,611
Malleco	10,133	5,592	187	7,485	4,951
Cautín	21,228	8,979	920	11,921	12,587
Valdivia	12,387	6,791	637	11,559	7,545
Osorno	8,318	5,524	156	5,542	2,770
Llanquihue	7,430	4,304	219	4,056	6,075
Chiloé	6,146	4,621	157	3,689	1,559
Aisén	1,229	1,027	44	1,261	953
Magallanes	1,285	2,791	151	6,708	2,857
Total	389,948	192,110	41,305	356,499	255,777

of the Chilean electorate set the stage for another close contest in which the Socialist-Communist candidate, Salvador Allende, fell just short of victory.

The presidential elections of 1958 brought to office Jorge Alessandri, son of ex-President Arturo Alessandri and an experienced conservative economic minister. Having won the presidency with a scant plurality over Salvador Allende, Alessandri could not count upon a docile Congress or even the temporary popular base achieved by Ibáñez in 1952. A year after he took office, the Cuban Revolution injected a whole new concern into Chilean politics and American foreign policy. In an effort to counteract the appeal of the Cuban

Revolution throughout the rest of Latin America, the United States proposed the Alliance for Progress, which included commitment to agrarian reform—the single policy most bitterly resisted by the Chilean Right during the previous thirty years. Although Alessandri attempted to maintain the essential administrative and legislative impediments to agricultural unionism and rural labor conflict, he found himself under rapidly mounting pressure from Marxist and Christian Democratic political organization among the rural labor force.

The electoral successes of the FRAP coalition in the countryside in the 1958 presidential election and the disappearance of the Law for the Permanent Defense for Democracy renewed interest among Socialists and Communists in political mobilization of rural workers. In addition, the growing strength of the Christian Democratic party in the early 1960s sent groups of Catholic organizers to rural areas to compete with the Marxists. Penetration of Marxist parties and Christian Democrats into the countryside, combined with the electoral reform of 1958, produced a fundamental alteration in Chilean politics in the 1961 congressional elections. For the first time in the twentieth century the Conservatives and the Liberals failed to gain one-third of the seats in Congress. FRAP obtained more votes than any other single party list and controlled 27.5 percent (40) of the seats in the Chamber of Deputies and elected thirteen senators (of a total of 45). The Christian Democrats, originally a small group that had broken away from the Conservative party in the late 1930s, for the first time polled more votes than the Conservatives.

The outcome of the 1961 congressional elections left the incumbent Alessandri administration dependent upon the Radical party. The Radicals, hoping to win back the presidency in 1964, demanded ministerial participation in exchange for support of the government in the legislature. In addition, the Radicals now became advocates of "land reform." United States diplomats also put pressure on the Alessandri government to adopt a land reform program as part of the Alliance for Progress.

Alessandri, a firm believer in the benefits of private enterprise and diminishing government "interference" in the economy, opposed the reformist elements that demanded sweeping social and economic changes in Chilean life. However, loss of congressional influence by Conservatives and Liberals, along with pressures from the Alliance for Progress and mounting Marxist/Christian Democratic political activity, forced certain changes upon the administration. In defense of their political base in the countryside, Conservatives and Liberals attacked the Alliance for Progress and argued that increased Chilean

TABLE 19. SUMMARY OVERVIEW OF LANDOWNER-GOVERNMENT RESPONSE TO RURAL LABOR ACTIVISM IN CHILE, 1932-57

Presidential Election	Landowner Reaction	Government Responses	Landowner Follow-up
1932-33			
Presidential election (1932). First legally organized rural unions formed in Chile; several rural labor conflicts.	Pressure from SNA and other landowner associations on President Alessandri, claiming unionization in countryside not legal.	Circular 4060-4061 "temporarily" suspends rural unionization; remains in effect until 1937-38.	Workers involved in first legal unions around Molina (Talca Province) dismissed and evicted; workers presenting labor petitions (1934-35) arrested, dismissed, evicted.
1938-39			
Popular-front candidate Pedro Aguirre Cerda elected. First large wave of rural unionization, labor conflicts.	Landowner associations publish numerous editorials railing against communist agitation; send letters to Pedro Aguirre Cerda. (Example: Landowners of Pirque claim: "Professional agitators have created discontent among workers and are forming unions, inciting social indiscipline. We have initial stages of a State of Revolution. Request that the government suspend for now all procedures leading to rural unionization.")	Ministerial Order 34* "temporarily suspends" rural unionization; remains in effect until 1946. * Clearly illegal, unconstitutional.	*Intendente of Curicó:* "Due to labor petitions presented by agricultural workers, the majority of affected landowners in this province are dismissing workers who participated. Workers whose families have lived on these farms for generations being forced to leave." *Intendente of Linares:* "Landowners have organized movement to evict on a massive scale rural workers from farms in this region."

1946–47			
Gabriel González Videla elected President with Communist support. Communists occupy ministries; massive wave of rural (and urban-mining) labor conflicts, strikes, unionization.	Numerous editorials in SNA journal, *El Campesino*, denouncing agitations in the country. (Examples: November, December, 1946; March, 1947). Move in Congress to pass "special law" to regulate rural labor—with support of Gabriel González Videla.	Law 8811 (1947) restricts rural labor conflicts; outlaws strikes in agriculture; makes rural unionization almost impossible. Law 8987 (Law for the Permanent Defense of Democracy) outlaws Communists; "cleanses" labor movement—destroying most rural labor organizations.	Labor Department receives communications from all over the country reporting massive dismissals and evictions of rural workers—especially those active in labor conflicts or labor leaders.
1952–53			
Carlos Ibáñez elected President with support of Socialists; campesino strike at Molina; march on Santiago; isolated conflicts elsewhere.	Calls for government intervention; application of Law 8987.	Application of Law 8987 against leaders of Molina strike; eventual negotiated settlement.	Dismissal of labor leaders in Molina farms—but during 1953-57 conflicts continue, in gradually reduced number.

participation in the profits of the copper industry would do far more for the country than land reforms, tax reforms, or other redistributionist measures sponsored by the Alliance. In language that would become more familiar after the military coup of 1973, one Conservative senator cautioned that the potential for demagoguery in the Alliance for Progress threatened the basic values of the "Western and Christian world."

Attacked by both the Left and the Right, the American copper companies felt the impact of the first tentative measures that ultimately resulted in nationalization. Taxes on the industry increased by 10 to 15 percent, and a Conservative minister proposed a plan whereby the companies would be forced to raise production considerably as well as to increase drastically (to 90 percent) the amount of copper refined in Chile. Although this plan was blocked through cabinet reshuffles and negotiations between the companies and Alessandri, the political position of both the American copper companies and the Chilean landowners seemed ever less tenable.

The growing need to import food, inflation, and a mounting press campaign by leftist and reformist newspapers and intellectuals isolated the landowners politically and identified them in the public mind as the group largely responsible for Chile's social and economic backwardness. Intensified organizational activity by Marxists and Christian Democrats in the countryside reminded landowners of the labor crises and union struggles of 1939-41 and 1946-47. Once again editorials appeared in the major SNA publication warning of the threat of communism and anarchy if rural workers were allowed to unionize. Now, however, landowners lacked the political strength in Congress and the urban alliances necessary to prevent the first step toward transformation of the Chilean countryside.

In 1962, the year after the Right lost its veto power in Congress, and under pressure from Alliance for Progress officials who controlled the American "foreign aid" program, Chile adopted an agrarian reform law that began a decade-long assault upon the hacienda system. Law 15020 created three government agencies to administer programs of land reform, agricultural extension, and agricultural planning. Though under the Alessandri administration the government failed to carry out extensive agrarian reform, the legislation did provide a legal basis for more extensive transfers of land from large estates to small holders. In addition, two of the new government agencies— the Agrarian Reform Corporation (CORA) and the Institute for Agrarian and Livestock Development (INDAP)—would later play a revolutionary role in transforming Chilean agriculture and Chilean politics. In the short run (1962-64), the Alessandri government carried out what many Chileans called a "flower pot reform" (*reforma de macetero*), converting 60,000 hectares of public lands and well-recompensed private estates into small and medium-size farms.

By the end of the Alessandri administration a three-way battle was shaping up for the 1964 presidential election. FRAP again supported the candidacy of Salvador Allende. The Christian Democrats, who obtained extensive financing from covert American sources, offered Eduardo Frei. The Right (*Frente Democrático*) presented Julio Durán, a member of the conservative wing of the Radical party. In March 1964 a congressional by-election to replace a popular Socialist congressman in Curicó was interpreted by the three contending forces as a barometer of electoral strength for the upcoming presidential elections. However accurately the Curicó by-election reflected national political sentiment, FRAP's decisive victory disheartened the Right which finished third behind the Christian Democrats. The Frente Democrático dissolved and, in an effort to prevent a "communist" victory, threw its support to Eduardo Frei.

In the presidential campaign that followed both the Christian Democrats and FRAP promised agrarian reform, rural unionization, and enforcement of labor law in the countryside. Both Marxists and Christian Democrats courted rural votes, supported rural strike committees, helped organize rural unions, and promised an end to the hacienda system. To the landowners the Christian Democrats were the lesser of two evils.

When the Christian Democrats won the presidential election, and found themselves in competition with the Marxists for rural votes in the upcoming congressional elections of 1965, the viability of the new government came to depend upon greatly increasing party representation in Congress. To achieve this, some Christian Democratic candidates adopted the most drastic tactics previously used by Marxists in the rural sector, including sponsorship of illegal agricultural strikes and land occupations. The rural votes that had guaranteed the political power of the hacendados in national politics now provided the impetus for a frontal attack on the hacienda system by the Christian Democratic administration, as well as by the Marxist opposition.

This attack on the hacienda system would first erode the political and economic arrangement that had held the Chilean party system together between 1932 and 1964, and would then intensify polarization of political conflict and so bring to an end Chile's vaunted political stability.

Chapter 9 • Christians and Marxists

1964

Competition for the presidency in 1964 pitted against each other the Christian Democrats and the Marxist Frente de Acción Popular, both of which rejected the basic assumptions of capitalist liberal democracy. The Marxist-dominated FRAP coalition offered the ultimate prospect of creation of a socialist society in Chile. The Christian Democrats proclaimed that Chilean society required fundamental, even revolutionary, changes, but that these changes could be carried out through legal, peaceful means. To emphasize the difference between themselves and the Marxists, they adopted as the slogan of their program, "Revolution in Liberty."

The Christian Democrats criticized the evils of capitalism and materialistic socialism, offering in their stead a vaguely defined "communitarian" society or Christian socialism. Based upon writings of the French philosopher Jacques Maritain and upon Catholic social doctrine, a communitarian society would supposedly end class conflict through new types of "worker enterprises" that harmonize labor and capital. It would combine social pluralism and civil liberties with a just redistribution of wealth and income. But just as Marxist-Leninists lack any detailed description of the works of a truly communist society, Christian Democrats had various visions of a communitarian society.

Marxist parties had played an active role in Chilean politics since the second decade of the twentieth century. Communists, Socialists, and Trotskyists could trace their ancestry to the labor movement of the late nineteenth century, the Partido Demócrata (1887), and the Partido Obrero Socialista (POS) led by Recabarren and his comrades after 1912. Although the Communist party dated only from 1922 and the Socialist party from the early 1930s, an indigenous Marxist movement linked to international Marxism had struggled for at least half a century to reform or destroy Chilean formal democracy.

In the labor movement the Marxists had created a firm base of popular support. Just as some families passed Catholicism from generation to generation, so other families transmitted loyalty to the Communist or the Socialist party. Party-oriented youth movements, retail shops, sports clubs, doctors, and even barber shops allowed most of such people's daily lives to go on within a network of party loyalists. Of course, not all party members or sympathizers so restricted their lives or committed themselves to party work, but both Communists and Socialists had established strong roots in Chilean soil.

The FRAP coalition's presidential candidate in 1964, Salvador Allende, was a savvy, well-known politician. During the popular-front years Dr. Allende served as minister of health and subsequently gained valuable political experience in the Congress. In 1952 and 1958, respectively, Allende lost presidential elections to Carlos Ibáñez and Jorge Alessandri. The slim margin of his loss to Alessandri in 1958 badly scared the traditional political parties, the Catholic Church, and policymakers in the United States.

In contrast to the Marxist parties, the Christian Democrats could trace their official existence back only to 1957. Prior to that time, however, the ideological and organizational evolution of Christian Democracy stemmed from Catholic social doctrine and from dissident and more progressive elements within the Chilean Conservative party. In particular, the papal encyclicals *Rerum Novarum* (1891) and *Quadragesimo Anno* (1931) established the foundations of official Catholic response to the dilemmas of industrial society and the international challenge of Marxism. Pope Leo XIII noted in *Rerum Novarum* that the process of industrialization and capitalist development concentrated production and wealth into the hands of "a small number of opulent and wealthy men and put upon the innumerable multitude of proletarians a yoke that differed little from slavery." Without organizations to defend them the workers found themselves "alone and defenseless . . . against the inhumanity of their masters." This critique of capitalist development did little immediately to influence the Latin American or Chilean Catholic hierarchy, but nonetheless provided doctrinal justification for initial efforts by progressive Catholic laypersons and clerics to improve the lot of the working classes.

Forty years later, at the depths of the world depression, Pope Pius XI reconfirmed the Church's concern for the plight of the working classes in a harsh attack on capitalism and international imperialism. Pius XI's *Quadragesimo Anno* went further than Leo XIII and specifically referred to the misery of the landless laborers of the countryside, indirectly placing the Church on the side of those advocating agrarian reform to bring about social justice.

These encyclicals and other doctrinal statements placed the Church in opposition to the economic and political liberalism upon which the institutions of Western capitalist democracy rested. Progressive Catholic social theorists rejected the legitimacy of labor market determination of wages, insisting upon a just wage sufficient to guarantee a decent standard of living for the worker and the worker's family. The Church also officially recognized the importance of workers' organizations—not as vehicles of class struggle, but as "instruments of concord and peace," guided by Christian principles in the solution of the social question. Despite this pacific orientation, *Rerum Novarum* recognized that harsh working conditions, long hours, and low pay sometimes justified workers in resorting to strikes or other forceful means to better their conditions.

In the first two decades of the twentieth century a small number of Catholic politicians and churchmen in Chile responded to the social question with proposals for reform inspired by the social doctrines elaborated in *Rerum Novarum*. Based in the Jesuit college of San Ignacio, Father Fernando Vives de Soler and Father Jorge Fernández Pradel influenced a group of future political leaders, priests, and bishops who later played a leading role in the development of Chilean Christian Democracy. By 1917 Father Vives and his colleagues had established a "Social Secretariat" and were engaged in unionization efforts among small numbers of workers in industry, transport, and commerce in Santiago. Objections by leading Conservative politicians undermined these first efforts and periodically forced the temporary European exile of controversial clerics.

Against the background of the post-World War I economic crisis in Chile, and the growing sentiment favoring separation of Church and State, the Chilean archbishop and prominent historian Crescente Errázuriz delivered a pastoral message entitled "On Social

Action." Archbishop Errázuriz took note of the misery of many Chilean workers and, in particular, of the lamentable condition of the campesinos. Speaking several years before the military coup of 1924 forced the "social laws" upon a recalcitrant Chilean Congress, the archbishop accepted the necessity of workers' organizations in order "to obtain for the workers the benefits to which they have a right."

Coincident with the Church's increased concern with the plight of Chilean workers and campesinos after World War I, it also faced pressures for separation of Church and State. In June 1923 President Alessandri proposed legislation to Congress intended to protect religious freedom for all Chileans and to insulate the Catholic Church from its traditional role in partisan politics. Quoting Bishop Valdivieso (1859), the president pointed to the dangers associated with linking the "future of the Church, the most precious interests of religion, . . . to the fortunes of a [political] party." Negotiations between Church officials and the Alessandri administration assured the former title to its extensive property holdings, financial assistance, and the right to maintain or expand its role in education, public health, and charitable activities. Thus, when the Constitution of 1925 officially separated Church and State, the archbishop of Santiago could comment in his pastoral that "It is just to note that the authorities in Chile, in establishing this separation, have not been motivated by the spirit of persecution which characterizes other countries where Catholicism has been attacked. . . . The State is separated from the Church; but the Church is not separated from the State, and will always be ready to serve it."

Archbishop Errázuriz' effective leadership in the Church-State separation matter left the Church in a relatively unblemished political position. He averted direct confrontation between Liberals, Radicals, and Conservatives, thereby allowing these groups, along with the Church, to focus upon the threatening implications of the social question.

Pastoral messages and other doctrinal statements on the social question by leading intellectuals of the Chilean Church derived both from a real concern for the condition of the Chilean poor and also from the growing Marxist influence among the country's working classes. Catholic leaders, grounded in the Church's philosophical and theological rejection of "individualistic liberalism," attempted to forge a response to the social question that would be an alternative to the millenarian Marxist vision of a classless society. Indicative of this anti-Marxist motivation for part of the Church's concern with the social question, the bishop of Temuco in 1933 presented a paper at the Third Congress of Catholic Men entitled "A Study of the Practical Manner of Combatting Communisn in Chile."

Anticommunism and sincere commitment to Catholic social doctrine provided the foundation of the education received at San Ignacio and Santiago's Catholic University by the generation of students in the late 1920s and early 1930s who would become the principal leaders of Chilean Christian Democracy. These young progressive Catholics—Bernardo Leighton, Manuel Garretón, Ignacio Palma, Radomiro Tomic, Eduardo Frei—served their political apprenticeship in the youth movement of the Conservative party. They became so active in carrying out the social doctrine of the Church that finally the Conservative party could not tolerate them, and in 1938 they broke away to form a new party, the Falange Nacional.

In the year that the Falange emerged as an independent political party, the Catholic Church created the Secretariado Nacional Económico Social (National Economic and Social Secretariat) in response to the social agitation associated with the growing strength of the Chilean popular front. Under the direction of Oscar Larson, who had previously worked with the Catholic Students Federation (ANEC), the Secretariat moved into direct social action, including organization of rural workers. Emilio Tagle, later the archibishop of Valparaíso, and Oscar Larson supported the formation of the Unión de Campesinos among rural workers in the region around Buin (Santiago province). By 1941 this Catholic rural labor union was reported to have 300 members in twelve rural estates. It was hardly a massive organizational drive, especially when compared with the national effort to unionize rural workers by Communists and Socialists from 1939 to 1941. Nevertheless this first Catholic support of rural workers' organizations infuriated the Conservative party, traditionally the Church's closest political ally.

In Fundo Huelquen, owned by a deputy of the Conservative party, a Falange lawyer and clerics assisted the workers in presentation of a labor petition to the landowner. The landowner attacked the clerics who participated in the workers' movement, suggesting that they leave determination of the workers' salaries to God and the conscience of the *patrón*. Subsequently the Conservative party demanded that the efforts of Larson, Tagle, and their colleagues be stopped and that the Unión de Campesinos be disbanded. The Church hierarchy acquiesced; Larson left for missions outside of Chile. Despite their immediate victory, the landowners recognized the threat of social movements inspired by Catholic social doctrine. They complained that "the *falangistas* are worse than the Communists, since we know how to defend ourselves against the Communists, but not so against the *falangistas*. . . ."

During the next decade the Falange remained a small, elitist social Christian party with a populist orientation. Occasionally Falange deputies made the critical difference in forging electoral or legislative coalitions or gave dramatic speeches in the Congress. For example, in 1947 Falange deputy Jorge Rogers Sotomayor bitterly denounced the rural unionization law (Law 8811) that reaffirmed the repression of rural workers. From time to time also, Falange leaders served in cabinet posts, beginning with Bernardo Leighton's brief stint as minister of labor (1938) in the second Alessandri administration. Progressive elements within the Church also continued with small-scale leadership-formation programs among workers and youth organizations. Neither in the political nor labor arena, however, did these progressive Catholics gain a mass following or exercise great national influence.

Complicating further the evolution of social Catholicism as a political force, new divisions within the Conservative party led to the foundation in the 1940s of the Partido Conservador Social Crístiano (Conservative Social Christian party). Somewhat more conservative than the Falange, and led by more established ex-Conservative politicians, the Conservative Social Christian party outpolled the Falange in national and local elections into the 1950s. The eventual dissolution in 1957 of the Partido Conservador Social Crístiano, however, united most progressive Catholics, along with ex-members of the Agrarian Labor party, into the Christian Democratic party (PDC) in anticipation of the 1958 presidential election.

After World War II a concern on the part of the Holy See and the United States about the advance of Marxism in Chile gave new impetus and financial support to Catholic organizations among workers, students, women, and peasants. Middle-class reformers, professionals, and technicians found in the Falange an alternative to the unmoving conservatism of the traditional parties and to the opportunism of the Radicals. With a heterogeneous base, the Falange developed as a multiclass movement under the continued direction of the generation of leaders who had founded it in the late 1930s. Slowly the Falange gained in national prestige and visibility, as it advocated extensive reforms consistent with the social doctrine of the Church.

Before 1953 the Falange was more active in urban areas and universities than in the countryside, but it would be the rural organizing activity of the Falange and Catholic labor leaders that did the most

TABLE 20. ELECTORAL EVOLUTION OF FALANGE NATIONAL
PARTIDO DEMÓCRATA CRISTIANA, CHAMBER OF DEPUTIES

Year	Total Votes	Percent of Electorate	Number of Deputies Elected
1941	15,553	3.5	3
1945	10,527	2.2	3
1949*	18,221	3.9	3
1953	22,353	2.8	3
1957	82,710	9.2	17
1961†	213,559	16.	23
1965	989,626	41.6	82

* In 1949 the Social Christian Party polled 2,018 votes without electing a deputy.
† Christian Democrats.
(Source: Adapted from Germán Urzua Valenzuela, *Los Partidos Políticos Chilenos*, Santiago, Editorial Jurídica, 1968, pp. 124-25.)

to boost the political credibility of the Catholic reformers. In 1952 Falange politician Emilio Lorenzini began to organize rural labor around the town of Molina in Talca province with the Federación Sindical Cristiana de la Tierra. The vineyards of the Molina region had seen a number of rural labor conflicts between 1919 and 1952. As late as 1946-47 headline-making legal strikes occurred in the region's farms—before Law 8811 and the Law for the Permanent Defense of Democracy suppressed the rural labor movement. It was ironical that in applying the latter law the government had banished Communist leaders, such as José Campusano, to the Molina district. Tense cooperation in the fields between Falange and Communist cadres set the stage for fierce competition in later years.

Emilio Lorenzini affiliated the Federación Sindical Cristiana de la Tierra with the major Catholic labor organization, Acción Sindical Chilena (ASICH). Formed in 1947 under the leadership of Jesuit Alberto Hurtado—after special authorization by the Jesuit general and Pope Pius XII—ASICH was a thorn in the side of both the Marxists and the traditional political parties in Chile. In the rural district around Molina, supported by Bishop Manuel Larraín (an early colleague of Father Hurtado in the awakening of the Catholic labor movement in the 1920s), ASICH and the Federación Sindical Cristiana de la Tierra provided campesinos with legal services, literacy and leadership training, and assistance in labor conflicts.

In October 1953, Lorenzini organized the Primer Congreso Sindical de los Obreros Campesinos de Molina, where rural workers and union leaders drew up labor petitions to present in the vineyards of Molina in November (prior to the harvest). When the landowners refused to negotiate in good faith with the workers, the campesinos declared a strike. Illegal under the terms of Law 8811, the strike brought government repression. Lorenzini and other union leaders went to jail for offenses specified in the Law for the Permanent Defense of Democracy; the government dealt with progressive Catholics by applying legislation intended to control "communist" activities.

Unwilling to accept defeat, ASICH organized a march to Santiago by the Molina campesinos. The political effect of this march in the early days of the new Ibáñez administration forced the government to release Lorenzini and other union leaders as well as to pressure the landowners to negotiate with the farm workers—despite the fact that the strike was clearly illegal. For both the numbers of workers involved and its psychological impact on national politics, the Molina strike is generally cited as the most important rural labor conflict in Chile prior to 1964. More important in the long run, however, were the campesino leaders who emerged in the Molina region, and the spread of the Catholic rural labor movement throughout the central valley, which provided Falange and Catholic reformers with a growing base in the Chilean countryside. In addition, after years of sporadic Marxist political and labor activity in the rural districts, the Church, Falange politicians, and Catholic-oriented rural labor unions had carried out the most important agricultural strike in Chilean history. The Molina strike and the subsequent activism of Catholic rural organizations gave credibility to Falange claims that they favored land reform, social justice, rural unionization, and sweeping social change.

Only four years after the Federación Sindical de la Tierra emerged in Molina, the Jesuit general in Rome, at the request of the Chilean Church, sent to Chile the Belgian Jesuit and social scientist, Roger Vekemans. The Chilean Church wanted help in the battle against communism; Vekemans would spearhead the anticommunist offensive for the next decade. Vekemans recruited Belgian businessman J. N. A. Sierens to begin social research in Chile. Sierens put together a systematic survey of Chilean institutions, with special attention given to "communist penetration." Noting the slim defeat of Allende in the 1958 presidential elections, Sierens recommended coordinated action by the Church to prevent a potential Marxist victory in 1964.

Vekemans, at the head of the Centro Bellarmino, directed an intellectual, organizational, and political campaign under the aegis of a "research and development foundation," called by its acronym DESAL. Large grants from Western European governments, private foundations, and Christian Democratic parties, as well as funds from the United States Central Intelligence Agency, via the conduit of the International Development Foundation, funded DESAL and other Catholic intellectual and organizing efforts. Vekemans, along with Father Zañartu (affiliated with the University of Notre Dame in the United States) and other Jesuits, gave doctrinal direction to the campaign against Marxism in Chile. A thorough study of this international politico-religious penetration of Chilean politics by David E. Mutchler* documented an intricate web of financial arrangements and organizational ties emanating from Vekemans and his colleagues. In this web were entangled the mass media, labor, business, the American AID mission, CIA, Western European governments, political parties, and private foundations.

Complementing its research activities and elaboration of a new "development ideology," the Catholic Church's anti-Marxist offensive resulted in the creation of numerous neighborhood organizations, unions, farm committees, discussion groups, women's organizations, and quasi-political groups that could be mobilized for the 1964 election campaign. In the meantime, ASICH formed the Unión de Campesinos Cristianos in 1960 to unite isolated farm unions and worker's committees and to expand the rural labor movement. Moreover, parallel operations by Acción Católica Rural (Rural Catholic Action) and the Institute for Rural Education (IER)—also partially financed with American funds and partially staffed with Peace Corps volunteers—gave rise to the Asociación Nacional de Organizaciones Campesinas (ANOC), or the National Association of Campesino Organizations. After completing their training at the IER, ANOC leaders received salaries from the institute while they led rural labor conflicts, created Christian-inspired rural organizations, and opposed communism in the countryside.

These Catholic-oriented rural labor leaders mobilized thousands of Chilean campesinos into new organizations and inspired a growing rural activism. Though some leaders of the movement may have understood the international and the national political implications of their ties with IER, ACR, and the Christian Democrats, later events would demonstrate that many participants were more independent

* *The Church as a Political Factor in Latin America* (New York: Praeger, 1971).

and more militant than their unknown patrons desired. Internal debates and conflicts over strategy and direction of the movement in the mid-1960s and after made clear that these campesino organizations were far more complex and less manipulable than their early directors had imagined. In the short term, however, these organizations proved an important resource in the campaign against Marxism in Chile.

As the political situation of the Alessandri government deteriorated after 1961, the rising Catholic rural labor movement, in alliance with the newly founded Christian Democratic party, represented a major alternative to the Marxist-dominated FRAP coalition of Communists, Socialists, and smaller reformist parties. The most prominent Christian Democratic leaders, including Eduardo Frei, had been schoolmates of important officials of Vekemans' Centro Bellarmino. Personal ties reinforced doctrinal and ideological connections between the Christian Democrats and the Jesuit intellectuals.

In 1962 the Chilean bishops entrusted Vekemans and Renato Poblete, an old schoolmate of Eduardo Frei, with preparation of a "pastoral plan" that would help Frei against Allende in the 1964 election. Also in 1962 the Chilean bishops initiated their own land reform experiments, anticipating the legislation passed by the Alessandri government later that year. Almost simultaneously the Church distributed a pastoral letter entitled "The Social and Political Duty." This pastoral made clear that "communism deprives man of his liberty, suppresses all dignity and morality of the human person; it denies to the individual all natural rights. . . . Communism destroys any bond between mother and child." During the 1964 election campaign Christian Democrats distributed thousands of copies of this pastoral letter and papered the walls of Chile with posters depicting the foreheads of Chilean children being branded with the hammer and sickle. The international Catholic offensive (1957-64) thus contributed to the domestic political campaign against the Marxists.

Meanwhile, Fidel Castro's sister, Juana Castro, came to Chile to tell the Chilean people, especially Chilean women, of the horrors of communism in Cuba. These developments combined with the psychological effect of the by-elections of Curicó—that prompted support by the Right for Frei's candidacy—and with millions of dollars in covert campaign contributions from American agents and European Christian Democrats, to give the Christian Democrats the presidency in 1964.

If anticommunism was the rationale for massive U.S., West German, and Church support for Chile's Christian Democrats, there existed within the Christian Democratic party many sincere reformers and even a small number of committed revolutionaries. President Frei's call for "Revolution in Liberty" was not empty rhetoric. The Christian Democrats intended to alter dramatically the very foundations of Chilean society, to redistribute income and wealth, to improve the living standards of, and to broaden opportunities for, the nation's workers and peasants, and to democratize the country's political and social life.

Faced with the many social and economic problems inherited from the process of economic development after 1930 and the historical legacy of a highly stratified class society, the Christian Democratic administration attempted to carry out a sweeping reform program encompassing every area of Chilean life. All the persistent problems of the Chilean economy received government attention—including efforts to control inflation, to improve the nation's balance of payments through stimulation of exports, to carry out large-scale agrarian reform, to enact meaningful tax reforms, and to make significant investments in public health, education and vocational training, and to expand the services of the Labor Department.

Almost every aspect of the government's program threatened either the political and economic privileges of the traditional elite or menaced leftist influence over organized labor and the urban and rural poor. No way existed for the Christian Democrats to implement their program without alienating the support of the rightist parties whose votes had elected President Frei. Similarly, no matter how successful the government was in implementing social and economic reforms, the FRAP parties could urge more rapid or more extensive changes in Chilean society; they could point to areas of policy failure and push working-class and peasant organizations into direct action that impelled the administration to move either faster than it desired or to use police to halt illegal land occupations or strikes.

Unfortunately for the Christian Democratic government, official policymakers clearly and precisely outlined the administration's short- and long-term goals in overly optimistic terms. Even with the Christian Democrats' stunning victory in the 1965 congressional elections, which gave them majority control of the House of Deputies, FRAP and rightist representatives in the Senate still managed to delay significantly passage of key legislation. Every major component of the government's program—"Chileanization" of the copper industry, agrarian reform/agricultural unionization, tax reform, wage-price stabilization, and proposals to stimulate industrial growth—faced the scrutiny and obstructionism of the opposition. This was, of course,

merely a new version of the historical struggle between executive coalitions and Congress that had characterized Chilean politics in the
parliamentary period and also after 1932—complicated now by the
facts that a single party rather than a coalition controlled the executive and that traditional political forces considered some Christian
Democrats *prepotentes*, or uncompromising.

Only in 1966-67, after considerable negotiation and compromise,
did the copper legislation, agrarian reform, and agricultural unionization legislation clear the Congress. Predictably, the Marxists opposed
any effort by the government to restrain inflation through limitations
on wage readjustments. The Right, enraged at the government-sponsored mobilization of rural workers into unions and cooperatives as
well as at the prospect of a real agrarian reform, held hostage the
copper legislation in an effort to weaken the administration's agrarian
program. The Right also exacerbated relations with the United States
by joining the Marxists in a call for outright nationalization of the
copper industry instead of the acquisition by the Chilean government of majority interest in the companies that the government
called "Chileanization." Only half facetiously, leading Conservative
and Liberal politicians suggested compensating the companies just as
the United States-approved agrarian reform would compensate Chilean landowners for their expropriated holdings—with government
bonds payable in thirty years.

The ambitious scope and the specificity with which the Christian
Democrats set out their program made its effective implementation
through legal means in a six-year period a practical impossibility. Notwithstanding greatly increased copper prices, due in part to the war
in Vietnam, and substantial assistance from the Alliance for Progress,
internal political opposition and the structural constraints of the
Chilean socio-economic situation prevented total success. Thus, even
the sometimes impressive accomplishments of the regime fell far
short of its publicly announced objectives. Moreover, the severe
drought of 1967-68 seriously disrupted agricultural production, thereby
adding to the nation's economic difficulties. The discrepancy between
stated objectives and actual attainment allowed both the rightist and
the FRAP opposition to point to the failure of the Christian Democratic administration.

In one area, especially, Christian Democratic policies led to dismal
failure. Rather than decreasing Chile's economic dependence and reducing the influence of foreign capital on its economy, the Frei government created numerous incentives to attract foreign investors and
subordinated public policy to conditions imposed by United States

TABLE 21. COMPARISON OF POLICY OBJECTIVES AND
PERFORMANCE OF "REVOLUTION IN LIBERTY"

Policy Objectives	Time Frame	Targeted Increase	Actual Increase
Retail prices	1965	25%	29%
Retail prices	1966	15%	23%
Retail prices	1967	10%	18%
Nonagricultural prices	1965	Less than 20%	28%
Money supply	1965	25%	65%
Real GNP	1964-70	23%	30%
Exports	1964-70	94%	94%
New farm ownerships	1964-70	100,000	28,000
New housing units	1964-70	360,000	260,000
Copper output	1964-70	90%	10%
Real GDP	1965-70	31%	18%
Per capita real GDP	1965-70	20%	5%
Gross investment	1965-70	70%	22% (through 1969)
Domestic saving	1965-70	100%	52% (through 1969)
Exports	1965-70	55%	68%
Copper exports	1965-70	70%	107%
Imports	1965-70	31%	63%

(Source: After Thomas L. Edwards, *Economic Development and Reform in Chile: Progress Under Frei, 1964-1970,* Latin American Studies Center, Michigan State University, 1972, p. 50.)

and international lending agencies. The incentives to foreign capital included generous profit-remittance arrangements and liberalized import regulations for firms establishing themselves in Chile. Promise of tax stability and exchange-control advantages also served to encourage foreign investment. In response to these incentives multinational enterprises substantially increased their investments in Chile, especially in the industrial sector. By 1970 over one hundred United States corporations had investments in Chile, among them twenty-four of the top United States-based multinationals.

Foreign investment brought with it high technology, capital-intensive production units that made little contribution to the government's efforts to reduce unemployment. Indeed, for the decade 1960-70, industry provided an average of only 15,000 new job opportunities per year—nowhere near enough to absorb the continuing tide of migrants from the countryside to the urban areas. This migration enlarged the rings of misery surrounding Santiago and other major cities, as the shantytowns and squatter settlements (*callampas,* or "mushroom towns") grew at alarming rates. In Santiago alone the *callampas* and squatter settlements sheltered nearly one-half million people, or 20 to 25 percent of the city's population.

Living conditions in these urban settlements varied from poor to deplorable. Most lacked basic urban services and amenities, including sewers and potable water. Unemployment levels ranged well above the official national figure of 8 percent, and underemployment disguised the desperate situation of families without any steady, dependable source of income. As in the rest of Latin America, these urban poor lacked meaningful unemployment insurance or welfare services that might guarantee even a "floor to misery." They endured a daily struggle for survival. Lacking also the protection of unions or private charitable relief, thousands of slum dwellers and residents of the shantytowns of Santiago received the political messages of the "Revolution in Liberty" without obtaining the material benefits it promised.

When the government did respond to the physical needs of the urban poor with self-help housing projects (*operación sitio*), encouragement of *centros de madres* ("mothers' centers") or *juntas de vecinos* ("neighborhood councils"), construction of waterworks or installation of electric lines, there always remained those who felt left out. The admittedly partisan process that determined which groups of urban poor would benefit from government programs, whether because of party affiliation or the high visibility of political mobilization in particular settlements, further undermined the government's efforts. For every successful program there were more people left out than included. The backlog of need and poverty made even significant improvements in the living conditions of some groups of the urban poor a political defeat for the incumbent administration, just as distribution of land to some 30,000 campesinos alienated many times that number who did not receive land from the government program.

In part, the extremely favorable treatment afforded the multinationals by the Frei administration, and the constraints on the government's program of reform, stemmed from the negotiated "solution" to Chile's immediate balance of payments crisis facing the Christian Democrats when they came to office. Chile's accumulated international obligations in 1964, over $1 billion, required almost 40 percent of copper export earnings for debt service alone. To support the Frei government's "Revolution in Liberty," the United States and ten other creditor nations agreed to a "rollover" or credit relief plan of approximately $100 million for a two-year period and a grace period that allowed for a five-year repayment schedule beginning in 1968.

Chile pledged in exchange to facilitate transfer of payments on the renegotiated debt and also to relax controls on foreign exchange for purchase of certain types of imports. In turn, AID provided large loans and other assistance to the Chilean administration; in 1964-65 AID accounted for almost 15 percent of Chile's national budget. Thus the financial feasibility of the Christian Democratic reforms depended not only upon the hope for better copper prices, but also upon the good will of U.S. policymakers and the cooperation of the multinational enterprises. Touting the "Revolution in Liberty" as a positive alternative to the Cuban revolutionary model, United States policymakers sought to buttress the Christian Democrats as well as to support American business interests in Chile. This strategy, reminiscent of the American decision to underwrite the initial CORFO projects in 1939 and 1940—only now on a much grander scale—entangled the Christian Democratic administration in the web of American foreign policy, including the war in Vietnam. It also exacerbated the internal divisions within the government party as the Christian Democratic youth movement and the more populist elements of the party rejected any identification with foreign capital, imperialism, the American embassy, or the Vietnam War.

Apart from its uneven record with respect to its announced social and economic objectives, the Christian Democratic government mobilized hundreds of thousands of women, students, workers, and campesinos into new unions, cooperatives, and community organizations. These organizations depended upon government encouragement or subsidies and came to expect continual economic benefits or expanded government services. Distribution of consumer goods, credit, agricultural inputs, and jobs through political agencies like Promoción Popular (Popular Promotion) and INDAP created a vast network of patronage and spoils tying bureaucrats, party hacks, slum dwellers, and campesinos to government pursestrings. Immediate benefits such as new sewing machines for a *centro de madres* or seed and fertilizer for a campesino cooperative helped convince the underclasses of the government's concern for their plight. Accompanied by promises of increasing material benefits by government enthusiasts who staffed the mushrooming public sector, these initial spoils of reform also created high expectations of rapid, often unobtainable, changes in lifestyle and of economic opportunities.

To a great extent the Christian Democratic program of political mobilization and deliberate "consciousness raising" (*concientización*) made impossible the attainment of its other major economic objectives such as control of inflation, increases in productivity, and higher

TABLE 22. DISTRIBUTION OF LABOR FORCE BY ECONOMIC SECTOR, 1960-1970 (1000s)

	1960	1961	1962	1963	1964	1965	1966	1967	1968	1969	1970	Percent
Agriculture	711.1	668.6	687.7	704.0	680.8	709.8	717.7	750.0	736.4	731.7	738.0	24.2
Mining	92.5	94.9	91.7	88.7	91.7	93.4	93.6	94.0	94.5	97.7	99.2	3.3
Industry	412.6	439.7	450.4	464.5	477.9	506.7	527.7	534.4	544.6	550.7	562.9	18.8
Construction	130.5	135.6	158.6	158.5	188.8	183.1	186.3	169.0	168.5	172.0	177.5	6.0
Electricity, Gas, and Water	10.8	11.0	11.1	11.8	12.3	12.5	11.9	11.9	11.8	11.8	11.8	0.3
Commerce	260.3	265.5	279.0	294.1	311.1	330.0	351.0	375.0	404.2	428.5	451.5	15.1
Transport	121.2	126.0	135.0	139.0	143.8	148.0	149.5	156.2	161.8	167.4	175.6	5.9
Services	578.0	587.6	592.5	613.6	630.9	640.0	665.0	721.4	757.5	761.3	777.7	26.0
Total	2,317.0	2,348.9	2,406.0	2,474.2	2,546.3	2,623.5	2,702.7	2,811.9	2,879.3	2,921.1	2,994.2	100.0

(Source: Odeplan, Chilean Planning Agency.)

levels of domestic savings and investment. With their hopes aroused by both the government's propaganda and the even more alluring Marxist vision in which redistribution of wealth and land would greatly improve the lot of the masses, Chilean workers and peasants could hardly be expected to accept government proposals for wage restraints, forced-savings plans, and moderation in labor disputes.

Moreover, as the government generally refused to use police or the military against slum dwellers, organized labor, or campesinos, illegal land occupations and even worker-declared "expropriation" of farms and factories occurred more frequently. Whereas the leftist press indignantly publicized the small number of cases in which the government did use force to halt labor conflicts or to remove trespassers—especially when workers died or were injured as in Puerto Montt in early March 1969—the political Right noted the government's reluctance to guarantee private property rights and organized white guards to defend its interests. No administrative decree or government policy could effectively limit popular mobilization once set in motion; only police or the military sufficed. With its unwillingness to adopt clearly repressive tactics, especially given the numerous divisions within the Christian Democratic party itself, the government found a lawful "Revolution in Liberty" to be illusory. If the government chose to uphold the law, it necessarily employed force against workers, peasants, and students acting illegally to accelerate the program of reform.

The Marxist parties, recognizing this dilemma, lost no opportunity to exacerbate it by proclaiming their support for land occupations, farm seizures (tomas), and widespread illegal strikes. If in order to

TABLE 23. ILLEGAL STRIKES, URBAN LAND INVASIONS,
FACTORY SEIZURES, AND FARM SEIZURES

	1966	1967	1968	1969	1970
Urban land invasions		13	8	73	220
Factory tomas	n.d.	n.d.	5	24	133
Illegal strikes	936	878	901	771*	1,085
Farm tomas	36**	9	27	148	271

* First nine months only.

** 1960-1966.

(Source: Chilean Labor Department Annual Report for each year; Solon Barraclough and J. A. Fernández, Diagnóstico de la reforma agraria Chilena, Mexico, Siglo Veintiuno, 1974; Walden F. Bello, "The Roots and Dynamics of Revolution and Counterrevolution in Chile," unpublished doctoral dissertation, Princeton University, 1975.)

demonstrate its commitment to reform, the government invariably refused to halt these activities, then legal reform would have given way to an uncontrolled and uncontrollable revolutionary situation. Just as the leftists deliberately confronted the government with this choice between suppression of popular movements and chaos, so the rightists challenged the legality of the agrarian reform process and organized sometimes violent resistance to the government's legal reforms.

Complicating this situation, a minority element within the Christian Democratic party encouraged mass mobilization and political activism beyond the limits officially set by the Frei administration. In particular, Jacques Chonchol, director of INDAP, believed it necessary to go beyond the bounds of existing law in the unionization of rural labor and in support for agrarian reform. While the government sought to squeeze new legislation out of Congress (1964-67), Chonchol, via INDAP, promoted large numbers of agricultural labor conflicts and organized multifarm unions in direct violation of existing legislation. Not to be outdone, Communist and Socialist organizers competed with INDAP in the effort to mobilize the rural labor force against the landowners and to accelerate agrarian reform.

These efforts overwhelmed the Labor Department, which lacked sufficient personnel and resources to administer properly the mounting number of requests to form agricultural unions or to process efficiently the hundreds of agricultural labor disputes. After frequent appearances in its offices of INDAP organizers (*promotores*) representing campesino groups, the Labor Department ruled that INDAP officials "do not have the legal right to intervene in the presentation of labor petitions and in the process of negotiation of labor conflicts in the agricultural sector." In response, INDAP personnel received instructions to limit their intervention in rural labor conflicts to "informal" support or assistance. In addition, the new peasant organizations and even the Catholic rural labor movement, generated by ASICH and the Institute for Rural Education, pressured CORA, the agency responsible for implementing land reform, to speed up the expropriation and redistribution of agricultural land. Administrative inability to keep pace with the tide of popular mobilization and rising expectations made the government appear unwilling to fulfill its promises to the urban and the rural poor. It also made credible Marxist attacks on the government for failing to carry out completely its promised program. Added to criticism from the Right, united in the Partido Nacional after merger of Conservatives and Liberals in 1965, the dissident Christian Democrats and Marxist swamped the government reform program in sectarian politics and obstructionism.

The debate within the Christian Democratic party over the pace, character, and objectives of agrarian reform typified the basic contradictions that eventually proved fatal to the "Revolution in Liberty." The essential constraints on Chilean development could not be overcome without both improved distribution of wealth and income *and* increased production of goods and services. If redistribution occurred at the cost of current investment and reduced productivity, then any gains to the workers and peasants could only be temporary. Rising demands for goods and services without concomitant expansion of domestic production and export earnings could only lead to a renewal of the inflationary spiral. Under these conditions an ever more militant, politicized rural labor force became a serious obstacle to the government's overall economic program at the same time as it was a major social and political accomplishment of governmental policy.

More than any other aspect of the government program, official encouragement and often subsidization of the formation of thousands of organizations among Chile's urban and rural poor upset the equilibrium of Chilean society. It also created political forces that the government could not or would not control. Consistent with the ambiguity that characterized its reform program, the government sometimes did and sometimes did not call in police to squelch illegal rural labor conflicts, strikes in the cities or mines, or land occupations; sometimes it used a labor conflict as a pretext to place one of its representatives (*inteventor*) in the farm where the conflict was taking place and to organize the campesinos for eventual expropriation of the property.

Thus the "Revolution in Liberty" proved to be neither a revolution nor entirely lawful. It also failed to solve the fundamental economic problems the Christian Democrats themselves had identified in 1964: slow economic growth, instability of prices (inflation), dependence upon foreign markets and capital, and unequal distribution of wealth and income. Nevertheless, it did improve the living conditions of thousands of rural workers, tenants, and other beneficiaries of land reform; it did enact critical political and administrative reforms; it instituted a tax system that generated substantial internal revenues; and it spread the belief that the Chilean state could offer real hope for improvement of the lot of the poor. In the areas of education and public health the Frei government also made impressive gains. Primary school enrollment increased by 46 percent, university enrollments doubled, and matriculation in technical schools quadrupled. Public health programs that established numerous rural clin-

TABLE 24. CHRISTIAN DEMOCRATIC AGRARIAN REFORM:
EXPROPRIATIONS, 1965–JULY 14, 1970

| Year | Number of Properties* | Area in Hectares | | Total Area |
		Irrigated	Unirrigated	
1965	99	41,260.1	499,923.0	541,183.1
1966	265	57,877.4	468,326.0	526,203.4
1967 (Law 15.020)	131	20,141.8	115,155.4	136,297.2
1967 (Law 16.640)	86	30,443.1	119,285.4	149,728.5
1968	223	44,681.1	612,566.3	657,247.4
1969	314	54,478.8	807,361.8	861,840.6
1970 (to July 14)	201	30,986.6	604,181.5	635,168.1†
Total	1,319	279,868.9	3,128,919.4	3,408,788.3

* Some *asentamientos* (land reform settlements) were formed by combining two or more properties.

† Error in original reads 535,163.1.

(Source: CORA, *Reforma agraria chilena*, 1965-1970, Santiago, CORA, 1970, p. 36.)

ics and trained community health leaders cut Chile's atrocious infant mortality rate and also bettered other general health conditions.

The reformist legislation of the Frei years and the massive organizational drive encouraged by the Christian Democratic administration provided substantial leverage for further fundamental reforms in Chilean society. In this sense the Christian Democrats definitively destroyed the cornerstone of Chilean formal democracy as it had functioned since 1932, without providing anything but the vaguely conceived notion of a "communitarian" society to replace it.

As the 1970 presidential elections approached, the Unidad Popular coalition, with Salvador Allende as its presidential candidate, offered a "transition to socialism" as their answer to this dilemma. The Christian Democratic candidate, Radomiro Tomic, urged an intensification of the "Revolution in Liberty." Jorge Alessandri, now an old man running as an "independent," appealed to the old elites and alienated middle-class sectors with the prospect of restoration of law and order.

From the perspective of the political Right the drastic nature of the Christian Democratic reforms between 1964 and 1970 prevented them from again supporting the Christian Democratic candidate as the lesser of two evils. In any case, most political analysts, including those in the American embassy in Santiago, predicted a victory for

Alessandri. When Salvador Allende emerged with a slim plurality, Chile plunged into three years of dramatic change, punctuated by increasing polarization, political violence, and American intervention in Chilean politics. Christian Democracy's broad-front reformist projects proved to be both too much and too little of what Chile required to become a more Christian and more democratic society.

In the last year of the Christian Democratic administration political tension mounted. A "strike" (the so-called *tacnazo*, because it involved the Tacna regiment) among the officers and men of the Tacna and Yungay regiments of the army resulted in demands for the ouster of the minister of defense and for better pay and materiel for the armed services. Led by retired general Roberto Viaux, this military movement temporarily controlled the main arsenal, the non-commissioned officers' school, and the principal recruiting station; it reminded many Chileans of the events of 1924. Though the movement sputtered and dissolved after the resignation of the defense minister and government promises to attend to the military's economic demands, there was talk of a possible Viaux presidential candidacy after his incarceration—in striking parallel to the 1934 Senate campaign of Maramaduque Grove when the campaign slogan "From jail to the senate" inspired the Chilean Left. Members of the Socialist party took the opportunity to support military aspirations for improved pay and materiel despite their distrust of the reactionary tendencies of Viaux and his comrades.

Shortly thereafter the government pushed legislation through Con-

TABLE 25. GROWTH OF CAMPESINO COOPERATIVE MOVEMENT, 1965-70

Year	Number	Members	Federations	Cooperatives Affiliated	Confederations	Federations Affiliated
1964	24	1,718				
1965	43	3,204				
1966	84	7,802				
1967	123	11,452				
1968	171	18,456				
1969	222	30,034	7	51		
1970*	250	37,675	9†	81	1	9

* To October 22.

† Does not include five federations in formation which would include 45 affiliated cooperatives.

(Source: INDAP, 1964/1970, n.p.)

TABLE 26. UNION MEMBERSHIP IN CHILE—1964 AND 1970

| | 1964 | | 1970 | |
	Number	Members	Number	Members
Industrial or Plant Unions	632	142,958	1,437	197,651
Professional or Craft Unions	1,207	125,926	2,569	239,323
Agricultural Unions	24	1,863	510	114,112
Totals	1,863	270,542	4,006	551,086

(Source: Chilean Labor Department Annual Report for each year.)

gress to pacify the military. Even so, on November 19, 1969, the government felt compelled to issue an official declaration threatening severe sanctions against anyone seeking to subvert the discipline of the armed forces. The declaration also emphasized that the commanders of the armed forces and *carabineros* had reaffirmed their loyalty, discipline, and respect for democratic institutions. To confirm this, President Frei declared a "state of emergency" under the questionable authority granted to the executive in cases of "public calamity." This decree allowed the commander of the armed forces to take action to "prevent the commission of crimes or the occurrence of events affecting the security of the state."

At the same time that the Frei government was facing Chile's first serious overt breach of military discipline since the popular-front period, revolutionaries and pseudorevolutionaries incited an already highly politicized population to take matters of economic and social change into their own hands. The Movimiento de Izquierda Revolucionaria (MIR), or Left Revolutionary Movement, a relatively new revolutionary organization which rejected electoral politics, spread

TABLE 27. IMPROVEMENTS IN PUBLIC HEALTH DURING
THE FREI ADMINISTRATION

	1964	1969
General Mortality (per 1000)	11.1	8.9
Infant Mortality (per 1000 births)	102.9	79.0
Measles (per 100,000)	38.6	3.5
Typhoid Fever (per 100,000)	2.1	0.9
Tuberculosis (per 100,000)	48.8	29.6

(Source: Presidential message to the National Congress, Santiago, May 21, 1970; Sergio Molina, *El Proceso de Cambio en Chile*, Santiago, Editorial Universitaria, 1972, p. 89.)

its inflammatory ideology among the Mapuche and the campesinos of southern Chile and into the *callampas* of the urban centers. Favoring direct action, MIR cadres, often university students from the University of Concepción, joined with the Mapuche in land "recuperation" movements that were met, not unexpectedly, by landowner resistance. Elements of the Socialist party and MAPU (a radical splinter group from the Christian Democratic party) and even certain Communists also turned to overt attacks on the rights of landed proprietors, industrial enterprises, and owners of urban land and housing projects.

Part of this mass mobilization owed its inspiration to the usual pre-presidential election rhetoric and vote seeking of the Marxist parties and the Christian Democrats. The Marxists, now in alliance with most of the Radical party and with a number of smaller parties, had again chosen Salvador Allende as their presidential candidate and formed a new version of the popular front called *unidad popular* (UP), or "popular unity." The popular unity electoral program called for revolutionary changes in Chile's political, economic, and social structure to overcome the exploitation and misery imposed upon the country by monopoly capitalism, imperialist exploitation, and class privilege. In the introduction to the UP electoral program, the parties of the coalition told the Chilean people that:

> Chile is a capitalist country, dependent on the imperialist nations and dominated by bourgeois groups who are structurally related to foreign capital and cannot resolve the country's fundamental problems—problems which are clearly the result of class privilege which will never be given up voluntarily.

The program criticized the Christian Democratic government as "nothing but a new government of the bourgeoisie, in the service of national and foreign capitalism, whose weak efforts to promote social change came to a sad end in economic stagnation, a rising cost of living, and violent repression of the people." According to the UP parties, the results of the Frei government demonstrated that reformism could not solve the problems of Chile's people.

To solve Chile's problems, the UP coalition proposed a peaceful transition to socialism. This required replacement of Chile's existing political institutions with a unicameral legislature, or people's assembly, to root out the evils of presidentialism and parliamentarism; reorganization of the judiciary and educational system; and greatly increased participation of workers and peasants through union and community organizations in national and local policymaking. Further, the program called for restructuring the economy by greatly increasing the scope of the "social" or public sector, by expropriating all agricultural estates of more than the equivalent of eighty hectares of irrigated land, and by nationalizing the financial system (banks and insurance companies) as well as "all those activities which have a strong influence on the nation's social and economic development." This last category seemed to open the door to a broad program of socialization of the means of production and of distribution channels. The UP indicated that with the dominant "social" sector of the economy there would coexist a "mixed" sector in which enterprises would combine public and private capital; and that, at least in the short run, small private firms could continue to operate. However, uncertainty among the country's small businesses concerning the eventual limits of the UP program, and the coalition's inability to reach internal agreement upon such limits, would produce serious political problems for the UP government (1970-73).

Opposing the UP coalition in the 1970 presidential election, the Christian Democrats chose as their candidate Radomiro Tomic. Tomic, ex-Chilean ambassador to the United States and one of the founders of the Falange, was considered an uncompromising leftist by the Chilean Right. Whereas other potential Christian Democratic candidates might have been able to reconstruct the alliance between the Partido Nacional, other conservative forces, and the Christian Democrats who elected Eduardo Frei in 1964, Tomic declared his unwillingness to cooperate with either the Right or the Radicals who refused to participate in the UP coalition. In a seeming attempt to appear even more revolutionary than Allende, Tomic highlighted his campaign with promises to complete agrarian reform by expropriating all the large rural estates "from the Andes to the sea" (*desde la cordillera hasta el mar*). Repeatedly Tomic emphasized that a victory in coalition with the Right was a victory *for* the Right. In contrast to his harsh attacks on the Partido Nacional and its candidate, Tomic's campaign speeches treated the possibility of an Allende victory as an alternative opportunity for progressive forces in Chile to unite and carry out fundamental social change.

If the Tomic candidacy, rather than that of a more moderate Christian Democrat, made rightist support for the Christian Democrats impossible, political polls showing ex-President Jorge Alessandri the likely victor in a three-way race for the presidency in 1970 whetted the appetite of the Chilean law-and-order forces for a return to "the stick" that Portales had once recommended to cure a nation's "bad habits." The combined support of the Partido Nacional, alienated middle-class groups, and a large number of urban and rural workers still attracted by the appeal of Alessandri's name, made his candidacy appear destined for success. Unfortunately for Alessandri and his supporters, his age and lack of vitality became embarrassingly evident in Chile's introduction to television politics. The image of a tired, inarticulate politician broadcast via television to many of the nation's voters reinforced the outhouse humor of UP election posters that caricatured Alessandri on a toilet with the caption "NICA or Ni cagando, politely translated as "No way!"

Alessandri's weakness as a campaigner and the Christian Democratic decision to go it alone split the vote three ways. Salvador Allende received a slim plurality. Notwithstanding the addition of Radicals and other small parties to the old FRAP coalition, the UP's share of the vote actually decreased slightly from that achieved by FRAP in the 1964 election. More than a mandate for Allende, the election clearly demonstrated the extreme political divisions within Chilean society in 1970, with the "centrist" candidate finishing last.

According to the Chilean constitution, when no presidential candidate received a majority of the votes, Congress could choose as president one of the two candidates with the highest vote total. Since the Christian Democrats controlled the deciding votes in Congress, Alessandri proposed to exchange an immediate resignation for congressional designation of him as president. This would have allowed Eduardo Frei, ineligible to succeed himself immediately, to enter new elections and refashion a Rightist-Christian Democratic alliance to prevent Allende from becoming president. While this plan attracted some Christian Democrats, most of the party's congressional representatives and Radomiro Tomic opposed it firmly. Instead, they demanded passage of a package of constitutional guarantees with UP support prior to the congressional vote on Chile's next president: among these, guarantees of the multiparty system, maintenance of civil liberties and freedom of the press, access by all parties to government-controlled TV stations, protection for the armed forces against political purges or the creation of militia, continued existence of, and public subsidies for, the private educational system, autonomy of the university system, protection for government employees—many added during the Frei administration—against dismissals or political persecution. In short, the Christian Democrats sought to buttress with constitutional amendments Chile's existing *political system* against the in-coming Allende administration's plans for a new institutional order. The Christian Democrats insisted that only approval of these

TABLE 28. PRESIDENTIAL ELECTIONS, 1964 AND 1970

Political Parties and Candidates	1964 Total	1964 Percentage	1970 Total	1970 Percentage
FRAP/UP (Salvador Allende)	977,902	39.5	1,070,344	36.3
Christian Democrats (Eduardo Frei, 1964 Radomiro Tomic, 1970)	1,409,102	55.5	821,801	27.8
Julio Duran*	125,233	5.0		
Jorge Alessandri			1,031,159	34.9

* Durán withdrew his candidacy before the election but still received 5% of the vote.

amendments with the votes of UP deputies and senators would allow them to vote for Allende as president.

As the Christian Democrats bargained with the UP parties for constitutional amendments to limit the future course of an Allende government, Right-wing extremist groups, such as Patria y Libertad ("Fatherland and Freedom"), and United States business and diplomatic groups plotted to prevent Allende's inauguration. International Telephone and Telegraph, one of the largest American-based multinationals with interests in Chile, took the initiative in approaching the CIA with a plan to destabilize the Chilean economy through international economic pressure, delays, or cancellation of loans and credits, and by fomenting panic among Chile's private businesses. Covert efforts to bankrupt savings banks and to induce unemployment also figured in the American scheme to prevent Allende's confirmation by the Chilean Congress. Later, congressional hearings in the United States made clear that President Nixon and his closest foreign policy advisers, including Henry Kissinger, played an active role in this effort to subvert the work of Chile's Congress.

Despite the behind-the-scenes machinations of ITT and American policymakers, the UP bargain with the Christian Democrats on the package of constitutional amendments seemed to assure an Allende victory in the congressional voting. Nevertheless, two days before the Congress was to decide on Chile's next president, extreme right-wing groups, allegedly with CIA backing, made a desperate effort to kidnap the commander-in-chief of the Chilean army. Apparently they hoped to cast the blame for the abduction on MIR or on the UP— and thereby change the Christian Democratic votes in the Congress or provoke military intervention. This ploy backfired. General Schneider resisted his assailants, and they mortally wounded him in an exchange of gunfire. Schneider died on October 25, 1970, the day after the Chilean Congress confirmed Salvador Allende as Chile's next president.

Proclaiming that with him the people (*el pueblo*) of Chile entered into the presidential palace, Salvador Allende received the presidential sash on November 3, 1970. Less than three years later Allende's body would be carried from La Moneda, testimony to his unsuccessful struggle to take Chile down the peaceful road to socialism.

Salvador Allende inherited the political mythology and constitutional legitimacy of a system no longer viable without substantial modifications. The increasing violence, including political terrorism and "expropriation" of money from banks by *Miristas*, as well as the challenge to civilian authority represented by the *tacnazo* in the last year of the Frei administration, reflected the decomposition of the political arrangements that had held together the old order. President Allende lacked a revolutionary army to carry out his will; he headed a precarious multiparty coalition lacking both internal cohesiveness and underlying agreement on the pace and character of change to be implemented by the *unidad popular* government. Like all reformist Chilean presidents in the twentieth century, President Allende faced a hostile Congress and entrenched bureaucracy. And he lacked even the popular mandate President Aguirre Cerda had achieved after the election won by the popular front in 1938.

Worse still, Allende was a Marxist whose program evoked the intense hostility of the majority of the Chilean electorate as well as the uncompromising and active opposition of the United States. From the outset, American foreign policy, both covert and diplomatic, sought to disrupt the Chilean economy, to cut off or stifle credit from international lending agencies, to provide financial and moral support for the regime's opponents—and to maintain friendly relations with the Chilean military. Viewed as a "test case" of the viability of elected Marxist governments not only in Latin America but also in Western Europe (especially France and Italy), the Allende government potentially threatened the integrity of the NATO alliance as well as the southern cone of South America. Friendly and expanding relations with Cuba and Eastern Europe, when added to the government's eventual expropriation of American copper companies and other foreign investments, persuaded hard-line American officials that every effort be made to "destabilize" the Chilean economy and oust the UP government. The concentration in Santiago of numerous leftist intellectuals and political exiles from other Latin American countries made the Chilean capital a center of revolutionary activity, closely scrutinized by secret police and military intelligence agents from Brazil, Bolivia, Uruguay, and Argentina.

Ironically, the very successes of certain of the UP government's programs, and the economic consequences of these successes, so polarized Chilean society that less than three years after Allende's inauguration (August, 1973) the congressional opposition called upon the military to re-establish the "rule of the constitution and the law." In a setting quite different from the confrontation between President Balmaceda and Congress before the civil war of 1891, the confrontation between the UP coalition and the old order nevertheless adopted the familiar rhetoric and charges of Chilean politics: the president had violated his constitutional authority, and Congress sought to uphold its constitutional mandate, to assure respect for the constitution, and to prevent executive tyranny. Censure of government ministers and impeachment proceedings in Congress, so reminiscent of the structure of political conflict in the parliamentary period, now served as a reminder that the effort to implement socialism through legal means faced the challenge of the numerous checks and balances of liberal democracy inherent in the Chilean polity. Less than three weeks after Congress appealed to the armed forces to preserve Chilean democracy from presidential excess, a military coup on September 11, 1973, splattered the peaceful road to socialism with blood.

The popular unity government's short-term economic policies attempted to effect a massive income redistribution program through differential wage and salary readjustments to benefit the poorest sectors of Chilean society. In marked contrast to the stabilization schemes of the Ibáñez or Alessandri periods, the UP policymakers hoped to stimulate demand by providing significantly higher-than-inflation salary increments to the urban and rural poor. Added to increases in real income for the mass of Chilean workers, impressive increases in government expenditures and monetary expansion stimulated the stagnant economy. The administration's policymakers expected these meaures to increase effective demand and, thereby, to convince Chilean entrepreneurs to utilize the excess capacity that idled numerous workers. Thus, through a combination of income redistribution, increase in effective demand, and reduction of unemployment, the UP govern-

ment hoped to bring the country out of the economic recession inherited from the Frei government and to increase popular support for
the Allende coalition.

Unfortunately for the government, the monopolistic structure of
Chilean industry, rapidly expanding demands by workers for expropriation of farms and factories, and the corresponding distrust by private investors of the government's ultimate intentions toward private
firms, all militated against substantial private investment programs.
This meant that despite short-term improvements in industrial production and in worker consumption, the UP's programs of income redistribution in the context of a "transition to socialism"—with capitalist owners still making investment decisions—led inevitably to
shortages, rising prices, and black markets. Instead of investing for
the future, private entrepreneurs sold off their inventory at speculative
prices or, in agriculture, disposed of farm machinery and cattle herds.
They invested in dollars, German marks, or other hard currencies.
Under these conditions rising demand, escalating emissions of currency, and deficit spending fueled an inflation of extraordinary magnitude. By mid-1973 the annual rate of inflation exceeded 300 percent
and reduced the real income of workers and salaried employees to
levels below those of late 1970 when the UP had taken office.

Every short-term success of government policy involved contradictions that led ever more rapidly to political and economic disaster. In
part, this resulted from the disunity of the UP coalition. Acting as if
the coalition were simply another executive-electoral alliance, each
party demanded its share of the spoils. The government filled important administrative posts through an elaborate quota system which
assigned personnel designated by the political parties to positions
throughout the administration. Employment opportunities in the
firms nationalized, "intervened," or requisitioned by the government
became plums with which to reward party stalwarts or to combat unemployment. These difficulties led to precipitate declines in productivity throughout the economy.

In the rural sector, debate over the types of agricultural production
units to establish on the expropriated farms created uncertainty among
the campesinos and smallholders. Attacks on the *asentamiento* system introduced by the Christian Democrat administration alienated
the beneficiaries of the Frei agrarian reform, while experiments with
variations on collective farms, state farms, and regional production
units resulted in virtual disorganization of the agricultural economy.
After a good harvest in 1970-71, agricultural production declined seriously. As a result the government was forced to use scarce foreign ex-

change to import foodstuffs needed to meet the increased demand occasioned by higher worker incomes and to make up for the reduction in domestic production.

The government's methods for dealing with shortages, carrying out agrarian reform, and constructing the "social" or public sector of the economy exacerbated political tensions and intensified the economic crisis. In an attempt to minimize the problems of urban supply, the government organized public entities to compete with the private sector in wholesale and retail distribution. DINAC, a public enterprise constituted by the amalgamation of several large distribution agencies acquired by CORFO, made efforts to gain control of wholesale distribution, while thousands of private supply and price committees *juntas de abastecimiento popular* (JAP) were organized to cooperate in local distribution of articles of consumption to urban neighborhoods. These JAP committees assisted inspectors from DIRINCO, the agency charged with enforcing price controls, in their efforts to prevent private retail merchants from evading such controls. Subsequently, the supply of "people's marketbaskets," or *canastas populares*, to the JAP for distribution to the people of the shantytowns and worker neighborhoods directly threatened the viability of Chile's more than 125,000 retail merchants and uncounted ambulatory vendors. The JAPs also served as a potential organizational mechanism for administering a direct, mandatory system of rationing as well as for monitoring the activities of opposition elements at the local level. None of these implications were lost upon the opposition which attacked the inefficiency, corruption, and "political criteria" with which the JAPs distributed the *canastas populares*.

TABLE 29. THE AGRARIAN SECTOR

EXPORT OF GOODS AND AGRICULTURAL IMPORTS 1965-70
(YEARLY AVERAGE), 1971 AND 1972 (MILLIONS OF DOLLARS)

	1965-70	1971	1972
Total Exports	$939	$964	$836
Agricultural Exports	$ 24	$ 29	$ 19
Agricultural Imports	$184	$311	$468
Agricultural Imports as Percentage of Total Export Earnings	19.6%	32.2%	56.0%

(Source: Stefan de Vylder, *Allende's Chile*, Cambridge University Press, 1974, p. 202.)

Ideological and political fragmentation within the UP government heightened the economic uncertainty. Unable to control the activities of MIR, certain members of his own Socialist party, and the militant Mapucistas, President Allende failed to halt the acceleration of farm and factory seizures and illegal strikes in which workers demanded nationalization or expropriation of the enterprises where they were employed.

In the first eighteen months of the UP government, campesinos temporarily or permanently occupied some 1700 rural properties. In Article 171 of the agrarian reform law enacted by the Christian Democratic government, the Allende government found a legal mechanism to convert farm seizures or illegal strikes into de facto transfers of managerial responsibility for rural estates. Article 171 provided that "in case of lock-out or illegal work stoppage that, for any reason, suspends exploitation of a rural enterprise, the President of the Republic can order resumption of labors [reanudación de faenas] with the intervention of the civil authority . . . and the support of police if necessary." The law gave the government official [interventor] assigned to "intervene" the farm "all the prerogatives necessary to continue operation of the enterprise." With this authority government interventores could hire new personnel, incur new liabilities or pay old debts, and decide what crops to plant or animals to sell. A short period of intervention could easily bankrupt any farm or at least make most owners quite willing to sell their farms to CORA on favorable terms. Thus, Article 171 of the agrarian reform law could be used by the Popular Unity government as a flexible legal tool to speed up the agrarian reform process—if only campesinos intensified the process of illegal farm occupations or strikes. In practice this tactic was used on so many farms that the administration soon ran out of party loyalists in the agrarian bureaucracies to assign as interventores.

In the urban sector the government resorted to application of the all-but-forgotten Decree Law 520, a vestige of the "Socialist Republic" of 1932. As indicated in Chapter 8, this decree law allowed the government to requisition, intervene, or expropriate any private enterprise that failed to comply with laws regulating price controls, speculation, stockpiling in anticipation of increases in official prices for particular commodities, interruption of production, or refusal to utilize efficiently installed capacity when the government decided there existed a "shortage" of a particular commodity. Legislation against lockouts also gave the government leverage in labor conflicts. As in the agricultural sector, requisitions or interventions in industry

TABLE 30. REQUISITIONS AND INTERVENTIONS,
NOVEMBER 1970–NOVEMBER 1972

Period	Interventions	Requisitions	Total
November-December 1970	37	1	38
January-February 1971	23	—	23
March-April 1971	1	5	6
May-June 1971	12	12	24
July-August 1971	9	6	15
September-October 1971	24	7	31
November-December 1971	21	9	30
January-February 1972	13	6	19
March-April 1972	14	7	21
May-June 1972	16	3	19
July-August 1972	7	18	25
September-October 1972*	23	48	71
November 1972	2	4	6
Total	202	126	328

* During the October strike a large number of enterprises were subjected to intervention or requisition for participation in the general lockout. Most of these companies were later returned to their owners.

(Source: Based on Instituto de Economía, *La Economía Chilena en 1972*, pp. 116ff. After Stefan de Vylder, *Allende's Chile*, Cambridge University Press, 1974, p. 146.)

could quickly bankrupt the legal owners and facilitate transfer of the affected industry to the public sector.

Under these conditions the predictions made in 1938 by Polish economist Oscar Lange proved entirely accurate. Indeed Lange's analysis is perhaps the most appropriate epitaph, as well as explanation, for the domestic economic failures of the UP government.

An economic system based on private enterprise and private property of the means of production can work only as long as the security of private property and of income derived from enterprise is maintained. The very existence of a government bent on introducing socialism is a constant threat to this security. Therefore, the capitalistic economy cannot function under a socialist government unless the government is socialist in name only.

. . . Owners threatened with expropriation have no inducement to make the necessary investments and to manage them efficiently. And no government supervision or administrative

TABLE 31. INDUSTRIAL ESTABLISHMENTS CONTROLLED BY THE CHILEAN STATE

Form of control	November 1970	December 1971	December 1972	May 1973
State ownership*	31	62	103	165
Under Intervention or Requisition	–	39	99	120
Total	31	101	202	285

* Both social and mixed areas and including six new industries that were created by the Chilean state after November 1970.
(Source: Stefan de Vylder, *Allende's Chile*, Cambridge University Press, 1974, p. 145.)

measures can cope effectively with the passive resistance and sabotage of the owners and managers.

No administrative device adopted by the government could cope with the resistance of the opposition. Black markets, shortages, and rampant inflation undermined confidence in the government and hardened the opposition forces against the de facto socialization of the economy. At the same time that the activities of MIR and the most radical members of the government coalition convinced the government's enemies that only violent resistance could halt consolidation of a new political reality, the Communists and Allende sought to negotiate a de-escalation of conflict with the Christian Democrats in exchange for clearly defined limits on the extent of socialization in industry and agriculture. Neither those who believed that socialism could be established only through force and popular mobilization, nor the Partido Nacional and the growing movement of economic and professional associations (*gremios*) committed to violent counterrevolution, gave any breathing room to the government's efforts to arrive at a pacific resolution of the crisis.

As the political and economic situation deteriorated, supply and distribution problems in the urban areas sent into the streets thousands of women from upper-, middle-, and even working-class homes, banging on pots and pans to symbolize the government's inability to resolve the economic crisis. In response, organized workers and their families facetiously offered to share their food with the *momios* (literally, "mummy," a term UP sympathizers applied to the supporters of the old order) if they were really unable to feed themselves. Moving their struggle against the government to the streets, leaders of the major trade associations and economic interest groups such as the SNA and the SFF allied themselves with extreme right-wing political organizations such as Patria y Libertad, PROTECO, and Soberania, Orden y Libertad (SOL). These recently organized movements established white guard vigilantes to resist farm and factory seizures and to recover occupied private property in *retomas*. By mid-1972 the opposition had united in a so-called *gremialista* movement. A massive strike in October of 1972 mobilized shopkeepers, professional and economic associations, bank clerks, students, and even certain working-class and campesino groups in an effort to shut down the Chilean economy. The strike was precipitated by the demand of the 40,000 members of the independent truckers' association that the government suspend its plans to create a state-owned trucking enterprise, but it quickly became openly political and directly challenged the UP government and its program.

Recognizing the critical political moment, ex-President Eduardo Frei personally influenced the Christian Democratic party to support the strike and mobilize its followers in opposition to the government. On October 15, 1972, the party's secretary general, Renán Fuentealba declared that the government was "acting openly in defiance of the constitution and the laws, as well as of fundamental human rights," and that this circumstance was "dangerous for all our citizens." In light of this danger, Fuentealba affirmed the Christian Democrats' adherence to the truckers' movement. Predictably, the Partido Nacional aggressively supported the strike, maintaining that only organized civil disobedience could overcome the government's effort to impose communism on Chile.

Faced with a situation bordering on insurrection, the UP government declared a partial state of emergency. This meant that military officers took over the responsibility for maintaining order, for enforcing temporary censorship on the opposition media, and, in effect, for shoring up the UP coalition's fragile position. By October 21, the newly created *comando gremial* confronted the government with a sweeping set of demands that, if accepted, would have amounted to abrogation of the UP program. Despite the serious economic effects of the strike (the government later estimated the loss to the country at almost $300 million), continued production in the factories and support by UP loyalists prevented a complete economic shutdown. The *gremialista* movement failed to win a definitive victory. In addition, the emergence of new working-class organizations, or *cordones industriales*, among the factory workers in Santiago's "industrial belts"—

such as Los Cerrillos, Puente Alto, and Vicuña MacKenna—threatened the development of real popular militias and institutions of "parallel power." Pursuing a more revolutionary course than the leadership of the CUT, the Communist party, or President Allende, a nucleus of revolutionary workers in the *cordones industriales* began preparing for armed confrontation.

Coincident with the October strike, the opposition moved on the legislative front to impeach four of Allende's ministers. Faced with a loss of key advisers and the resurrection of the political tactic of censure and impeachment of ministers, President Allende made a critical political decision. He invited the army commander-in-chief, Carlos Prats, to serve as minister of interior while at the same time continuing in his army post. The president also included an air force general and an admiral in his new cabinet. Jacques Chonchol, the ex-Christian Democrat who served as Allende's minister of agriculture and was probably the member of the Allende ministerial team most hated by the opposition (because of his leadership in the agrarian reform process), left the cabinet.

Declaring their full confidence in General Prats, the leaders of the truckers' strike negotiated a settlement in early November that included promises by the government to return enterprises occupied by workers during the strike and also not to nationalize the transport and wholesale trade sectors of the economy. Although the government did not entirely fulfill these promises, the October strike had made the military the arbiter of the nation's political conflicts.

General Prats emphasized that the two most important tasks facing the new cabinet consisted of restoration of order and administration of peaceful, honest congressional elections in March 1973. In the aftermath of the truckers' strike, however, speculation abounded about the extent of American financial support and CIA involvement in the events of October. Meanwhile the opposition looked to the March 1973 elections as an opportunity to win the two-thirds majority in the Congress that would permit Allende's impeachment. The presence of General Prats in the interior ministry seemed to guarantee the integrity of the March elections, but it also inspired harsh condemnation from those on the left who proposed "getting on with the Revolution."

Concentrating their efforts on the upcoming elections, the Christian Democrats, the Partido Nacional, and other opposition forces forged an electoral alliance called the Democratic Confederation, or CODE. The results of the March elections, however, proved a victory for no one. CODE obtained 55 percent of the votes but actually lost seats in the Congress to the UP coalition. The opposition *was* a majority, but it now faced three years of the Allende administration before the presidential elections scheduled for 1976. Notwithstanding the veracity of CODE's claims of electoral fraud and the abnormal delay in reporting the election returns, there could be no doubt that the UP coalition retained significant popular support. Despite the economic crisis, shortages of consumer goods, and the opposition's media offensive against the government, the UP coalition still could count on more than 40 percent of Chile's voters—an increase over its electoral support in the 1970 presidential elections.

Between March 1973 and September 1973, intensified militancy by MIR and certain elements within the UP coalition, as well as public threats by Socialist leader Carlos Altamirano to infiltrate and subvert the armed forces, were juxtaposed to counterrevolutionary economic sabotage and terrorism. The galloping inflation rate increased the number of strikes, including an extremely costly work stoppage by the miners at the El Teniente copper mine in Rancagua. Workers who in the past had looked to Marxist union leaders now followed a Christian Democrat in a strike condemned by the UP government. Lasting more than two months, the strike drew support from thousands of university students and members of the Federation of Secondary Students in Santiago. It also directly pitted the UP government against an important group of organized workers—not against *momios*.

Amidst rampant inflation, political and economic crises, and the rising pitch of government and opposition rhetoric, unsuccessful negotiations between the government and the Christian Democrats continued—even after an abortive coup d'état by the second tank regiment in Santiago in June 1973. The quick defeat of this *tancazo* seemed to reaffirm General Prats' commitment to defense of the constitutional government. Gradually, however, Prats' apparent political ambitions, rumors that he would emerge as the UP presidential candidate in 1976, and an incident in which he reportedly threatened a woman driver with death for sticking out her tongue at him as he motored through Santiago, all combined to erode his support among fellow officers.

The political situation grew even worse in late July with new strikes by the truckers and the *gremialista* movement. After a temporary absence, representatives of the armed forces again returned to the cabinet to restore order (August 9, 1973). Now all three service commanders, as well as the commander of the national police force (*carabineros*), occupied ministries. Intensified implementation of the provisions of the gun control law, passed in 1972, sent military units to factories and shanty towns to disarm workers and forestall a popular insurrection. These searches for arms, or *allanamientos*, also served to collect intelligence on the quantity of arms available in the *cordones industriales*, and to train army units in tactics for confrontation with the civilian population at factory work sites, union halls, party offices, and in the *poblaciones*. The number of *allanamientos* increased gradually after early 1973. Less attention was given to the armed vigilantes organized by the *gremialista* and right-wing political movements. In July 1973, according to pro-*unidad popular* sources, only two of twenty-four *allanamientos* involved "groups of armed fascists"; all the rest were directed against factories, offices of *unidad popular* parties, government offices, or other supporters of the Allende government. By the first part of August, when the new military-based cabinet was organized, the *allanamientos* were coordinated operations of army, air force, and naval units moving against leftists throughout the nation.

In the meantime the *gremialista* strike movement continued, supported by the entire political opposition and students at the Catholic University. Unable to negotiate an end to the trucking strike and annoyed by obstacles put in his way by Allende's civilian supporters, air force General César Ruiz Danyau abruptly resigned from the cabinet only days after accepting the portfolio of transport and public works. President Allende's quick acceptance of Ruiz's resignation as minister *and as air force commander-in-chief* provoked a new political crisis, involving agitation among the general's air force colleagues.

Violence in the streets of Santiago, political terrorism by leftists and rightists, and an imminent state of political chaos elicited a call by the majority opposition in the Chilean Congress for the military to intervene to guarantee institutional stability, civil peace, security, and development. The same day, hundreds of wives of military officers gathered outside of General Prats' residence to demand his resignation. Prats resigned the next day and was followed by his military colleagues General Guillermo Pickering and Mario Sepúlveda (commander of the Santiago garrison). Now President Allende was at the mercy of General Augusto Pinochet Ugarte.

On September 11, 1973, General Pinochet and his fellow service commanders led a well-coordinated, brutal, and highly successful military movement that ended the UP government and resulted in the death of President Salvador Allende. According to the military, Salvador Allende committed suicide after surviving aerial bombardment of the presidential palace.

More has been written about Chile between 1970 and 1973 than about all the rest of Chilean history. The *unidad popular* experience raised important theoretical questions for socialist intellectuals and politicians concerning the viability and correct tactics of the "peaceful road to socialism." These leftists who believe(d) in the possibility of such a process have sought to determine where the Allende government went wrong, how the process could have been salvaged, how European Communists and Socialists can prevent the "fascization" of the middle class which was the social base of the counterrevolution in Chile.

Although congressional investigations in the United States have made available incontrovertible evidence of extensive U.S. efforts to undermine the Allende government, many Marxists still insist that the "real" key to the failure of the UP administration was the activities of the ultra-leftists." Typical in this respect, an important article in *World Marxist Review* (July 1974) noted that "the working class was gradually forced into isolation and the intermediate strata became, objectively, allies of the country's enemies. . . . The Chilean experience has reaffirmed anew that ultra-leftism is a boon for imperialism and reaction." In the year after the military coup, leaders of the Chilean Communist party who escaped the military intelligence's dragnet, still insisted that "at times of crisis we worked in alliance with the patriotic part of the Army faithful to the constitution and this played a decisive role in suppressing the October 1972 conspiracy [the truckers' strike]. This alliance could have developed were it not for the spread of ultraleftism."

In contrast, Trotskyists and other militant revolutionaries have seen in the Chilean experience new evidence that there can be no peaceful road to socialism. They argue that Allende should have armed and unleashed the workers and peasants in a violent revolutionary movement to destroy Chile's liberal democracy and the capitalist state. How the military would have reacted to such a move by President Allende in 1970 or 1971—and the inevitable massacre that would have occurred—is usually omitted from these "revolutionary" postmortems.

For the Right and the Christian Democrats, of course, there was little interest in explaining why Allende failed to take Chile down the peaceful road to socialism. Like the Marxists and other UP supporters, however, they found soon enough that the military coup that ousted President Allende brought neither relief from economic crisis nor restoration of constitutional order. Instead, the Chilean military imposed a highly authoritarian, repressive political regime that effectively eliminated every basis of civil liberty and political freedom stipulated in the Chilean constitution of 1925.

The ultimate tragedy of *unidad popular*, then, was that President Allende lost the opportunity to carry out important social reforms while maintaining the political liberty that had evolved in Chile after 1932. United States diplomacy, economic pressure, and covert subversion of Chile's domestic politics played an important role in the failure of the UP coalition. However, American or other outside pressures could not by themselves have ensured this failure. Short of military intervention, the United States did not have enough leverage, even with the variety of economic and political screws it tightened, to guarantee Allende's failure. Whereas the Agency for International Development (AID), the Export-Import Bank, the Inter-American Development Bank, and the World Bank rejected Chile's requests for credit during 1971 and 1972, short-term credits from Western Europe, the Soviet Union, and the Socialist bloc more than made up for the withdrawal of financial support by the United States. A large foreign exchange surplus inherited from the Frei government even allowed temporary increases in imports to buttress the government's short-term emphasis on improved consumption for the working classes. This was so despite declines in copper prices that portended extreme balance-of-payment problems in 1971. By the end of 1971 the government's principal economic strategist, Pedro Vuskovic, alleged that lack of foreign exchange constituted the main constraint on further realization of the UP program. This constraint originated not in a net decrease in available foreign credits, but rather in circumstances occasioned largely by the government's own economic policies.

Whatever the full extent of United States complicity in the tragedy of September 1973, and whatever the impact of international economics, the most critical factor of all in the failure of the Allende administration was bad politics. Bad politics—the spouting of revolutionary rhetoric without the force to impose a revolutionary program—produced a politico-economic crisis. Bad politics prevented conciliation and compromise with the Christian Democrats, the small shopkeepers, the truckers, the beneficiaries of the Frei agrarian reform—in short, with all the elements of the middle strata, working class, and peasantry who had nothing to lose and much to gain by an attack on economic monopolies and foreign corporations. President Allende failed because he lacked the power to impose a revolutionary socialist regime yet insisted on employing the rhetoric of revolution. He failed also because there is no peaceful road to the socialism envisaged by Marxist-Leninists in a liberal democratic polity. By pursuing an illusion that threatened the livelihood of broad sectors of the population, President Allende's *unidad popular* coalition set the stage for a counterrevolution that imposed upon Chile a regime of coercion, intolerance, and brutality unequaled since the era of conquest.

Chapter 10 • Dictatorship

Not even the shrillest political rhetoric of leftists and rightists between 1970 and 1973 prepared Chileans for the ferocity of the military coup of September 11, 1973. Accustomed as they were to the gross hyperbole of propaganda from all political parties and movements since the early 1930s, most Chileans did not really believe that a military *Putsch* would occur; fewer still anticipated installation of a military-dominated government that would become the longest-lived administration in Chilean history.

Called upon by opposition groups in the Congress to restore the constitutional order purportedly violated by the Popular Unity government, the military leadership instead closed the legislature, curtailed activities by political parties, and outlawed the political organizations that had supported the government of President Allende. Press censorship, suspension of civil liberties, and fierce repression of leading politicians, labor leaders, academics, and other supposed Marxist sympathizers merged into a "holy war" against what the military called the "Marxist cancer."

Initial resistance to the coup in factories, workplaces, homes, and in the streets proved hopeless against the overwhelming power and brutality of the military forces which hunted down and attacked Allende supporters and other "subversives." Thousands of Chileans died in the first days after the coup, while accounts of torture in the improvised detention centers throughout the nation became so widespread as to be routine.

The military junta directed its avenging wrath not only at political leaders but also at symbols of the cultural and institutional foundations of Chilean democracy. When Chilean Nobel prize-winning poet and Communist party activist Pablo Neruda died of cancer—and grief—eleven days after the coup, his house was ransacked and the library vandalized. Though his funeral procession became a spontaneous protest against the junta, the circumstances of his death also symbolized the junta's determination to eradicate all vestiges of the political left. Literature, sculpture, painting, and even popular songs now became targets of the junta's violence. The murder of intellectual and folksinger Victor Jara at the National Stadium (turned into a prison and torture center) initiated an era in which listening to records or tapes by "subversive" artists would be quiet acts of resistance.

General Augusto Pinochet justified the coup and the new government's repressive measures in part by alleging that the Allende coalition had a plot (*plan zeta*) to murder military and civilian opposition leaders in order to impose communism definitively upon Chile. Moreover, the general maintained:

> The greatest possible enforcement and highest respect for Human Rights implies that these must not be exercised by those individuals who spread doctrines or commit acts which in fact seek to abolish them. This makes it necessary to apply restrictions as rigorous as the circumstances may require to those who defy the juridical norms in force. . . . Our attitude must necessarily remain inflexible for the good of Chile and its people.

In addition to justifying its violent extirpation of subversives, the Chilean junta pointed to the international significance of its victory over communism. Reminding Chileans of the glories of independence, General Pinochet declared that "Chile was one of the first countries in the world to abolish slavery. Now our country has broken the chains of totalitarian Marxism, the great Twentieth-Century Slavery, before which so many bow their heads without the courage to defeat it. We are thus once again pioneers in Humanity's fight for liberation."

The military pioneers in "Humanity's fight for liberation" did not limit their attacks to supporters of the Allende government. Once the initial campaign of terror and assassination gave way to gradual institutionalization of a military-police state, the regime's leaders made clear that they intended to write the final epitaph for Chilean democracy and to transform the moral and intellectual foundations of

Chilean life. Military rectors replaced academic administrators in the universities; Chilean higher education faced a thorough pogrom which practically wiped out departments and schools in the social sciences, philosophy, education, and other disciplines touched by Marxist or liberal influences. Social and ideological pluralism disappeared.

In a fashion reminiscent of the military's heroes—Portales and Ibáñez—the junta declared its contempt for "old style" democracy, for politics, and for politicians. Rekindling the embers of the military movement of 1924 and Ibáñez' theme of anti-politics in the 1952 election, the junta replaced Ibáñez' symbolic broom with torture and death—and promised to end forever the immorality, corruption, and ineptitude of civilian democratic politics which had allowed the assumption of the Popular Unity government.

As the initial fury of September 11, 1973 subsided, the military junta turned to the task of imposing a new social and political order upon Chile. In retrospect, it is possible to identify several overlapping stages in the evolution of the policies of the military junta and its civilian supporters in their efforts to carry out a thorough "modernization" and "cleansing" (*depuración*) of the Chilean polity. In the first stage, the government implemented essentially *ad hoc* measures of political repression and economic retrenchment to establish political control and achieve economic stabilization. By 1975, a second stage began as the regime institutionalized the new security apparatus and intensified repression against the leadership of the targeted leftist parties and movements. When the limited success of the economic measures became evident, the junta adopted a more drastic economic "shock treatment." This second stage—consolidation of General Pinochet's control through the secret police and security apparatus and adoption of the shock treatment—brought a radical application of orthodox monetary and fiscal policy combined with a number of politically motivated cuts in particular government agencies and public enterprises.

During these first two stages in the evolution of military policy, key leaders began to enunciate a longer term program for political and economic transformation of Chile. First, in a "Declaration of Principles of the Government of Chile" (1974), the junta proclaimed its intention to "take upon itself the historic mission of giving Chile new governmental institutions that [would] embody the profound changes occurring in modern times." In order to do this the government "guided by the inspiration of Portales, . . . [would] energetically apply the principle of authority and drastically punish any outburst of disorder or anarchy." Anticipating later policies, the "Declaration of Principles" also emphasized the task of "reorganizing the economy, destroyed to its very roots by Marxism," and "imposing authority and discipline in production and labor relations."

Further elaborating on these themes in 1975, the government published *National Objectives of the Chilean Government.* Once again emphasizing the linkage of its political vision with Chile's Portalian legacy and the country's national heritage, the junta declared that a new political system would require "formation of new generations steeped in the concepts of love of God, the Fatherland and the family . . ." This declaration hinted at the strong push for a new curriculum that the junta would later introduce into the nation's primary schools, emphasizing patriotism, morality, and anti-communism. The new political system would also involve a strengthening of presidential authority and a "rationalized, modern and functional public administration purified of all political and party influence. . . ." Without specifying further the precise character of this new political system, the government made clear that it would be *depoliticized,* technocratic, efficient, and free from Marxist influence.

A third phase in the development of the military junta's political objectives began almost simultaneously with implementation of the "shock treatment." No longer satisfied with emergency decrees, and seeking to create an apparent juridical legitimacy, the junta introduced a series of "constitutional acts," which amended or eliminated certain parts of the Constitution of 1925—without fully replacing it. Lacking any legal basis, these "constitutional acts" proved of little use in legitimizing the military dictatorship. However, changing economic and political conditions within Chile from 1976 to 1980 led, in 1980, to a fourth stage of post-1973 institutional development: a national plebiscite on a new constitution and its implementation in 1981. In the period after 1981, the government sought to institutionalize the program of socio-economic and political transformation initiated with the coup in 1973. This included the so-called seven modernizations announced in 1979 (see below) and implementation of the new constitution. In this stage General Pinochet sought to manage a resurgence of political opposition amidst an economic recession (1981-84) and then to complete the presidential term which ended in 1989 according to the 1980 constitution.

Though recognizable in retrospect as overlapping stages in the development of post-1973 Chile, the contradictory tendencies within the military government, among both military and civilian elites, as well as the concerted struggle of opponents against the dictatorship, made the everyday history of this evolution far from inevitable. Following that process in some detail provides a framework for understanding the conflictive, polarized society that emerged in Chile in the late 1980s.

In 1973 no fundamental consensus existed within the military regarding the appropriate duration of military rule or upon a comprehensive alternative political regime. Civilian supporters of the military government also disagreed as to the type of political system that ought to follow military rule. Some preferred a relatively quick restoration of civilian government under a more restrictive liberal democracy which excluded Marxist and leftist participation. Others favored replacing liberal democratic institutions with a more corporatist system based on functional representation through occupational associations or *gremios*. (The term *gremio* in Chile was used broadly to refer to professional and occupational associations as diverse as truckers, white-collar employees, and retail merchants. *Gremios* had constituted the main social base of opposition to the Popular Unity government.)

Despite lack of agreement on the type of political system with which to replace that established under the Chilean constitution of 1925, a general consensus within the military blamed "politics" and the "political class" for the crisis of 1970-73 and for the economic disaster the country had experienced. According to this view, the defects of Chilean democracy and the unpatriotic, self-interested maneuverings of politicians had permitted the penetration of Marxism into Chilean national life. This threatened the nation's historical traditions as well as its national security and sovereignty. The junta leadership and its supporters viewed the military coup as the beginning of a salvational crusade to wrest *la patria* from the abyss.

A narrower, technocratic critique of Chilean development from the 1930s until 1973 emanated especially from a group of economists influenced by conservative academics in the United States. Many of these Chileans had received advanced professional education at the University of Chicago or studied in Chile under Chicago-influenced professors as part of an exchange program with the Catholic University established in the 1950s. In Chile they were soon nicknamed "the Chicago Boys" or, more generically, the neo-liberal economists. These economists focused upon the inefficient allocation of resources that resulted from politicization of the economy, overregulation, excessive protectionism, and the burden of unprofitable public enterprises. Underlying these defects was a *political system* that spawned irresponsible demands and demagogic promises.

In the short run, a melding of anti-political sentiment, anti-Marxism, and the technocratic orientations of the junta's policy advisers led to a combination of ferocious repression of the opposition and, by 1975, to economic shock treatment.

In the period 1973 to 1975, the junta seemed to have the support of a majority of Chileans in the effort to restore political order and reconstruct the economy. Professional organizations, the *gremios*, a number of women's organizations sharing the banner of *poder feminino*, and the major non-Marxist political parties—in short, the social base of the opposition to the Popular Unity government—viewed the military junta as the only short-term solution to the political and economic crisis facing the nation. Even most religious leaders initially supported the military intervention. The hierarchy of the Catholic Church, at odds with the Popular Unity government over proposed educational reforms, called upon the Chilean population to cooperate with the new regime in restoring order, even though the Permanent Committee of the Episcopal Conference lamented the violence and bloodshed of the coup. In a 1975 study done by researcher Brian Smith, almost all of the bishops of the Chilean Catholic Church indicated that they believed the coup had been necessary.

Only slowly and with painful moderation did the majority of Chilean social and political groups begin to challenge even the most extreme measures of the military government. MIR, which had predicted a coup all along and criticized the naiveté of a "peaceful road to socialism," declared that socialism had not been defeated, but rather that a "reformist illusion" had come to an end. The military security apparatus made MIR activists a special target; penetration of the organization by military security, torture of captured *Miristas*, and murder of many militants significantly weakened the MIR organization by 1976. Likewise, the government targeted the Communist party leadership as well as party-affiliated labor union, student, and community organizations. Systematic persecution resulted in the deaths of many Communist party members and the capture of almost the entire internal leadership in 1976. By then, however, the party had created a clandestine apparatus within Chile. It had also created a parallel party organization in Europe, with the Central Committee leadership operating in the Soviet Union. Thus, the

Communists, albeit with difficulty, maintained contacts with worker, peasant, student, and community organizations.

Divided even before the military coup, the Chilean Socialist party fragmented further after 1973. Debates over the cause of the coup and proper goals for the party under the dictatorship left two major factions—one supporting an alliance with the Communists and another favoring a more moderate role in alliance with non-Marxist Leninist democratic parties. In many ways, in the initial periods after the coup, the Socialist party suffered the most serious disintegration and divisions of all Chilean political movements.

In contrast to the leftist parties and movements, a majority of Christian Democrats initially approved of the military ouster of President Allende. While expressing their regret for the departure from Chile's constitutional traditions, party leaders nevertheless laid blame for the coup on "the economic disaster, institutional chaos, armed violence and the profound moral crisis to which the deposed government led the nation." Christian Democratic leaders called upon their supporters to "contribute to the new government their technical, professional, or functional cooperation." The Christian Democrats expected a brief military interlude and then elections which would allow ex-President Frei to assume again the executive office.

In its 1974 "Declaration of Principles," however, the military leaders affirmed that ". . . it is imperative to change the mentality of Chileans. . . . The Government does not intend to be a mere caretaker. . . . The Government of the Armed Forces aspires to initiate a new era in the national destiny. . . ." This declaration and subsequent actions taken against Christian Democratic leaders and party members destroyed the illusions of Christian Democrats who had supported the coup. It also vindicated the judgment of a minority of Christian Democrats who denounced the coup from the first instance. Christian Democratic leaders finally understood that it would be impossible to implement their own programs through the junta, or to convince the military leaders to step aside. Gradually, the full scope of the military repression and the realization that democracy would not be restored pushed most of the Christian Democrats into active opposition to the military government. In turn, General Pinochet felt entrenched enough to dispense with the façade of a legal political party opposition. By 1977 the military would no longer tolerate Christian Democratic or other organized opposition and decreed the "dissolution" of *all* political parties.

Meanwhile, some groups and individuals within the Catholic Church also opposed and confronted military repression. In October

1973 the Committee of Cooperation for Peace (COPACHI) began to provide legal services, food, medical assistance, and sanctuary to victims of the persecution unleashed by the military and the new security apparatus, *Dirección Nacional de Inteligencia* (DINA). Gradually a national network of safehouses and underground resistance emerged, oftentimes using Church buildings or the homes of courageous Chileans willing to risk their lives to save others from death or torture. With the Church and Chilean Catholics sorely divided, however, some religious leaders withdrew from COPACHI after evidence surfaced of its linkages to clandestine activities. Under pressure from conservative Catholics and from General Pinochet, Cardinal Silva dissolved COPACHI in 1975.

Soon thereafter Cardinal Silva Henríquez established the Vicariate of Solidarity, which from 1976 onwards became the single most important source of moral opposition to the dictatorship. At the same time, it provided a partial umbrella of protection for numerous community organizations, research institutes, and human-rights defense groups. In particular, small groups of women, partially sheltered against the regime's wrath by the moral umbrella of the Church and partially protected by their status as "women, mothers, and wives," became visible leaders in the struggle against human rights abuses. In practice, neither the moral umbrella of the Church nor the supposedly elevated role of mothers and wives in a society which the military and their civilian allies claimed was based on the privileged place of the family, entirely protected human rights activists and other women viewed as subversives from hideous psychological torture, rape, and worse in the regime's detention centers. Nevertheless, the permeable umbrella of the Church permitted *some* protection against the systematic campaign of political repression. The Vicariate also extended material support to the urban and rural poor, provided technical assistance to small farmers, published magazines for popular education, and maintained records on political detainees and "disappeared" persons (people killed or detained and unaccounted for by the government).

Consolidation of the military junta's political power occurred simultaneously with the gradual evolution of a program of economic stabilization and deregulation. In the first eighteen months, economic policy, like the government's political initiatives, had an "emergency" character. Bringing a halt to hyperinflation along with deregulating the economy and reducing the entrepreneurial role of the state (thereby reducing the large losses in public enterprises) received primary attention. To achieve these objectives the government devalued the Chilean currency, removed price controls from almost all commodities (October 1973), postponed scheduled wage increases (and then adjusted wages in relation to a doctored consumer price index), freed interest rates for capital market transactions, and modified taxes. To encourage investment the government eliminated capital gains taxes and reduced taxes on corporate profits. A new value-added tax of 20 percent was introduced to raise revenue. In addition, the government returned to private ownership more than two hundred firms incorporated into the public sector under the Popular Unity government. The junta also took initial steps to liberalize trade and capital flows by reducing tariff barriers and passing a new foreign investment law (Decree Law 600, 1974) that gave foreign investors equal treatment with domestic investors. Reduced tariff barriers were supposed to make imported goods less expensive for the Chilean consumer and also to encourage efficiency and modernization of Chilean industry. Perhaps most importantly, the junta drastically reduced government expenditures and employment in the public sector.

Unfavorable international economic trends, including increasing prices for imported oil, sharply falling prices for Chilean exports, especially copper, and rising interest rates limited the success of the *junta's* economic policies. The unfavorable international trends, combined with the government's focus on reducing public sector expenditures, led to dramatic increases in unemployment, which exceeded 14 percent of the labor force by official estimates in 1975. Real wages declined sharply as did labor's share of gross domestic income. Inflation, though reduced, continued at levels over 300 percent per year in 1975. While still blaming the difficult economic situation on the legacy of the Popular Unity government, the military leadership and a group of civilian advisers decided to shift from its "gradualist" approach to the earlier mentioned economic "shock treatment."

In previewing the shock program, Minister of Economy Sergio de Castro declared that the misery and suffering experienced by Chileans in the period 1974-75 "[was] the result of the years of demagogy and erroneous economic policies, the consequence of an exaggerated statism, the result of exaggerated protectionism that guaranteed monopoly profits . . . the result of policies made to benefit special interest groups to the detriment of the majority of the population." The shock treatment was intended to eliminate inflation and institutional barriers to economic growth quickly and dramatically through intensification of the stabilization program already in place and the addition of new more radical policies. Minister of Finance Jorge Cauas, in announcing the shock program in April 1975, told the nation:

The President of the Republic and the Honorable Government Junta have asked me to design and carry out an economic
program with the fundamental purpose of eradicating the inflation that has affected our country for more than seventy years
and which recently has become extreme as a result of the dema-
gogical economic policy carried out by the former government.
. . . The main objective of this program is, as we have already stated, to put a brake on inflation by the end of this year.
For this reason, certain basic measures have been approved. Although these measures imply continued sacrifice on the part of
the community in the coming months, the compensations will
be economic stability which will permit adequate economic development. This will mean that in the not too distant future
poverty will be stamped out and all Chileans will be able to
benefit from the advantages of the modern world.
. . . The way to recovery, although it is short and well
known, is fraught with sacrifices and denials. . . .

What followed included reductions of between 15 to 25 percent
in government expenditures and drastic decreases in the size and role
of the public sector; a temporary 10 percent increase in income taxes;
a series of tax revisions to increase government income; and tightened
monetary policy. Approximately 80,000 government employees lost
their jobs and unemployment grew throughout the economy, while
industrial output dropped 25 percent in 1975. However, inflation declined precipitously (from over 300 percent per year in 1974 to 84
percent in 1977) and the government deficit practically disappeared
by the end of 1975.
In many respects these government policies achieved their short-
term objectives. Declines in the rate of inflation, improvement in
government revenue collection, and elimination of large government
deficits all encouraged government policymakers. Hyperinflation disappeared, but inflationary expectations lingered. In 1976 the government resorted to revaluation of the Chilean peso by 10 percent, with
subsequent pre-announced exchange-rate adjustments to convince
the Chilean people that inflation was truly under control. Though
very impressive improvement did occur, inflation remained above 30
percent per year.
Numerous technical critiques of the shock treatment emerged
among opponents of the military government as well as among some
supporters who disagreed both with the severity of the economic
measures and with the impact these policies had on key sectors of

the economy. The most evident and widespread impacts involved massive unemployment, reaching approximately 20 percent of the labor force, and a steep decline in gross domestic product—down officially by 13 percent in a single year. Grim, desperate impoverishment afflicted millions of Chileans.

The recession and unemployment also began to induce a restructuring of the labor force. More and more poor Chileans performed occasional services ("guarding" cars, wiping windshields, shining shoes, working as domestic servants) and/or became itinerant vendors (*ambulantes*) of combs, gum, candy, pens, foodstuffs, or other low value commodities. Increasing participation in small-scale commerce and services created a more isolated, disorganized labor force, while contributing to feelings of social dislocation and to a preoccupation with survival on a daily basis. Reinforced by the political repression, secret police raids on homes and *poblaciones*, and the intensity of government efforts to eradicate community, student, and labor organizations, these conditions cast a pall of despair over the urban shantytowns and small provincial towns. Restitution of farmland to former owners and dismantling of the agrarian reform cooperatives (see Chapter 1) pleased many recipients of the new farm properties, but also left 35,000 to 40,000 landless workers who failed to qualify for the military program of land parcelization. Scattered makeshift settlements or *villorrios* in the rural areas cropped up around the country, and rural-urban migration accelerated without providing either jobs or solace to the migrants.

As a result of the desperate economic situation, the growth of the informal and service sectors, and the loss of jobs in certain parts of the industrial sector of the economy, labor force participation by women—and particularly poor women—greatly increased. The recession made working outside the home a necessity for survival. This trend, which would continue into the late 1980s, contributed to a further breakdown in traditional family patterns, both by inducing an increased "independence" of many women and by eroding the self-esteem of men unable to perform their expected role of "protectors and providers" in the nuclear family. Thus, while the military government proclaimed its intentions to reaffirm and support the traditional patriarchal family as the basic unit of Chilean society, government policies and the economic crisis confronted many Chilean women and the families they sustained with quite another reality.

In efforts to palliate the urgent situation of hundreds of thousands of Chilean families, the military government introduced a program of make-work public works projects and miscellaneous jobs called the *Programa de Empleo Mínimo* (PEM). Initiated in March 1975 with some 19,000 participants, it had grown to over 150,000 by late 1976 (over 5 percent of the economically active labor force). These workers received small "salaries" and, in about 30 percent of the cases, food rations (funded by the U.S. AID program and Catholic Relief—*Caritas*) for janitorial, service, maintenance, reforestation, and construction jobs. They were not counted among the *officially* unemployed. For hundreds of thousands more Chileans the recession induced by the shock treatment allowed not even the meager buffer of PEM.

Economic stabilization, reducing the role of the public sector, deregulation, and "opening" of the economy merged gradually into a coherent neo-liberal program for restructuring the Chilean economy. Policies utilized to achieve these ends included monetary restraints, budget reductions, and privatizing public assets (selling most of the 492 firms owned by CORFO and almost all the previously nationalized banks as well as much publicly held agricultural land). Inasmuch as the divestiture program occurred in a depressed economic environment, a select group of national and foreign firms acquired these enterprises at very favorable prices. The process also led to concentration of financial and productive assets in the hands of a small number of new diversified financial groups such as Grupo Vial, Grupo Cruzat-Larraín, Grupo Yarur, Grupo Matte, Grupo Puig, and Grupo Edwards.

Implementation of the economic program and consolidation of the regime's political control brought efforts to legitimize the *junta*'s authority with something beyond the original emergency decrees. By 1975 the junta and its civilian collaborators were actively planning a "new institutional order" to replace the outmoded institutions of Chilean democracy. Four "constitutional acts" adopted between December 1975 and September 11, 1976, moved Chile in the direction of a constitutional military dictatorship.

The apparent contradiction of this three-word characterization will not surprise readers familiar with *Alice in Wonderland* or George Orwell's *1984*. Only by reading these constitutional acts can one appreciate fully the unintentional irony promulgated into law by Chile's military dictators. To illustrate, Constitutional Act Number 3 (September 4, 1976) stipulated, among other intriguing provisions:

> Article 1. Men are born free and equal in dignity. This constitutional act guarantees all individuals:

11. Liberty of conscience, and expression of all creeds and free exercise of all religions, as do not violate moral principles, good behavior or public order . . .

12. Freedom of opinion and information, in all ways and by all means, without prior censorship, notwithstanding responsibility under the law for offense or abuse as may be committed in use of these freedoms. However, the courts may prohibit publication or circulation of opinions or information affecting moral principles, public order, national security or the private life of individuals.

. . . Individuals who may have been at any time convicted or found guilty of threatening the institutional order of the Republic may not own, direct, or manage mass communications media, nor may they in any way participate in functions connected with the publication or broadcast of opinions or information.

Article 2. No individual may invoke any constitutional or legal precept whatsoever to violate the rights or freedoms established hereunder, or to threaten the integrity or operation of the state of law or the established regime.

Any act of individuals or groups directed to disseminate doctrines which threaten the family, or which promote violence or the concept of a society based on class struggle, or as may be otherwise contrary to the established regime or the integrity or operation of the state of law, is illicit and in violation of the institutional organization of the Republic.

If these sections read like a tongue-in-cheek Orwellian invention, Constitutional Act Number 4 (promulgated at the same time as the act above) seems to go further than even Orwell. To combat "latent subversion," this act authorized the president of the republic to declare "a state of defense against subversion." Under such conditions, the president "may only restrict personal freedom, freedom of information, and the right of assembly." If the president declared a state of "internal or external war" or a "state of internal commotion," his authority was still greater, including the power to deprive Chileans of their citizenship and "to suspend or restrict all of the rights or guarantees set forth in Constitutional Act Number 3. . . ."

By the end of 1976 the Chileans were living in a juridical Wonderland; but the enforcement mechanisms of the military junta could hardly be characterized as a house of cards. And no Chilean could merely wake up to escape the nightmare.

The "constitutional acts" remained emergency measures rather than a legitimate foundation of a new political order. With growing Church denunciations of the activities of DINA and the new focus of U.S. foreign policy under President Carter on human rights, supporters of the military government engaged in internal discussions concerning the desirability and need to establish a more permanent alternative political system. Within the military government, and among its civilian supporters, disagreement existed over the precise features of a new institutional order. Nevertheless, consolidation of the regime, weakness of the opposition (including abolition of all political parties in March 1977), and pressure for moderation of the repressive policies from the United States as well as some European nations, made expedient a vague commitment to a transition to a less political regimen.

From 1973 onward, government-sponsored constitutional study groups and official agencies had debated a new institutional order, but General Pinochet had made no specific commitment to adopt a new constitution nor to a timetable for military withdrawal from a tutelary role in national politics. In July 1977, General Pinochet announced the "Chacarilla Plan," promising movement toward a new system of "protected democracy." Apparently acting without full consultation with other junta members, General Pinochet provided in the Chacarilla Plan a framework for gradual transition from military rule to a new political system. During a lengthy transition period basic legislative reforms in the areas of labor, social welfare, education, and public administration would provide the foundations for the new political order, while the military and selected civilian leaders would share responsibility for policymaking. Ultimately, the new system would use a restrictive and indirect system of electing a new president, and reserve to the armed forces the mission of protecting, guaranteeing, and supervising national security and modernization.

Shortly after announcing the Chacarilla Plan, General Pinochet abolished the DINA. This action served as a symbolic indication that the "emergency" situation of 1973-76 had ended and that the regime was moving toward institutionalization of a new political order. In addition, abolition of the DINA served to mollify critics in the United States and Europe, where this agency had carried out assassinations and attacks on prominent Chileans. In its place, however, Pinochet created the National Information Center (CNI), an agency with the same general purpose and practices—but now with formal authority and jurisdiction.

The outlawing of the political parties, unilateral announcement of the Chacarilla Plan, and reorganization and institutionalization of the secret police all evidenced General Pinochet's emerging predominance within the junta. By combining political adeptness, application of "the stick and the cake" in the fashion of his hero—Portales—and skillful manipulation of internal incentives within the armed forces, he gradually achieved control over the junta, the security apparatus, and the main administrative centers of power. With the national budget as an instrument for policy initiatives, and for rewarding supporters, especially the armed forces which had long felt neglected and unappreciated by civilian politicians, General Pinochet astutely modified spending priorities and the perquisites of armed service personnel.

In the first two years of the military *junta*, with public expenditures declining by some 40 percent, military expenditures *increased* by over 30 percent. Officers achieved great economic gains and privileges, while the national police (*carabineros*) gained in status and benefits with their transfer from the ministry of interior and "elevation" to co-equal participants in the junta with the other armed forces. International disputes and the potential for armed conflict with Bolivia and Peru in the mid-1970s and, later, with Argentina, focused national concern on re-equipping and modernizing the armed forces while providing narrow professional national defense missions for the military commanders. The government also encouraged development of a more diversified Chilean arms industry to protect the country against the vagaries of international supplies. In this context, the intelligence branches and *investigaciones* assumed a more important role in domestic politics and came to serve as a key source of power and control for General Pinochet. The dictatorship became less a government *of* the armed forces and more a regime of military leaders and civilian technocrats, led by General Pinochet, supported *by* the armed forces. In this arrangement the security apparatus gained autonomy and became a key element in assuring political control.

Over time, however, disagreements within the military institutions over government policy and professional issues came to the surface. In 1973 the coup leaders had purged high ranking officers who appeared most likely to resist the coup and a number of others were killed, imprisoned, or retired. Enlisted personnel who refused to participate in the coup also suffered execution, incarceration, or other punishment. Later, General Prats, ex-commander-in-chief and a potential challenger to Pinochet's control, was assassinated in Buenos Aires.

Consolidation of General Pinochet's hegemony through the opera-

tions of DINA and, later, the CNI alienated certain sectors within
the armed forces, but modifications of the career and promotion system in the army made officers increasingly reliant upon the patronage
and good graces of Pinochet himself. Nevertheless, some officers resisted the neo-liberal economic program, favoring a more nationalist
and populist alternative to resolve the country's crisis. Disproportion-
ately large increases in expenditures for internal security and the army
distressed some navy and air force officers. Before 1976-77, however,
this distress did not translate into open challenges to General Pinochet
or the military junta.

Announcement of the Chacarilla Plan opened the door to debate
concerning the character of the regime, timing of movement to an
alternative political model, and the role of political parties, labor, and
other organizations in the new political system. This debate eventually involved high ranking military officers and even members of the
junta. Conflicts with Air Force General Gustavo Leigh over the pace
of political "normalization" and the process of junta decision-making
resulted in the latter's removal from the junta and, in 1978, a number of forced retirements within the air force.

Meanwhile Chilean exiles around the world continued to wonder
if they could ever return to their homeland, or if Chile would ever
again be free of military rectors in the universities, military censors
over the media, military masters over a civilian population. In the
face of a United Nations charge of human rights violations in Chile,
General Pinochet called a national referendum in the first week of
1978, in which Chilean citizens were asked to vote "no" or "yes" on
the following resolution:

> In the face of the international aggression unleashed against
> the government of the fatherland, I support [General] Pinochet
> in his defense of the dignity of Chile, and I reaffirm the legiti-
> mate right of the republic to conduct the process of institution-
> alization in a manner benefiting its sovereignty.

With the opposition repressed and the mass media muffled, the government claimed that more than 75 percent of the electorate had expressed support for Pinochet. Based on this overwhelming "mandate," General Pinochet announced that there would be no further
elections for a decade, and he told Chile's politicians, "It's finished
for you."

In response to the consolidation of the regime's position as well as
to apparent support reflected in the January 1978 plebiscite, General

Pinochet lifted the "state of siege" in March and replaced it with the somewhat less restrictive "state of emergency." Under the "state of emergency," the military tribunals were theoretically subject to review by the Supreme Court, and civil liberties were partially restored. The following month (April 5, 1978) Pinochet announced an amnesty for political prisoners and exiles. However, the amnesty decree contained enough exceptions—for example, it excluded those guilty of misuse of public funds and other "economic crimes"—to make it largely a public relations measure. Moreover, the official translation of Pinochet's announcement distributed by the Chilean embassy in Washington, D.C., made clear the general's firm intentions to prevent renewed political opposition:

> I wish to announce tonight that I have decided to pardon prison sentences or commute them to exile—that is, abandonment of the country—for all persons sentenced by military courts for crimes against the national security committed before or after September 11, 1973.
>
> Although it is entirely improper to refer to persons found guilty of a crime as political prisoners, now, as a result of the amnesty decree which is inspired by humanitarian motives, no one will be able to say that there are persons deprived of their freedom in Chile because of political happenings.
>
> I hope that this decision by my Government will be understood as a sign of pacification and not one of weakness, for anyone who falls into error in that respect runs the risk from now on of suffering full application of the law.

As General Pinochet secured his control over the country, the economic shock treatment gave way to impressive economic growth based upon improved international prices for Chilean products, increases in agricultural, industrial, and mining exports, and large inflows of foreign investment and loans. A rush of financial and real estate speculation generated enthusiasm in elite circles in Santiago, Valparaíso, and other urban centers. New office buildings and shopping centers dotted both downtown Santiago and the fashionable neighborhoods of the capital. Luxury condominiums decorated the coastline at Valparaíso and Viña del Mar. Road and highway construction, port modernization, improvements in bus and rail transport, all seemed to justify the confidence of the junta and the neo-liberal economic team in the correctness of their program and in Chile's future. Import duties, initially reduced to an average of 15 percent, and then to 10 percent in 1979, spurred a consumption frenzy among Chileans able to pur-

TABLE 32. AVAILABILITY OF GOODS AND SERVICES PER 10,000 POPULATION, 1970-81

	1970	1971	1972	1973	1974	1975	1976	1977	1978	1979	1980	1981
Automobiles	189	203	223	228	216	251	253	279	313	354	413	494
Television Sets	138	186	197	129	242	167	139	418	435	459	477	454
Refrigerators	72	68	64	52	39	27	31	49	72	132	156	171
Washing Machines	52	61	58	53	64	46	43	48	69	100	127	150
Telephones	415	438	455	461	466	466	475	483	523	536	541	555
Residential Electricity consumption (thousand kilowatts)	988	1,077	1,269	1,376	1,397	1,366	1,344	1,380	1,476	1,546	1,625	1,709
Liquefied Gas	302	345	370	387	395	379	393	415	413	411	412	413

(Source: Bela Balassa "Policy Experiments in Chile 1973-1983" in Gary M. Walton, ed., *The National Economic Policies of Chile*, Greenwich, Conn., 1985, pp. 222-23.)

chase imported goods previously exorbitantly expensive due to tariff protection. Improving economic conditions reaffirmed support for the military government despite stories of torture and international criticism of the Pinochet government. Television sets, calculators, stereos, computers, and more esoteric imports were justification enough for many Chileans of the overthrow of the Popular Unity government.

Selected macroeconomic indicators also affirmed the government's success: inflation reduced from over 600 percent per year to 30 percent in 1979; solid growth of domestic production after 1977; dramatic decreases in budget deficits; impressive expansion of non-traditional exports to a diversified list of European, Asian, and Western Hemisphere markets; positive balance of payments after 1978; and increasing levels of foreign investment and international confidence in the Chilean economy.

With the economic recovery Chile's affluent and middle-class sectors enjoyed what came to be called "the Chilean Miracle." Boasting of its success in *Chile, 1980 Economic Profile*, the government declared: "Five years ago Chile boldly embarked on a course to revitalize its weakened economy, replacing protectionism with free-market policies . . . the average GDP growth rate over the last five years has been 7.3%. . . . A diversified economy capable of functioning at an internationally competitive level has now been established, thereby assuring economic stability and offering excellent opportunities for domestic and foreign investors."

In contrast to the government's pride in "the miracle," a number of dissident intellectuals, artists, and writers such as Fernando Alegría, Poli Délano, Ariel Dorfman, Antonio Skármeta, and Hernán Valdés produced work with subtle ironies and/or horrific detail which focused on the human cost of the supposed economic miracle. In the press, magazines, and dramatic presentations seemingly innocuous messages encoded scathing critiques of the military dictatorship, as regime opponents attempted to walk the precipice between the wrath of censors and secret police and the temptations of self-censorship. In some cases folk art in the *poblaciones* or provincial towns served both to earn a survival wage for artisans who created decorative appliqué and embroidered pieces (*arpilleras*) while expressing resistance to the government's programs. In a less subtle effort, Chilean writer Pablo Huneeus published "The New Economist's Creed." This satirical spoof offended some readers with its seeming parody of religious beliefs, but it also reflected the cynical claims by the Pinochet government of defending the "Western-Christian Tradition." The "New Economist's Creed" read, in part:

TABLE 33. SELECTED ECONOMIC INDICATORS, 1973-1982

Year	1973	1974	1975	1976	1977	1978	1979	1980	1981	x73-81	1982
Growth Rate Real GDP (%)	−5.6	1.0	−12.9	3.5	9.9	8.2	8.3	7.8	5.7	2.6	−14.3
Inflation (%)[1]	508.1	375.9	340.7	174.3	63.5	30.3	38.9	31.2	9.5	156.5	20.7
Government Deficit as % of GDP	24.7	10.5	2.6	2.3	1.8	0.8	−1.7	−3.1	−1.7	4.0	2.3
Exports FOB (millions of dollars)	1,309	2,151	1,590	2,116	2,185	2,460	2,835	4,705	3,836	2,687	3,706
Imports FOB (millions of dollars)	1,288	1,794	1,520	1,473	2,151	2,886	4,190	5,469	6,513	3,032	3,643
Commercial Balance (millions of dollars)	21	357	70	643	34	−426	−355	−764	−2,677	−344	63
Balance of Payments (millions of dollars)	−21	−55	−344	414	113	712	1,047	1,244	67	353	−1,165
Long- and Medium-term Foreign Debt (millions of dollars)	3,261	4,026	4,267	4,274	4,510	5,923	7,507	9,413	12,553	6,193	13,815

[1] Change in Consumer Price Index (INE), December-December each year.

(Source: Banco Central de Chile, *Informe Económico de Chile*, 1983, p. 46.)

x = average, 1973-81

I believe in the all powerful dollar, creator of heaven and earth;

I believe in Milton Friedman, His only son, our God, conceived by the grace of the University of Chicago;

Born of the Stock Market . . . expropriated, died and buried;

Descended into the hell of Socialism;

In the Third Year, returned to life, ascending the 11th [day of the military coup in September 1973]

I believe in the Holy Spirit, sacred private enterprise and Japanese cars;

I believe in the capital markets, the *financieras* and Pierre Cardin shirts;

I believe that Adam Smith lives, Keynes is dead, and Marx was a nightmare

I believe in selling the factories, mines and forests of the country

I believe there are too many journalists and public opinion counts for nothing

I believe that sociologists are a plague and the poor a necessary evil

I believe in tennis, long lunches and comparative advantage;

I believe in international prices, domestic salaries and Argentine shoes;

I believe Carter is a communist, the Cardinal is a communist and the communists are communists;

I believe in the communion of the market, forgiveness for our sins, the appearance of the "disappeared" [unaccounted for political prisoners] and in the eternal Junta.

Amen.

Opponents and critics of the military government pointed out that while the so-called miracle amounted to economic recovery, it was a recovery in which unemployment remained over 15 percent, the gains in consumption were concentrated among the top 20 percent of income earners in the country (though real wages were improving), and the foreign debt was burgeoning. Wild financial and real estate speculation provided a façade of "boom" while portending disaster. The traditional industrial sector, battered by competition from imports, failed to recover its vigor despite stimulation of export-oriented industries such as wood and paper products, fishmeal, minerals, and processed fruit. With financial intermediation between the domestic economy and foreign commercial banks among the most profitable of enterprises, *real* interest rates remained very high while domestic investment stayed very low. Indeed, the most profitable sector of the economy seemed to be in the ever more complex pyramid of financial speculation which utilized paper assets as security for secondary and tertiary credit lines. The same financial groups at the center of the speculative boom also controlled over 60 percent of total private exports by 1980. Critics also pointed to the growing foreign indebtedness—particularly short-term loans attracted by the high *real* domestic interest rates—and the increased vulnerability of the economy to fluctuations in the international marketplace.

However, this list of constraints and defects in the economic model paled in comparison with the highly visible "miracle." As economic growth and the glitter of new construction and public works bolstered the government's confidence and base of support, General Pinochet announced further institutional initiatives. In September 1979 he declared that the government would adopt a program of national modernization, involving radical changes in the areas of labor policy, education, social security, health, regional decentralization, justice, and agriculture. What came to be called "the seven modernizations" paved the way for the eventual institutionalization of the authoritarian system in a constitutional plebiscite in 1980.

Most important of the seven modernizations was the 1979 "Labor Plan." The culmination of a six-year attack on organized labor, the new labor plan focused on permanent depoliticization and demobilization of labor in Chilean society. In the first months after the coup, the military government had banned strikes, prohibited collective bargaining, and suspended the processing of all labor petitions. It outlawed the CUT, prohibited union elections, and assigned military officers to mediate labor disputes between workers and employers. Other measures barred union meetings held without prior approval by the police.

From the outset, the military junta defined these innovations as "emergency measures" that would be revised as the regime developed a program to modify the old Labor Code. The Minister of Labor declared in 1976 that "it is not possible to introduce a new industrial relations system until the evils that brought us to this social crisis are extirpated. For this reason collective bargaining and union elections have been suspended." The emergency measures remained in place until the Labor Plan of 1979.

Organized labor's initial responses to the military government involved primarily non-Marxist groups which the junta allowed to function as evidence that government policy was not antilabor, but rather anticommunist and antipolitical. In 1974, public employees, maritime workers, bank employees, health workers, and even some members of the metallurgical federation, who were affiliated with the National

Workers' Central (CNT), attempted to obtain government recognition as the official voice of labor. The CNT, which included Christian Democrats and *gremialistas*, failed to achieve any immediate mass support. It also failed to reconcile the conflicts between those who wholeheartedly supported the junta and those who preferred the role of "responsible" (versus Marxist) opposition. The existence of the CNT initially served the government's need to establish alternative procedures for industrial relations and to demonstrate to the International Labor Office that labor rights and interests in Chile were being respected. In addition, the junta's second labor minister, Air Force General Nicanor Díaz, and some of his colleagues sought to put into place a corporatist and populist model of industrial relations rather than merely repress labor for the benefit of employers.

Meanwhile, the CUT constituted an external directorate in Paris and made efforts to maintain clandestine contacts with the outlawed political parties and their supporters in the workplace. Illegal strikes in 1974, by both ex-Popular Unity supporters and more conservative workers, challenged the military's policies but they also provoked harsh reactions against union leaders and rank and file. Speaking at the May 1, Labor Day celebration in 1975, the minister of labor proclaimed that "September 11 detained Marxism, it did not destroy it; we must now destroy Marxism."

In June 1975 a group of labor federations previously affiliated with the CUT, including Christian Democrats who rejected collaboration with the military regime, created a loosely organized alternative to the CNT which they called the National Union Coordinating Committee (CNS). The government, however, viewed the CNS as an effort to resurrect the politicized, leftist labor movement of the past; its leaders suffered periodic arrests, harassment, and sometimes death or "disappearance."

Toward the end of 1975, a so-called Group of Ten, predominantly Christian Democratic labor leaders, also became active. This group included relatively moderate labor opponents to the military regime, and even some personalities whom the dictatorship had designated to represent Chile at International Labor Organization (ILO) meetings outside the country. In May 1976 the Group of Ten published an open letter criticizing the government's labor policies, and in 1977 took the lead in rejecting General Pinochet's proposals for a "protected democracy" in the Chacarilla Plan.

In response to the renewed activism of labor, and emulating in some ways the labor policies of General Ibáñez's first administration (1927-31), the junta attempted to establish a heterogeneous base of *gremios* in a new National Gremialist Secretariat (1976) and a National Unity Labor Front. It also sponsored parallel unions within firms or economic sectors where labor opposition existed, for example, among copper and port workers and within the National Electricity Industry (ENDESA). Most of these efforts fell short of government aspirations, although certain labor leaders and workers repeatedly manifested support for the junta. Finally, in 1978, the military government attempted to create a new officialist labor organization called the National Union of Chilean Workers (UNTRACH), but this organization could not garner any mass support despite its moderate criticisms of government policy.

Renewed strike activity from 1977 to 1978, including job actions, absenteeism, and hunger strikes in the copper mines, ports, and among textile, chemical, metallurgical, and transportation workers, was met with a variety of repressive measures. Authorities arrested numerous labor leaders, fired participants in the job actions, sentenced some activists to internal exile (*relegación*), and dissolved seven union federations affiliated with the CNS. Not only did these measures fail to end the strikes before the workers attained some of their goals, but, more importantly, the high visibility of the strikers and of the government response focused international attention anew on Chilean politics and provoked both official and grass roots support for the opposition in Europe and the United States. President Carter's emphasis on human rights in U.S. foreign policy collided directly with the Chilean government's practices, and the possibility of a boycott by the AFL-CIO in the United States threatened the very basis of the export-led economic recovery promoted by the government.

Inability to control workers in government-owned copper mines which produced the single most important source of foreign exchange for the country, together with the threat of isolation from U.S. markets by refusal of American workers to offload Chilean cargoes, pushed the Pinochet government toward new labor policies. Beginning with an abrupt call for union elections in 1978 and Decree Law 2200, the Chilean military regime redesigned the Chilean industrial relations system. Thus, the Labor Plan, heralded as one of the seven modernizations initiated in 1979, represented the Pinochet government's efforts to clarify and codify the role and limits of labor in the evolving system of "protected democracy."

The new labor regimen legalized a system of collective bargaining and guaranteed yearly wage readjustments tied to the official rate of inflation. Union organization and bargaining between employers and workers were recognized as basic to modern industrial relations. However, the new regulations limited collective bargaining and strike action to individual plant unions or, in agriculture, to unions in individual farms. Strikes were limited to sixty days, after which time employees who refused to return to work "are considered to have resigned . . . but will be eligible for unemployement subsidies." (This provision led eventually to a number of 59-day strikes, followed by brief interludes and then subsequent return to strike action.) In contrast to previous legislation which allowed for federations and confederations to act at regional or national levels, the new labor laws forbade these types of organizations from participating in collective bargaining and a number of other "political" activities. To avoid the possibility of simultaneous labor disputes or strikes, the new regulations specified a timetable for labor negotiations in particular firms or sectors of the economy, and published a long list of firms and sectors where strikes were prohibited. The laws authorized the government to dissolve labor organizations for participating in "monopolistic practices" (presenting similar labor petitions in several firms at the same time), engaging in "political" activities, or carrying out activities beyond the scope of "union functions."

In the case of agricultural unions this meant the loss of all the gains achieved during the Christian Democratic and Popular Unity administrations. Permitted to organize unions only in farms with fifteen permanent workers (or nine in some special cases), farmworkers faced restrictions on organization more severe than those enacted in 1947 and were subject to layoff at the whim of the employer. Simply by refusing to hire more than fourteen *full-time* workers, agricultural employers could avoid unionization. As a result, in 1981, agricultural workers unions claimed fewer than 30,000 members nationwide—approximately 15 percent of the membership they had at the end of 1973. In addition, agricultural policies which both reversed the agrarian reform and added to rural unemployment made the plight of rural labor and the problems of the rural labor movement even more difficult. Indeed, no group of workers suffered more, or lost more, under the military regime than the Chilean campesinos.

Supplementary labor decrees allowed work days of up to twelve hours, without overtime scales, so long as total hours worked per week did not exceed forty-eight. The government also eliminated the traditional system of labor courts and even abolished the old *colegios profesionales*, essentially professional associations of doctors, lawyers, pharmacists, or journalists, and replaced them with *gremialista* associations. Officially, these policies were adopted to eliminate restraints on the market and inefficiencies in the economy; in practice they coincided with the government's ongoing efforts to depoliticize Chilean society by fragmenting organized labor and professional associations and limiting their activities to narrow, geographically specific actions.

In addition to the "Labor Plan," the other "modernizations" also had both economic and political objectives. Modernization of the educational system involved decentralization of educational administration by placing the primary schools under the direction of municipal authorities. The national government retained supervisory control over the content of education—emphasizing basic skills, Chilean history and geography, and civic duties and responsibilities. This emphasis had emerged early in the military administration with declarations in the *Objetivo Nacional del Gobierno de Chile* (1975) that "education should strengthen and transmit love for *la patria* and national values, . . . appreciation of the family as the basic cell of society, acceptance of the idea of national unity. . . ." Constitutional Act No. 3 (1976) had also emphasized "promoting among students a sense of moral, civic, and social responsibility, love of *la patria* and its fundamental values . . . and the spirit of brotherhood among people and among nations." This emphasis on morality and national values carried forward to the announced plan for educational modernization, set forth in the "Presidential Directive for Education" (March 5, 1979).

Beginning in 1980-81, municipal governments took over responsibility for administering the public primary schools, with curriculum and budgets supervised by the Ministry of Education. The government emphasized the need to strengthen primary education where, in 1973, fewer than 60 percent of the students enrolled in grade one completed grade eight (the last year of public, obligatory education). In addition, expanded preschool and day-care programs, coordinated with nutrition programs, greatly improved the situation of young children and some working mothers. The government also emphasized the need to expand technical and vocational education.

Transfer of responsibility for school administration to the municipalities practically destroyed the enormous political and social influence of the 90,000-member National Teachers Union (SUTE). Bargaining over salary and working conditions became essentially "local" matters, with teachers subjected to personnel policies at the municipal rather than the national level, as well as regulated by national labor law prohibiting strikes in the public sector.

Established in 1970 after many years of organizational development in the educational sector, SUTE affiliated teachers and administrators employed by the Ministry of Education. It had obtained legal recognition from the Popular Unity government and had participated actively in formulating educational policy. After the coup of 1973, General Pinochet declared that it was necessary to purge public education of subversive elements. To achieve this objective new policies eliminated most of the employment security won for teachers over the last fifty years. In December 1973 the government ended payroll check-offs for SUTE and froze the union's funds. A year later, both SUTE and smaller teacher organizations lost their legal status (Decree Law 1284) and recognition.

To replace SUTE and other teacher organizations the government created a new association called the *Colegio de Profesores* (Decree Law 678, 1974). This organization would supposedly register all teachers in the public and private sector, regulate professional and ethical conduct of teachers, and set standards for teacher preparation and licensing. It would also assist in the government program to depoliticize the teaching profession in Chile. Many of the old headquarters and social centers of SUTE were transferred to the new Colegio. The Colegio de Profesores was itself subsequently dissolved when the government decreed abolition of all the professional *colegios* in 1981. Though the Colegio was replaced in late 1981 by a new Chilean Educators Gremialist Association (AGECH), teachers lost control over professional standards and national educational policy, while at the same time they faced a fragmented, localized labor market that fit the model of the economy favored by neo-liberal policymakers.

In the areas of secondary and university education, reforms introduced by the military government emphasized rationalization of the national system to eliminate competing and overlapping programs, more specialization, and reduction of subsidies for higher education. A decree law in December 1980 redefined the functions of Chilean universities, including the types of degrees they could award, while allowing other educational institutions, such as *centros de educación superior*, to offer programs previously reserved to the universities. Subsequent decrees refined and elaborated the new educational policies, with the general thrust toward *self-financing* and a relative shift of resources from higher education to primary and technical education prevailing. In 1974 higher education absorbed 47 percent of the national education budget. This share fell to 33 percent in 1978, 27 percent in 1980, and 20 percent in 1982. Thus, the corollary of the government's commitment to allocate increasing resources to preschool and primary education was the relative decline in support of higher

education. In many ways this policy represented a highly positive redistribution of opportunities in favor of poorer sectors of the population; yet the increased fees at the level of secondary (and university)
education frustrated the ambitions of those with lesser means as they
graduated from the eighth year of free public education. Encouraging the proliferation of private educational institutions, institutes,
and technical training, the government reduced expenditures on the
university system, made fewer openings available to entry-level students, and gradually increased the extent to which student fees accounted for university income. By 1982, some 18 percent of university
income came from student fees, which averaged over $1300 per year.
Moreover, the technical universities, primarily catering to lower income students in the past, also raised fees to levels ranging from $600
to $1200 per year. These fees made higher education inaccessible to
many thousands of students. The previous commitment to free or
low-cost higher education had disappeared.

The military program for modernization of education entailed a
fundamental contradiction between a long overdue focus on more resources for primary and technical education and a contraction of opportunities in the system of higher education. In the long run, this
contradiction could not be maintained without incubating a growing
dissatisfaction among Chilean youth and exacerbating class antago-
nisms as the door to opportunity for social mobility slammed in the
faces of large numbers of the younger generation.

Educational "modernization" represented not merely a technical,
rationalizing effort but also an integral part of the military government's move toward a new political order. An expanding system of
preschools allowed the government to establish a presence in numerous neighborhoods and communities, as well as to deliver nutrition
and health services, along with its political message, to thousands
of poor families. In the primary schools, an emphasis on "basics,"
and also on morality and patriotism, clearly coincided with the regime's self-defined mission of preparing new generations of Chileans
"steeped in a love of the fatherland." Military administrators in the
universities, purges of the faculties and student bodies, more competitive admission policies, and increases in student fees all evidenced
the concern with depoliticizing university life and refocusing student
efforts on narrow professional and vocational goals. The "modernization" of the educational system, along with the political purges, also
significantly reduced the traditional participation by students in
national and university politics. Only after 1984, with the brief politi-

cal opening or *apertura* tolerated by the government, did students re-emerge, along with labor and party activists, as a vocal force in opposition to the government.

Educational reform measures coincided with other policy initiatives in health and social security in shaping the social framework for "protected democracy." Modernization of the health care and social security systems also emphasized privatization and rationalization. Worker pension payments were shifted from a large number of specialized public funds to a relatively smaller number of private companies called pension administration funds (Administradoras de Fondos de Pensiones or AFP). The law required worker contributions, but allowed freedom of choice regarding where they deposited their money. Lacking good information about the new system and the companies involved, most participants chose the new large financial conglomerates which also managed pension funds. Older workers and the infirm remained under public plans, thus taking paying members of the system to the private sector and leaving the public sector saddled with already incurred obligations. Several public agencies retained responsibility for licensing and regulating the AFP; limited public liability existed in case of bankruptcy of the insurance companies or in cases when pensions did not amount to a legislated minimum. The pension system reform added greatly to concentration of financial assets within the economy. After two months of operation of the system the two largest financial conglomerates controlled 75 percent of the pension assets.

In the area of health policy, the military government inherited a relatively sophisticated National Health Service which paralleled a good quality system of private health care. To make the National Health Service (SNS) more efficient, the government adopted Decree Law 2763, "Restructuring of the Health Sector." This administrative reform created twenty-seven regional agencies, with directors appointed by the president, and with a mandate to reduce costs and to improve service. Priority was given to programs of maternal and infant care, along with nutrition education and feeding programs. Inasmuch as the new social security and pension system allowed workers to choose private health care providers under private insurance schemes, the SNS would become a provider of services to those least able to provide for their own health services—a provider of last resort.

Although the majority of doctors in Chile initially seemed to favor drastic reform of the National Health Service and the move toward privatization, some doctors and medical students protested the new system. These protests, along with the technical and administrative barriers to complete evisceration of the SNS, spared the health system total dismantlement. Public investment in new health facilities dropped as did refurbishment of old installations. Nevertheless, the SNS and other government agencies carried out effective programs of prenatal and postnatal care, as well as nutritional supplement programs, which allowed the country to reduce infant mortality and malnutrition-related disease. Redirection of health priorities toward these objectives by the military government, and the generally high quality training and performance of Chilean health professionals, overcame many of the constraints imposed by budget reductions. This was achieved despite economic conditions that might have led to increased malnutrition and nutrition-related disease among infants and young children. The long-term effects of these administrative and technical reforms in the health care system require more time for valid analysis, but significant gains from particular government programs were evident by the early 1980s.

In the area of judicial and criminal justice administration, the government also moved forward with "modernization." This program included building a number of new combination court–penal facilities, appointing large numbers of new judges, improving judicial compensation, and liberalizing rules of evidence to "allow all sorts of evidence useful in establishing the truth . . . photos, tapes, films, cassettes, videos, etc." New provisions regarding civil procedures, juvenile justice, and legal assistance also were implemented from 1981 to 1983. In 1983 the government claimed that 30 percent of all courts ever created in Chile had been established since 1973. The government also proudly displayed similarly impressive statistics for new offices of Civil Registry and Notaries which it claimed made civil and criminal justice administration more efficient and more accessible to the Chilean population.

With the "seven modernizations" under way and the economic recovery in full swing, General Pinochet moved toward the fourth stage of post-1973 development: efforts to legitimize both the political and economic initiatives of the regime through the adoption of a new constitution. Heralded as the "Constitution of Liberty," after the book written by the neo-liberals' intellectual hero, conservative economist Friedrich Hayek, the constitutional project enshrined the notion of "protected democracy" and gave constitutional protection to the basic features of the "seven modernizations." The government submitted the constitution to plebiscite on September 11, 1980 (the

TABLE 34. NUTRITION, HEALTH, AND EDUCATION INDICATORS, 1970-82

	1970	1971	1972	1973	1974	1975	1976	1977	1978	1979	1980	1981	1982
Nutrition													
Calorie consumption per capita	2,282	2,645	2,819	2,642	2,243	2,290	2,565	2,511	2,603	2,634	2,655	2,675	2,627
Protein per capita (grams)	67.1	73.8	78.8	70.7	64.3	62.7	66.3	65.8	67.8	68.6	65.5	68.5	70.2
Health													
Physicians per 1,000 population	75	76	77	78	80	83	85	90	92	94	95	97	n.a.
Hospital beds per 1,000 population	3.8	3.8	3.9	3.8	3.8	3.8	3.6	3.6	3.5	3.6	3.4	3.3	3.3
Medical visits per capita	1.08	1.22	1.14	1.03	0.92	0.88	1.05	1.07	1.09	1.13	1.13	1.14	1.19
Adult visits per capita	0.99	1.12	1.00	0.87	0.73	0.70	0.86	0.87	0.89	0.93	0.93	0.93	n.a.
Pediatric visits per child	1.04	1.22	1.16	1.09	1.08	1.01	1.15	1.18	1.22	1.26	1.26	1.30	n.a.
Obstetrical visits per woman of child bearing age	0.26	0.26	0.33	0.31	0.27	0.27	0.27	0.33	0.35	0.35	0.35	0.36	n.a.
Crude death rate per/1,000	8.9	8.8	9.0	8.2	7.8	7.3	7.8	7.0	6.7	6.8	6.7	6.2	6.1
Infant mortality rate per/1,000	82.2	73.9	72.7	65.8	65.2	57.6	56.6	50.1	40.1	37.9	33.0	27.0	23.6

Life expectancy (years)	64.2	64.5	64.8	65.1	65.4	65.7	65.9	66.2	66.5	66.7	67.0	67.3	67.5
Education (per age group)													
Preschool (%)	11.8	13.9	16.0	16.6	19.9	20.0	21.7	23.8	25.3	25.2	26.8	26.5	26.7
Primary school (%)	107	114	117	120	121	119	117	118	119	120	118	115	111
Secondary school (%)	39.6	46.3	49.4	50.9	50.1	48.0	48.9	50.5	52.5	54.9	55.3	56.9	54.8

(Source: Bela Balassa "Policy Experiments in Chile, 1973-1983," Gary Walton, ed., *The National Economic Policies of Chile* Greenwich, Conn., 1985, pp. 222-23; INE, Compendio Estadistico, 1984, 1985.)

seventh anniversary of the coup of 1973) amidst forceful publicity campaigns and severe restrictions on opposition organization and access to the media. Claims of vote fraud and intimidation by opponents of the new constitution did little to mitigate the impact of the apparently overwhelming acceptance of the new constitution. The government reported that with 93 percent of Chile's eligible voters participating in the plebiscite, more than two-thirds of the voters had given their approval. The government also noted that some 30 percent of the voters rejected the new constitution, an indication that opposition claims of intimidation and fraud had not prevented large numbers of Chileans from voting against the government's proposal.

While it was impossible to know with certainty the extent of fraud or intimidation involved in the plebiscite, the size of the *negative* vote gave seeming credibility to the government's victory. General Pinochet and his advisers had either achieved an impressive electoral affirmation of their policies or they had proven themselves extraordinarily astute politicians in their reporting and manipulation of the plebiscite outcome. It was even possible that the government had both won the plebiscite *and* skillfully fabricated the reported results to enhance the credibility of the plebiscite process.

Most importantly, the new constitution marked the end of the *ad hoc* emergency decrees, defined the institutional character of "protected democracy," and established a new juridical framework for national life. Government policy now derived from a constitutional process apparently sanctioned by a majority of the Chilean electorate. Future changes in process or policy depended upon modification or elimination of this new legal system. The constitution also legitimized the continuation of General Pinochet's personalist administration *until 1989*, with the possibility of his re-election to a new term of office lasting until 1997.

Decree Law 1150 (October 21, 1980) promulgated the new Political Constitution of the Republic of Chile. Implementation began in 1981. Much of the language of the constitution, as well as the basic concepts, had been drawn from the "Declaration of Principles" (1974), the National Objectives of Government (1975), the "Constitutional Acts" (1976), the decrees concerning regional administration, the Labor Plan, and the other "modernizations" undertaken in the late 1970s. Matters of continuing controversy within the government, or areas of implementation which required additional legislation or regulations, were treated in "interim provisions." For example, *all political party activity remained outlawed* until an "organic constitutional law" regulating party activity could be adopted. (No law appeared until 1987.)

The Constitution of 1980 institutionalized anti-politics, anti-Marxism, and the new socio-economic order. It also reaffirmed traditional Hispanic values and practices and explicitly emphasized the role of the patriarchal family as the basic unit of a hierarchically organized society. It did this in the name of Western-Christian values, patriotism, and *national security*. Every citizen was obligated to "honor the fatherland, defend its sovereignty, and contribute to the preservation of national security and the essential values of Chilean tradition (Art. 22). The same section of the constitution made military service obligatory and provided for mandatory firearms registration with the military authorities. While the constitution also provided a long list of civil rights and liberties of all Chileans (Art. 19), these were limited by the requirements of national security. For example, the right of free association was subject to the provision that "all groups contrary to morality, public order or security of the State are prohibited."

The Constitution nowhere specifically defined "national security," but the text assigned the armed forces the mission to "guarantee the institutional order of the republic" (Art. 90). Indeed, the new constitution officially made the armed services a dominant political force in Chile. This constitutional development paralleled the growth in personnel of the armed forces (especially the army) and their growing share of government expenditures. In addition, a National Security Council, responsible for a number of advisory and policymaking tasks (Arts. 95-96), inserted military officers into legislative and administrative functions. Each of the armed services received direct representation on the regional development councils which appointed mayors, thereby controlling or monitoring both municipal administration and the reformed educational system. Provision for eventual election of a new Congress, after adoption of a law regulating political parties, also included *designees* of the National Security Council as senators (ex-commanders of each of the three military branches and the *carabineros*). In short, the new constitution provided for permanent militarization of Chilean politics.

The constitution also ratified the social and economic initiatives of the period 1973-81. Article 19 required special legislative approval for the state to engage in entrepreneurial activities. Article 62 reserved to presidential initiative any law to impose, eliminate, or reduce taxes, or to create new public services or new positions in the public administration. This provision was intended to limit severely the role of a "political" legislature and also to focus attention on any efforts to increase the size or expand the functions of the government. The president also had such authority with respect to determination of remuneration in the public sector and in the contracting of foreign loans by any public entity. These provisions, along with a number of others, greatly enhanced the authority of the president and emasculated the legislative branch—a further irony of the military government since the overthrow of President Allende, like that of President Balmaceda in 1891, had been carried out partly in the name of limiting executive abuse of authority and re-establishing the balance between Congress and the president.

The constitution also reaffirmed and institutionalized the labor and social security "modernizations." Articles 8, 15, 16, and 19 prohibited "propagation of any doctrines that . . . advocate violence, or a conception of society or of the state, or of the juridical order of a totalitarian character, or founded on the idea of class conflict . . ."; made unconstitutional all movements, organizations, or political parties that advocated such ideas; outlawed all political party participation in union affairs; and outlawed participation in political parties by labor leaders. In addition, any future congressman or senator who attempted to influence labor negotiations, administrative proceedings, or labor court cases could be removed from office.

The period between approval of the new constitution and March 1981 marked a high point in General Pinochet's administration. Economic expansion, political institutionalization, and the advent of the more supportive administration of President Ronald Reagan in the United States, all seemed to favor the continuity and the strengthening of the Chilean regime. Instead, between March 1981 and the end of the year a combination of international and domestic developments brought economic collapse and financial panic, erosion of political support both among the government's staunch supporters and the social base of the regime, and renewed pressures for rapid transition to a less authoritarian political system.

A complex interaction of international economic trends and internal economic developments provoked the worst economic depression in Chile since the early 1930s. Recession in the United States and Europe, along with tightened monetary and credit policies and skyrocketing interest rates all affected Chile drastically. Chilean firms and private parties had contracted large amounts of dollar-denominated loans at a fixed exchange rate. Short-term foreign indebtedness more than tripled from 1979 to 1982; medium- and long-term debt doubled in the same period. Even more importantly, while public foreign indebtedness had represented more than 50 percent of such obligations in 1979, the private sector indebtedness reached more than 66 percent of the more than 17 billion-dollar total foreign debt by 1982. Since consumption, speculation in real estate, financial pyramids, and flight capital accounted for considerable portions of this private debt, investment and increased productive capabilities grew much too slowly to finance the growing interest payment burden. Shifting government policies on exchange rates (devaluation of 18 percent in June 1982, subsequent pre-announced mini-devaluations, until September 1982, with a floating exchange rate thereafter) exacerbated the crisis, with the result that the Chilean private sector all but collapsed.

According to the government's orthodox policymakers this collapse should have been allowed to "correct itself." Indeed, many of the doctrinaire "Chicago Boys" blamed the financial collapse to a great extent on the government's failure to implement more fully the neo-liberal reforms. These critics pointed out that as early as 1976 the government had rescued the Bank of Osorno, rather than allowing bankruptcy, thereby undermining the discipline of the market in rationalizing the economy. Moreover, according to this viewpoint, fixing the exchange rate in 1979 discriminated against Chilean exporters (since internal inflation exceeded international inflation) and overvalued the Chilean peso. This made Chilean agricultural and industrial products uncompetitive. Further, indexing wages to the consumer price index in the new labor legislation had prevented Chilean employers from "bargaining freely" concerning the cost of labor. Thus, according to the neo-liberals, the reforms had neither been carried far enough nor implemented thoroughly enough.

Others pointed out that lack of careful regulation of the financial activities of the major conglomerates had allowed accumulation of a private foreign debt of an immense magnitude, secured only with fragile, sometimes clearly fraudulent, paper assets. Rising interest rates and drastic reductions in the inflow of foreign loans and investments that had fueled the financial "boom" made it impossible to continue the debt service. Declining prices for Chilean exports as a consequence of the international recession (including a decline in copper prices of over 40 percent from its peak in early 1980 to mid-1982) and a growing balance of payments deficit (15 percent of gross domestic product in 1981) contributed to the debacle. Tariff reductions that had practically eliminated protection for Chilean industries and agriculture allowed consumer goods to flood the country from nations whose industries received a variety of tariff and non-tariff protection from their own governments.

The highly visible sugar firm, Compañía Refinería de Azucar de Viña del Mar (CRAV), part of the financial empire of a prominent businessman, collapsed in May 1981. A seemingly isolated event, this business failure was a warning of things to come. In mid-1981 the Pinochet government began responding to certain portents of the coming crisis. In part these responses stemmed from concern for illegal, corrupt financial practices and in part from the resurgence of a type of "interest group" politics in which sectors of industrialists, agricultural interests, and others lobbied for more favorable, special treatment. First, a new banking law prohibited loans by banks to their owners and affiliate firms; eliminated common stock as an acceptable part of bank capital, and otherwise sought to regulate the rash of financial pyramiding and Ponzi schemes. Too late to prevent the coming collapse, these new laws at least pointed at one source of the impending disaster. Meanwhile, four banks and finance companies went bankrupt in November 1981. The government responded by arresting the principals for financial irregularities and assumed control of the banks.

A largely symbolic change in finance minister, followed by further devaluation of the peso, did nothing to arrest the downward economic spiral. Significantly, the government directed the national sugar enterprise, IANSA, to adopt new price and subsidy policies for sugar-beet growers and imposed tariffs on specific goods to protect Chilean firms from "dumping" by foreign competitors. Agriculture and mining, in selected regions, also received energy subsidies.

In January 1983 the crisis forced the government to "intervene" (take over management and operations of) the largest private banks in the country, assume responsibility for privately contracted debt, and begin a public rescue of the mangled private sector. General Pinochet lamented his failure to deport the speculators and corrupt bankers whom he called "paper emperors," but it would be the hundreds of thousands of unemployed and homeless Chileans who would pay the highest price for the gigantic swindles and the destruction of the Chilean economy.

The Chilean economy declined in gross domestic product by over 14 percent in 1982; unemployment rose to over 20 percent with an additional 450,000 Chileans participating in two government makework programs—PEM, and the newly created Job Program for Heads of Household, or POJH. By the end of 1983 over 500,000 Chileans

TABLE 35. FOREIGN DEBT, DEBT AS PERCENT OF EXPORTS OF GOODS AND
SERVICES, RATIO OF INTEREST PAYMENTS TO EXPORTS OF GOODS AND SERVICES

	1981	1982	1983	1984	1985	1986*
Debt (millions of dollars)	15,591	17,159	18,037	19,669	20,413	20,690
Interest Payments/Exports of Goods and Services (%)	38.8	49.5	38.9	48.0	43.5	39.2
Debt as percent of Exports of Goods and Services	311	370	390	438	454	426

* Preliminary estimate.

(Source: CEPAL, "Preliminary Review of the Latin American Economy," 1986.)

depended upon PEM or POJH for subsistence. With the interest
burden of the debt almost 50 percent that of the value of annual
exports, and rising, General Pinochet and his advisers called upon
the people of Chile to tighten their belts and to make even more
sacrifices for the future of their children and their nation. The private
debts which had served to enrich small numbers of Chileans would
now be collectivized. The nation would renegotiate the debt with
international bankers and international financial organizations. Government control over the country's credit system, the "intervened"
(bailed out) banks, and major firms associated with financial conglomerates, along with continued government operation of public

TABLE 36. WORKERS INSCRIBED IN PEM, POJH

	PEM	POJH (begins Oct. 1982)	Percent of Labor Force
1975	72,695		2.3
1976	157,836		5.0
1977	187,647		5.9
1978	145,792		4.2
1979	133,933		3.9
1980	190,673		5.2
1981	175,607		4.9
1982	225,290	102,772 (Dec.)	9.0
1983 (Oct.)	286,751	225,264	14.0

(Source: Jaime Ruiz-Tagle and Roberto Urmeneta, Los trabajadores del programa
del empleo mínimo, 1984, pp. 24, 168; Instituto Nacional de Estadísticas, Compendio Estadístico, 1984.)

enterprises in the copper, petroleum, coal, and other sectors, the ports, telecommunication, transportation, and international trade, was a further irony of a program dedicated since 1973 to emphasis on market decision-making and privatization.

Mockingly, opponents of the Pinochet government, and even ex-supporters, termed this process the "Chicago road to Socialism." Government policymakers, in contrast, claimed that the interventions would be temporary and looked forward to "reprivatization." In reality, the extent to which government policymakers had determined the character of economic opportunities in the private sector, together with the official and unofficial participation of representatives of the major economic groups in making public policy, resembled much more closely the customary patterns of Hispanic capitalism in Chile than any brand of socialism. As in the past, private enterprise and profit depended upon government policies which allowed coercion of labor, concentration of wealth in a limited number of firms and families, and collusion between government authorities and a small number of private actors in managing the economy. Admittedly, the government had declared its intent to liberalize the economy, just as Chilean Conservatives and Liberals had done during the nineteenth century. In both cases, however, economic liberalism coincided with political authoritarianism and elitist processes of policymaking. General Pinochet, like his heroes Portales and Ibáñez, had imposed policy initiatives through force, in collaboration with civilian advisers and technocrats, while denying the value and denigrating the legitimacy of democratic institutions. As particular policies failed or proved defective, whether neo-liberal or otherwise, these could be dropped or modified without implying any fundamental departure from the basic elements and assumptions of Chile's updated version of Hispanic capitalism.

Begining in late 1981, the collapse of the economic "miracle" precipitated widespread political realignment. *Gremialistas*—old-time members of the National party, middle-class professionals, and an array of small businessmen—suffered the consequences of the depression and expressed open, if cautious, opposition to government policies. Groups which had railed vociferously against President Allende, and which had been closely asssociated with the *junta* in its early years, now called the Pinochet regime "the worst government in the country's history." Prominent leaders of the truckers, Chamber of Commerce, retail merchants, and professional organizations verbally attacked General Pinochet in harsh, even insulting language. Some went to jail and others suffered harassment and beatings by unidentified "civilians." Still violently anti-Marxist and unwilling to form a coalition with Communists and Socialists, even for the limited and temporary purpose of ousting Pinochet, these groups now called for a change in government policies—and sometimes for a more rapid transition to democracy. However, many of these groups still preferred authoritarian government to the threatened "return to chaos" which the government-controlled media and propaganda constantly assured Chileans would follow if the military government passed from the scene. Although the occasion of ex-President Eduardo Frei's death in 1982 sparked a massive demonstration against General Pinochet's regime, it also underlined the lack of viable civilian opposition leadership with which to replace him.

With the political parties still outlawed and traditional political leaders unable to assemble an effective opposition movement to confront the dictatorship, organized labor took a new and central role in seeking to reactivate and mobilize opposition forces. The most important group of organized workers in Chile, the Copper Workers Confederation (CTC), notwithstanding internal divisions and parallel government unions within its membership, confronted the Pinochet regime head on in 1981. A lengthy strike at the El Teniente mine in Rancagua created extremely tense relations with the government. In 1982, copper workers joined with the Coordinadora Nacional Sindical (CNS), the Confederation of Private Sector Employees (CEPCH), and the independent Catholic-inspired Unitary Workers Front (FUT) in sending a letter to General Pinochet requesting modification of the Labor Plan and many of the government's economic policies. The Copper Workers Confederation threatened the government with another strike and even discussed the possibility of a call for a general strike in May 1983. After reconsideration, the CTC instead joined forces with other labor organizations, community organizations, and professional groups in sponsoring a national day of protest (May 11, 1983). All over Chile, and especially in Santiago, Chileans kept their children home from school, absented themselves from work, and—as the opposition had done in the time of protests against the Popular Unity government—banged on pots and pans, while screaming insults at Pinochet and calling for his ouster.

Following the success of this day of protest, labor made another effort at achieving a loose unity in the creation of a National Workers' Command (CNT). Though unable to overcome long-standing ideological and organizational conflicts, a broad spectrum of workers' organizations, ranging from the National Association of Public Em-

ployees (ANEF) to the Maritime Confederation and the Confederation of Private Sector Employees united in public opposition to the
Pinochet government. In the process, some labor leaders suffered
incarceration or even assassination, for example, Tucapel Jiménez,
a leader of ANEF.

A second national day of protest on June 14, 1983, proved even
more successful, but a national strike called for later in the month
failed to achieve the desired impact. Repeated "days of protest" followed these initial acts of mass public opposition. Each protest left
a small toll of dead and many injured in confrontations between
civilians and the security forces. In August 1983, General Pinochet
deployed thousands of troops in Santiago to control a mass demonstration called by a coalition of labor organizations and the outlawed
political parties. *Pobladores* lit fires and built barricades in the
shantytowns; the armed forces invaded neighborhoods of the poor,
made mass arrests, and attacked protesters, while demonstrators in
middle-class neighborhoods experienced the indiscriminate use of
tear gas and random shooting. In addition to the mass demonstrations, small groups of Chileans organized numerous quick, mobile
protests at designated times and places, with participants arriving on
pre-arranged schedule and rapidly dispersing to avoid detention by
carabineros.

Having taken the initiative in 1983, labor organizations continued
to resist government policy. In 1984 ten leaders of the CNT signed
an open letter to Pinochet calling for a return to the constitution of
1925, repeal of the Labor Plan, and reversal of the government's economic policies—in short, a comprehensive change of regime and
policy. Thus, the government's effort to depoliticize labor had actually resulted in an admittedly divided labor movement assuming a
central role in national politics previously performed by the now
outlawed political parties. As in the case of economic policy, the
results of government labor policy proved in many ways contrary to
government objectives.

As mounting public protests against the government occurred in
1984-85, labor groups played a key coordinating role. At the plant
level, individual unions refocused their energies on demands for
improved wages and working conditions. Outside the organized labor
movement, which had lost many members to unemployment and
repression, a variety of women's groups, local committees, agricultural
cooperatives, and *ad hoc* shantytown associations carried on self-help
and anti-regime activities all over Chile. Many of these groups main-

tained some connections with clandestine party networks, Church-related organizations, and labor unions. In other cases they operated in relative isolation, attempting to feed the hungry, hide the persecuted, improve local distribution of consumer goods, and maintain community or local solidarity.

Aware of the mounting frustration and, in some cases, political organization of hundreds of thousands of shantytown dwellers, the government carried out recurrent night-time raids to demobilize anti-government groups active in the *poblaciones*. The urban poor had long constituted a dilemma for Chilean political leaders, but now the cumulative effects of the military government's economic and internal security policies had the effect of radicalizing many shantytown dwellers, particularly the young and unemployed. The extreme social segregation between the urban poor and the residents of middle- and upper-class neighborhoods of Santiago made the apparent radicalization of these groups of great concern to many elements in the capital. Lack of knowledge and contact among rich and poor reached levels never before experienced in Chile, producing an eerie if imperfect analogue to racial ghettos in the United States. The fear of unleashing the stored-up hatred of the *pobladores* limited the willingness of many opposition groups with middle-class constituencies to adopt an insurrectionary style in efforts to replace General Pinochet with a more moderate administration.

At the same time, contradictory as it might seem, a significant minority of *pobladores* continued to support General Pinochet, whether because they had benefited directly from the government's public works and housing programs, or their children had received nutritional and day care services, or because they remembered negatively the intense politicization of daily life from 1970 to 1973. Support for the government within the *poblaciones* and elsewhere also resulted, in part, from General Pinochet's successful efforts to transform the pre-existing network of mothers' clubs (*centros de madres*) into a clientelistic base of support. Affiliated nationally in an organization called CEMA, headed officially by General Pinochet's wife (CEMA had customarily been headed by the wives of Chile's civilian presidents), CEMA provided an instrument for mobilizing a feminine social base for the regime. Wives of military officers were assigned to coordinate local groups, distribute patronage, carry out educational programs, and enlist women in the crusade to purify the nation and to restore the order and harmony so necessary for family life. These appeals to morality, patriotism, and feminine virtue, along with material benefits customarily distributed through the CEMA network since the 1960s, garnered significant, if minority, support for the regime from women of all social classes.

Differences of opinion within the *poblaciones*, as well as among women's organizations and community groups, were symptomatic of persistent political and ideological cleavages within Chilean society. The wave of protests initiated in 1983 eventually gave rise to the resurgence of the three major political blocks characteristic of Chile since the 1930s. On the political right, a so-called Group of 8 allied a range of *gremialista*, "nationalist," and more traditional conservative politicians who provided a civilian face for the social base of the Pinochet government. Eventually some of these groups would seek to distance themselves from the government and form a new united rightist political party (in 1987) so as to appear as likely participants in a transitional coalition when Pinochet passed from the scene. In the short term, however, the political right supplied ministers and advisers to the junta.

In 1983, in an effort to contain the wave of mass protests and demonstrations, General Pinochet appointed the ex-leader of the National party, Sergio Onofre Jarpa, as minister of interior. Feigning a willingness to negotiate with the "responsible" (non-Marxist) opposition, General Pinochet deftly utilized the rightist politicos as shills in a so-called political opening, or *apertura*. In reality, Jarpa had no power and certainly no ability to meet the most important demands of the opposition: General Pinochet's resignation and the immediate return to democracy. Nevertheless, the participation of civilian politicians from the rightist parties and movements as figureheads of the administration gave a veneer of legitimacy and a hint of flexibility to the Pinochet government. It also served to reinforce divisions between centrist and leftist opponents of the regime inasmuch as the government seemed to accept the existence of the Christian Democrats and their allies *de facto*, if not *de jure*, so long as the left remained excluded from dialogue or participation in the political process.

The political center, including the Christian Democrats, Social Democrats, Radicals, part of the Socialist party, and other smaller groups united in the Alianza Democrática (AD). The Alianza repeatedly called for Pinochet's resignation and favored rapid transition to a more democratic system. However, it rejected the use of violence to oust Pinochet and opposed a coalition with Marxist parties and movements in any transitional government alternative to the junta. With a diverse and multi-class social base, the parties and movements of the Alianza occupied a tenuous, shifting middle ground between the junta's program of anti-politics and their own desire to limit leftist influence in Chile while, at the same time, restoring most civil liberties, electoral politics, and a set of government initiatives closer to the developmentalist and redistributionist policies of the 1960s. Frustrated in its negotiations with Minister Jarpa, the parties and movements which had made up the Alianza Democrática, and particularly Christian Democrats, continued to view themselves as the obvious successors to Pinochet in any transition from authoritarian rule— either within the bounds of the 1980 constitution or through a return to the constitution of 1925.

On the left, the Communist party, MIR, and a part of the Socialist party identified with ex-Popular Unity Minister, Clodomiro Almeyda, formed the Movimiento Democrático Popular (MDP). The MDP called for all forms of resistance against the dictatorship and still insisted upon the ultimate goal of a socialist society in Chile. Operating both clandestinely and also "above ground," when conditions permitted, the MDP's revolutionary objectives and declarations gave credibility to General Pinochet's repeated warnings to Chileans of a "return to chaos" should his administration succumb to the demands of the politicians for a return to the past. Likewise, the MDP's tactics and strategic objectives separated the left from the political center just as had been the case since the 1930s. Between the MDP and the AD, a "Socialist bloc" (some socialists, left Catholics, and other smaller groups) represented an ideological transition between the revolutionary Marxist left and the political center.

After more than a decade of a dictatorship dedicated to depoliticizing Chilean society, the major ideological and organizational tendencies—which had emerged in the 1930s, dominated national life from 1930 to 1973, been blamed by the military and its supporters for the crisis of 1970-73, and suffered concerted attacks since 1973— survived, reasserted themselves, challenged the regime, and continued unable to draw forth a consensual basis for Chilean politics and society. Even among the groups firmly opposed to the new Constitution and to the thrust of government policies, historical animosities and basic disagreements over an alternative to the Pinochet government prevented formation of a unified opposition movement. General Pinochet well understood and skillfully utilized these divisions amongst the opposition to maintain himself in power.

To some extent, the new constitution assisted Pinochet in this effort, as did changes in internal politics and the foreign policies of the United States. United States policy toward Chile had shifted considerably from President Nixon's support and assistance in the early years of the military government—juxtaposed to congressional legislation restricting military and other aid—to President Carter's public condemnation of human rights abuses, to President Reagan's reemphasis on anti-communism. Never, however, had U.S. foreign policy prevented General Pinochet from obtaining private foreign loans or investments. This had proved especially important during the height of the economic "miracle," and it proved critical once again in the mid-1980s.

In particular, United States support for millions of dollars' worth of credits, loans, and loan guarantees by the World Bank, Inter-American Development Bank, and large syndicates of private commercial banks helped to buffer Chile's debt burden and financed public works, new investments, and palliative make-work programs. The earthquake of 1985 (see Chapter 1) complicated the country's economic recovery, but also justified major new loan programs from international agencies for reconstruction of ports, highways, bridges, housing, and other physical infrastructure. All these projects helped to alleviate social and economic pressures. They also allowed General Pinochet to claim the confidence of the international banking community in his efforts to maintain himself in power and to institutionalize the new political order.

Dramatic declines in oil prices, plunging international interest rates, and economic recovery in the United States and Europe in the mid-1980s also provided breathing space for Pinochet by bolstering the Chilean economy. Economic recovery, again based on export expansion and imported capital, allowed unemployment to drop to "only" 10 percent in 1987. As the value of exports climbed to over $4 billion and the country achieved a trade balance of approximately $1 billion, enthusiastic government policymakers reaffirmed the validity of the export-driven model of economic growth. Stimulation of nontraditional exports reached new "highs" in late 1986 when the government announced that "a company that markets bathroom fixtures under the Fanaloza trade mark, has just shipped a trial order of 2,175 toilet-and-tank units to the United States. . . . The company's general manager said that this is one of Fanaloza's most exciting export operations since it started shipping yacht bathroom fixtures in 1984."

Along with renewed export growth, an innovative debt-equity conversion scheme enhanced the regime's international credibility. This scheme permitted investors to purchase government "foreign debt notes" at a discount, outside of Chile, and to exchange them at full face value in pesos to pay debts, acquire stock or fixed assets, or assets received in payment of foreclosure, or to finance new investments in Chile. The debt-equity conversion process which, according to official estimates, involved $1.96 billion from mid-1985 to June 1987, both helped to retire some of the 20 billion-dollar foreign debt and to *re-privatize* assets obtained by the government as a result of the collapse in the early 1980s. Hailed by officials of the United States Treasury and by international lenders as a model of innovation for other Latin American debtors, the Chilean government also persisted in its efforts to attract new foreign investment and to revitalize the private sector of the economy. Indeed, CORFO sold stock in government-owned companies to foreign investors and to the major private pension funds in order to raise money and to renew the divestiture program. Significant new investments from private companies and banks from Canada, New Zealand, Australia, West Germany, France, Spain, the United Kingdom, and the United States, together with new credit lines from the World Bank, InterAmerican Development Bank, and private foreign financial institutions, added to the Pinochet administration's optimism about the economy. Though a new United States ambassador to Chile openly discussed with members of the opposition the possibility of General Pinochet's departure from government, public and private economic policymakers in the United States provided encouragement and substantial leverage for General Pinochet in his efforts to survive the challenges to his administration.

Notwithstanding the post-1985 economic upturn, public opinion polls in Chile in 1986-87 evidenced less than 20 percent support for General Pinochet's administration. Increasing frustration on the part of the disunited opposition juxtaposed to the uncompromising insistence by General Pinochet on fulfilling his term of office and following "constitutional" procedures (the constitution of 1980) generated ever more bitterness and violence.

By the time General Pinochet had successfully orchestrated the constitutional plebsicite of 1980, frustration and desperation had already led to escalation in the tactics used by some elements of the opposition in efforts to rid the country of an ever more personalist dictatorship. The evident ineffectiveness of the centrist and rightist opposition, along with the need to re-establish its own credibility, led the Communist party of Chile to call publicly for the use of *all* types of struggle against the dictatorship. A commitment to armed struggle, as a part of an overall resistance to the Pinochet government, allied the Communists with MIR and certain sectors of the Socialist party. The 1979 victory of the Sandinistas in Nicaragua against the Somoza dictatorship gave this tactic some credibility, despite the obvious differences between Nicaragua and Chile. In addition, the new Reagan administration in the United States shifted emphasis in U.S. policy away from a focus on human rights issues and clearly supported the Pinochet government in international forums. Lack of viable internal alternatives to Pinochet, and the loss of hope for U.S. pressures on the regime for changes in policies, made the new Communist tactic understandable, if very unlikely to achieve success. However, it also made it practically impossible for Christian Democratic leadership or other democratic movements to join in a unified opposition coalition even for the limited purpose of ousting General Pinochet.

Lack of unity did not prevent growing levels of opposition among all strata of the Chilean population after the collapse of the "miracle" in 1981. Reversals of economic policy and disputes among diverse entrepreneurial groups over corrective measures fragmented the "nonpolitical" social base of the government. The resurgence of labor protests and strikes, calls both for Pinochet's resignation and for restoration of democracy from all the old political parties (theoretically nonexistent under the new constitution), and increasing numbers of "days of protest" all raised the hopes of opposition forces that General Pinochet's regime had run its course. By mid-1984, expectations were high for a quick end to the dictatorship. Daring headlines in opposition newspapers even declared in bold print: "He doesn't want to leave"—and in smaller print—"We'll have to throw him out." A year later, in August 1985, a temporary opposition coalition hammered out a "National Accord for Transition to Full Democracy." This *Acuerdo* called for immediate termination to the states of "constitutional exception" (state of siege, state of emergency, state of internal commotion" etc.), restoration of university autonomy, an end to political banishment and exile, and constitutional reforms that eliminated the main elements of the "Constitution of Liberty." The *Acuerdo* also called for programs of economic reactivation, abandonment of the neo-liberal policies, creation of jobs, and *an active role for the state in reshaping the Chilean economy*. In short, the opposition asked General Pinochet to surrender both his office and the major changes he had introduced since 1973.

Surrender was not acceptable. Instead, Pinochet announced that the 1980 constitution would remain in effect, that he would complete his term of office scheduled to end in 1989, and that he had not yet decided whether he would be a candidate, as the constitution allowed, for the term which would end in 1997. Opposition newspapers, magazines, and other publications, which had appeared in the "political opening" allowed by Pinochet from 1983 to 1984, again were censored or closed down. Selective detentions and harassment reminded the opposition of the limits to the general's tolerance. On the political left, declarations that the *Acuerdo* was no substitute for armed struggle reinforced General Pinochet's determination and frightened many middle- and upper-class Chileans who were bombarded with the threat of "Cubanization" and "Nicaraguanization" of Chile. Groups which preferred some measure of liberalization, *without Marxist participation* in Chilean politics, saw no obvious alternative to Pinochet's continuation in office. Christian Democratic, social democratic, and more conservative political groups found themselves without a concrete program for temporary or long-term replacement of Pinochet and the new system of "protected democracy." Nor could they patch together a workable formula for accommodating the reality of the persistence of the left in Chilean society and politics. General Pinochet had not succeeded in depoliticizing Chile, but the perpetuation and intensification of political polarization served his interests in the mid-1980s, if only by preventing the opposition from uniting effectively against him.

A key to General Pinochet's political survival remained his control over the military, and especially over the army and the internal security forces. Through manipulations of command assignments, modification of the career and retirement system, and personalist patronage, General Pinochet had established a base of support in the army. As commander-in-chief of the armed forces, he relied upon respect for hierarchy and military discipline to maintain formal control over the other services. Certain elements within the military had adopted a radical anti-Marxism as a collective political commitment, and this base of ideologically oriented officers provided further support for General Pinochet's stance against a return to the past. Further, Chilean sociologists Arturo Chacon and Humberto Lagos reported, in a study called *La Religión en las Fuerzas Armadas y de Orden*, that by 1986 some 15,000 members of the Chilean armed forces had joined evangelical churches, and become "zealous proselytizers, anti-Catholic, anti-communist and anti-Marxist."

These new trends within the military institutions after 1973 also introduced contradictions which led to difficulties for the Pinochet government. Disagreements over economic policy and over the permanent political role of key officers, if not the entire armed forces, under the new constitution, bothered some Chilean military professionals who still preferred a narrower focus on external defense, force modernization, and professional careers *apart from* responsibil-

ity for policymaking. Other officers resented the personalization of
the government, the relative dominance of the army and security
forces, and the civilian population's understandable antagonism for
what ex-*gremialista* leader, Orlando Sáenz, now called Chile's military institutions: "an occupying force." A number of officers even
held a real preference for civilian, democratic institutions, though
most shared concern about the participation of the left in a democratic system.

By the early 1980s some officers were well aware of the advantages
to the armed forces of negotiating some sort of extrication from the
military's political role *at minimal damage to the military institutions*. But with whom could military officers negotiate such an extrication? No civilian coalition or political force had emerged that
could effectively challenge General Pinochet, present an alternative
program widely enough shared to offer some chance of success, or,
most importantly, comply with any agreement negotiated with the
military as a way to initiate a transition to a more democratic, civilian
government. The profound ideological and organizational divisions of
the Chilean polity, the lack of any obvious personage (after the death
of Eduardo Frei in 1982) with whom to replace General Pinochet,
and the lack of effective guarantees against persecution, trials, and
loss of career (as occurred in some cases in Argentina after restoration of civilian government in 1983), all restrained the efforts of military officers who might otherwise have sought a gradual process of
accommodation with certain civilian parties and movements. Nevertheless, dissent within the air force and navy took the form of public
criticisms, leading to forced retirements and changes in command assignments. This public criticism continued even after an assassination
attempt against General Pinochet in early September 1986 in which
a number of his military escort were wounded or killed.

Responding to the assassination attempt, to dissent within the military institutions, to the reported discovery of a large arms cache in
northern Chile, and to civilian calls for his ouster, General Pinochet
ordered a new campaign of repression, murder, and detentions against
targeted civilians. He replaced the army member of the *junta* with
the director of the secret police and forced a number of generals into
retirement. General Pinochet reiterated his intention to remain in
office until 1989 and to institutionalize the new political order. Providing a symbolic gesture to domestic and external critics, he
ended the "state of siege" (reduced to a "state of emergency") and
promulgated a new law on political parties in early 1987—with the
expected limitations on party functions and the exclusion of Marxist

and other "subversive" organizations. Like his hero, Portales, Pinochet deftly applied the "stick and the cake" to maintain the new
political order.

Ultimately, only military acquiesence in the removal of General
Pinochet, or an unexpected problem with his health, appeared to offer any chance of cutting short the constitutionally prescribed term
ending in 1989. In a further irony of the military regime, civilian politicians once again looked to the military to remove a president by
other than constitutional means, in order to achieve the objective
they believed would be attained in 1973: restoration of democratic
government with exclusions on participation by Marxists and the left.
However, democracy without the participation of more than 30 percent of the Chilean population remained as much a contradiction in
1987 as it had forty years earlier with adoption of the "Law for the
Permanent Defense of Democracy" in the administration of President González Videla.

Unable to unite, unable to provide the military with assurances of
institutional integrity and immunity from prosecution for abuses of
human rights, and unable to agree upon a formula for short-term
transition or for a new political system, the opposition to General Pinochet was openly discouraged at the beginning of 1987. Groups on
the political right sought to find some new common ground in anticipation of the politics of succession in 1989; the center continued
criticizing government policies and seeking new temporary coalitions
and agreements as a basis for restoring democracy, though the Socialist party withdrew from the Alianza Democrática at the end of 1986;
the left, divided as always, gave some support to the centrist projects
while the more revolutionary groups advocated political mobilization
and, where possible, armed resistance against the regime.

An historic papal visit to Chile in early April, 1987, preceded by
unprecedented levels of political posturing and maneuvering by government and opposition forces, focused the world's attention once
again both on the abuses of the Pinochet government and the divisions among the opposition to the regime. At the behest of John
Paul II, opposition forces from left to right, including the Communist
party, signed a vague pledge to work for a peaceful transition to democracy and met together to consider the possibilities of the political
moment. However, this unusual meeting of leaders from Chile's fragmented opposition had much less impact than the fierce military and
police repression against regime opponents who defiantly protested
government policies during a papal mass attended by hundreds of
thousands of Chileans in Santiago. Televised around the world, the

violent disruption of the papal ceremony symbolized the stalemate of Chilean politics in 1987. General Pinochet blamed the violence on Communist agitators; the opposition took heart from the Pope's message of peace and solidarity with those who suffered from injustice, unemployment, and misery, but were unable to agree on the "true" message of the Pope or to translate the Pope's spiritual solidarity into political power. Thus, in the short term, the Pope's visit to Chile did little to change the reality of the dictatorship's hold on the country.

By mid-1987, government and opposition preparations for the plebiscite to select a president for the term 1989-97, as required by the 1980 constitution, took center stage in Chile's political drama. Even as destructive storms ravaged central Chile in July 1987, leaving a toll of human death and injury as well as extensive damage to roads, bridges, farms and housing, opposition groups debated the most effective tactics for confronting the dictatorship in the upcoming plebiscite. Some favored refusal to register, abstentionism, selection of an alternate candidate to oppose whomever the government selected (despite constitutional provisions for a single candidate in 1989), or pressuring the government to allow "free and competitive elections." Others dismissed the feasibility of electoral opposition and urged continued armed resistance.

While the moderate opposition discussed electoral tactics, and the Manuel Rodríguez Patriotic Front carried out a variety of armed actions against the government, General Pinochet insisted upon compliance with the transitory provisions of the 1980 constitution. This meant exclusion of Marxists and other "subversives" from the political process and institutionalization of the authoritarian political order. In October 1987 the dictatorship again made clear its commitment to these objectives in new repressive legislation. In an obvious effort to limit political debate and bulwark the regime against a new wave of protests and labor activism, the military *junta* sought to bar employment of "Marxists" in education and journalism, provided for fines against news media which propagated "Marxist" ideas, and even threatened penalties against groups and individuals who cooperated politically or proposed coalitions with Marxist movements or parties.

In these circumstances, the insights reportedly offered by President Salvador Allende to opposition leader Orlando Sáenz, about a month before Allende's death, seemed ever more prophetic:

> Let me tell you something. . . . You are looking for a military dictatorship. And from somewhere, not that I believe there's anything after death, but still, if there is, I shall look down on

you all and find you all together, casting about for ways to get
out of power the military man you replace me with. I shall see
you all there, plotting and planning it, but with a great deal
more difficulty than you are having now, how to get rid of the
soldier you put in my place. Because it won't cost you much to
get him in. But by heaven, it will cost you something to get
him out.

In the late 1980s, as in so many critical moments in Chilean history, the struggle for human dignity, improved living conditions, democratization and participation of the majority of the population in
making decisions about matters that affected their daily lives faced
the barrier of calls for order, discipline, and economic efficiency. Confrontations between bearers of alternative visions of society, of politics, of the past, and of the future had led to institutionalization of
an agonizing reconquest of Chile, replete with its own version of
inquisition.

Yet this new conquest and new inquisition could not ultimately
achieve its mission. Chile could not be "purified" (*depurado*); politics could not be ended; the struggle for a better life could not be terminated by decree or through terror. In a sense, the ultimate failure
of the government's policies since 1973 was the survival of all political forces and movements of the 1970s and the creation of new ones
despite state terrorism. This failure, however, left Chilean society
even more polarized and lacking in consensus than in 1973. Recognition that the constitution of 1980 could not survive much beyond
General Pinochet himself did not in itself provide the basis for an alternative model of society and politics. Obviously, the *personal* dictatorship of General Pinochet would eventually pass from the scene.
Nevertheless, Chileans looked to the future with uncertainty, no
longer confident of their special knack to be different within Latin
America, no longer able, even with their dry, biting humor, to suppress the grisly reality of the last fifteen years. Long years of personal,
social, and political reconciliation would be required to erase the scars
of military dictatorship.

Political Chronology

1534
King of Spain names Diego de Almagro governor of Neuva Toledo, extending approximately from Ica to just north of Tal Tal.

1535-36
Almagro expedition enters Chile and reconnoiters into the central valley. Finding no great source of wealth as in Peru, Almagro returns to Cuzco to contest the spoils of conquest with the Pizzaros.

1539
Pizzaro authorizes Pedro de Valdivia to lead expedition of conquest to Chile, which he baptizes Nuevo Extremo or Nueva Extremadura.

1540-41
Pedro de Valdivia's expedition arrives at the Mapocho river in December; Santiago founded February 12, 1541, and within the month Valdivia creates the first cabildo. September 11, 1541, local Indians attack the new town, practically destroying it and most of the settlers' provisions.

1540-53
Initial settlement and warfare with indigenous population under leadership of Valdivia. First towns founded: La Serena (1544); Concepción (1550); La Imperial, Valdivia, Villarrica (1552); Los Confines (1553).

1553
Battle of Tucapel, Valdivia killed by Indians led by cacique Lautaro—his ex-groom.

1553-57   Disputes among Valdivia's lieutenants over control of the colony. Continued warfare with Indians. Spanish defeated at Marigueñu (1554), settlements abandoned. Three years later Spanish destroy Lautaro's forces at Peteroa (1557).

1557-61   Viceroy at Lima names his son, García Hurtado de Mendoza, governor of Chile and sends an army financed out of the royal treasury to secure Chile. Alonso de Ercilla y Zuñiga, author of the epic poem, *La Araucana*, arrives with this expedition to Chile.

1557-59   Exploration of territory from Concepción to the south. Osorno founded (1558), and expedition under command of Juan Ladrillero penetrates to the Strait of Magellan. Fort at Tucapel reconstructed and Concepción resettled.

1559   Tasa de Santillán—ordinances seeking to regulate Indian labor and personal service to the Spanish—prohibits use of Indians as beasts of burden and require sufficient daily food for Indian workers. Ordinances largely ignored, despite application in mines at Quilacoya near Concepción.

1561-63   Administration of Governor Francisco de Villagra. Creation of Diocese of Santiago (1561). Bartolomé Rodrigo González Marmolejo appointed first Bishop. Fray Gil de González preaches "defensive war," unsuccessfully seeking to defend Indians.

1563-65   Interim administration of Pedro de Villagra. Pope Paul IV creates Diocese of La Imperial (1563). Philip II decrees establishment of Chile's first *audiencia* at Concepción (1565).

1565-67   Interim administration of Rodrigo de Quiroga. Audiencia installed at Concepción and town of Castro founded (1567) after expedition of exploration and conquest to island of Chiloé.

1567-75   Chile governed by Bravo de Saravia. Bishop of La Imperial advises king to suppress the audiencia (1570) because of its failure to help pacify the territory and deal firmly with abuses against the Indians. Despite continued efforts by the Bishop and royal decrees, *encomenderos* continue to evade regulations. Audiencia at Concepción abolished (1573).

1575-70   Rodrigo de Quiroga, one of the area's first conquistadors and lieutenant of Valdivia, assumes political leadership, supports encomenderos, and urges king to approve "personal service" of Indians to Spaniards. Carries out large expeditions of war against Indians in southern region. Prisoners are maimed to prevent their escape.

1580   Chillán founded.

1580-83   Interim administration of Ruíz de Gamboa, Quiroga's son-in-law. In effort to secure permanent appointment, Ruiz de Gamboa cooperates with Bishop Medillín in promulgation of Tasa de Gamboa (1580) which sought to abolish "personal service." Gamboa fails to win decisive victory over Araucanians, and the Spanish king sends Alonso de Sotomayor, a veteran soldier, as governor of Chile.

1583-92   Administration of Alonso de Sotomayor. Gradual revocation of Gamboa's reforms; forced labor—personal service reinstated. Stimulation to mining economy in Quillota and Choapa valleys. Despite harsh campaigns against Araucanians, Indians remain unsubdued. Sotomayor's secret marriage to a Creole woman leads to his downfall.

1592-99   Administration of Martín García Oñez de Loyola, nephew of the viceroy of Peru and relative of Ignatius de Loyola, founder of the Society of Jesus (Jesuit order). Renewal of official concern with conditions of Indians. Outlaws sale of Indian captives or their transport from the south to northern mines or to Peru.

1598   Indian uprising under cacique Pelantaru. Oñez de Loyola is killed and decapitated in valley of Curalava. Nine years later his head is returned by Indians to Governor Alonso García Ramón. Philip II dies.

1599-1601   Several interim administrations. Abandonment of Spanish settlements in the south. Beginning of permanent royal subsidy (*situado real*) to finance war against Araucanians (1600).

1601-05   Administration of Alonso de Ribera. Permanent army is established in Chile (1603). Diocese of La Imperial moves to Concepción (1603). Indian offensive continues with Spanish defeats at Santa Cruz, Valdivia (1599), La Imperial and Angol (1600), Villarrica (1602), Osorno and Arauco (1604). Spanish respond with renewed sorties south. Southern economy totally disrupted.

1605-10   Administration of García Ramón. Accompanied to Chile by the Jesuit, Luis de Valdivia. Luis de Valdivia preaches "defensive warfare." García Ramón continues offensive against Indians, suffering humiliating defeat in 1606. King authorizes perpetual slavery for captured Indian rebels (1608). Pope Paul V authorizes war against the Araucanians. Jesuit Luis de Valdivia arrives in Spain to seek official acceptance of "defensive warfare" (1609). In the same year a new audiencia established in Santiago.

1610-11   Interim administrations of Merlo de la Fuente and Jara Quemada. Luis de Valdivia's influence results in reappointment of Alonso de Ribera as governor of Chile. Valdivia named as *visitador general*.

1612-17   Administration of Alonso de Ribera. Political intrigue between governor and Luis de Valdivia. Murder of Jesuit missionaries at Elicura provides pretext for renewed warfare (1614) despite official policy to the contrary.

1617-24   Interim administration of five different governors. Luis de Valdivia leaves Chile in 1619. "Defensive warfare" largely discredited. Tasa de Esquilache (1620) again seeks to regulate Indian labor—generally unsuccessful.

1625-29   Administration of Fernández de Córdoba. King of Spain authorizes renewed warfare against Araucanians and slavery for captives. Governor allows branding of Indian captives. Spaniards suffer new military defeats, notably at Las Cangrejeras near Yumbel.

1629-39   Administration of Lazo de la Vega. Spanish defeat Araucanians at La Albarrada (1631) and Philip IV officially abolishes "personal service" (1633). New regulations—Tasa de Lazo de la Vega (1635)—issued concerning Indian labor. Abolishes personal service but "allows" Indians to pay tribute in labor and "rent" their services. Widespread abuses.

1639-46   Administration of the Marquis de Baides. Governor attempts to negotiate with Araucanians. Pact of Quillín recognizes sovereignty of Araucanians. In exchange Indians agree to receive missionaries. Peace treaty terms violated. Warfare resumes, though Indians help Spaniards repel invasion of southern Chile by Brouwer expedition (1643).

1646-49   Administration of Martín de Mujica. Earthquake destroys Santiago (1647). Followed by typhoid epidemic. Viceroy at Peru temporarily suspends certain taxes in Chile. Pact of Quillín renewed.

1650-56   Administration of Acuña y Cabrera. Cunco Indians kill crew of ship carrying situado to Valdivia (1651). Punitive expedition destroyed by Indians (1653). Nepotism and corruption weaken Spanish military. Indian uprising in 1655; vecinos of Concepción "depose" Acuña y Cabrera. Indians again push Spaniards out of southern settlements. Southern economy in shambles.

1656-63   Three interim administrations. King Philip IV prohibits future slave raids and military expeditions into hostile territory without prior approval. Viceroy at Lima appeals decisions to protect Peruvian labor supply.

1664-68   Administration of Francisco de Meneses. Governor in disputes with Church and audiencia. Corruption prevails as governor and supporters loot public administration, sell favors, and engage in slave raids (*malocas*) and trade. Peruvian viceroy, Count of Santistéban, supports continued enslavement of Araucanians.

1668-70   Two interim administrations succeed Meneses after he leaves Chile in disgrace.

1670-81   Administration of Juan Henríquez. Debate over treatment of Indians continues. Writings of Diego de Rosales gain influence. Queen Regent Mariana of Austria officially abolishes slavery in 1674. Henríquez and audiencia develop *depósito* system to circumvent abolition (1676). King Charles II reaffirms abolition decree of 1674 and orders freed Indians transported for their "care" to Peru (1679). King reverses his decree in response to Governor Henríquez's letters defending Chilean interests (1683). Pirates under Bartholomew Sharp sack La Serena (1680).

1682-92   Administration of José de Garro. Governor proposes massacre of Araucanian leaders. Viceroy and King reject Garro's proposal (1686). New pirate attacks at Coquimbo and La Serena (1686). Earthquake at Lima (1687) stimulates Chilean wheat production, increase in prices and temporary economic expansion.

1692-1700   Administration of Tomás Marín de Poveda. Royal decree of 1693 authorizes Indians to pay tribute in money or kind instead of personal service. Decree evaded as others in the past. Renewed efforts to pacify Araucanians through negotiations and missions—unsuccessful as in the past.

1700   Death of Charles II. Beginning of Bourbon era for Spanish America. Charles II leaves no successor. Throne is willed to Philip of Anjou (Philip V of Spain), grandson of Louis XIV of France.

1701-14   War of the Spanish Succession ended by the treaties of Utrecht and Rastadt. Philip V, King of Spain, renounces claim to French throne.

1713   England granted the *asiento* or monopoly on slave trade with Spain's colonies.

1701-08   Administration of Governor Francisco Ibáñez de Peralta. Corruption involving the situado. Civil war with rebels calling for ouster of governor. Rebellion suppressed. Increasing levels of contraband trade. Numerous complaints against governor lead to his removal by Philip V.

1709-16   Administration of Governor Juan Andrés de Ustáriz. Large scale commercial corruption involving French merchants after Ustáriz buys post of Chilean governorship for 24,000 pesos. Pirates under Captain Rogers find Alexander Selkirk ("Robinson Crusoe") on the island Más a Tierra in the Juan Fernández Archipelago.

1717-33   Administration of Governor Gabriel Cano y Aponte. Moderate policies pursued toward Mapuches. Period of relative peace with exception of rebellion in 1723. Earthquake provokes great damage to Santiago (1730) and affects seriously most of central Chile. Earthquake is followed by tidal wave at Valparaíso causing serious losses. Smallpox epidemic (1731).

1734-37   Interim administration of Manuel de Salamanca.

1737-45   Administration of Governor José Antonio Manso de Velasco. Founding of new towns in mining and agricultural districts, including San Felipe (1740), Los Angeles, Canquenes, San Fernando (1742), Melipilla, Rancagua, Curicó (1743). In recognition of his service, Manso de Velasco is made viceroy at Lima.

1745-55   Administration of Governor Domingo Ortiz de Rozas. Real Universidad de San Felipe inaugurated (1747) and La Moneda begins to function (1749). For his service in founding new settlements—Quirihue and Coelemu (1749), La Florida (1751), Casablanca and Petorca (1753), and Ligua (1754)—the king confers title upon Ortiz de Rozas. Ortiz de Rozas dies (1756) on return to Spain.

1751   Earthquake and tidal wave destroy Concepción.

1755-61   Administration of Governor Manuel de Amat y Junient. University of San Felipe begins operation (1757). Violent repression of prison rebellion in Santiago (1758). Amat y Junient becomes viceroy at Lima upon leaving Chilean post.

1761-68   Administration of Governor Antonio de Guill y Gonzaga. Foundation of Rere (1765). Yumbel (1766), and Tucapel el Nuevo (1765). Jesuits expelled from Chile (1767). Governor delegates much authority to *corregidor* Zañartu who imposes a reign of repression against criminals and indigents in Santiago. According to Francisco Encina, the slogan for Zañartu's program "By Reason or by Force" anticipated the slogan on the Chilean national escutcheon.

1768-73   After the death of Guill y Gonzaga, several interim administrations follow. New Indian uprisings and Spanish losses force negotiation of still another treaty (Paz de Negrete, 1770) in which Spanish give Indians compensation in money and cattle.

1773-80   Administration of Agustín de Jáuregui. Establishment of viceroyalty of Buenos Aires (1776), opening of direct commerce to Chile (1778), separation of Cuyo from Chile (1779). Governor introduces Draconian criminal legislation in efforts to curb violence, robberies, cattle rustling, and drunkeness. First significant census taken in Chile (1778). Like several of his predecessors, Jáuregui leaves Chile to become viceroy at Lima.

1780-87   Administration of Governor Ambrosio de Benavides. Administrative reorganization—introduction of intendant system (1782) with Chile divided into two intendencies: Santiago and Concepción. Upon the death of Benavides, the Intendant of Concepción, Ambrosio de O'Higgins, becomes governor of Chile.

1783   Earth tremor and flooding in Santiago as Mapocho River rages through the city. Entire neighborhoods disappear.

1787-96   Administration of Governor Ambrosio O'Higgins. Foundation of numerous new towns and mining centers. Public works, road construction, and beautification of Santiago. Encomiendas abolished (1791). New treaty with Indians in south (Parlamento of Negrete, 1793). Foundation of the *Consulado* (1795). O'Higgins becomes viceroy at Lima in 1796.

1796-1802   Administration of Governor Gabriel de Avilés y del Fierro and several interim administrations. Threat of war against England preoccupies the colony with preparations for defense against invasion. After brief tenure in Chile, Avilés becomes viceroy at Buenos Aires and then at Lima. Interim governors follow until 1802.

1802-08   Administration of Governor Luis Muñoz de Guzmán. Continuation of public works programs in Santiago. Buenos Aires occupied by English (1806). Beginnings of political unrest in Chile. Vaccinations introduced in Chile (1805). Muñoz de Guzmán dies in 1808.

1808-10   Interim administration of Francisco Antonio García Carrasco. Unrest intensifies and governor is replaced by Mateo de Toro y Zambrano.

Sept. 18, 1810   Cabildo Abierto creates first junta, beginnings of Chilean independence movement.

1811-13   "Dictatorship" of José Miguel Carrera. Offspring of slaves born in Chile declared free (1811). Appearance of Chile's first newspaper, *La Aurora de Chile* (1812). Civil war in Chile.

1814   Treaty of Lircay. *Patria Vieja* ends after defeat of insurrectionists at Rancagua. Chilean forces retreat to Mendoza.

1814-17   *La Reconquista*—temporary restoration of Spanish authority as military expeditions from Peru defeat rebel forces.

1817   General San Martín and Bernardo O'Higgins lead army from

Argentina into Chile and defeat Spanish forces at Chacabuco (February 12, 1817).

1817-23   Dictatorship of Bernardo O'Higgins. Continued war against Spanish forces south of Santiago. Expeditionary force leaves Chile to liberate Peru (1820). Peruvian independence declared (1821) as San Martín occupies Lima. Titles of nobility abolished (1817).

1823-30   Period of chaos and political uncertainty dominated by liberal, federalist experiments and personality of Ramón Freire. Slavery abolished (1823). Federalist experiment (1826-28).

1828-30   Renewed civil war.

1830   Battle of Lircay (April 17, 1830). Conservative forces emerge victorious.

1831-41   Two five-year terms of President Joaquín Prieto. Constitution of 1833 adopted. Chile defeats Peru-Bolivia Confederation (1836-1839). Initiation of "Portalian State."

1842   University of Chile founded.

1849   Emergence of Liberal party.

1850   Sociedad de Igualdad established under leadership of Francisco Bilbao to contest election of Manuel Montt.

1841-51   Two five-year terms of President Manuel Bulnes, hero of the war against Bolivia and Peru. Civil War of 1851 mars succession, but Bulnes successfully defends his chosen successor, Manuel Montt.

1851-61   Two five-year terms of President Manuel Montt. Civil wars in 1851 and 1859 fragment ruling elite. Formation of Conservative party (1857). Economic boom as a consequence of gold strike in California. Expansion of Chilean commerce, mining and agriculture. Political challenge to clerical forces and old Conservative elite.

1861-71   Two five-year terms of President José Joaquín Pérez. Coalition governments incorporate Liberals and Conservatives into government as President breaks with party that elected him. Radical party formed in 1861 by Pedro León Gallo and the Matta brothers. Radical party becomes proponent of political reforms. "Theological Question" becomes a key issue in Chilean politics.

1871-75   Administration of President Federico Errázuriz Zañartu. Errázuriz dismisses Conservative members of coalition (1873) and forms cabinet entirely of Liberals, Radicals, and Nationals—the so-called Liberal Alliance. Religious question dominates domestic politics.

1876-81   Administration of President Aníbal Pinto. Severe economic crisis facing country "alleviated" by victory in the War of the Pacific (1879-1883). Chile acquires nitrate fields from Peru and Bolivia, increasing territory by more than one-third.

1883   Creation of the Sociedad de Fomento Fabril.

1881-86   Administration of President Domingo Santa María. Attempted renewal of political authoritarianism and anticlericalism. Suffrage extended to all males over 25 years of age.

1886-91   Administration of José Manuel Balmaceda. Growth of nitrate and export trade accompanied by expansion of public works programs, government bureaucracy, educational opportunities. Conflict between President Balmaceda and Congress over government policies and constitutional issues leads to civil war. Balmaceda commits suicide as term ends. Congressional victory inaugurates period of "parliamentary republic" (1891-1924).

1887   Formation of Partido Demócrata.

1888   Establishment of the Catholic University.

1889   Creation of Pedagogical Institute.

1890-91   Civil War.

1891-96   Administration of Jorge Montt. Leader of the opposition against Balmaceda, Montt attempts to restore peace in Chile. Incipient industrialization brings pressures for protectionist legislation. Partido Demócrata, elects first deputy to Congress (1894).

1896-1901 Administration of Federico Errázuriz Echaurren. Diplomacy avoids conflict with Argentina. Tariff legislation and cattle tax (1897) provoke intense opposition. "Social question" emerging in Chilean politics with growth of workers' press and labor organizations. First electric trolley in Santiago (1900). President dies in office (1901).

1901-06   Administration of Germán Riesco Errázuriz. Campaigns with slogan "I am not a threat to anyone." Promulgation of Code of Civil Procedure (1902) and Criminal Procedure (1906). Peace treaty signed with Bolivia (1904). Strikes in Valparaíso (1903) and "meat strike" protesting cattle tax erupt into violence in Santiago—"Red Week" 1905. Earthquake devastates Valparaíso (1906).

1906-10   Administration of Pedro Montt. Worker protest, wave of strikes in 1907-09. Stockmarket crash (1907). Massacre of workers at Santa María de Iquique (1907). TransAndean railroad completed (1910).

1907   Massacre of workers at Santa María de Iquique.

1909   Organization of Gran Federación de Obreros de Chile. By 1917 becomes a militant labor organization (FOCH) and eventually affiliates with RILU.

1910-15   Administration of Ramón Barros Luco. Famous for his remark "There are only two kinds of political problems, those that solve themselves and those without solution." Barros Luco faces military conspiracy (1912). Initial impact of World War I on economy brings recession and worker activism.

1912   Creation of Socialist Workers Party (POS) founded by Luis Emilio Recabarren and supporters.

1913   General strike in Valparaíso, led by anarchists.

1915-20   Administration of Juan Luis Sanfuentes. World War I impacts Chilean society and economy, increasing industrialization and labor organization. Economic crisis after war brings urban protests in Santiago and labor activism.

1917   Port strike in Valparaíso. Government declares martial law; Yáñez decree seeks to regulate industrial relations.

1918   AOAN rally in Santiago.

1919-20   Wave of labor activism, AOAN rally in Valparaíso (January); Congress gives President Sanfuentes emergency powers; tram strike in Santiago; ADAN rally in Santiago (August); Police raid IWW headquarters in Valparaíso and attack Student Federation (FECH) headquarters in Santiago. Arrests and detention of labor and POS leaders. Workers and police die in labor conflict in Puerto Natales (1919) and Magallanes (1920).

1920 Arturo Alessandri assumes Presidency (December).

1920-24 First administration of President Arturo Alessandri. Alessandri, after populist campaign, is unable to move reforms through Congress. Military "coup" pushes social and labor legislation through Congress with a "rattling of sabers." Alessandri leaves the country.

1922 Establishment of Chilean Communist party.

1925 New Constitution approved. President Alessandri returns to Chile only to leave again after conflict with Defense Minister, Carlos Ibáñez.

1925 Massacre of striking nitrate workers at Oficina La Coruña in Antofagasta.

1927-31 Ibáñez takes control of government after a period of "tutelage." Controlled elections provide a compliant congress. Massive public works program induces temporary prosperity as Ibáñez represses opposition. Stock market crash and depression bring Ibáñez's downfall.

1932-38 Arturo Alessandri returns to presidency after more than a year of juntas, insurrections, and uncertainty which includes the 100 days of a Chilean "Socialist Republic." Alessandri restores order, imposes the 1925 constitution, and utilizes fiscal conservatism to improve public finances. In departure from earlier (1920s) rhetoric, Alessandri presides over a Conservative regime.

1933 Creation of Socialist Party of Chile.

1934 Massacre of peasants at Ranquil.

1935-38 Formation of the Falange Nacional with splinter of Conservative youth group from Conservative party. Falange eventually (1957) becomes the Chilean Christian Democratic Party.

1936	Formation of Popular Front as prelude to 1938 presidential elections.
1938	Massacre of Nazis involved in protest movement (September 5) and incarceration of their leader, González Von Marées.
1938-41	Administration of Pedro Aguirre Cerda with support of Popular Front coalition. Reformist programs follow, including creation of Chilean Development Corporation (CORFO). Rural activism frightens political right; Popular Front parties agree to "suspend" rural unionization. Aguirre Cerda dies in 1941.
1942-46	Administration of President Juan Antonio Ríos. Popular Front dissolved but variety of coalitions follow. Communists and Socialists dominate labor movement but competition for control eventually divides leftist parties. President Ríos dies in 1946; new elections bring fellow Radical, González Videla, to the presidency.
1946-52	Administration of President Gabriel González Videla. Initial coalition of Radicals, Liberals, and Communists breaks up. González Videla, with support by the United States, moves against Communists. Communist party outlawed in 1948 and labor organizations purged. Chile becomes Cold War battleground.
1947	New legislation restricts rights of rural labor. Conflicts in labor movement lead to divisions between Communist- and Socialist-led unions.
1948	Coal strikes and labor agitation. Law for the Permanent Defense of Democracy outlaws Communist party.
1952-58	Administration of President Carlos Ibáñez. Ibáñez elected on "anti-political" platform. Economic difficulties after the Korean War plague Ibáñez. High inflation rates and foreign advisers' stabilization programs undercut Ibáñez's popularity. Ibáñez approves electoral reform and relegalization of Communist party before leaving office.
1958-64	Administration of President Jorge Alessandri. After barely winning election over Salvador Allende, the candidate of the Leftist Coalition (FRAP), Alessandri presides over a conservative administration that introduced a number of minor reforms. Anti-inflation programs are relatively successful, but

alienate workers, peasants, and part of the middle class. Under pressure from Alliance for Progress, a land reform law passes in 1962.

1964-70   Administration of President Eduardo Frei. Frei presides over the Christian Democratic "Revolution in Liberty" that dramatically alters Chilean politics and society. Mobilization of workers, peasants, slum-dwellers, and women destabilizes Chilean politics—and the government is unable to deliver on all its promises. Renewed inflation, economic stagnation, and seizures of farms, urban lots, and housing projects punctuate the last years of Christian Democratic government.

1970-73   Unidad Popular administration of President Salvador Allende. A program to put Chile on the peaceful road to socialism is met with bitter resistance by domestic and international opponents. Political polarization finally results in a bloody military coup, September 11, 1973.

1973-8?   Military dictatorship directed by General Augusto Pinochet. Political parties outlawed and civil liberties restricted. Severe repression of opposition. Military regime seeks to create new political system; 1980 constitution "institutionalizes" new regime of "protected democracy." Drastic economic and social policy changes emphasize privatization and foreign investment. Economic boomlet (1977-81) followed by intense recession (1982-85). Support for military government erodes but opposition unable to forge unified coalition. Assassination attempt on Pinochet in late 1986. Country remains under "state of emergency" into 1987.

Selective Guide to
the Literature on Chile

This bibliography is intended as a starting point for the general reader in locating* materials on Chilean history and society. It is hoped that the specialist on Chile may also find in the topical bibliographic treatments a useful foundation for more intensive study of particular periods or themes in Chilean history. In general, the bibliography emphasizes published books. Manuscript sources, documents, and professional articles are listed in special cases or where I have relied upon particular works in the present volume.

In some respects Chilean historiography is extremely rich, detailed, and voluminous. For example, a comprehensive listing of works on colonial Chile, Chilean independence, or Chilean agriculture and rural society would require an extremely lengthy format merely for an alphabetical listing. Bibliography on the Unidad Popular period (1970-73) has reached massive proportions. In contrast, much remains to be done on pre-Hispanic Chile; no recent general history is available.

With this in mind, the bibliography that follows integrates chronological and thematic headings, beginning with a list of basic reference works and data sources, then moving to treatment of Chilean geography, population and natural resources, followed by studies on pre-Hispanic Chile through materials on the 1980s. In addition to suggestions for reading on particular topics or historical periods, an effort is also made to de-

* Place of publication for Chilean sources is Santiago, Chile, unless otherwise noted.

note sources with especially helpful bibliographies of their own for those interested in specialized topics. Inasmuch as the present bibliography is *selective* rather than comprehensive, I have sought to cite sources for further research rather than to provide comprehensive lists of references for experts on specific themes or historical periods.

Even with this limited objective some readers will note the absence of a work they consider "basic" to the treatment of a particular topic or period, or even the absence of a topic they would have liked to have seen covered in the bibliography. While I hope these deficiencies will be minimal, I certainly welcome suggestions for additions to the selective bibliography for future editions of this history.

In 1970 the National Statistical Institute (INE) published the *Guía de Publicaciones Estadísticas*, a list of current and historical statistical information on Chile divided into periodical publications, census, and individual booklets on special topics (for example, electoral data on particular elections, statistical abstracts, industrial or manufacturing census). In addition, this publication lists periodical and serial documents from other government agencies (for example, Social Security Administration, Central Bank, National Health Service). This exhaustive list of government publications makes the *Guia* an indispensable starting point for locating geographical, economic, social, and specialized historical data on Chile.

The following sources provide basic geographical, demographic, economic, social, and statistical material on Chile, as well as biographical dictionaries.

Area Handbook for Chile, Washington, D.C., U.S. Govt. Printing Office, 1982;

Banco Central de Chile, *Informe Económico de Chile*, 1983, 1984; *Indicadores Económicos y Sociales 1960-1982*;

Russell H. Bartley, *Latin America in Basic Historical Collections: A Working Guide*, Stanford, 1972 (information on manuscript holdings in libraries and collections);

M. L. Bohan and M. Pomerantz, *Investment in Chile: Basic Information for United States Businessmen*, U.S. Dept. of Commerce and Bureau of Foreign Commerce, 1960;

Jean Borde and Romulo Santana-Aguilar, *Le Chili: la terre et les hommes*, Paris, 1980;

CORFO, *Chile Economic Report*, New York (monthly review and update on the economy circulated by the Chilean government);

Chile, Economic Profile (Annual survey of the economy based on data from the Central Bank, National Planning Office (ODEPLAN), National Statistical Institute (INE), the National Copper Corporation (CODELCO), and individual Chilean government ministries; *Cuentas nacionales, 1940-1949* (also, *1950-1960*);

CORFO (Corporación de Fomento de la Producción), *Geografía económica de Chile*, texto refundido, 1967;

Corporación de Investigaciones Económicas para Latinoamérica (CIEPLAN) *Colección Estudios CIEPLAN*, 1979- (a periodical publication which contains a large number of articles and statistical information on the Chilean economy and public policy);

Lía Cortés and Jordi Fuentes, *Diccionario político de Chile: 1810-1966*, 1967;

Diccionario biográfico de Chile, 5th ed., 1944;

Pedro Pablo Figueroa, *Diccionario biográfico de Chile: 1550-1887*, 3 vols., 1897-1902; *Diccionario biográfico de extranjeros en Chile*, 1900;

Virgilio Figueroa, *Diccionario histórico, biográfico y bibliográfico de Chile: 1800-1931*, 5 vols., 1925-31;

Ronald Hilton (ed.), *Who's Who in Latin America Part IV: Bolivia, Chile, and Peru*, Stanford, 1947;

Jordi Fuentes, Lía Cortés, Fernando Castillo I., and Arturo Valdés P., *Diccionario Histórico de Chile*, 7th ed., 1982;

Jack Hopkins, ed., *Latin America and Caribbean Contemporary Record*, annual. 1983- (Vol. 1 covers 1981-82), New York (provides current overviews of politics and economic change, by country);

Instituto Geográfico Militar, *Atlas de la República de Chile*, 2nd ed., 1983; *Geografía de Chile*, 8 vols., 1983-84: I. *Fundamentos geográficos del territorio nacional;* II. *Geomorfología;* III. *Biogeografía;* IV. *Población y sistema nacional de asentamientos urbanos;* V. *Geografía de los suelos;* VI. *Geografía de los fondos marinos;* VII. *Geografía industrial;* VIII. *Hidrografía;*

Instituto Nacional de Estadísticas (INE), *Anuario de Demografía* (demographic yearbook); *Compendio Estadístico*, 1985 (annual statistical compendium with demographic, economic, and social data);

Markos Mamalakis, "Historical Statistics of Chile: An Introduction" *Latin American Research Review* 13:2 (1978), 127-37, provides a brief summary of source material on historical statistics, including national accounts, demography, agriculture, industry, mining, the public sector, money and banking, trade and balance of payments, accompanied by a useful list of specific references. Mamalakis has contributed greatly to historical research in Chile with *Historical Statistics of Chile: National Accounts* (1978); *Demography and Labor Force* (1980); *Forestry and Related Activities* (1982); *Money, Prices and Credit Services* (1984); *Money, Banking and Financial Services* (1985);

Oficina de Planificación Nacional (ODEPLAN), *Cuentas Nacionales de Chile; Informe social;*

Rosa Quintero Mesa, comp., *Latin American Serial Documents* #7, Chile, 1973 (titles of publications by Chilean government agencies in alphabetical order; also includes titles of numerous journals published in Chile);

Sara de Mundo Lo, *Index to Spanish American Collective Biography*, Vol. I. *The Andean Countries*, Boston, 1981 (short biographies of prominent persons indexed by subject, e.g. medicine, philosophy, sports);

Servicio Nacional de Salud (SNS, National Health Service), *Anuario de nacimientos y de defunciones y causas de muerte;*

Otto Neuberger, comp., *A Guide to Official Publications of the Other American Republics: Chile*, Washington, D.C., 1947 (entries arranged by name of Chilean government ministry);

Republic of Chile, Embassy in Washington, *Statistical Profile of Chile:* 1967, Washington, D.C., 1967 (mimeo);

República de Chile: *Dirección de estadística y censos* (census for 1940, 1952, 1960, 1970); *Dirección de estadística y censos: síntesis estadística*, 1968; *Dirección de estadística y censos: población total por provincias, Chile: 1885-1960*, 1964; and *Dirección general de estadística: estadística chilena* (monthly 1960-70);

República de Chile, Oficina Central de Estadística, *Censo de 1854, 1865, 1875, 1895, 1907* (19th- and early 20th-century census reports);

Statistical Abstract of Latin America, Univ. of Calif., Los Angeles–Center for Latin American Studies;

El pasado republicano de Chile: o sea Colección de discursos pronunciados por los presidentes de la República ante el Congreso nacional al inaugurar cada año el período legislativo, Concepción, 1899 (collection of state of the nation addresses by presidents 1832-99);

World Bank, *Chile, An Economy in Transition*, Washington, D.C., 1979 (overview of the development of the Chilean economy in the 1970s with extensive statistical appendices).

BASIC GENERAL HISTORIOGRAPHICAL AND BIBLIOGRAPHICAL SOURCES

Fidel Araneda Bravo, "Los estudios históricos en Chile," *Atenea 113*, Nov.-Dec. 1953;

Horacio Aránguiz Donoso, *Bibliografía histórica: 1959-1967*, 1970 (surveys of literature in 50 journals and books published between 1959 and 1967);

Ramón Briseño, *Estadística bibliográfica de la literatura chilena*, 2 vols.,

1862-79 (includes a listing of newspapers by city and public documents arranged by presidential administration);

Paul Drake, "El impacto académico de los terremotos políticos: investigaciones de la historia chilena en inglés, 1977-1983," *Alternativas*, Jan.-April 1984, 56-78;

Herminia Elgueta de Ocsenius, *Suplemento y adiciones a la bibliografía de bibliografías chilenas*, 1930 (updates Laval's work (see below) to 1930, bringing total of titles reviewed to almost 600);

Guillermo Feliú Cruz, *Historia de las fuentes de la bibliografía chilena*, 3 vols., 1956-58 (evaluates contributions of all major bibliographers to 1958);

Hernán Godoy Urzúa "El ensayo social: notas sobre la literatura sociológica en Chile," *Anales de la Universidad de Chile*, No. 120, Oct.-Dec. 1960;

Julio César Jobet, "Notas sobre la historiografía chilena," *Atenea* 291-292, Sept.-Oct. 1949; *Temas históricos chilenos*, 1973 (historiographical interpretation of selected themes in Chilean historical literature);

Ramón Laval, *Bibliografía de blibliografías chilenas*, 1915;

Luis Montt, *Bibliografía chilena*, 3 vols., 1904-21;

Robert Oppenheimer, *Chile: A Bibliography*, Los Angeles, 1977;

Nicolás Enrique Reyes and L. J. Silva Arriagada, *Ensayo de una bibliografía histórica y geográfica de Chile*, 1902 (lists works published to 1900; good source for locating local or regional studies);

William Sater, "A Survey of Recent Chilean Historiography 1965-1976," *Latin American Research Review* 1979 (an extensive overview and synthesis of recent scholarship on Chile);

Peter J. Sehlinger, *A Select Guide to Chilean Libraries and Archives*, Bloomington, Ind., 1979;

John Tepaske, ed., *Research Guide to Andean History*, Durham, N.C., 1981;

Jack Ray Thomas, "The Impact of the Generation of 1842 on Chilean Historiography, *The Historian* 41:4 (Aug. 1979);

Emilio Vaisse, *Bibliografía general de Chile.*

A number of anthologies and critical surveys offer introductions to Chilean art, literature, journalism, and music as well as biographical material on Chilean intellectuals and artists.

Fernando Alegría, *Literatura chilena del siglo XX*, 2nd ed., 1962; and *La poesía chilena; orígenes y desarrollo del siglo XVI al XIX*, Berkeley, 1954;

Homero Castillo and Raúl Silva Castro, *Historia bibliográfica de la novela chilena*, Charlottesville, 1961;

Samuel Claro and I. Urrutia, *Historia de la música en Chile*, 1973;

Luis E. Délano and Edmundo Palacios, *Antología de la poesía social de Chile*, 1962;

Julio Durán Cerda, *Panorama del teatro chileno: 1842-1959*, 1959;

David William Foster, *Chilean Literature: A Working Bibliography of Secondary Sources*, Boston, 1978;

Gaspar Galáz and Milan Ivelić, *Historia de la pintura chilena desde la colonia hasta nuestros días*, Valparaíso, 1981;

Mario Godoy Quezada, *Historia del cine chileno*, 1966;

Cedomil Goic, *La novela chilena*, 1968;

Mariano Latorre, *La literatura en Chile*, Buenos Aires, 1941;

Samuel A. Lillo, *Literatura chilena*, 7th ed., 1952 (official text on Chilean literature for secondary schools);

Hugo Montes and Julio Orlandi, *Historia de la literatura chilena*, 10th ed., 1982;

Eugenio Pereira Salas, *Historia de la música en Chile: 1850-1900*, 1957;

Arturo Torres Rioseco, *Breve historia de la literatura chilena*, Mexico, 1956;

Manuel Rojas, *Historia breve de la literatura chilena*, 1964;

Antonio Romera, *Historia de la pintura chilena*, 1960;

Vicente Salas Viu, *La creación musical en Chile: 1900-1951*, 1951;

Raúl Silva Castro, *Panorama literario de Chile*, 1961; and *Prensa y periodismo en Chile: 1812-1956*, 1961; *Evolución de las letras chilenas, 1810-1960*, 1960; *Antología general de la poesía chilena*, 1959; *Antología de cuentistas chilenos*, 1957;

Gastón Somoshegyi-Szokol, *Contemporary Chilean Literature in the University Library at Berkeley*, Berkeley, 1975 (partially annotated bibliography, and bibliographical guide to general anthologies and literary studies);

Arturo Torres Rioseco and Raúl Silva Castro, *Ensayo de bibliografía de la literatura chilena*, Cambridge, Mass., 1935;

Fernando Uriarte, "La novela proletaria en Chile," *Mapocho* 4, 1965;

José Zamudio, *La novela histórica en Chile*, 1949;

Hernán Godoy (ed.), *El carácter chileno*, 1981, and *La cultura chilena*, 1982, provide a number of views of popular culture and intellectual development in Chile from colonial times to the 1980s.

Geography, Population, and Natural Resources

From the time Pedro de Valdivia wrote to the Emperor Charles V in 1545 that, "this land is such that there is none better in the world for living in and settling," the role played by Chilean geography in shaping the territory's socio-economic and political development has been apparent to many writers on Chile. Early, now classic, accounts are Abbé Don J. Ignatious Molina, *The Geographical, Natural, and Civil History of Chile* (2 vols., trans. from the Italian with notes from the Spanish and French versions by the English editor, London, 1809) and Claudio Gay, *Historia física y política de Chile: documentos sobre la historia, estadística y la geografía* (26 vols., Paris, 1844-55). The best short summary of the relation between Chilean geography and historical development is Harold Blakemore, "Chile," in Harold Blakemore and Clifford T. Smith (eds.), *Latin America: Geographical Perspectives* (London, 1971). Other useful geographic and demographic summaries include *Area Handbook for Chile* (U.S. Govt. Printing Office, 1969); *Manual para invertir en Chile*, published by the Chile-California project, 1967 (see esp. Chap. 1, "Visión general de Chile"); George Pendle, *The Land and the People of Chile* (London, 1964); Preston James, *Latin America* (4th ed., New York, 1964); Overseas Economic Surveys, *Chile* (London, 1958); Gilbert J. Butland, *Chile: An Outline of Its Geography, Economics and Politics* (London, 1956); Francis Maitland, *Chile: Its Land and People* (London, 1941); Benjamín Subercaseaux, *Chile: A Geographic Extravaganza* (trans. of *Chile: o una loca geografía*) New York, 1943. Robert McCaa has added concern for methods and sources for social and demographic history in "Chilean Social and Demographic History: Sources, Issues and Methods," *LARR* 13:2, 1978, 104-26. McCaa discusses Chilean demographic and social history as well as providing valuable basic references. A much more detailed and technical summary also useful for its bibliography can be found in CORFO, *Geografía económica de Chile*, texto refundido (1967). Dated, but historically essential, is the classic by Enrique Espinosa, *Geografía descriptiva de la república de Chile*, 5th ed. (1903). Standard geographical treatments are provided in Elías Almeyda Arroyo, *Geografía de Chile* (1955); Sociedad Chilena de Historia, *Geografía de Chile: física, humana y económica* (1968); Pedro Cunill, *Geografía de Chile*, 7th ed. (1978); Augusto Pinochet Ugarte, *Síntesis geográfica de Chile* (1963). Many descriptions of selected Chilean regions are also available. The most well known deal with the desert north, the central valley, and Antarctica: Isaiah Bowman, *Desert Trails of Atacama* (New York, 1924); W. J. Dennis, *Tacna and Arica* (New Haven, 1931); George McBride, *Chile: Land and Society*—the classic description of

Chile's central valley agriculture and hacienda system—(New York, 1936); O. Pinochet de la Barra, *La antártica chilena* (1948). None of these last works is strictly speaking a geography, but all contain geographical information in addition to considerable historical, social, and economic material. Two useful works that treat Chilean boundaries are: Jaime Eyzaguirre, *Breve historia de las fronteras de Chile*, 4th ed. (1973) and Robert D. Talbott, *A History of the Chilean Boundaries* (Ames, 1974).

INDIGENOUS PEOPLES

Although pre-Hispanic Chilean history is not thoroughly researched, a number of basic contributions in the field provide detailed and often conflicting information. Julio M. Montané's *Bibliografía selectiva de antropología chilena: Primera parte—Araucanos, Pehuenches, Chiloé y territorios adyacentes; Segunda parte—generalidades: Zona norte y central*, 2 vols. (La Serena, 1963-64) contains approximately 400 references on Chilean Indians. Julian H. Steward (ed.), *Handbook on South American Indians*, Vol. II (New York, 1957), offers the best summary in English of Chilean indigenous civilization. Other well-known studies are Agustín Edwards, *People of Old* (London, 1929); F. L. Cornely, *Cultura diaguita chilena y cultura de El Molle* (1956); Jorge Dowling, *Religión, chamanismo y mitología mapuches* (1973); René León Echaíz, *Prehistoria de Chile Central* (Talca, 1957); Tomás Guevara, *Historia de Chile prehispánico*, 2 vols. (1925-27); *Historia de la civilización de Araucanía*, 7 vols. (1898-1913); Ricardo Latcham, *La prehistoria chilena* (1936) and *Organización social y creencias religiosas de los antiguos araucanos* (1924); Alejandro Lipschutz, *La comunidad indígena en América y en Chile* (1956); José T. Medina, *Los aborígenes de Chile* (1952); Greta Mostny, *Culturas pre-colombinas en Chile* (1960). Another very useful and readable overview of pre-Hispanic Chilean peoples appears in Francisco Esteve Barba, *Descubrimiento y conquista de Chile* (Madrid, 1946) along with a somewhat more extensive bibliography. As is the case with the study of pre-Columbian peoples in general, Julian Steward and Louis Faron, *Native Peoples of South America* (New York, 1959) offers a brief but helpful summary of knowledge on the natives of Chile, as does Wendell C. Bennett and Junius B. Bird, *Andean Culture History* (London, 1965). A more recent overview of pre-Columbian Chile by Osvaldo Silva appears in the first volume of a 4-volume work edited by Sergio Villalobos, *Historia de Chile* (a 1983 edition makes all four volumes available in a single book).

The Araucanian Indians' heroic resistance to the Spanish conquest inspired the first epic poem of Latin America, Alonso de Ercilla's *La Arau-*

cana. Much of the historical work, chronicles, and other literature of the colonial period (see below) reflects this interest in the Araucanian people and their war against the Spanish. Several 19th-century descriptions of the Araucanians provide insight into the social and economic conditions prevalent after centuries of warfare: Ignacio Domeyko, *Araucanía y sus habitantes* (1st ed., 1845, 2nd ed., Buenos Aires, 1971); Pedro Ruís Aldea, *Los araucanos i sus costumbres* (1st ed., 1856, Biblioteca de autores chilenos, Vol. 5, 1902); Edmund Reuel Smith, *The Araucanians, or Notes of a Tour among the Indian Tribes of Southern Chile* (London, 1855).

Recent scholarship on the Araucanians and Mapuche has been dominated by the work of Louis Faron: *Mapuche Social Structure* (Illinois, 1961); *Hawks of the Sun* (Pittsburgh, 1964); *The Mapuche Indians of Chile* (New York, 1968). All provide additional references. A mid-20th-century study by Mischa Titien, *Araucanian Culture in Transition* (Ann Arbor, 1951), provides insight into the dilemma of Chile's Indians in the 20th century; Alejandro Saavedra's *La cuestión mapuche* (1971) presents a much more dismal picture twenty years later—with significant political implications. José Bengoa and E. Valenzuela's *Economía Mapuche. Pobreza y subsistencia en la sociedad Mapuche contemporánea* (1983) is even more depressing.

Travel Accounts

Observations of travelers provide information and insight often lacking in other sources. For an overview of travel accounts see Guillermo Feliú Cruz, *Notas para una bibliografía sobre viajeros relativos a Chile* (1965). Accounts by Chileans, North Americans, Latin Americans, and Europeans from the 17th century onward are both interesting reading and valuable resources for the historical study of Chile. Among the most useful are:

Henry Willis Baxley, *What I Saw on the West Coast of South and North America*, New York, 1865;

R. Nelson Boyd, *Chile: Sketches of Chile and the Chilians 1879-1880*, London, 1881;

Henry M. Brackenridge, *A Voyage to South America, performed by order of the American Government in the years 1817, and 1818, in the Frigate Congress*, 2 vols., Baltimore, 1819;

Alexander Caldcleugh, *Travels in South America during the Years 1819, 1820, 1821*, London, 1825;

Vicente Carvallo y Goyeneche, "Descripción histórico-geográfica del reino de Chile," *Colección de Historiadores* 10, 1879;

Richard J. Cleveland, A Narrative of Voyages and Commercial Enter-
    prises, 2 vols., Cambridge, Mass., 1842;
Charles Darwin, The Voyage of the Beagle, Garden City, N.Y., 1962;
Thomas Cochrane Dundonald, Narrative of Services in the Liberation of
    Chile, Peru and Brazil from Spanish and Portuguese Domination, 2
    vols., London, 1859;
George Alexander Findlay, A Directory for the Navigation of the South
    Pacific Ocean, London, 1863;
M. Frezier, Relation du voyage de la mer du sud aux côtes du Chili et du
    Pérou, Paris, 1716;
Lt. J. Gilliss, The U.S. Naval Astronomical Expedition to the Southern
    Hemisphere during the Years 1849-1852, Washington, D.C., 1855,
    Vol. I (Chile);
María Graham, Journal of a Residence in Chile during the Year of 1822,
    London, 1824;
Thaddaeus Peregrinus Haenke, Descripción del reyno de Chile, 1942;
Samuel Haigh, Sketches of Buenos Ayres and Chile, London, 1829;
Basil Hall, Extracts of a Journal Written on the Coasts of Chile, Peru,
    and Mexico in the Years 1820, 1821, 1822, 2 vols., Edinburgh, 1826;
Adolph E. Howard, A Handbook or Guide to British Shipmasters and
    Others Trading to the Coast of Chile, Valparaíso, 1882;
Daniel J. Hunter, A Sketch of Chile, expressly prepared for the use of
    emigrants from the United States and Europe to that country, New
    York, 1866;
Samuel Burr Johnston, Cartas escritas durante una residencia de tres años
    en Chile, trans. by José Toribio Medina, 1917; and Diario de un
    tipógrafo Yanqui en Chile y Perú durante la guerra de la inde-
    pendencia, Madrid, 1919;
Gabriel Lafond de Lurcy, Viaje a Chile, 1970;
Mrs. C. B. Merwin, Three Years in Chile, New York, 1863;
John Miers, Travels in Chile and La Plata, 2 vols., London, 1826;
Fray Diego de Ocaña, "Relación del viaje a Chile: año de 1600," Anales
    de la Universidad de Chile, No. 120 (1960);
Vicente Pérez Rosales, Recuerdos del pasado, trans. as California Adven-
    ture, San Francisco, 1947;
Eduardo Poeppig, Un testigo en la alborada de Chile: 1826-1829, 1960;
Ignacio Richard, A Mining Journey Across the Great Andes, London,
    1863;
William S. W. Ruschenberger, Three Years in the Pacific: 1831-1834,
    Philadelphia, 1834;
W. H. Russell, A Visit to Chile and the Nitrate Fields of Tarapacá, Lon-
    don, 1890;

Domingo F. Sarmiento, *Chile: descripciones-viajes-episodios-costumbres,*
 Buenos Aires, 1961;
Peter Schmidtmeyer, *Travels into Chile over the Andes in the Years 1820-
 1821,* London, 1824;
Juan G. Serrato, *A través de Chile,* Buenos Aires, 1898;
William Bennet Stevenson, *A Historical and Descriptive Narrative of
 Twenty Years' Residence in South America,* 3 vols., London, 1825;
Thomas Sutcliffe, *Sixteen Years in Chile and Peru by the Retired Gov-
 ernor of Juan Fernández,* London, 1841;
Paul Truetler, *Andanzas de un alemán en Chile 1851-1863,* trans. by
 Carlos Keller, 1958;
*Useful Information for Captains of Merchant Vessels and Others Trading
 to the Port of Valparaíso,* Valparaíso, 1872;
George Vancouver, *A Voyage of Discovery to the North Pacific Ocean
 and Round the World,* 3 vols., London, 1789;
Viajeros en Chile: 1817-1847, 1955 (Samuel Haigh, Alexander Cald-
 cleugh, Max Radiguet).

CHILEAN HISTORY

Two historians, Diego Barros Arana and Francisco Encina, establish the
framework for Chilean historical studies. The foremost Liberal historian
of the 19th century, Diego Barros Arana produced the *Historia general de
Chile,* 16 vols. (1884-1902), the starting point for almost all Chilean historiography through 1833, including the conservative, revisionist *Historia
de Chile desde la prehistoria hasta 1891* by Francisco Encina, 20 vols.
(1940-52). A 3-volume summary of the Encina history by Leopoldo
Castedo—*Resumen de la historia de Chile*—has gone through several editions and makes the Encina history somewhat more accessible to readers
unwilling to read or to acquire the 20-volume edition (1st ed., 1954).
Charles C. Griffin, "Francisco Encina and Revisionism in Chilean History," (*HAHR* 36, Feb. 1957) is an important critical review of the
Encina history. Ricardo Donoso's *Barros Arana: educador, historiador y
hombre público* (1931) provides an overwhelming bibliography of Barros
Arana's historical scholarship, including works on the independence movements and the Portalian period. A doctoral dissertation by Gertrude
Yeager Matyoka, *Diego Barros Arana and the Historia Jeneral de Chile*
(Texas Christian University, 1972) provides a more recent critical analysis of Barros Arana's work as well as insight into 19th-century Chilean development. Also useful are Domingo Amunátegui Solar's 2-volume *Historia de Chile* (1933)—intended as a secondary school textbook—and
Jaime Eyzaguirre's *Historia de Chile,* 2 vols., 2nd ed. (1973), covering the

period from pre-Columbian times until 1861. Also of importance are Eyzaguirre's earlier works, *Fisonomía histórica de Chile* (1948) and *Historia de Chile: génesis de la nacionalidad* (1965). More recent general histories are Sergio Villalobos R., Osvaldo Silva G., Fernando Silva V., and Patricio Estellé M., *Historia de Chile*, 4 vols. (available in a single volume), 1983; and Gonzalo Vial, *Historia de Chile*, 2 vols. (1981-83). Luis Galdames, *Estudio de la historia de Chile*, 8th ed. (1938), translated into English as *A History of Chile* (Chapel Hill, 1941), is a one-volume survey ending shortly after the Great Depression. An earlier narrative in English, A. U. Hancock, *History of Chile* (Chicago, 1893), is largely a political history, ending with the civil war of 1891. A brief narrative by Isaac Joslin Cox, "Chile" in A. Curtis Wilgus's *Argentina, Brazil and Chile since Independence* (New York, 1963), traces major events from 1808 until the mid-1930s. Ricardo Donoso's *Breve historia de Chile* (Buenos Aires, 1963) is the briefest general history in Spanish. A secondary school text by Francisco Frías Valenzuela, based on the author's longer multivolume work, provides an important indication of what Chilean students learn of Chilean history, *Manual de historia de Chile*, 5th ed. (1960). Jay Kinsbruner's *Chile: A Historical Interpretation* (New York, 1973) is the closest thing in print to a recent English-language history of Chile, but the author makes it clear that this work is an interpretation of key developments in Chilean history rather than a history in the conventional sense.

In general, 20th-century history is not well developed in the available Chilean histories. However, one collection of articles edited by Hernán Godoy, *Estructura social de Chile* (1971), offers an excellent selection of materials on Chilean society, economy, and politics from the time of the conquest to the 1970s. In addition, this anthology contains an exceptionally good topical bibliography organized by historical period. A collaborative effort by Mariana Aylwin, Carlos Bascuñán, Sofía Correa, Cristián Gazmuri, Sol Serrano, and Matías Tagle, *Chile en el siglo XX* (1983), offers a fresh interpretation of Chilean history from 1900 to 1970. Alejandro Foxley's *Redistributive Effects of Government Programmes: The Chilean Case* (Oxford, 1979) offers a more specialized analysis of the impact of government policies in Chile in the 20th century, with emphasis on the post-1960 years.

CONQUEST AND THE FORMATION OF CHILEAN SOCIETY

The single most important source of primary materials on the conquest of Chile is the series "Colección de historiadores de Chile y documentos relativos a la historia nacional (CH)," 51 vols. (1861-1953). This collection of chronicles, documents, and histories of the conquest has received priority from a number of Chile's most prominent historians and includes most of the key contributions to Chilean history in the early colonial period. Newer editions of some of the more salient works have been reissued in paperback in abbreviated form in a series called "Escritores coloniales de Chile," including Alonso de Góngora Marmolejo, *Historia de Chile desde su descubrimiento hasta el año 1575;* Alonso de Ovalle, *Histórica relación del reyno de Chile;* Alonso González de Nájera, *Desengaño y reparo de la guerra de Chile;* Francisco Núñez Pineda y Bascuñán, *Cautiverio Felíz* (an account of life among the Araucanians by a captured Spaniard); and Diego de Rosales, *Historia general del reino de Chile.* Other key works in the "Colección de historiadores" are Vicente Carvallo Goyeneche, *Descripción histórico-geográfica del reino de Chile;* and Miguel de Olivares, *Historia militar, civil, y sagrada de Chile.* As in the rest of Spanish America, many of these early writers on Chile were members of religious orders, especially the Society of Jesus (Jesuits).

A major figure in the creation of the "Colección de historiadores," José Toribio Medina, also made available large quantities of primary materials to scholars through his energetic archival research. Major published contributions include: *Cartas de Pedro de Valdivia que tratan del descubrimiento y conquista de Chile* (1953)—letters from Valdivia to Charles V; *Colección de documentos inéditos para la historia de Chile desde el viaje de Magallanes hasta la batalla de Maipo, 1518-1818,* 30 vols. (1888-1902); and *Cosas de la Colonia* (1952). Other sources of primary materials include the *Archivo de la Capitanía Jeneral; Archivo de la Real Audiencia; Archivo del Arzobispado de Santiago;* and the *Archivo Nacional de Chile.* In addition, the "Actas del cabildo de Santiago de 1541 a 1557 y de 1558 a 1577" can be found in the "Colección de historiadores," vols. 1 and 17.

Historical treatments of the period of conquest are numerous, ranging from biographies of Pedro de Valdivia and other conquistadores to comprehensive and detailed monographic studies. Among the most useful of the latter, Francisco Esteve Barba's *Descubrimiento y conquista de Chile* (Madrid, 1946) stands out as a reliable summary with helpful bibliography following each chapter. The set of histories from the Catholic point of view, by Catholic historian Crescente Errázuriz offers a comprehensive treatment of the period from the conquest to the late 16th century and an interpretation somewhat different than the Liberal orientation of Barros Arana, whose volumes—*Historia de Chile, Pedro de Valdivia,* 2 vols. (1911-21); *Historia de Chile sin gobernador 1554-1557* (1912); *Historia de Chile, Don García de Mendoza: 1557-1561* (1914); *Historia de Chile, Francisco de Villagra 1561-1563* (1915); *Historia de Chile, Pedro de Villagra 1563-1565* (1916); and *Seis años en la historia de*

Chile, 1598-1605 (1908)—contain a wealth of detailed information. A doctoral dissertation at the University of Florida, Thomas Braman, *Land and Society in Early Colonial Santiago* (1977), synthesizes much of the older materials on the early years of conquest and includes a good working bibliography for this period.

On Pedro de Valdivia, his companions, and the conquest of Chile, a handful of well-known studies summarizes existing knowledge: Rosa Arciniega, *Don Pedro de Valdivia: Conquistador de Chile* (1943); Jaime Eyzaguirre, *Ventura de Pedro de Valdivia* (1963); Hugh R. S. Pocock, *The Conquest of Chile* (New York, 1967); Joaquín Santa Cruz, *Problemas históricos de la conquista de Chile* (1902); Luis Silva Lezaeta, *El conquistador Francisco de Aguirre* (1953); Ida W. Vernon, *Pedro de Valdivia: Conquistador of Chile* (New York, 1969). A sympathetic treatment of Valdivia's mistress, later wife of another Chilean governor, can be found in Stella B. May, *The Conqueror's Lady: Inéz de Suarez* (New York, 1930). Other historians have taken the biographies of major Indian chiefs as a point of departure, for example René León Echaíz, *El toqui Lautaro* (1971).

The ongoing warfare between Spaniards and the Araucanians of Chile gave to Chilean colonial society a unique character, influencing settlement patterns, social and economic institutions, and the composition of its population. The best single volume interpreting the relationship between the frontier status of Chile and the evolution of Chilean society is Alvaro Jara's *Guerra y sociedad en Chile* (1971, translated from a French edition published ten years earlier). Jara's other work on colonial labor systems and Spanish-Indian relations complements the monograph and serves as a basis for colonial labor history: "Fuentes para la historia del trabajo en Chile" (*BACH* 54, 55, 58, 51, 1956-57, 1959); *El salario de los indios y los sesmos del oro en la Tasa de Santillán* (1961); *Los asientos del trabajo y la provisión de mano de obra para los no-encomenderos en la ciudad de Santiago: 1586-1600* (Estudios de historia económica americana, trabajo y salario en el período colonial, No. 1, 1959); "Salario en una economía caracterizada por las relaciones de dependencia personal," (*RCHG 133*, 1965). The only available interpretation of Spanish-Indian confrontation in English is Eugene H. Korth's, *Spanish Policy in Colonial Chile* (Stanford, 1968). Written from a Jesuit perspective, Korth's study includes an admirable bibliography of primary sources as well as secondary treatments on the Spanish conquest and settlement of Chile. It is an essential starting point for any further work on this period of Chilean history. An earlier article by Louis de Armond, "Frontier Warfare in Colonial Chile," *Pacific Historical Review* (May 1954), is still an interesting introductory reading on the Chilean frontier.

Among the most valuable secondary sources on the Indian question and early colonial society are Domingo Amunátegui Solar, *Las encomiendas de indíjenas en Chile*, 2 vols. (1909); Miguel Luis Amunátegui, *Descubrimiento y conquista de Chile* (1862); Guillermo Feliú Cruz and Carlos Monje Alfaro, *Las encomiendas según tasas y ordenanzas* (Buenos Aires, 1941); Kalky Glauser R., "Orígenes del régimen de producción vigente en Chile," *Cuadernos de la Realidad Nacional*, No. 8 (1971); Mario Góngora, *El estado en el derecho indiano, época de fundación: 1492-1570* (1951); "Vagabundaje y sociedad fronteriza en Chile: Siglo XVIII a XIX," *Cuadernos del Centro de Estudios Socioeconómicos*, No. 2 (1966); *Encomenderos y estancieros, estudios acerca de la constitución social aristocrática de Chile después de la conquista: 1580-1660* (1970); Néstor Meza Villalobos, *Políticas indígenas en los orígenes de la sociedad chilena* (1951); *La formación de la fortuna mobiliaria y el ritmo de la conquista* (1941); María Isabel Gonzáles Pomes, "La encomienda indígena en Chile durante el siglo XVIII," *Historia* 5 (1966); Jorge Randolph, *Las guerras de Arauco y la esclavitud* (1966); Manuel Salvat Monguillot, "El régimen de encomiendas en los primeros tiempos de la conquista," *RCHG*, No. 132 (1964); Fernando Silva Vargas, *Tierras y pueblo de indios en el reino de Chile* (1962).

The most important Marxist contribution to conquest historiography is Luis Vitale, *Interpretación marxista de la historia de Chile*: Tomo 1: *Las culturas primitivas, la conquista española* (1957). One Chilean historian, Tomás Thayer Ojeda, has given special attention to the origins of the so-called "raza chilena" more generally. Major works include: *Elementos étnicos que han intervenido en la población de Chile* (1919); *Formación de la sociedad chilena y censos de la población de Chile entre los años 1540 a 1565, con datos estadísticos, biográficos, étnicos, y demográficos*, 3 vols. (1939-41); *Los conquistadores de Chile*, 2 vols. (1908); with Carlos J. Larraín, *Valdivia y sus compañeros* (1950).

COLONIAL SOCIETY AND CULTURE

Central to the development of Chilean society, as in the rest of Spanish America, the Catholic Church and its representatives played a critical role in conquest, social organization, education, and public policy. Eugene Korth's already mentioned study is a basic source in English for an overview of the role of the Church in shaping Spanish colonial policy in Chile. Among the numerous Spanish-language sources are: Diego Barros Arana, *Riquezas de los antiguos jesuitas de Chile* (1872); Francisco Enrich, *Historia de la compañía de Jesús en Chile*, 2 vols. (Barcelona, 1891); Crescente Errázuriz, *Los orígenes de la iglesia chilena: 1540-1603* (1873);

José Ignacio Victor Eyzaguirre, *Historia eclesiástica, política y literaria de Chile*, 3 vols. (Valparaíso, 1950); Elías Lizana and Pablo Maulen (eds.), *Colección de documentos históricos recopilados del archivo del arzobispado de Santiago*, 4 vols. (1919-21); José Toribio Medina, *La inquisición en Chile*, 2 vols. (1890); Policarpo Gazulla, *Los primeros mercedarios en Chile: 1535-1600* (1918); Carlos Silva Cotapos, *Historia eclesiástica de Chile* (1925).

Insight into colonial art, literature, and music in Chile can be found in Fernando Alegría, *La poesía chilena; orígenes y desarrollo del siglo XVI al XIX* (México, 1954); Luis Alvarez Urquieta, *La pintura en Chile durante el período colonial* (1933); Alfredo Benavides Rodríguez, *La arquitectura en el virreinato del Perú y en la capitanía general de Chile*, 2nd ed. (1961); Alejandro Fuenzalida Grandón, *Historia del desarrollo intelectual de Chile: 1541-1810* (1903); *Historia de la literatura colonial*, 3 vols. (1878); Eugenio Pereira Salas, *Los orígenes del arte musical en Chile* (1941); *Historia del arte en el reino de Chile: 1541-1776* (1965); Luis Roa Urzúa, *El arte en la época colonial de Chile* (1929); Tomás Thayer Ojeda, "Las bibliotecas coloniales en Chile," *Revista de bibliografía chilena y extranjera* 1, No. 11 (1943).

Colonial education and pastimes are treated in Miguel Luis and Gregorio Amunátegui, *De la instrucción pública en Chile* (1856); José Toribio Medina, *La instrucción pública en Chile desde sus orígenes hasta la fundación de la universidad de San Felipe de Santiago de Chile*, 2 vols. (1928); Eugenio Pereira Salas, *Juego y alegrías coloniales en Chile* (1947).

COLONIAL ECONOMY AND SOCIETY

Nineteenth-century treatments of the colonial economy of Chile reflect the struggle between liberalism and the Hispanic-Catholic tradition. More recent interpretations reflect the global confrontation between supporters of market economies, capitalism, and Marxism. The works by Alvaro Jara and Mario Góngora cited earlier provide the foundation for an understanding of Chile's colonial economy and economic institution. Eugene Korth's already mentioned work, *Spanish Policy in Colonial Chile* contains references to good primary sources. Articles on specialized themes on colonial society and economy as well as documents with commentary appear periodically in *RCHG, BACH,* and *Historia*.

Marxist interpretations of colonial society include José Cademartori, *La economía chilena* (1968) esp. chaps. 2 and 3; André Gunder Frank, *Capitalism and Underdevelopment in Latin America* (1969); Julio César Jobet, *Ensayo crítico del desarrollo económico-social de Chile* (1955); Hernán

Ramírez Necochea, *Antecedentes económicos de la independencia de Chile* (1959); Marcelo Segall, *Desarrollo del capitalismo en Chile* (1953); "Las luchas de clases en las primeras décadas de la República de Chile," *Anales de la Universidad de Chile*, No. 125 (1962); Luis Vitale, *Interpretación marxista de la historia de Chile: La colonia y la revolución de 1810* (1969).

A survey of historiographical literature on colonial Chile in the 19th century, with portraits of the most well-known Chilean historians and facsimiles of the title pages of important works, is Guillermo Feliú Cruz, *Historiografía colonial de Chile*, Tomo I, 1796-1886 (1958); Armando de Ramón and José Manuel Larraín's *Orígenes de la vida económica chilena*, 1659-1808 (1982) adds a wealth of empirical data on prices, production, commerce, and patterns of economic change in the 17th and 18th centuries. To this must be added the studies of Rolando Mellafe, *Las primeras crisis coloniales, formas de asiento y origen de la sociedad chilena, siglos XVI y XVII* in *Siete Estudios*, Homenaje de la Facultad de Ciencias Humanas a Eugenio Pereira Salas (1975), and *Latifundio y poder rural en Chile en los siglos XVII y XVIII* (1980).

Among the great number of works on colonial society and economy, including social and economic institutions and patterns of commerce, are the following basic studies:

Sergio Bagú, *Economía de la sociedad colonial*, Buenos Aires, 1949; and *Estructura social de la colonia*, Buenos Aires, 1952;

Marcello Carmagnani, *Les Mécanismes de la vie économique dans une société coloniale: le Chili* (1680-1830), Paris, 1973;

Miguel Cruchaga, *Estudio sobre la organización económica y la hacienda pública de Chile*;

Mario Góngora, "Los 'hombres ricos' de Santiago y La Serena a través de las cuentas del quinto real," *RCHG*, No. 131, 1963;

Eugenio Pereira Salas, *Buques norteamericanos a fines de la era colonial: 1778-1810*, 1936;

Demetrio Ramos, *Trigo chileno, navieros del Callao y hacendados limeños*, Madrid, 1967;

Ruggiero Romano, *Una economía colonial: Chile en el siglo XVIII*, Buenos Aires, 1965;

Agustín Ross, *Reseña histórica sobre el comercio de Chile en la era colonial*, 1894;

René Salinas, "Raciones alimenticias en Chile colonial" *Historia* 12 (1974-75);

Sergio Sepúlveda, *El trigo chileno en el mercado mundial*, 1959;

John Tepaske and Herbert Klein, *The Royal Treasuries of the Spanish*

Empire in America: Chile and the Rio de la Plata, Durham, N.C., 1982;

Sergio Villalobos, *El comercio y la crisis colonial: un mito de la independencia*, 1968, and *Comercio y contrabando en el Río de la Plata y Chile: 1700-1811*, Buenos Aires, 1965.

On mining in particular, the reader may consult:

J. Bruggen, *Bibliografía minera y jeológica de Chile*, 8 vols., 1919-27;

Alberto Herrmann, *La producción en Chile de los metales y minerales más importantes de las sales naturales, del azufre y del guano desde la conquista hasta fines del año 1902*, 1903;

Augusto Orrego Cortés, *La industria del oro en Chile*, 1890;

Francisco San Ramón, *Reseña industrial e histórica de la minería y metalurgia de Chile*, 1899;

José Joaquín (Jotabeche) Vallejo, *Costumbres mineras*, 1943;

Benjamín Vicuña Mackenna, *El libro de la plata*, 1882; *El libro del cobre y del carbón de piedra*, 1883; and *La edad del oro en Chile*, 2 vols., 1932.

Studies on social themes in the colonial period, including the role of ethnic and cultural minorities in colonial Chile, are:

Domingo Amunátegui Solar, *Historia social de Chile*, 1936; and *La sociedad chilena del siglo XVIII: mayorazgos y títulos de castilla*, 3 vols., 1903-04;

Gunter Bohm, *Nuevos antecedentes para una historia de los judíos en Chile colonial*, 1963;

Marcello Carmagnani, "Colonial Latin American Demography: Growth of Chilean Population, 1700-1830," *Journal of Social History*, No. 2, 1963; and *El salariado minero en Chile colonial, su desarrollo en una sociedad provincial: el norte Chico; 1690-1800*, (1963);

Guillermo de la Cuadra Gormaz, *Origen de doscientas familias coloniales de Santiago*, 3 vols., 1941-47; *Origen y desarrollo de las familias chilenas*, 1948-49; and "Censo de la capitanía general de Chile en 1777," *BACH*, No. 12, 1940;

Enrique Eberhardt, *Historia de Santiago de Chile*, 1916;

Guillermo Feliú Cruz, *La abolición de la esclavitud en Chile*, 1942;

Alejandro Fuenzalida Grandón, *La evolución social de Chile: 1514-1810*, 1906;

Mario Góngora, *Origen de los inquilinos de Chile central*, 1960; and "Urban Social Stratification in Colonial Chile," *HAHR* 55, 1975;

with Jean Borde, *Evolución de la propiedad rural en el valle del Puange*, 2 vols., 1956;

Eugene Korth and Della M. Flusche, *Forgotten Females: Women of African and Indian Descent in Colonial Chile, 1553-1800*, Detroit, 1983;

Elías Lizana, *Colección de documentos históricos de archivo del arzobispado de Santiago*, 4 vols., 1919-21;

Rolando Mellafe, *La introducción de la esclavitud negra en Chile*, 1959;

Humberto Muñoz, *Los movimientos sociales en el Chile colonial*, 1945;

William F. Sater, "The Black Experience in Chile," *Slavery and Race Relations in Latin America*, R. Toplin (ed.), Westport, Conn., 1974;

Gonzalo Vial Correa, *El africano en el reino de Chile*, 1957.

On the cabildo and the effects of administrative reforms in the colonial period, see:

Julio Alemparte, *El cabildo en Chile colonial*, 1940;

Miguel Luis Amunátegui, *El cabildo de Santiago desde 1573 hasta 1581*, 3 vols., 1890-91;

Jacques Barbier, "Elite and Cadres in Bourbon Chile," *HAHR*, Aug. 1972 (clearly the most important recent revisionist work on the effects of the Bourbon reforms on colonial administration and society); *Imperial Reform and Colonial Politics: A Secret History of Late Bourbon Chile*, Ph.D. diss. (Univ. of Connecticut, 1973); *Reform and Politics in Bourbon Chile, 1755-1796*, Ottawa, 1980;

David H. Edwards, *Economic Effects of the Intendency System in Chile: Captain General Ambrosio O'Higgins as Reformer*, Ph.D. diss., (Univ. of Virginia, 1973);

Della M. Flusche, "The Cabildo and Public Health in Seventeenth Century Chile," *TA* 29, 1972; and "City Councilmen and the Church in Seventeenth Century Chile," *Records of American Catholic Historical Society of Philadelphia 81*, No. 3, 1970;

Carlos Ugarte, "El cabildo de Santiago y el comercio exterior del reino de Chile en el siglo XVIII," *Estudios de las Instituciones Políticas y Sociales*, Vol. I, 1967.

INDEPENDENCE AND THE AUTOCRATIC REPUBLIC

The exceptionally researched study, *Ideas and Politics of Chilean Independence: 1808-1833* by Simon Collier (Cambridge, Eng., 1967), is without a doubt the most important source in English on late 18th-century

Chile, the independence movement, and the formation of the Portalian state. Collier's bibliography lists manuscript sources, contemporary newspapers and journals, as well as contemporary and modern scholarship on the period. I have relied heavily on Collier's work in my own discussion of this period in Chapter 4 and will not attempt here to replicate his bibliography. In addition, Collier's article "The Historiography of the Portalian Period 1830-1891 in Chile," *HAHR* (Nov. 1977) adds an important and systematic treatment of traditional and revisionist history on the independence period, formation of the Portalian state, and 19th-century Chilean historiography more generally.

Review of the historiography of the independence period is found in Gonzalo Vial, "Historiografía de la independencia de Chile," *Historia*, No. 4 (1965). Recent studies by American scholars have considerably expanded our knowledge of post-independence commercial affairs and the social composition of the Chilean oligarchy; Stanley Frederick Edwards, *Chilean Economic Policy Goals 1811-1829: A Study of Late Eighteenth Century Social Mercantilism and Early Nineteenth Century Economic Reality*, Ph.D. diss. (Tulane Univ., 1971); and John Rector, *Merchants, Trade and Commercial Policy in Chile: 1810-1840*, Ph.D. diss. (Indiana Univ., 1976); and "Transformaciones comerciales producidas por la independencia de Chile," *RCHG*, No. 143 (1975). The work of Roger Haigh, *The Formation of the Chilean Oligarchy: 1810-1821* (Salt Lake City, 1972) and of Mary Felstiner, *The Larraín Family in the Independence of Chile: 1789-1830*, Ph.D. diss. (Stanford, 1970), "Kinship Politics in the Chilean Independence Movement," *HAHR* 56 (Feb. 1976), offers insight into the nature and behavior of the Chilean oligarchy in the early 19th century. For accounts of the evolution of Chile's political elite in the 19th century see the classic work by Alberto Edwards Vives, *La fronda aristocrática* (1936) and the more recent study by Gabriel Marcella, *The Structure of Politics in Nineteenth Century Spanish America: The Chilean Oligarchy 1833-1891*, Ph.D. diss. (Univ. of Notre Dame, 1973).

The independence period and formation of the "Portalian" state have produced a voluminous literature. On the independence movement and its leaders see: Julio Alemparte, *Carrera y Freire* (1903); Miguel Luis Amunátegui, *La crónica de 1810*, 3 vols. (1876); *Don Manuel de Salas*, 3 vols. (1895); *Los precursores de la independencia de Chile*, 3 vols. (1919); with Benjamín Vicuña Mackenna, *La dictadura de O'Higgins* (Madrid, 1920); *La revolución de la independencia* (1945); and *Nacimiento de la república de Chile: 1808-1833* (1930); Stephen Clissold, *Bernardo O'Higgins and the Independence of Chile* (New York, 1969); Agustín Edwards, *The Dawn* (London, 1931); Francisco Antonio Encina,

Portales: Introducción a la historia de la época de Diego Portales: 1830-1891, 2 vols. (1934); Fernando Errázuriz, *Chile bajo el imperio de la constitución de 1828* (1861); Jaime Eyzaguirre, *Ideario y ruta de la emancipación chilena* (1957); and *O'Higgins,* 3rd ed. (1950); Guillermo Feliú Cruz, *El pensamiento de O'Higgins* (1954); Jay Kinsbruner, *Bernardo O'Higgins* (New York, 1968); William R. Manning (ed.), *Diplomatic Correspondence of the United States Concerning the Independence of Latin American Nations.* 3 vols. (New York, 1925); José Toribio Medina, *Actas del cabildo de Santiago de Chile durante el período llamado de la patria vieja: 1810-1814* (1910); Néstor Meza Villalobos, *La actividad política del reino de Chile entre 1806 a 1810* (1968); Bartolomé Mitre, *Historia de San Martín y de la emancipación sudamericana,* 3 vols. (Buenos Aires, 1887-88); Ricardo Montaner Bello, *Historia diplomática de la historia de Chile* (1961); Francisco José Moreno, *Legitimacy and Stability in Latin America: A Study of Chilean Political Culture* (New York, 1969) (the study by Moreno emphasizes the conflict between the "authoristic" tradition and the liberal principles espoused in the independence period and the 19th cenutry); A. Orrego Luco, *La patria vieja,* 2 vols. (1935-57); Eugenio Orrego Vicuña, *O'Higgins: vida y tiempo* (Buenos Aires, 1946); Hernán Ramírez Necochea, *Antecedentes económicos de la independencia de Chile* (1959) (a Marxist interpretation of the independence movement); Raúl Silva Castro, *Egaña en la patria vieja* (1959); *Ideas y confesiones de Portales* (1954); and (ed.), *Escritos políticos de Camilo Henríquez* (1960); Benjamín Vicuña Mackenna, *El ostracismo de los Carrera* (1938); and *Tradición y reforma en 1810* (1961); Donald E. Worcester, *Sea Power and Chilean Independence* (Gainesville, 1962).

For post-1810 political development until the Constitution of 1833, the following sources are a good foundation: Benjamín Vicuña Mackenna, *Pipiolos y pelucones* (1939); Diego Barros Arana and Benjamín Vicuña Mackenna, et al., *Historia de la república de Chile: 1810-1830,* 5 vols. (1866-82); Ricardo Donoso, *Desarrollo político y social de Chile, desde la constitución de 1833,* 2nd ed. (1942); *Las ideas políticas en Chile,* 2nd ed. (1967) (This last work is perhaps the most important statement by a Chilean author of the struggle between liberalism and Hispanic values as a constant issue in Chilean history.); Alberto Edwards, *La organización política de Chile: 1810-1833,* 2d ed. (1955); Jaime Eyzaguirre, "Las ideas políticas en Chile hasta 1833," *BACH* 1 (1933); Jay Kinsbruner, *Diego Portales: Interpretive Essays on the Man and Times* (The Hague, 1967); Daniel Martner, *Estudio de política comercial chilena e historia económica nacional,* 2 vols. (1923); Paul V. Shaw, *The Early Constitutions of Chile* (New York, 1930); Ramón Sotomayor Valdéz, *Historia de*

Chile bajo el gobierno del general don Joaquín Prieto, 4 vols. (1900-1903); Benjamín Vicuña Mackenna, *Don Diego Portales,* 2 vols. (Valparaíso, 1863); Carlos Walker Martínez, *Portales* (Paris, 1879); José Zapiola, *Recuerdos de treinta años: 1810-1840,* 5th ed. (1902).

NINETEENTH-CENTURY CHILE

Simon Collier's "The Historiography of the 'Portalian' Period: 1830-1891 in Chile," *HAHR* (Nov. 1977) must be consulted when treating this period of Chilean history. Allen Woll's *A Functional Past: The Uses of History in Nineteenth Century Chile* (Baton Rouge and London, 1982) summarizes the ideological currents influencing 19th-century Chilean historiography and offers important insights into 19th-century Chilean society.

In general, historical studies on 19th-century development in Chile have come to rely less on the classical Chilean sources as American, British, Chilean, and European scholars produce monographs on particular themes, and Marxist historians and non-Marxist revisionists offer conflicting versions of socio-economic and political development in 19th-century Chile.

On Chilean social and economic development in the 19th century, Arnold J. Bauer, *Chilean Rural Society from the Spanish Conquest to 1930* (Cambridge, Eng., 1975) provides a useful overview along with a valuable bibliography. Harold Blakemore's *British Nitrates and Chilean Politics: 1886-1896* (London, 1974), a much broader work than its title suggests, offers a crucial interpretation of socio-economic development and Chilean politics, including a controversial treatment of the martyred president Balmaceda. For a radically different view, readers should consult Hernán Ramírez Necochea, *Historia del imperialismo en Chile* (1960); *La guerra civil de 1891: antecedentes económicos* (1953); and *Balmaceda y la contrarrevolución de 1891,* 2nd ed. (1969). Frederick Pike's *Chile and the United States: 1880-1962* (Notre Dame, 1962) interprets much of 19th- and early 20th-century Chilean history and is probably the most readable overview available in English. A controversial revisionist interpretation of political and economic development in the 19th century is Maurice Zeitlin, *The Civil Wars in Chile* (Princeton, 1984). On the role of women viewed through the educational system, see Gertrude M. Yeager, "Women's Roles in Nineteenth-Century Chile: Public Education Records, 1843-1883," *Latin American Research Review 18,* No. 3 (1983).

On 19th- and early 20th-century Chilean politics, Pike's work cited above is a useful summary. A more recent, revisionist view of post-1861 political developments is Julio Heise González, *Historia de Chile: el período parlamentario 1861-1925* vol. I (1974), vol. 2 (1982). This study is essential for understanding institutional evolution, the issues and myths surrounding the civil war of 1891, and early 20th-century political history. Heise's bibliography lists most of the important primary and secondary works on Chilean political and constitutional development from the early 19th century to the 1930s. Fernando Campos Harriet, *Historia constitucional de Chile*, 6th ed. (1983), covers the institutional development of the country from precolonial times until 1970, with detailed accounts of the 19th-century administrations, legislation, public policy, and extensive bibliographical references in the notes. In *Diagnóstico de la burocracia chilena: 1818-1969*, Germán Urzúa Valenzuela and Ana María García Barzellatto provide a synthesis of the growth of the Chilean state apparatus since independence and the political implications of bureaucratic expansion, including developments in the 19th century. Also of value is Germán Urzúa Valenzuela, *Evolución de la administración pública chilena* (1818-1968), 1970. Ricardo Donoso's polemical *Desarrollo político y social de Chile desde la constitución de 1833* and *Las ideas políticas en Chile*, 2nd ed. (1967) are both among the key secondary works on the 19th century. For a Marxian interpretation, also the source of much revisionist history on the 19th century, see Julio César Jobet, *Ensayo Crítico del desarrollo económico-social de Chile* (1955). Another important contribution to social history is Guillermo Feliú Cruz, "Un esquema de la evolución social de Chile en el siglo hasta 1891," in *Chile: visto a través de Agustín Ross* (1950).

In general, studies on the 19th century are much more specialized than those on earlier periods of Chilean history. As Chile was integrated into the web of expanding European and North American economies, it became itself a more complex and specialized society. Among the facets of this complexity examined by scholars are participation in the California and Australian gold rushes, growth of the mining and nitrate industry of the north, the beginnings of industrialization and intensified urbanization, immigration, transportation developments, war and military issues, diplomacy, intellectual development, and the emerging social question.

Such diversity makes topical categorization quite difficult. In the broad area of socio-economic evolution, including works on particular areas of the Chilean economy, social stratification and class conflict, the social question, technological change and international economic relations, one school of historical scholarship has recently emphasized the "dependency" of Chilean development upon events in Europe and North America. Complementing more traditional Marxist treatments of Chilean socio-economic trends in the 19th century and Francisco Encina's earlier laments concerning the direction and character of Chilean development in *Nuestra inferioridad económica* (1955), the dependency theorists trace most problems facing Chile to this pattern of international exploitation in the past centuries. Key works in this tradition include Ramírez Necochea's already mentioned study, *Historia del imperialismo en Chile* (1960); Marta Harnecker and Gabriela Uribe, *Imperialismo y dependencia* (1972); and three doctoral dissertations Roger Burbach, *The Chilean Industrial Bourgeoisie and Foreign Capital 1920-1970* (Indiana Univ., 1975); Charles G. Pregger Román, *Dependent Development in Nineteenth Century Chile* (Rutgers Univ., 1975), and Jacqueline Spencer Garreaud, *A Dependent Country: Chile 1817-1861* (Univ. of California, San Diego, 1981). A related but more balanced approach is Aníbal Pinto Santa Cruz, *Chile: un caso de desarrollo frustrado* (1959).

Markos J. Mamalakis's conservative interpretation, *The Growth and Structure of the Chilean Economy: From Independence to Allende* (New Haven and London, 1976), stands in sharp contrast to the dependency theorists. Buttressed by data for the 19th century as well as the twentieth, along with thorough research in secondary sources, his conclusions concerning the role and effect of foreign investment in Chile offer a significant counter to the dependency theorists. Carmen Cariola Sutter and Osvaldo Sunkel, *Un siglo de historia económica de Chile, 1830-1930* (Madrid, 1982), offers interpretive essays on a century of Chilean economic evolution, useful statistical appendices, and an important annotated thematic bibliography.

Henry W. Kirsch, *Industrial Development in a Traditional Society, The Conflict of Entrepreneurship and Modernization in Chile*, Gainesville, 1977, is an excellent reassessment of Chilean industrial development and includes a wealth of descriptive material and bibliographical references related to individual sectors and firms in the Chilean economy. Other key sources on industrialization include Jack Pfeiffer, "The Development of Manufacturing Industry in Chile, 1820-1940," Ph.D. diss. (Univ. of Chicago, 1947); Oscar Alvarez A., *Historia del desarrollo industrial de Chile*, 1936; special issue of *Colección Estudios CIEPLAN*, No. 12 (March 1984) "Perspectivas históricas de la economía chilena: del siglo XIX a la crisis del 30" (includes a suggestive article by Carlos Hurtado R. T., "La economía chilena entre 1830-1930: sus limitaciones y sus herencias," which re-evaluates Chilean economic policy and the role of the state in the 19th century). Another important contribution to the reassessment of Chilean industrial and economic development is J. Gabriel Palma, *Growth and Structure of Chilean Manufacturing Industry from 1830 to 1935: Origins and Development of a Process of Industrialization in an Export Economy*, Ph.D. diss. (Univ. of Oxford, 1979). Also of use on the 19th-century development of the Chilean economy are Luis Ortega, *Change and Crisis in Chile's Economy and Society*, *1865-1879*, Ph.D. diss. (Univ. of London, 1979); "Acerca de los orígenes de la industrialización chilena, 1860-1879" *Revista Nueva Historia*, No. 2 (1981), and P. S. Conoboy, *Money and Politics in Chile*, *1878-1925*, Ph.D. diss. (Univ. of Southhampton, 1977).

For particular sectors or regions of the Chilean economy and economic issues in the 19th century the following sources are of considerable value: Marcello Carmagnani, *Sviluppo Industriale e Sotto-Sviluppo Económico: il caso cileno 1860-1920* (Turin, 1971); C. W. Centner, "Great Britain and Chilean Mining: 1830-1914," *Economic History Review*, No. 12 (1942); Henry William Kirsch, *The Industrialization of Chile: 1880-1930*, Ph.D. diss. (Univ. of Florida, 1973); Santiago Machiavello Varas, *El problema de la industria del cobre y sus proyecciones económicas y sociales* (1923); Markos Mamalakis and Clark Reynolds, *Essays on the Chilean Economy* (Homewood, Ill., 1965); Santiago Marín Vicuña, *Los ferrocarriles en Chile* (1912); Max Nolff, "Industria manufacturera," CORFO, *Geografía económica de Chile* (1967); Robert B. Oppenheimer, *Chilean Transportation Development: The Railroads and Socio-economic Change in the Central Valley*, Ph.D. diss. (Univ. of California, Los Angeles, 1976); "National Capital and National Development: Financing Chile's Railroads in the 19th Century," *Business History Review*, 54 (Spring 1982); Luis Ortega, "The First Four Decades of the Chilean Coal Mining Industry," *Journal of Latin American Studies* 14 (May 1982); L. R. Pederson, *The Mining History of the Norte Chico: Chile* (Evanston, 1966); John Whaley, *Transportation in Chile's Bío Bío Region: 1850-1915*, Ph.D. diss. (Indiana Univ., 1974). Whaley's work, an excellent economic history of the Bío Bío region, also discusses primary sources and railroad statistics.

On nitrates, the most important sector of the economy in the late 19th century, see in addition to the Blakemore work already mentioned, Oscar Bermúdez, *Historia del salitre desde sus orígenes hasta la guerra del Pacífico* (1963); G. Billinghurst, *Los capitales salitreros de Tarapacá* (1889); Manuel Cruchaga, *Guano y salitre* (Madrid, 1929); J. R. Brown, "Nitrate Crisis: Combinations and the Chilean Government in the Nitrate Age," *HAHR*, No. 63 (1963); "The Chilean Nitrate Railways Controversy," *HAHR*, No. 38 (1958); M. B. Donald, "History of the Chile Nitrate Industry," *Annals of Science* 1 (Jan. 1936); and 2 (April 1936); Thomas F. O'Brien, *The Nitrate Industry and Chile's Crucial Transition: 1870-1891* (New York, 1982); Michael Monteón, *Chile in the Nitrate Era, The Evolution of Economic Dependence, 1880-1930* (Madison, 1982); Charles Bergquist, *Labor in Latin America, Comparative Essays on Chile, Argentina, Venezuela and Colombia* (Stanford,

1986); J. F. Rippy, *British Investments in Latin America: 1822-1949* (Hamden, Conn., 1966). A doctoral dissertation at Indiana University (1978) by Laurence Stickell, *Migration and Mining: Labor in Northern Chile in the Nitrate Era, 1880-1930*, will surely stand as the most important social and labor history of the nitrate industry.

Each of the "major" events and international conflicts of Chile's 19th-century history has occasioned its own historical literature. This includes, of course, the war against the Peru-Bolivia confederation early in the century, participation in the gold rushes of California and Australia, the civil wars of 1851 and 1859, the War of the Pacific, the civil war of 1891, and the effects of each economic boom or depression.

On the California gold rush's impact on Chile see Jay Monaghan, *Chile, Peru and the California Gold Rush of 1849* (Berkeley, 1973). A Marxist treatment of the civil wars of 1851 and 1859 is Luis Vitale's, *Las guerras civiles de 1851 y 1859 en Chile* (Concepción, 1971). Useful specialized studies on fiscal, financial, and public-sector performance include: Roberto Espinoza, *Cuestiones financieras de Chile* (1909); *La reforma bancaria y monetaria* (1913); Carlos T. Hamud, *El sector público chileno entre 1830-1930* (1969); and Agustín Ross, *Chile: 1851-1910: sesenta años de cuestiones monetarias y financieras y de problemas bancarios* (1911). Another ostensibly specialized study is Claudio Véliz, *Historia de la marina mercante de Chile* (1961), a work which goes well beyond history of the merchant marine, representing a basic source for Chilean economic history in the 19th century.

Immigration to Chile in the 19th century has also received limited, but careful attention in Carl Solberg, *Immigration and Nationalism: Argentina and Chile 1890-1914* (Austin, 1970); Jean Pierre Blancpain, *Les Allemands au Chili: 1816-1945* (Cologne, 1974)—a massive study of the German experience in Chile and the German contribution to Chilean society; Mark Jefferson, *Recent Colonization in Chile* (New York, 1921); George Young, *The Germans in Chile: Immigration and Colonization 1849-1914* (New York, 1974).

For the most systematic and detailed discussion of Chile in world affairs in the 19th century, and the domestic impact of these events, see the award-winning volume by Robert N. Burr, *By Reason or Force: Chile and the Balancing Power in South America 1830-1905* (Berkeley and Los Angeles, 1965). Burr's bibliography lists a wide range of official publications and other primary sources for Chilean international relations in the 19th century as well as materials on domestic development. An earlier but still useful look at Chilean diplomacy in the 19th century is Henry Clay Evans, *Chile and Its Relations with the United States* (Durham, N.C., 1927). Evans's book also surveys domestic socio-economic development in the 19th century. Other diplomatic studies include the classic by Mario Barros, *Historia diplomática de Chile 1541-1938* (Barcelona, 1970), which provides an overview from the colonial period to the Popular Front; William R. Sherman, *The Diplomatic and Commercial Relations of the United States and Chile: 1820-1914* (Boston, 1926). The war with Spain in the 1860s is treated in William Columbus Davis, *The Last Conquistadores* (Univ. of Georgia, 1950). Of great value for the War of the Pacific and late 19th-century Chile is William Sater's careful study, *The Heroic Image in Chile: Arturo Prat, Secular Saint* (Berkeley and Los Angeles, 1973). Sater's bibliography and notes contain numerous references to primary sources and government documents related to the War of the Pacific and Chilean economic and political development in the 19th century as well as newspaper and journal sources. Sater's article, "Chile during the First Months of the War of the Pacific," *Journal of Latin American Studies* 5 (1973) is helpful for background on the Chilean situation as the country entered the War of the Pacific. Sater has also contributed *Chile and the War of the Pacific* (Lincoln, Neb., 1986), which details conditions in Chile during the war and its effect on domestic politics and economy. Of related interest is Thomas Bader, *A Willingness to War: A Portrait of the Republic of Chile during the Years Preceding the War of the Pacific*, Ph.D. diss. (Univ. of California at Los Angeles, 1967).

The War of the Pacific and the subsequent diplomatic conflicts involving Chile, Peru, and Bolivia are the subjects of a large number of patriotic diatribes and some scholarly study. For varying interpretations of the war and polemical discussion of culpability the following list of sources may be consulted:

Pascual Ahumada Moreno, *Guerra del Pacífico*, 8 vols., Valparaíso, 1884-1891;

Jorge Basadre, *Historia de la República del Perú*, 6th ed., Lima, 1968 (Basadre is Peru's most eminent historian);

Gonzalo Bulnes, *Guerra del Pacífico*, 3 vols., Valparaíso, 1911;

Andrés A. Cáceres, *La Guerra del 79: sus compañas. Redacción y notas por Julio C. Guerrero*, Lima, 1973 (the memoirs of Peru's leading general and hero of the War of the Pacific); and *La guerra entre el Perú y Chile: 1879-1883*, Buenos Aires, 1924;

Edmundo H. Civiti Bernesconi, *Guerra del Pacífico: 1879-1883*, 2 vols., Buenos Aires, 1946;

W. J. Dennis, *Tacna and Arica: An Account of the Chile-Peru Boundary Dispute and the Arbitration of the United States*, New Haven, 1931;

Francisco García Calderón, *Memorias del cautiverio: prólogo y notas de Ventura García Calderón*, Lima, 1949 (account of this Peruvian ex-president's capture and imprisonment by the Chileans after the occupation of Lima);

V. G. Kiernan, "Foreign Interest in the War of the Pacific," *HAHR* 35 (1955);

Francisco A. Marchuca, *Las cuatro campañas de la Guerra del Pacífico*, 4 vols., Valparaíso, 1926;

Sir Clements R. Markham, *The War between Peru and Chile: 1879-1882*, London, 1882;

Herbert Millington, *American Diplomacy and the War of the Pacific*, New York, 1948;

Mariano Felipe Paz-Soldán, *Narración histórica de la guerra de Chile contra el Perú y Bolivia*, Buenos Aires, 1884.

The last decades of the 19th century brought the social question to Chile. In addition to the numerous contemporary accounts, political proclamations, and other writing, the following works are useful to the understanding of the social question and the labor movement in Chile: Robert Alexander, *Communism in Latin America* (New Brunswick, 1957); and *Labor Relations in Argentina, Brazil and Chile* (New York, 1962); Alan Angell, *Politics and the Labour Movement in Chile* (London, 1972); Jorge Barría Seron, *Breve historia del sindicalismo chileno* (1967); *Trayectoria y estructura del movimiento sindical chileno* (1963); and *El movimiento obrero en Chile* (1972); César A. DeLeon, "Las capas medias en la sociedad chilena del siglo XIX," *Anales de la Universidad de Chile*, No. 132 (1964); Peter DeShazo, *Urban Workers and Labor Unions in Chile, 1902-1927* (Madison, 1983); Julio César Jobet, *Recabarren, los orígenes del movimiento obrero y del socialismo chileno* (1956); Patricio Manns, *Breve síntesis del movimiento obrero* (1972); Michael Monteón, *The Nitrate Mines and the Origins of the Chilean Left: 1880-1925*, Ph.D. diss. (Harvard, 1974); James Oliver Morris, *Elites, Intellectuals, and Consensus: A Study of the Social Question and the Industrial Relations System in Chile* (Ithaca, N.Y., 1966)—this book provides the most complete list of references to newspaper, periodical and contemporary literature on the social question as well as secondary sources. It is the single most important reference source in English—; Hernán Ramírez Necochea, *Historia del movimiento obrero en Chile: siglo XIX* (1956); Alberto Varona, *Francisco Bilbao: revolucionario de América*, Buenos Aires (1973).

For a useful sample of contemporary sources on the social question and early labor histories see:

Juan Enrique Concha, *Cuestiones obreras,* 1899;

Luis Malaquías Concha S., *Sobre la dictación de un código del trabajo y de la previsión social,* 1907;

Javier Díaz Lira, *Observaciones sobre la cuestión social en Chile,* 1904;

Marcos Gutiérrez Martínez, *La cuestión obrera i el derecho de propiedad,* 1904;

"Informes de los Señores Concha y Quezada," *Boletín de la sociedad de fomento fabril 20,* 1903;

Tulio Lagos V., *Bosquejo histórico del movimiento obrero en Chile,* 1947;

J. Lawrence Laughlin, "The Strike at Iquique," *The Journal of Political Economy 17,* 1909.

Augusto Orrego Luco, "La cuestión social en Chile," *Anales de la Universidad de Chile 119.* Primero y segundo trimestre, 1961, No. 121 y 122;

Moisés Poblete Troncoso, *El derecho del trabajo y la seguridad social en Chile,* 1949;

J. Valdés Cange (pseudonym used by Alejandro Venegas), *Cartas al Excelentísmo Señor Don Pedro Montt,* Valparaíso, 1909;

Benjamín Vicuña Subercaseaux, *Socialismo revolucionario y la cuestión social en Europa y Chile,* 1908.

Political histories of Chile in the 19th century are numerous. Available to a lesser extent are summaries of the terms of individual presidents. Simon Collier's earlier cited article on the historiography of the Portalian period (*HAHR,* Nov. 1977) reviews the major work on this period while Harold Blakemore's "The Chilean Revolution of 1891 and Its Historiography," *HAHR 45* (Aug. 1965) is the single most important review of sources on the civil war of 1891, Balmaceda, and Chilean society at the turn of the century.

Many of the Chilean histories of the 19th century represent Liberal attacks on Conservative or Portalian administrations or vice versa.

On individual presidential administrations see:

Juan Bautista Alberdi, *Biografía del general Don Manuel Bulnes: presidente de la República de Chile,* 1846;

José A. Alfonso, *Los partidos políticos en Chile,* 1902;

Alberto Edwards Vives, *El gobierno de don Manuel Montt: 1851-1861,* 1932;

Isidoro Errázuriz, *Historia de la administración Errázuriz,* 1935;

Jaime Eyzaguirre, *Chile durante el gobierno de Errázuriz Echaurren: 1896-1901,* 1957;

Germán Riesco, *Presidencia de Riesco,* 1950;

Ricardo Salas Edwards, *Balmaceda y el parlamentarismo en Chile*, 1914;
Ramón Sotomayor Valdés, *Historia de Chile durante los cuarenta años transcurridos desde 1831 hasta 1871*, 2 vols., 1875-76;
Benjamín Vicuña Mackenna, *Introducción a los diez años de la administración Montt, Don Diego Portales*. 2 vols., Valparaíso, 1863;
Cristián A. Zegers, *Aníbal Pinto: Historia política de su gobierno*, 1969.

The evolution of 19th-century political thought, parliamentary institutions, electoral reform, the crisis of the Balmaceda presidency, and the character of the Chilean oligarchy are treated in:

José A. Alfonso, *El parlamentarismo i la reforma política en Chile*, 1909;
Justo and Domingo Arteaga, *Los constituyentes de 1870*, 1910;
Abdón Cifuentes, *Un decenio de la historia de Chile*, 1905;
Malaquías Concha, *El programa de la democracia*, 1908;
Ricardo Donoso, *Alessandri, agitador y demoledor: cincuenta años de historia política de Chile*, 2 vols., 1952, 1954; and *Historia de las ideas políticas en Chile*, 1946;
Alberto Edwards Vives, *La fronda aristocrática*, 1936;
Rafael Egaña, *Historia de la dictadura y la revolución de 1891*, 1891;
Pedro Pablo Figueroa, *Historia de la revolución constituyente: 1858-1859*, 1889;
Maximiliano Ibáñez, *El régimen parlamentario en Chile*, 1908;
Abraham Konig, *La constitución de 1833 en 1913*, 1913;
José J. Larraín, *El derecho parlamentario chileno*, 2 vols., 1896-97;
José Victorino Lastarria, *La constitución política de la República de Chile comentada*, 1856;
José Maza, *Sistemas de sufragio i cuestión electoral*, 1913;
Hermógenes Pérez de Arce, *El parlamentarismo*, 1901;
Paul Reinsch, "Parliamentary Government in Chile," *APSR*, June 1909;
Manuel Rivas Vicuña, *Historia política y parlamentaria de Chile*, 3 vols., 1964—a key figure in Chilean parliamentary politics provides valuable insight into the parliamentary era—;
Ramón V. Subercaseaux, *Memorias de ochenta años*, 1936.

The class basis of Chilean 19th-century politics is introduced in:

Frederick Pike, "Aspects of Class Relations in Chile, *HAHR*, Feb. 1963;
Luis Emilio Recabarren, *Los albores de la revolución social en Chile*, 1921—the author is the most well-known early leader of the Chilean labor movement—; and *Ricos y pobres a través de un siglo de vida republicana*, 1910.

The Civil War of 1891

The civil war of 1891, with its relationship to the nitrate economy, and also the symbol of President Balmaceda, has generated considerable historical literature. Harold Blakemore's, "The Chilean Revolution of 1891 and Its Historiography," *HAHR* 14 (1965) reviews this literature and offers the reader the benefit of Professor Blakemore's astute interpretation of the Balmaceda years. Blakemore's book, *British Nitrates and Chilean Politics: 1886-1896* (1974), is by far the most important work on the Balmaceda period. Blakemore presents much new material and a marked contrast to earlier work by Chilean nationalists and Marxists on the War of the Pacific, the role of British investors in Chilean politics, and on the policies of the Balmaceda administration. Among the most important treatments of the Balmaceda period and the civil war of 1891 are:

J. Bañados Espinosa, *Balmaceda: su gobierno y la revolución de 1891*, 2 vols., Paris, 1894;

Aníbal Bravo Kendrick, *La revolución de 1891*, 1946;

J. Díaz Valderrama, *La guerra civil de 1891*, 2 vols., 1942;

O. Hardy, "British Nitrates and the Balmaceda Revolution," *Pacific Historical Review* 17, 1948;

Maurice Kervey, *Dark Days in Chile*, London, 1891-92;

Michael Meeropol, *On the Origins of the Chilean Nitrate Enclave*, Ph.D. diss. (Univ. of Wisconsin, 1973);

Crisóstomo Pizarro, *La revolución de 1891*, Valparaíso, 1971;

Hernán Ramírez Necochea, *Balmaceda y la contrarrevolución de 1891*, 2nd ed., 1969 (a Marxist interpretation of the Civil War of 1891);

J. Rodríguez Bravo, *Balmaceda y el conflicto entre el congreso y el ejecutivo*, 2 vols., 1921, 1926;

Edwards R. Salas, *Balmaceda y el parlamentarismo en Chile*, 2 vols., 1914, 1925;

J. Sears and B. W. Wells, *The Chilean Revolution of 1891*, Office of Naval Intelligence, Washington, D.C., 1893;

Ximena Vergara and Luis L. Barros, "La guerra civil del 91 y la instauración del parlamentarismo" *Revista Latinoamericana de Ciencias Sociales* 3 (June 1972);

J. M. Yrarrázaval, *El presidente Balmaceda*, 2 vols., 1940.

Economy and Society in the Twentieth Century

It is very difficult to find a discussion of the Chilean economy that fails to include discussion of Chilean politics. In an effort to provide a bibliographical overview of Chilean political economy in the 20th century, I have compiled a list of works covering the economy to approximately 1970. The works on this list include both general treatments and studies with a more specialized focus. In addition, separate lists of references follow for the agricultural sector, copper, and mining, due to the special importance of these sectors of the Chilean economy both in strictly economic terms and in regard to Chilean politics.

In addition to the recent work of Mamalakis (*The Growth and Structure of the Chilean Economy: From Independence to Allende*, 1976) mentioned earlier, the best synthesis of Chilean political economy and economic issues for the period 1952 to 1970 is Ricardo Ffrench Davis, *Políticas económicas en Chile: 1952-1970* (1973), which examines stabilization programs and economic policy from the time of the Klein-Saks missions to 1970. It also includes extremely useful data series and an excellent bibliography of technical literature on the Chilean economy. For general treatments of Chilean economic development and economic issues see:

Jorge Alessandri, *La verdadera situación económica y social de Chile en la actualidad*, 1955;
Marco Ballesteros and Tom E. Davis, "The Growth of Output and Employment in Basic Sectors of the Chilean Economy," *Economic Development and Cultural Change* 11, 1963;
Jere R. Behrman, *Macroeconomic Policy in a Developing Country: The Chilean Experience*, Amsterdam, 1977;
José Cademartori, *La economía chilena: un enfoque marxista*, 1968;
Alvin Cohen, *Economic Change in Chile: 1929-1959*, Gainesville, 1960;
Luis Correa Prieto, *Nuestra economía y sus flaquezas: análisis no comprometido*, 1963;
ECLA (CEPAL), *Antecedentes sobre el desarrollo de la economía chilena: 1925-1952*, 1954;
P. T. Ellsworth, *Chile: An Economy in Transition*, New York, 1945;
Instituto de Economía de la Universidad de Chile, *Desarrollo económico de Chile: 1940-1956*, 1956; and *La economía de Chile: 1950-1963*, 2 vols., 1963;
Julio César Jobet, *Ensayo crítico del desarrollo económico social de Chile*, 1955;
Nicholas Kaldor, "Economic Problems of Chile," *Essays on Economic Policies* 2, London, 1964;
Santiago Machiavello Varas, *Política económica nacional: antecedentes y directiva*, 2 vols., 1931;
Markos Mamalakis and Clark Reynolds, *Essays on the Chilean Economy*,

Homewood, Ill., 1965 (includes special contributions on copper and agriculture);

Daniel Martner, *Estudio de política comercial chilena e historia económica nacional*, 2 vols., 1923;

Aníbal Pinto et al., *Chile hoy*, 1970; *Chile: una economía difícil*, 1964; *Tres ensayos sobre Chile y América Latina*, Buenos Aires, 1971; and *Hacia nuestra independencia económica*, 1963;

Universidad de Chile, *Desarrollo de Chile en la primera mitad del siglo XX*, I. 1953;

Stefan de Vylder, *From Colonialism to Dependence: An Introduction to Chile's Economic History*, Stockholm, 1977;

Mario Zañartu and John Kennedy (eds.), *The Overall Development of Chile*, Notre Dame, 1969.

Public finance, monetary issues, and the continuing debate over inflation and stabilization policy are discussed in:

César Araneda Encina, *Veinte años de la historia monetaria de Chile: 1925-1945*, 1945;

Banco Central de Chile, *Evolución de las finanzas públicas de Chile: 1950-1960*, 1963;

Jorge Cauas, "Políticas de estabilización: el caso chileno," *Estudios monetarios 2*, 1970;

Tom E. Davis, "Eight Decades of Inflation in Chile: 1879-1959: A Political Interpretation," *Journal of Political Economy 81*, No. 4, 1963;

David Felix, "An Alternative View of the 'Monetarist-Structuralist' Controversy," *Latin American Issues: Essays and Comments*. A. Hirschman (ed.), New York, 1961;

Frank Fetter, *Monetary Inflation in Chile*, Princeton, 1931;

Herman Finer, *The Chilean Development Corporation*, Montreal, 1947;

Eduardo García, *Inflation in Chile: A Quantitative Analysis*, Ph.D. diss., M.I.T., 1964;

Joseph Grunwald, "The 'Structuralist' School in Price Stabilization and Economic Development: The Chilean Case," *Latin American Issues: Essays and Comments*, A. Hirschman (ed.), New York, 1961;

Albert O. Hirschman, "Inflation in Chile," *Journeys Toward Progress*, New York, 1963;

Rolf Luders, *A Monetary History of Chile 1925-1958*, Ph.D. diss. (Univ. of Chicago, 1968);

Misión Klein-Saks, *El programa de estabilización de la economía chilena y el trabajo de la Misión Klein-Saks*, 1958;

Ministerio de Hacienda, *Cuentas fiscales de Chile: 1925-1957*, 1959;

Max Nolff and Felipe Herrera, *La inflación: naturaleza y problemas*, 1954;

ODEPLAN, *Cuentas nacionales: 1960-1970*, 1971;

Enrique Sierra, *Tres ensayos de estabilización en Chile*, 1970.

Sectoral development in industry, agriculture, mining, banking, and tax or exchange rate policy receive treatment in:

Pedro Aguirre Cerda, *El problema agrario*, Paris, 1929; and *El problema industrial*, 1933;

Oscar Alvarez Andrews, *Historia del desarrollo industrial de Chile*, 1936;

Sergio Aranda and Alberto Martínez, *Industria y agricultura en el desarrollo económico*, Instituto de Economía de la Universidad de Chile, 1970;

Eric Baklanoff, "Model for Economic Stagnation: The Chilean Experience with Multiple Exchange Rate," *Interamerican Economic Affairs* 13, Summer 1959;

Solon Barraclough, "Reforma agraria: historia y perspectiva," *Cuadernos de la Realidad Nacional*, No. 7, 1971;

Sergio Bitar, "Política de desarrollo industrial," *Cuadernos de Economía*, No. 22, Dec. 1970;

Marcello Carmagnani and C. M. Hernández, "Evolución de la industria en Chile: 1860-1940," *Boletín del Centro de Estudios Socioeconómicos* 1, 1967;

CORFO, *Obreros industriales chilenos*, 1970;

F. Durán Bernales, *Población, alimentos y reforma agraria*, 1966;

Peter Gregory, *Industrial Wages in Chile*, Ithaca, N.Y., 1967;

Rodolfo Hoffman and F. Debuyst, *Chile: una industrialización desordenada*, 1966;

Instituto de Economía de la Universidad de Chile, *La tributación agrícola en Chile 1940-1958: algunas implicaciones del sistema tributario chileno*, 1960;

Ricardo Lagos, *La industria en Chile: antecedentes estructurales*, 1966;

Daniel Martner, *Estudio de política comercial chilena e historia económica nacional*, 2 vols., 1923;

Oscar Muñoz G., *Crecimiento industrial de Chile: 1940-1965*, 1968;

Oscar Muñoz, *Chile y su industrialización*, 1986; and et al., *Proceso a la industrialización chilena*, 1972 (collection of articles considering development under conditions of dependence, and various aspects of industrial development in Chile);

Mariano Puga Vera, *El petróleo chileno*, 1964.

Concern with foreign investment and concentration of wealth and power in Chile are found in:

Jorge Ahumada, *En vez de la miseria,* 1958;

Genaro Arriagada, *La oligarquía patronal chilena,* 1970;

Sergio Bitar, "La inversión extranjera en la industria chilena," *Trimestre Económico* 13, No. 4, Oct.-Dec. 1971;

CORFO, *Análisis de las inversiones extranjeras en Chile: 1954-1969,* 1972; and *La inversión extranjera en la industria chilena,* 1970;

F. Dahse, *El mapa de la extrema riqueza,* 1979;

Fernando Galofre, *Entrepreneurial and Governmental Elites in Chilean Development,* Ph.D. diss. (Tulane Univ., 1970);

Ricardo Lagos, *La concentración del poder económico, su teoría, realidad chilena,* 1961; and "La nueva burguesía chilena," *Revista APSI* (June 1981);

Maurice Zeitlin et al., "New Princes for Old? The Large Corporation and the Capitalist Class in Chile," *American Journal of Sociology* 80, July 1974.

Chilean Agriculture, Rural Life, and Agrarian Reform

Many writers have analyzed Chilean politics and society against the backdrop of the land tenure system, *inquilinaje,* deficient agricultural production, and the relationship between rural life and urban power. The literature on rural Chile is truly overwhelming. CIDA, *Chile: Tenencia de la tierra y desarrollo socio-económico del sector agrícola* (1966), and the annotated bibliography published by the Land Tenure Center at the University of Wisconsin at Madison—*Agrarian Reform in Latin America: An Annotated Bibliography* (1974)—are excellent sources of bibliographical references on agriculture, rural life, and agrarian reform in Chile. Key studies on rural Chile and the formation of the hacienda system include: Rafael Baraona et al., *Valle de Putaendo* (1960); Luis Correa Vergara, *Agricultura Chilena,* 2 vols. (1939); Ramón Domínguez, *Nuestro sistema de inquilinaje* (1867); M. Drouilly and Pedro Lucio Cuadra, "Ensayo sobre el estado económico de la agricultura en Chile," *Boletín de la Sociedad Nacional de Agricultura* 10 (1878); Mario Góngora, *Encomenderos y estancieros* (1970); *Origen de los "inquilinos" de Chile central* (1960) with Jean Border, *Evolución de la propiedad en el valle del Puange,* 2 vols. (1956); Silvia Hernández, "Transformaciones tecnológicas en la agricultura de Chile central: siglo XIX," *Cuadernos del centro de estudios socio-económicos,* No. 3 (1966); Gonzalo Izquierdo, *Un estudio de las ideologías chilenas: la sociedad de agricultura en el siglo XIX* (1968);

Carlos Keller, *Una revolución en la agricultura* (1956); George McBride, *Chile: Land and Society* (Baltimore, 1936); Tancredo Pinochet Le-Brun, "Inquilinos en la hacienda de su excelencia," *Antología chilena de la tierra*, Antonio Corvalán, ed. (1970); Moisés Poblete Troncoso, *El problema de la producción agrícola y la política agraria nacional* (1919); Teodoro Schneider, *La agricultura chilena durante los últimos cincuenta años* (1904).

Significant contributions include the long list of works published at ICIRA in Santiago under the direction of Solon Barraclough prior to the military coup of 1973. Perhaps foremost on the list is Almino Affonso et al., *Movimiento campesino chileno*, 2 vols. (1970). Among others are: Andrés Pascal, *Relaciones de poder en una localidad rural*; Solon Barraclough, *Notas sobre tenencia de la tierra en América Latina*; Pablo Ramírez, *Cambios en las formas de pago a la mano de obra agrícola*; A. Corvalán et al., *Reforma agraria chilena: seis ensayos de interpretación*; Antonio Corvalán (ed.), *Antología chilena de la tierra*; Alejandro Saavedra, *La cuestión mapuche*; Hugo Zemelman, *El migrante rural*; Brian Loveman, *El campesino chileno le escribe a su excelencia*.

Other important studies include: José Bengoa, *El Campesinado Chileno después de la reforma agraria* (1983); F. Broughton, *Chile: Land Reform and Agricultural Development*, Ph.D. diss. (Univ. of Liverpool, Eng., 1970); Jean Carrière, "Landowners and the Rural Unionization Question in Chile, 1920-48, *Boletín de Estudios Latinoamericanos y del Caribe*, No. 22 (June 1977); Joseph Collins, *Agrarian Reform and Counter-Reform in Chile* (San Francisco, 1979); Peter Dorner (ed.), *Land Reform in Latin America: Issues and Cases* (Madison, 1971); Roberto P. Echeverría, *The Effect of Agricultural Price Policies on Intersectoral Income Transfers*, Ph.D. diss. (Cornell Univ., 1969); Lovell S. Jarvis, *Chilean Agriculture under Military Rule, From Reform to Reaction, 1973-1980* (Berkeley, 1985); Kyle Steenland, *Agrarian Reform under Allende: Peasant Revolt in the South* (Albuquerque, 1977); Cristóbal Kay, *Comparative Development of the European Manorial System and the Latin American Hacienda System: An Approach to a Theory of Agrarian Change for Chile*, Ph.D. diss. (Univ. of Sussex, Eng., 1971); Robert R. Kaufman, *The Politics of Land Reform in Chile* (Cambridge, Mass., 1972); Brian Loveman, *Struggle in the Countryside: Politics and Rural Labor in Chile 1919-1973* (Bloomington, Ind., 1976); Terry L. McCoy, *Agrarian Reform in Chile: 1962-1968*, Ph.D. diss. (Univ. of Wisconsin, 1969); Marvin Sternberg, *Chilean Land Tenure and Land Reform*, Ph.D. diss. (Univ. of California, Berkeley, 1962); Jeannine Swift, *Agrarian Reform in Chile: An Economic Study* (Lexington, Mass., 1971); William Thiesenhusen, *Chile's Experiments in Agrarian Reform* (Madison, 1966);

Thomas C. Wright, *Landowners and Reform in Chile: The Sociedad Nacional de Agricultura 1919-40* (Urbana, 1982). In addition, the *Boletín de Estudios Agrarios* and the series of studies *Documentos,* published by the Grupo de Estudios Agro Regionales (GEA) and the research of the Grupo de Investigaciones Agrarias (GIA), provide much valuable material on Chilean agriculture, forestry, and labor organizations in the post-1973 period.

COPPER

Since 1930 copper has dominated Chile's economy. At the mercy of international economic forces and controlled until 1971 by foreign firms, the copper industry was the source of perpetual political conflict. No other study has done so much to put the Chilean copper industry into an international perspective as Theodore Moran, *Multinational Corporations and the Politics of Dependence* (Princeton and London, 1974). Another study, less sympathetic to Chile and more sensitive to the interests of the American firms—but nonetheless extremely careful and well researched—is Eric Baklanoff, *Expropriation of United States Investments in Cuba, Mexico, and Chile* (New York, 1975). By far the most detailed recent work relating the Chilean copper industry to American investment is George Mason Ingram IV, *Nationalization of American Companies in South America: Peru, Bolivia, Chile,* 2 vols., Ph.D. diss. (Univ. of Michigan, 1973). Ingram's massive study includes an extensive bibliography on foreign investment in Chile, as well as Peru and Bolivia, along with sources on the Chilean copper industry in particular. Other valuable works on copper in the Chilean economy include:

Gregorio Amunátegui, "The Role of Copper in the Chilean Economy," *Latin America and the Caribbean: A Handbook,* Claudio Véliz (ed.), London, 1968;

Eric N. Baklanoff, "Taxation of United States-owned Copper Companies in Chile: Economic Myopia versus Long-run Self-interest," *National Tax Journal,* No. 14, March 1961;

M. Castillo, H. Correa, and R. Gac, "Las empresas de la gran minería Sociedad Minera El Teniente" CORFO, *El Cobre Chileno,* 1973;

"Contribution of Copper to Chilean Economic Development: 1920-1967," *Foreign Investment in the Petroleum and Mineral Industries: Case Studies of Investor-Host Country Relations,* Raymond F. Mikesell et al., Baltimore and London, 1971;

Carlos Fortín, "The Copper Policy of the Chilean Junta" Working Papers, Latin American Program, The Wilson Center, No. 76;

Joanne Fox Przeworski, *The Decline of the Copper Industry in Chile and Entrance of North American Capital*, Ph.D. diss. (Washington University, 1978);

A. Fuenzalida, *El trabajo y la vida en el mineral El Teniente*, 1918;

Norman Girvan, *Copper in Chile*, Univ. of West Indies, Jamaica, 1972;

Joseph Grunwald and Philip Musgrove, *Natural Resources in Latin American Development*, Baltimore, 1970;

L. Hiriat, *Braden, Historia de una mina* (1964).

Markos Mamalakis, "The American Copper Companies and the Chilean Government, 1920-1967: Profile of a Foreign-owned Export Sector," *Foreign Investment in the Petroleum and Mineral Industries: Case Studies of Investor-Host Country Relations*, Raymond Mikesell et al., Baltimore, 1971;

Santiago Marín Vicuña, *La industria del cobre en Chile*, 1920;

Raymond Mikesell, "Conflict and Accommodation in Chilean Copper," *Foreign Investment in the Petroleum and Mineral Industries: Case Studies of Investor-Host Country Relations*, Raymond Mikesell et al., Baltimore, 1971;

Eduardo Novoa Monreal, *La nacionalización del cobre: comentarios y documentos*, 1972 (important source for copper policy under the Allende government);

C. W. Reynolds, "Chile and Copper," *Essays on the Chilean Economy*, M. Mamalakis and C. W. Reynolds (eds.), New Haven, 1966;

María Rosaria Stabili, "Relaciones de producción capitalista; los empresarios norteamericanos en la minería del cobre de Chile, 1905-1918," *Revista Latinoamericana de Historia Económica y Social*, VI (1985);

Thomas G. Sanders, "Chile and Its Copper," *AUFS West Coast South America Series 26*, No. 1, New York, 1969;

Paul Sigmund, *Multinationals in Latin America: The Politics of Nationalization*, Madison, 1980;

John V. Sweeney, An Economic Analysis of the Nationalization of the Gran Minería of Copper in Chile, Ph.D. diss. (Catholic University of America, 1977);

P. Vayassière, "La division internationale du travail et la desnationalisation du cuivre Chilien (1880-1920)," *Cahiers du Monde Hispanique et Luso-Brésilien*, No. 20 (1973);

Mario Vera Valenzuela, *La política económica de cobre en Chile*, 1961.

Regional and Local Histories, Urbanization

From colonial times the formation and growth of urban centers has inspired local and regional histories. In recent times rapid urbanization has become a most salient feature of Chilean life. Studies that focus on regional development or on Chilean urbanization more generally include: DESAL, *Poblaciones marginales y desarrollo urbano: el caso chileno* (1965); John Friedman and Thomas Lackington, "La hiperurbanización y el desarrollo nacional en Chile," *Estructura social de Chile*, H. Godoy, ed., (1971); Guillermo Geisse G., *Problemas del desarrollo urbano regional en Chile* (1968); Gabriel Guarda, "Influencia militar en las ciudades del reino de Chile," *Boletín de la Academia Chilena de la Historia* 33, No. 75 (1966); and "El urbanismo imperial y las primitivas ciudades de Chile," *Finis Terrae* No. 51 (1957) (these two articles describe the early urbanization in colonial Chile); Carlos Hurtado Ruiz-Tagle, *Concentración de población y desarrollo económico* (1966); Bruce Herrick, *Urban Migration and Economic Development in Chile* (Cambridge, Mass., 1965); Fernando Marín G. and B. Salamón Roseblitt, *La vivienda colonial urbana* (1956); Mario Francisco Rothschild, *Regional Development and Sectoral Specialization: The Chilean Case*, Ph.D. diss. (Cornell Univ., 1973); Eduardo Secchi, *La casa chilena hasta el siglo XIX* (1952); Jorge Gustavo Silva, *La nueva era de las municipalidades de Chile; recopilación histórica de la vida comunal del país* . . . (1931); Astolfo Tapia Moore, *Legislación urbanística de Chile: 1818-1959* (1961); Tomás Thayer Ojeda, *Las antiguas ciudades chilenas* . . . (1911); Frederick S. Weaver, Jr., *Regional Patterns of Economic Change in Chile: 1950-1964* (Cornell Univ. diss. series, 1968).

Numerous historical descriptions of the evolution of individual cities or towns also exist. For Santiago see: Guillermo Feliú Cruz, *Santiago a comienzos del siglo XIX: crónica de los viajeros* (1970) (excerpts from numerous travel accounts referring to physical environment, economy, and social life of Santiago in the early 19th century); Joseph Fichandler and Thomas O'Brien, "Santiago, Chile 1541-1581: A Case Study of Urban Stagnation," *TA* (1976); Vicente Grez, *La vida santiaguina* (1879). On the province of Valparaíso see: Roberto Hernández D., *Valparaíso en 1827* (Valparaíso, 1927); Carlos J. Larraín, *Viña del Mar* (1946); René M. Salinas, "Caracteres generales de la evolución demográfica de un centro urbano chileno: Valparaíso, 1685-1830," *Historia*, No. 10 (1971); *Población de Valparaíso en la segunda mitad del siglo XVIII* (Valparaíso, 1970); Benjamín Vicuña Mackenna, *Historia de Valparaíso*, 2 vols. (1936); and *Quintero: su estado actual y su provenir* (Valparaíso, 1874).

La Serena, Copiapó, Antofagasta, and other northern urban places are treated in: Domingo Amunátegui Solar, *El cabildo de La Serena: 1678-1800* (1928); Oscar Bermúdez, *Orígenes históricos de Antofagasta* (Antofagasta, 1966); and "Pica en el siglo XVIII; estructura económica y social," *RCGH* 3 (1973); Manuel Concha, *Crónica de la Serena desde su fundación hasta nuestros días: 1549-1870* (La Serena, 1971); Domingo Contreras Gómez, *La ciudad de Santa María de Los Ángeles*, 2 vols. (1972-44); Bernardo Cruz, *San Felipe de Aconcagua*, 2 vols. (1949-50); Eugenio Chouteau, *Informe sobre la provincia de Coquimbo presentado al supremo gobierno* (1887); Julio Figueroa G., *Historia de San Felipe* (San Felipe, 1902); Martin I. Glassner, "Feeding a Desert City: Antofagasta, Chile," *Economic Geography*, No. 45 (1969); Carlos Keller, "Los orígenes de Quillota," *BACH*, No. 61 (1959); J. Larraín de Castro, "Los orígenes de Zapallar, contribución a la historia de la propiedad territorial," *BACH*, No. 12 (1940); Joaquín L. Morales O., *Historia del Huasco* (Valparaíso, 1896); Andrés Sabella, *Semblanza del norte chileno* (1955); C. M. Sayago, *Historia de Copiapó* (Copiapó, 1854).

Leonardo Mazzei, "Ensayo de un recuento bibliográfico relativo a la zona sur de Chile: Talca-Magallanes: 1812-1912," *HGFC*, provides a comprehensive bibliography of regional studies for the territory from Talca south. Illustrative studies for urban centers and their hinterlands from the Central Valley south include: Armando Braun Menéndez, *Pequeña historia Magallánica*, 2nd ed. (Buenos Aires, 1954); Fernando Campos H., "Concepción y su historia," *BACH* (1970); Guillermo Cox y Méndez, *Historia de Concepción* (1822); Pedro Cunill, "Castro: centro urbano de Chiloé insular," *Antropología* 2, Primer semestre (1964); Gabriel Guarda, *La economía de Chile austral antes de la colonización alemana* (Valdivia, 1973); René León Echaíz, *Historia de Curicó*, 2 vols. (1975); S. Manuel Mesa, *Proyección histórica de la provincia de Linares* (Linares, 1965); Isabel P. Montt, *Breve historia de Valdivia* (Buenos Aires, 1971); Reinaldo Muñoz Olave, *Chillán: sus fundaciones y destrucciones: 1580-1835* (1921); Carlos Olguín B., *Instituciones políticas y administrativas de Chiloé en el siglo XVIII* (1971); S. Carlos Oliver, *El libro de oro de Concepción* (Concepción, 1950); Eduardo Pino Zapata, *Historia de Temuco* (Temuco, 1969); N. Alberto Recart, *El Laja un río creador* (1971); John H. Whaley, *Transportation in Chile's Bío Bío Region: 1850-1915*, Ph.D. diss. (Indiana Univ., 1974).

EDUCATION

The organization and role of education in Chilean society has received insufficient attention by historical researchers. Among the few significant

contributions in this area, the following sources are foundations for future
research:

Oscar Alvarez, "Aspectos sociológicos del problema educacional en Chile,"
   Revista Méxicana de Sociología 20, No. 3, 1958;
Domingo Amunátegui Solar, *Los primeros años del instituto nacional,
   1813-1835*, 1889; *Recuerdos del instituto nacional*, 1941;
Miguel Luis Amunátegui, *Estudios sobre instrucción pública*, 3 vols.,
   1897-98;
Manuel Ballesteros E., *Compilación de leyes y decretos vigentes en
   materia de instrucción pública*;
Manuel J. Barrera, "Trayectoria del movimiento de reforma universitaria
   en Chile," *Journal of Latin American Studies*, No. 10, 1968;
Rudolph C. Blitz, "Some Observations on the Chilean Educational Sys-
   tem and Its Relations to Economic Growth," *Education and Eco-
   nomic Development*, Chicago, 1965;
Margaret Campbell, "Education in Chile: 1810-1842," *Journal of Inter-
   American Studies* 1 (July 1959);
Fernando Campos Harriet, *Desarrollo educacional: 1810-1960*, 1960;
Raúl Cortés Pinto, *Bibliografía anotada de educación superior*, Universi-
   dad Técnica Federico Santa María, Valparaiso, 1967;
Ricardo Donoso, *Recopilación de leyes, reglamentos, y decretos relativos
   a los servicios de enseñanza pública*, 1937;
Ricardo Donoso, "El instituto pedagógico: tres generaciones de maestros,"
   Journal of Inter-American Studies 6 (Jan. 1964);
Kathleen Fischer, *Political Ideology and Educational Reform in Chile,
   1964-1976* UCLA, Los Angeles, 1979;
Manuel A. Garretón, "Universidad y política en los procesos de transfor-
   mación y reversión en Chile, 1967-1977, *Estudios Sociales 26*, No. 4
   (1980);
Clark C. Gill, *Education and Social Change in Chile*, Washington, D.C.,
   U.S. Govt. Printing Office, 1966;
Carlos Huneeus M. *La reforma en la universidad de Chile*, 1973;
Ivan Jaksic, *Academic Rebels*: Philosophy and Higher Education in Chile
   Since Independence, unpublished ms., Berkeley 1986;
Enrique Kirberg, *Los nuevos profesionales: educación universitaria de
   trabajadores en Chile*: UTE, 1968-1973, Guadalajara, 1981;
Amanda Labarca Hubertson, *Historia de la enseñanza en Chile*, 1939;
Daniel Levy, "Chilean Universities Under the Junta: Regime and Policy,"
   Latin American Research Review 21 (1986);
Ministerio de Educación Pública, *Bases generales para el planteamiento*

de la educación chilena, 1961; and *Algunos antecedentes para el planteamiento integral de la educación chilena*, 1964;

Enrique Molina, *El liceo y la formación de la élite*, 1933;

Roberto Munizaga Aguirre, *El estado y la educación*, 1953;

Máximo Pacheco Gómez, *La Universidad de Chile*, 1953;

Tancredo Pinochet, *Bases para una política educacional: al frente del libro de Amanda Labarca*, 1944;

Maximiliano Salas Marchant, *Reflexiones educacionales en torno a nuestra situación social*, 1942;

Danilo Salcedo, *La Universidad de Chile y su reforma inconclusa*, 1975;

Gabriel Sanhueza, "Panorama de la evolución de las ciencias pedagógicas y la investigación educacional en Chile: 1900-1960," *Anales de la Universidad de Chile* 120, No. 125, 1962;

Peter Sehlinger, *The Educational Thought and Influence of Valentin Letelier*, Ph.D. diss. (Univ. of Kentucky, 1969).

José Toribio Medina, *Historia de la Real Universidad de San Felipe de Chile*, 2 vols., 1928;

William Sywak, *Values in Nineteenth Century Chilean Education: The Germanic Reform of Chilean Public Education 1885-1910*, Ph.D. diss. (Univ. of California, Los Angeles, 1977);

Luis Terán, *Nuestra enseñanza secundaria: los problemas y las soluciones*, 1938;

Patricia Weiss Fagen, *Chilean Universities: Problems of Autonomy and Dependence*, Beverly Hills, 1973;

Allen L. Woll, "For God and Country: Historical Textbooks and the Secularization of Chilean Society: 1840-1890," *Journal of Latin American Studies*, No. 7, 1975.

POLITICS—POLITICAL HISTORY, MEMOIRS, AND
GENERAL INTERPRETATIONS OF CHILEAN
POLITICS IN THE TWENTIETH CENTURY

Chilean politics in the 20th century has attracted considerable attention from Chilean authors and foreign observers alike. Before 1973, scholars routinely depicted Chile as a permanent exception to the common pattern of caudillismo and military government in Latin America. In practice, Chilean formal democracy did seem to depart from the "typical" Latin American political experience. Not surprisingly therefore, much of the literature on Chilean politics focuses upon constitutional history, elections, the party spectrum, and the various presidential administrations. For the English-language reader, the most important pre-1970 description and analysis of Chilean politics remains Federico Gil, *The Political Sys-*

tem of Chile (Boston, 1966). For the period from the 1950s to 1973,
Arturo Valenzuela, *The Breakdown of Democratic Regimes: Chile* (Baltimore and London, 1978), is a valuable description and analysis of political polarization which led eventually to the military coup of 1973.
An insightful interpretive work on Chilean politics and society is Mario
Góngora, *Ensayo histórico sobre la noción de estado en Chile en los siglos
XIX y XX* (1981). Tomas Moulian, *Democracia y socialismo en Chile*
(1983), is an important retrospective analysis and critique of the development of Chilean democracy and the role of the leftist parties and movements through 1973. Moulian calls for a "secularization" of Chilean
Marxism. Other general works on Chilean politics, constitutional history,
policy dilemmas, and class conflict range from the memoirs of Chilean
presidents to careful studies of interest groups, the military or the Chilean
legislature. Listed below are a number of books and articles of general
interest to students of Chilean politics followed, in turn, by a list of
works concerned particularly with elections, the political party system,
and individual parties or movements:

Weston Agor, *The Chilean Senate: Internal Distribution of Influence*,
     Austin, 1971;
Jorge Ahumada, *La crisis integral de Chile*, 1966;
Arturo Alessandri, *Recuerdos de gobierno*, 3 vols., 1967;
Robert Alexander, *Arturo Alessandri: A Political Biography*, 2 vols., Ann
     Arbor, 1977; *The Tragedy of Chile*, Westport, 1978;
Carlos Andrade Geywitz, *Elementos de derecho constitucional chileno*,
     1963;
Mario Bernashcina, *Los constituyentes de 1925*, 1945; *Derecho municipal
     chileno*, 3 vols., 1952; and *Manual de derecho constitucional*, 1955;
H. E. Bicheno, "Antiparliamentary Themes in Chilean History: 1920-
     1970," *Allende's Chile*, Kenneth Medhurst (ed.), London, 1972;
Ricardo Boizard, *Cuatro retratos en profundiad: Ibáñez, Lafferte, Leigh-
     ton, Walker*, 1950 (brief biographies of leading political figures);
Frank Bonilla and Myron Glaser (eds.), *Student Politics in Chile*, New
     York, 1970;
Claude G. Bowers, *Chile Through Embassy Windows: 1939-1953*, New
     York, 1958;
Donald Bray, *Chilean Politics during the Second Ibáñez Government*,
     1952-1958, Ph.D. diss. (Stanford Univ. 1961);
Ben Burnett, *Political Groups in Chile*, Austin, 1972;
Fernando Campos Harriet, *Historia constitucional de Chile*, 1956;
César Caviedes, *The Politics of Chile: A Sociogeographical Assessment*,
     Boulder, Colo., 1979;

Peter Cleaves, *Bureaucratic Politics and Administration in Chile*, Berkeley, 1975;

Luis Correa, *El presidente Ibáñez: la política y los políticos*, 1962;

Ricardo Cruz-Coke, *Geografía electoral de Chile*, 1952;

Francisco Cumplido C., "Constitución política de 1925: hoy crisis de las instituciones políticas chilenas," *Cuadernos de la Realidad Nacional*, No. 7, Sept. 1970;

Charles H. Daughtery (ed.), *Chile: Election Factbook*, Washington, D. C., 1963;

Ricardo Donoso, *Alessandri, agitador y demoledor: cincuenta años de historia política de Chile*, 2 vols., Mexico, 1952-54; and *Desarrollo político y social de Chile*, 1943;

Paul Drake, "The Political Responses of the Chilean Upper Class to the Great Depression and the Threat of Socialism: 1931-1933," *The Well Born and the Powerful*, F. C. Jaher (ed.), Urbana, Ill., 1973; and *Socialism and Populism in Chile, 1932-1952*, Univ. of Illinois, 1978;

Guillermo Edwards Matte, *El Club de la unión en sus ochenta años, 1864-1944*, 1944;

Enzo Faletto, et al. (eds.), *Génesis histórico del proceso político chileno*, 1971;

Herman Finer, *The Chilean Development Corporation*, Montreal, 1947;

Patricio F. García, *Los gremios patronales*, 1973;

Jorge González von Marées, *El mal de Chile: sus causas y sus remedios*, 1940 (analysis of Chile's "problem" by Chilean Nazi leader);

José G. Guerra, *La constitución de 1925*, 1929;

Ernst Halperin, *Nationalism and Communism in Chile*, Cambridge, Mass., 1965;

Julio Heise González, *Historia constitucional de Chile*, 1954;

Phillip J. Houseman, *Chilean Nationalism: 1920-1952*, Ph.D. diss. (Stanford Univ., 1960);

Eduardo Goddard Labarca, *Chile invadido: reportaje a la intromisión extranjera*, 1968;

Elías Lafferte, *Vida de un comunista*, 1957;

Norbert Lechner, *La democracia en Chile*, Buenos Aires, 1970;

Frank Marshall Lewis, *The Political Effects of a Multi-Party System upon the Presidential Form of Government in Chile*, Ph.D. diss. (Univ. of Texas, 1955);

Armand Mattelart, et al., *La ideología de la dominación en una sociedad dependiente*, Buenos Aires, 1970;

Francisco José Moreno, *Legitimacy and Stability in Latin America: A Study of Chilean Political Culture*, New York, 1969;

Arturo Olavarría B., *Chile entre dos Alessandri*, 2 vols., 1962-65;

James Petras, *Politics and Social Forces in Chilean Development*, Berkeley and Los Angeles, 1969;

Frederick B. Pike, *Chile and the United States: 1880-1962*, Notre Dame, Ind., 1963;

Fernando Pinto, *Crónica política del siglo XX*, 1970;

Wurth Rojas, *Ibáñez, caudillo enigmático*, 1958;

Kalman Silvert, *The Chilean Development Corporation*, Ph.D. diss., Univ. of Pennsylvania, 1948; *Chile: Yesterday and Today*, New York, 1965; *The Conflict Society: Reaction and Revolution in Latin America*, New Orleans, 1961; "A Political-Economic Sketch of Chile," *AUFS Newsletter* 4, Jan. 1957; and "Some propositions on Chile," *AUFS West Coast South America Series* 11, No. 11 (Chile), New York, 1964;

Barbara Stallings, *Class Conflict and Economic Development in Chile, 1958-1973*, Stanford, 1978;

Osvaldo Sunkel, "Change and Frustration in Chile," *Obstacles to Change in Latin America*, Claudio Véliz (ed.), New York and London, 1965;

Germán Urzúa Valenzuela, *Diccionario político institucional de Chile*, 1984;

Arturo Valenzuela, *Political Brokers in Chile: Local Government in a Centralized Polity*, Durham, N.C., 1977;

Thomas C. Wright, *The Sociedad Nacional de Agricultura in Chilean Politics: 1879-1938*, Ph.D. diss. (Univ. of California, Berkeley, 1971);

Gertrude M. Yeager, "The Club de la Unión and Kinship: Social Aspects of Political Obstructionism in the Chilean Senate, 1920-1924," *The Americas* 35 (1979);

Jordan Marten Young, *Chilean Parliamentary Government: 1891-1924*, Ph.D. diss. (Princeton Univ., 1953);

Maurice Zeitlin, "The Social Determinants of Political Democracy in Chile," *Latin America*, J. Petras and M. Zeitlin (eds.), Fawcett, Conn., 1968.

POLITICS—ELECTIONS, POLITICAL PARTIES, AND POLITICAL MOVEMENTS

The evolution of Chilean political parties and the electoral system are treated in:

Roger Abbot, "The Role of Contemporary Political Parties in Chile," *APSR*, 45, June 1951;

Atilio Boron, "La evolución del régimen electoral en Chile," *Revista Latinoamericana de Ciencia Política* (Dec. 1972);

José Luis Castro, *El sistema electoral chileno*, 1941;

D. Corkhill, *From Dictatorship to Popular Front: Parties and Coalition Politics in Chile 1931-1941*, Ph.D. diss. (Univ. of Essex, Eng., 1974);

Alberto Edwards, *Bosquejo histórico de los partidos políticos chilenos*, 1936; ——— and Eduardo Frei Montalva, *Historia de los partidos políticos chilenos*, 1949;

Federico Gil, *Genesis and Modernization of Political Parties in Chile*, Gainesville, 1962;

Sergio Guilsasti Tagle, *Partidos políticos chilenos*, 2nd ed., 1964;

Daniel Hellinger, "Electoral Change in the Chilean Countryside: The Presidential Elections of 1958 and 1970," *Western Political Quarterly* 31:2, June 1978;

René León Echaíz, *Evolución histórica de los partidos políticos chilenos*, 2nd ed., 1971;

Charles Parrish, Arpad Von Lazar, and Jorge Tapia Videla, *The Chilean Congressional Elections of March 7, 1965: An Analysis*, Washington, D.C., 1965;

Karen L. Remmer, "The Timing, Pace, and Consequence of Political Change in Chile: 1918-1925," *HAHR*, No. 57, May 1977; *Party Competition in Argentina and Chile: Political Recruitment and Public Policy, 1890-1930*, Lincoln, Neb. 1984;

Fernando S. Silva, *Los partidos políticos chilenos*, 1972;

Peter Snow, "The Political Party System in Chile," *South Atlantic Quarterly*, No. 62, Autumn 1963;

Germán Urzúa Valenzuela, *Historia político electoral de Chile*, 1986;

Arturo Valenzuela, "The Scope of the Chilean Party System," *Comparative Politics* 4, January 1972;

J. Samuel Valenzuela, *Democratización vía reforma: la expansión del sufragio en Chile*, Buenos Aires, 1985;

On the Radical party and the Popular Front period, in addition to the excellent study by Drake mentioned above; see:

Salvador Allende Gossens, "Pedro Aguirre Cerda," *Arauco*, Jan. 1964;

Alberto Baltra Cortés, *Pedro Aguirre Cerda*, 1960;

Francisco Barría Soto, *El partido radical: sus historia y sus obras*, 1957;

Florencio Durán Bernales, *El partido radical*, 1958;

Juan C. Fernández, *Pedro Aguirre Cerda y el frente popular chileno*, 1938;

Gabriel González Videla, *El partido radical y la evolución social de Chile*, Gainesville, 1962;

Luis Palma Zúñiga, *Historia del partido radical*, 1967; and Pedro Aguirre
    Cerda: *maestro-estadista-gobernante*, 1963;
Darío Poblete and Alfredo Bravo, *Historia del partido radical y del frente
    popular*, 1936;
Eudocio Ravines, *The Yenan Way*, 1951 (ex-Comintern agent in Latin
    America recounts his role in formation of Chilean Popular Front and
    activities of Chilean Marxists);
Peter Snow, *El radicalismo chileno*, Buenos Aires, 1972;
John Reese Stevenson, *The Chilean Popular Front*, Philadelphia, 1942;
Richard R. Super, *The Chilean Popular Front Presidency of Pedro Aguirre
    Cerda: 1938-1941*, Ph.D. diss. (Arizona State Univ. 1975);
M. Salvador Valdés, *Cinco años de gobierno de izquierda: 1939-1943; las
    instituciones y las finanzas*, Puente Alto, 1944;

Chilean socialism is discussed in:

Agustín Alvarez Villablanca, *Objetivos del socialismo en Chile*, 1946;
Fernando Casanueva and Manuel Fernández C., *El partido socialista y la
    lucha de clases en Chile*, 1973;
Carlos Charlín, *Del avión rojo a la república socialista*, 1972 (excellent
    source of material on late 1920s and early 1930s);
Alejandro Chelén Rojas, *Trayectoria del socialismo*, Buenos Aires, 1967;
Salomón Corbalán, *El partido socialista*, 1957;
Paul Drake, *Socialism and Populism in Chile*, Urbana, 1978;
Mirian Hochwald, *Imagery in Politics: A Study of the Ideology of the
    Chilean Socialist Party*, Ph.D. diss., Univ. of California, Los Angeles,
    1971;
Julio César Jobet, *El partido socialista de Chile*, 2 vols., 1971; and Ale-
    jandro Chelén R., *Pensamiento teórico y político del partido socia-
    lista*, 1972; *Socialismo y comunismo*, 1952; and *El socialismo chileno
    a través de sus congresos*, 1965;
Benny Pollack, "The Chilean Socialist Party: Prolegomena to Its Ideology
    and Organization," *Journal of Latin American Studies*, May 1978;
Oscar Schnake Vergara, *Chile y la guerra: hacia una democracia dirigida*,
    1941 (Political commentary by leading Chilean socialist);
Jack Ray Thomas, "The Evolution of a Chilean Socialist: Marmaduque
    Grove," *HAHR* 47, No. 1, 1967;
Oscar Waiss, *Presencia del socialismo en Chile*, 1952.

Key works for understanding the origins and growth of the Chilean
Communist party include:

Andrew Barnard, *The Chilean Communist Party, 1922-1947*, Ph.D. diss.
(University of London, 1978); "Chilean Communists, Radical Presidents and Chilean Relations with the United States, 1940-1947,"
Journal of Latin American Studies 13 (November 1981);
Carlos Contreras Labarca, *La conspiración de los enemigos del pueblo*,
1940; and *Por la paz, por nuevas victorias del frente popular*, 1939;
Carmelo Furci, *The Chilean Communist Party and the Road to Socialism*, London, 1984;
Jorge Jiles Pizarro, *Partido comunista de Chile*, 1957;
Hernán Ramírez Necochea, *Orígen y formación del partido comunista
en Chile*, 1965.

The Conservative and Christian Democratic parties are studied by:

Ignacio Arteaga Undurraga, *Reseña histórica de las XVI convenciones del
partido conservador*, 1947;
Patricio Dooner, *Cambios sociales y conflicto político: el conflicto político
nacional durante el gobierno de Eduardo Frei (1964-1970)*, 1984;
Michael Fleet, *The Rise and Fall of Chilean Christian Democracy*,
Princeton, 1985;
George Grayson, *El partido demócrata cristiano chileno*, Buenos Aires,
1968;
Frank Mazella, *Party-Building in a Modernizing Society: A Study of the
Intermediate Leaders of the Chilean Christian Democratic Party*, 2
vols., Ph.D. diss. (Indiana Univ., 1972);
Bartolomé Palacios and Héctor Rodríguez de la Sotta, *El partido conservador y la democracia cristiana*, 1933;
Marcial Sanfuentes C., *El partido conservador*, 1957.

Michael Potashnik treats the Chilean Nazi movement in *Nacismo: National Socialism in Chile: 1932-1938*, Ph.D. diss. (Univ. of California, Los Angeles, 1974).

POLITICS—CATHOLIC CHURCH

The Catholic Church has played a significant but ambiguous role in recent
Chilean history. With leading Church intellectuals and dignitaries associated with the Christian Democratic government and a sweeping anti-Marxist campaign after 1962, Church activity took on an overtly political
character that contrasted markedly with its earlier linkage to the Conservative party. A number of studies captured this new reformist orientation of

the Church; only David Mutchler, *The Church as a Political Factor in Latin America; with Particular Reference to Colombia and Chile*, New York (1971), details the role of Church policy and programs in the Cold War, the Alliance for Progress, and the domestic anti-Marxist movement in Chile. Mutchler's book is essential to the understanding of the role of the Chilean church in national life. Brian H. Smith, *The Church and Politics in Chile* (Princeton, 1982), provides both a history of the Church and Church doctrine in Chile and an analysis of the Church's role in socio-economic and political change. It is required reading for an understanding of the Church since 1964; it also provides special insight into Chilean politics in the 20th century.

Other important works on the "new" church in Chile and the Catholic reformers include:

Isidoro Alonso, Renato Poblete, and Ginés Garrido, *La iglesia en Chile: estructuras eclesiásticas*, Madrid, 1961;

Fidel Araneda Bravo, *El Arzobispo Errázuriz y la evolución política y social de Chile*, 1956;

Virginia Marie Bouvier, *Alliance or Compliance: Implications of the Chilean Church Experience for the Catholic Church in Latin America*, Syracuse, N.Y., 1983;

William J. Coleman, *Latin American Catholicism: A Self Evaluation*, Maryknoll, N.Y., 1958;

John J. Considine (ed.), *The Church in the New Latin America*, Notre Dame, Ind., 1964;

William V. D'Antonio and Frederick B. Pike (eds.), *Religion, Revolution and Reform*, New York, 1964.

Michael Dodson, "The Christian Left," *Journal of Inter-American Studies and World Affairs* 21 (Feb. 1979);

Oscar Domínguez, *El campesinado chileno y la acción católica rural*, Fribourg, FERES, 1961;

Jaime Guzmán, "The Church in Chile and the Political Debate," in Pablo Baraona Urzúa, *Chile, A Critical Debate*, 1972;

Jorge Iván Hubner Gallo, *Los Católicos y la política*, 1959;

Ricardo Krebs (ed.), *Catolicismo y laicismo: Las bases doctrinarias del conflicto entre la iglesia y el estado en Chile, 1875-1885*, 1981;

Henry Landsberger and Fernando Canitrot, *Iglesia, intelectuales y campesinos*, INSORA, 1967 (an excellent study of the role of progressive Catholics in the Chilean rural labor movement);

Henry Landsberger (ed.), *The Church and Social Change in Latin America*, Notre Dame, Ind., 1970;

Kenneth Langton and Ronald Rapoport, "Religion and Leftist Mobilization in Chile," *Comparative Political Studies* 9 (Oct. 1976);

Alejandro Magnet, *El padre Hurtado*, 3rd ed., 1957;

J. Lloyd Mecham, *Church and State in Latin America*, Chapel Hill, 1966;

Frederick Pike, "Catholic Church and Modernization in Peru and Chile," *Journal of Interamerican Affairs*, 20, No. 2, Mar. 1966;

Renato Poblete, *La iglesia en Chile*, Fribourg and Bogotá, FERES, 1962;

Thomas G. Sanders, "The Chilean Episcopate," *AUFS Newsletter*, July 1968;

Thomas G. Sanders and Brian H. Smith, "The Chilean Catholic Church During the Allende and Pinochet Regimes," *AUFS West Coast South America Series 22*, New York, 1975;

Secretariado General del Episcopado de Chile, *La iglesia y el problema del campesinado chileno*, 1962;

Ivan Vallier, *Catholicism, Social Control and Modernization in Latin America*, New York, 1970.

THE MILITARY IN CHILEAN POLITICS AND SOCIETY

Many Chilean sources, including government publications, deal with the history of the armed forces or particular military institutions such as the Escuela Militar. A doctoral dissertation by Tommie Hillmon, Jr., *A History of the Armed Forces of Chile from Independence to 1920*, Syracuse Univ. (1963), provides seventy pages of annotated bibliographical references to primary sources and secondary materials on the Chilean military and diplomatic relations with its neighbors as well as detailed studies of military campaigns in the independence period, Chile's 19th-century wars, and the civil wars of 1851, 1859, and 1891. Hillmon's bibliography also contains a very extensive list of travel accounts of Chile from the 17th century onward and could be profitably consulted by scholars reviewing travel literature for Chile and Latin America more generally. Frederick Nunn's *Chilean Politics: 1920-1931*, cited earlier, is a key source on the important role of the military in Chilean politics and society in the first three decades of the 20th century. Nunn's selective bibliography is extremely helpful for materials on the military and Chilean politics in this period. The same author's *The Military in Chilean History*, Albuquerque (1976), explores the role of the Chilean military from 1810 to the military coup of 1973. Nunn has also contributed a number of articles on the Chilean military from the 19th century to the 1940s. Other especially useful sources on the Chilean military in politics in the 20th century include:

Arturo Ahumada, *El ejército y la revolución del 5 de septiembre 1924: reminiscencias*, 1931;

R. Aldunate Phillips, *Ruido de sables*, 1971?;

Genaro Arriagada H., *El pensamiento político de los militares* (CISEC), 1981;

Pablo Baraona Urzúa et al., *Fuerzas armadas y seguridad nacional*, 1973;

General Juan Bennett, *La revolución de 5 septiembre*, 1925;

General Jorge Boonen Rivera, *Participación del ejército en el desarrollo y progreso del país*, 1917;

Estado mayor del ejército, *Historia militar de Chile*, 3 vols., 1969;

Roy Hansen, *Military Culture and Organizational Decline: A Study of the Chilean Army*, Ph.D. diss., Univ. of California, Los Angeles, 1967;

Alain Joxe, *Las fuerzas armadas en el sistema político chileno*, 1970;

Alberto Lara, *Los oficiales alemanes en Chile*, 1969;

Carlos López V., *Historia de la marina de Chile*, 1929;

René Millar C., "Significado y antecedentes del movimiento militar de 1924," *Historia 2*, 1972-73;

Jorge Nef, "The Politics of Repression: The Social Pathology of the Chilean Military," *Latin American Perspectives (Chile: Blood on the Peaceful Road)*, Summer 1974;

Lisa North, *Civil-Military Relations in Argentina, Chile and Peru*, Berkeley, 1966;

Alberto Polloni Roldán, *Las fuerzas armadas de Chile en la vida nacional*, 1972;

Carlos Portales, "Militarization and Political Institutions in Chile," in P. Wallensteen, J. Galtung, and C. Portales, *Global Militarization*, Boulder and London, 1985;

Augusto Varas (ed.), *Transición a la democracia*, 1984;

Augusto Varas et al., *Estado y fuerzas armadas en el proceso político chileno*, 1982;

Augusto Varas, *Los militares en el poder* (forthcoming). (Varas kindly allowed me to read a draft of this manuscript which will add considerably to our knowledge of the Pinochet regime);

Augusto Varas and Felipe Agüero, *El proyecto político militar*, 1984;

General Carlos Sáez Morales, *Recuerdos de un soldado*, 3 vols., 1933-34 (good source for Chile's "Socialist Republic");

George Strawbridge, Jr., *Militarism and Nationalism in Chile: 1920-1932*, Ph.D. diss. (Univ. of Pennsylvania, 1968);

Terrence S. Tarr, *Military Intervention and Civilian Reaction in Chile: 1924-1936*, Ph.D. diss. (Univ. of Florida, 1960);

Augustín Toro Dávila, *Síntesis histórico-militar de Chile*, 2 vols., 1969.

CHRISTIAN DEMOCRACY

From 1964 to 1970 Christian Democratic ideology and leadership dominated Chilean society. For over three decades Christian Democratic intellectuals had proclaimed their doctrine, criticized Chilean society, and promised an alternative to capitalism and socialism. Key works of the Christian Democratic leaders provide some insight into their goals, values, and hopes for a new "communitarian" society in Chile:

Jaime Castillo Velasco, *Los caminos de la revolución*, 1972; and *Las fuentes de la democracia cristiana*, 1963;

Jacques Chonchol and Julio Silva Solar, *Hacia un mundo comunitario: condiciones de una política social cristiana*, 1951;

Eduardo Frei Montalva, *Chile desconocido*, 1937; *La verdad tiene su hora*, 1955; *El social cristianismo*, 1951; *Pensamiento y acción*, 1958; *La política y el espíritu*, 1940; and *Aún es tiempo*, 1942; and *El Mandato de la historia* (1975);

Oscar Larson, *La ANEC y la Democracia Cristiana* (1967);

Julio Silva and Bosco Parra, *Nociones para una política demócrata cristiana*, 1947;

William Thayer Arteaga, *Trabajo, empresa, y revolución*, 1968.

CHRISTIAN DEMOCRACY AND THE
REVOLUTION IN LIBERTY

Despite the idealism of some Christian Democrats, the hard realities of Chilean politics and the historical legacy of the Chilean social question obstructed implementation of their reformist program. Supported heavily by United States policymakers with loans and "foreign aid," the Christian Democrats found themselves caught between the strong forces of the past and the calls for revolution from the political left. The hard road of political reform—the successes, failures, and the ultimate electoral defeat in 1970—are documented in a large and still growing literature. Key sources include:

Alan Angell, "Chile: The Difficulties of Democratic Reform," *International Journal*, No. 24, 1969; and "Christian Democracy in Chile," *Current History*, No. 58, 1970;

Ricardo Boizard, *La democracia cristiana en Chile*, 1963;

Luis Corvalán L., *Chile hoy: la lucha de los comunistas chilenos en las condiciones del gobierno de Frei*, Buenos Aires, 1965 (analysis by leader of Chilean Communist party);

David Cusack, *The Politics of Chilean Private Enterprise under Christian Democracy*, Ph.D. diss. (Univ. of Denver, 1970);

Thomas Edwards, *Economic Development and Reform in Chile*, Michigan State Univ., 1972;

Eduardo Frei et al., *Reforma constitucional: 1970*, 1970;

Edward de Glab, Jr., *Christian Democracy, Marxism and Revolution in Chile: The Election and Overthrow of Allende*, Ph.D. diss. (Northern Illinois Univ., 1975);

George W. Grayson, Jr., "Chile's Christian Democratic Party: Power Factions, and Ideology," *Review of Politics*, No. 31, Apr. 1969; and "Significance of the Frei Administration for Latin America," *Orbis*, No. 9, Fall 1965;

Leonard Gross, *The Last Best Hope: Eduardo Frei and Chilean Democracy*, New York, 1967;

Norbert Lechner, *La democracia en Chile*, Buenos Aires, 1970;

David Lehman, "Political Incorporation versus Political Stability: The Case of the Chilean Agrarian Reform: 1965-1970," *Journal of Development Studies*, No. 7, July 1971;

Sidney Lens, "Chile's Revolution in Liberty," *Progressive*, No. 30, Oct. 1966;

Sergio Molina, *El proceso de cambio en Chile*, 1972;

Arturo Olavarría B., *Chile bajo la democracia-cristiana*, 6 vols., 1966-71;

James Petras, *Chilean Christian Democracy: Politics and Social Forces*, Berkeley, 1967;

Paul E. Sigmund, "Christian Democracy in Chile," *Journal of International Affairs*, No. 20, 1966;

Osvaldo Sunkel, "Change and Frustration in Chile," *Obstacles to Change in Latin America*, Claudio Véliz (ed.), New York and London, 1965;

William Thiesenhusen, "Grassroots Economic Pressures in Chile: An Enigma for Development Planners," *Economic Development and Cultural Change*, No. 16, April 1968;

J. Thome, "Expropriations in Chile Under the Frei Agrarian Reform," *American Journal of Comparative Law*, No. 10, Summer 1971;

Giles Wayland-Smith, *The Christian Democratic Party in Chile: A Study of Political Organization and Activity with Primary Emphasis on the Local Level*, Cuernavaca, 1969;

Edward J. Williams, *Latin American Christian Democratic Parties*, Knoxville, Tenn., 1967;

Luis Vitale, *Esencia y apariencia de la democracia cristiana*, 1964;

Arpad Von Lazar and L. Quirós Videla, "Christian Democracy: Lessons in the Politics of Reform Management," *Interamerican Economic Affairs* 21, No. 4, Spring 1968;

Sergio Vuskovć, *Problemática demócrata-cristiana, propiedad, revolución, estado*, 1968;

Ricardo A. Yocelevzky R., "La Democracia Cristiana chilena, trayectoria de un proyecto," *Revista Mexicana de Sociología* 47, April-June 1985 (offers a historical view of the party and describes the role of the party under the military).

Unidad Popular and After

Never has more been written about Chile than has appeared since 1970 with regard to the Popular Unity coalition and the subsequent military coup. The published literature is truly massive. Moreover, the number of books on non-political topics also mushroomed, creating a veritable wave of Chilean publications. Lee H. Williams, comp., *The Allende Years*, lists almost 3000 Chilean imprints held in selected North American libraries.

Existing materials on the Unidad Popular experience itself represent a mix of ideological and descriptive summaries of the events of the Allende years. A preliminary review of more than thirty of these analyses from differing ideological perspectives can be found in Arturo and J. Samuel Valenzuela, "Visions of Chile," in *Latin American Research Review* 10 (Fall 1975). This review article is an excellent starting point for understanding the literature on the Unidad Popular years.

A Marxist-oriented review of the early literature after the coup is found in Ron Chilcote and Terry Dietz-Fee, "Assessing the Literature since the Coup," *Latin American Perspectives* 1 (Summer 1974; a special issue, *Chile: Blood on the Peaceful Road*). The same issue also includes articles on theoretical aspects of the Unidad Popular experience, the military, the upper classes, short-term effects of the military's economic policies, and agrarian reform from 1964 to September 1973. Also of considerable interest are Samuel Chavkin, *Storm Over Chile* (Westport, 1985), an updated and revised version of *The Murder of Chile*, with description of the Popular Unity period and also interviews with key actors after their experience in the prisons of the junta; Federico Gil, Ricardo Lagos, and Henry Landsberger, *Chile at the Turning Point, Lessons of the Socialist Years, 1970-1973* (Philadelphia, 1979), an English translation of a book published in Spanish in 1977 which offers a number of valuable assessments by actors in the Popular Unity government, other prominent Chileans, and social scientists of the Allende administration's efforts and dilemmas. Two important books on the role of labor and working-class politics during the Unidad Popular administration are Peter Winn, *Weavers of Revolution* (New York, 1986) and Juan G. Espinosa and Andrew S. Zimbalist, *Economic Democracy, Worker Participation in Chilean Industry, 1970-1973* (New York, 1978).

To date, if forced to choose a single volume from among the hundreds of books, edited collections, and articles that analyze the Allende years, a good choice would be Stefan de Vylder's *Allende's Chile, The Political Economy of the Rise and Fall of the Unidad Popular* (Cambridge Univ., London and New York, 1974). This book is a careful and extremely well-developed analysis of the political, economic, and social context of the Allende experience and the factors leading up to the military coup of 1973.

An important source of materials for insight into the situation and position of the Catholic left, some Christian Democrats and others who left the party, during the Allende administration, is Jaime Ruiz-Tagle P., *Poder político y transición al socialismo: tres años de la unidad popular*. Published in September 1973, just before the coup, the volume includes a number of articles published in *Mensaje*, the Jesuit journal in Santiago, during the Unidad Popular years. In addition to offering a clear insight into the perceptions of the Catholic left during these years, its bibliography lists some 400 titles—most from Chilean journals, newspapers, magazines, and books from 1970 to 1973. Arrangement of titles by topic—transition to socialism, agrarian reform, the problem of power, classes and social groups, political parties and interest groups, etc.—facilitates use by researchers.

An extremely useful, edited collection on Chile in the 1960s and early 1970s is Arturo and J. Samuel Valenzuela, *Chile: Politics and Society* (New Brunswick, N. J., 1976), which includes an introductory assessment of the constraints upon the Allende government and articles treating electoral politics, public opinion, the labor movement, agrarian reform, foreign capital in the Chilean economy, and the "invisible blockade" by the United States against the Unidad Popular government. Walden F. Bello, *The Roots and Dynamics of Revolution and Counterrevolution in Chile*, Ph.D. diss. (Princeton Univ., 1975), provides a detailed political-historical analysis in the context of theories on economic development and class conflict. Bello's bibliography includes hundreds of periodical and journal articles on the Unidad Popular years. Paul Sigmund's *The Overthrow of Allende and the Politics of Chile, 1964-1976* (Pittsburgh, 1977), offers an extremely readable analysis of Chilean politics from the mid-1960s through the Unidad Popular years, with brief treatment of the military regime.

Beyond these basic sources the following works offer a diversity of treatments of the Unidad Popular years:

Salvador Allende, *La lucha por la democracia económica y las libertades de difusión de la Presidencia de la República,* 1972; and *El mensaje del Presidente Allende ante el Congreso pleno,* Messages delivered May 21, 1971, 1972, 1973;

Juan E. Azcoaga, *El horizonte chileno,* Buenos Aires, 1973;

Genaro Arriagada H., *De la vía Chilena a la vía insurreccional,* 1974;

Lois Edwards Athey, *Government and Opposition in Chile during the Allende Years:* 1970-1973, 2 vols., Ph.D. diss. (Columbia Univ. 1978);

Pablo Baraona Urzúa, *Chile: A Critical Survey,* 1972;

A. Bardón, et al., *Itinerario de una crisis política económica y transición al socialismo,* 1972;

Peter Camejo *Allende's Chile: Is It Going Socialist?,* New York, 1971 (Trotzkyist assessment of Unidad Popular program);

Gustavo Canihuante, *La revolución chilena,* 1971;

Fernando Castillo et al., "Las masas, el estado y el problema del poder en Chile," *Cuadernos de la Realidad Nacional,* April 1973;

Jacques Chonchol, "La reforma agraria en Chile: 1970-1973," *El Trimestre Económico,* No. 53, 1976;

Luis Corvalán, *Camino de la victoria,* 1971;

Régis Debray, *Conversations with Allende,* 1971;

Andrés Echeverría and Luis Frei (eds.), 1970-1973: *la lucha por la juricidad en Chile,* 3 vols., 1974;

Les Evans (ed.), *Disaster in Chile,* New York, 1974 (Trotskyist view of 1970-73);

Richard E. Feinberg, *The Triumph of Allende: Chile's Legal Revolution,* New York, 1972;

Alejandro Foxley, et al., *Chile: búsqueda de un nuevo socialismo,* 1971;

Joan Garcés, 1970: *La pugna política por la presidencia de Chile,* 1971; *El estado y los problemas tácticos en el gobierno de Allende,* Madrid, 1973 (analysis by Allende's political adviser); and (ed.), *Nuestro camino al socialismo—la vía chilena,* Buenos Aires, 1971 (excerpts from speeches and writings of Salvador Allende);

Federico Gil, Ricardo Lagos and Henry Landsberger (eds.), *Chile, 1970-1973: lecciones de una experiencia,* Madrid, 1977;

Instituto de Economía, *La economía chilena en 1971,* Universidad de Chile, 1972;

Sergio Onofre Jarpa, *Creo en Chile,* 1973 (analysis by right-wing político);

Dale C. Johnson (ed.), *The Chilean Road to Socialism,* New York, 1973;

Eduardo Labarca Goddard, *Chile al rojo,* 1971;

Gonzalo Martner (ed.), *El pensamiento económico del gobierno de Allende,* 1971;

Kenneth Medhurst (ed.), *Allende's Chile*, London, 1972;

Hernán Millas and Emilio Filippi, *Chile 1970-1973: crónica de una experiencia*, 1974;

Orlando Millas, *Exposición sobre la política económica del gobierno y del estado de la hacienda pública*, Ministerio de Hacienda, Folleto No. 122, 1972;

Carlos Mistral, *Chile: del triunfo popular al golpe fascista*, Mexico, 1974;

Robert Moss, *Chile's Marxist Experiment*, Abbot Devon, Eng., 1973;

North American Congress on Latin America, "Chile: Facing the Blockade," *Latin America and Empire Report*, New York, 1973;

Lois Oppenheim, *The Quest for Unity on the Left: Allende's Chile and the Socialization of the Economy*, Ph.D. diss. (Washington Univ., 1980);

Neal Tannanhill "Allende and the Chilean Armed Forces," *Armed Forces and Society* 5:3 1979;

Claudio Orrego, *El paro nacional*, 1972;

Ian Roxborough, Phillip O'Brien, and Jackie Roddick, *Chile: The State and Revolution* (contains a very helpful "chronology of main events" 1969-September 11, 1973, and Marxist-oriented analysis of the Unidad Popular experience), 1977;

Unidad Popular, *Programa básico del gobierno de la Unidad Popular*, 1970;

Florencia Varas, *Conversaciones con Viaux*, 1972.

A variety of explanations for the failure of the Unidad Popular administration appear in:

Solon Barraclough, "The State of Chilean Agriculture before the Coup," *Land Tenure Center Newsletter*, No. 43, Jan.-March 1974;

Sergio Bitar, *Transición, socialismo y democracia: la experiencia Chilena*, México, 1979;

François Borricaud, "Chile: Why Allende Fell," *Dissent*, Summer 1974;

René Castillo, "Lessons and Prospects of the Revolution," *World Marxist Review*, No. 17, June 1974;

Nathaniel Davis (ex-U.S. Ambassador to Chile), *The Last Two Years of Salvador Allende*, Ithaca, 1985;

Pío García (ed.), *Las fuerzas armadas y el golpe de estado en Chile*, Mexico, 1974;

D. Holden, "Allende and the Myth Makers," *Encounter, Jan.* 1974;

Robert Kaufman, *Transition to Stable Authoritarian-Corporate Regimes: The Chilean Case?* Beverly Hills, 1976;

Brian Loveman, "Allende's Chile: Political Economy of the Peaceful Road to Disaster," *New Scholar*, 1978;

Gary MacEoin, *No Peaceful Road: The Chilean Struggle for Dignity*, New York, 1974;

North American Congress on Latin America, "Chile: The Story Behind the Coup," *Latin America and Empire Report*, Oct. 1973;

Philip O'Brien (ed.), *Allende's Chile*, New York, 1976;

General Carlos Prats González, (ex-Commander-in-Chief), *Memorias*, 1985 (offers special insight into the personalities, issues and daily confrontations that led up to the military coup of 1973);

David Plotke, "Coup in Chile," *Socialist Revolution*, No. 3, 1973;

Paul N. Rosenstein-Rodan, "Why Allende Failed," *Challenge*, May-June 1974;

Alan Touraine, *Vida y muerte del Chile popular*, México, 1974;

Armando Uribe, *The Black Book of American Intervention in Chile*, Boston, 1975;

L. Whitehead, "Why Allende Fell," *World Today*, Nov. 1973.

Official explanations by the Chilean military of the rationale for the *golpe* and information on subsequent policies can be found in:

Chile, 11 de septiembre de 1975;

Chile, Junta de Gobierno, *Declaración de principios del gobierno de Chile*, 1974; *Algunos fundamentos de la intervención militar en Chile*, 2nd ed., 1974; and *Libro blanco del cambio de gobierno en Chile*, 1974;

Chilean Foreign Investment Law, 1976 (includes new investment code and analysis of special fishery policy);

Chilegram (monthly with "News from 'Chile'." Government propaganda and right wing views);

Constitutional Acts Proclaimed by the Government of Chile, Sept. 11, 1976;

Gerardo Cortés Rencoret, "Introducción a la seguridad nacional," *Cuadernos del instituto de ciencia política*, Universidad Católica de Chile, Feb. 1976;

Enrique Ortúzar Escobar, "La nueva institucionalidad chilena," *Cuadernos del instituto de ciencia política*, Universidad Católica de Chile, Jan. 1976;

"Primero de Mayo 1976," Speech by Minister Sergio Fernández on Labor Day, 1976 (includes decrees related to labor).

Accounts of repression by the military regime and the impact of their policies on the Chilean working classes are numerous. The following sources provide an overview of this literature:

Alan Angell, "Counter-revolution in Chile," *Current History*, Jan. 1974;

Chile: masacre de un pueblo, cristianos frente a los hechos, resistencia y solidaridad, Lima, 1974;

IDOC, *Chile Under Military Rule*, New York, 1974;

Phillipe Labreveux, *Chile bajo las botas-crónicas del terror*, Buenos Aires, 1973;

Ricardo Lagos and Oscar Rufatt, "Military Government and Real Wages in Chile," *LARR*, Summer 1975;

North American Congress on Latin America, "The United States Propping Up the Junta," *Latin America and Empire Report*, Oct. 1974;

Pablo Santillana, *Chile: análisis de un año de gobierno militar*, Buenos Aires, 1974;

"Terror in Chile," *New York Review of Books*, May 30, 1974;

Víctor Villanueva, *Modelo contrarrevolucionaria chileno*, Lima, 1976 (analysis by Peru's foremost expert on the military and politics);

Sergio Villegas, *Chile-El estadio: los crímenes de la junta militar*, Buenos Aires, 1974.

CHILE UNDER THE MILITARY, 1973-

There is a growing literature on Chile under the military government which tends to be highly partisan—whether the topic is human rights, economic performance, or social change. A critical view of the first ten years of military rule is J. Samuel and Arturo Valenzuela (eds.), *Military Rule in Chile, Dictatorship and Oppositions* (Baltimore, 1986). An ongoing assessment of politics, economic policy, and social development in Chile since 1973 (along with other topics) can be found in the articles in the periodical *Colección Estudios CIEPLAN* (1979-   ). Alejandro Foxley's *Latin American Experiments in Neo-conservative Economics* (Berkeley, 1983) and *Para una democracia estable, economía y política* (1985) are important examples of the prolific work of the CIEPLAN academics. Somewhat of a counterpoint is the periodical *Estudios Públicos*, which publishes many articles by the "Chicago Boys" and other conservative economists. Articles in *Chile-America* (Rome) also offer a running commentary from a number of ideological perspectives on Chile since 1973. In addition, a variety of Chilean news and opinion magazines (when they aren't censored or closed) provide analysis and updates. These include *Análisis, Apsi, Cauce, Cosas, Ercilla, Estrategia, Hoy, Pa-*

norama, Qué Pasa. Gary M. Walton (ed.), *The National Economic Policies of Chile* (Greenwich, Conn., 1985), provides a synthesis in English of economic policy, predominantly from the viewpoint of conservative economists, but with a minority position on distributive issues. Work on Chilean art and literature after the coup, as well as literature published in exile and in Chile, reflects the tragedy of human suffering and the continuing sharp divisions in Chilean society. Examples of these trends can be found in Fernando Alegría, *Chilean Writers in Exile* (Trumansburg, N.Y. 1982); Poli Délano et al., *Primer coloquio sobre literatura Chilena (de la resistencia y el exilio)* (México, D.F. 1980); and Antonio Skármeta, *Joven narrativa chilena después del golpe* (Clear Creek, Ind., 1976). From exile the reviews *Literatura chilena en el exilio* and *Araucaria de Chile* have been the most well-known forums for Chilean writers, while publications like *La bicicleta* have struggled to survive within the country. Three of the most moving testimonial works concerning repression by the junta and conditions in the prisons are Hernán Valdés, *Tejas Verdes* (Barcelona, 1974); Alejandro Witker, *Prisión en Chile* (México, 1975); and Aníbal Quijada Cerda, *Cerco de Púas* (1977). Grinor Rojo, *Muerte y resurrección del teatro chileno, 1973-1983* (Madrid, 1985), documents the evolution of the Chilean theater under the Pinochet regime. The following books treat social, economic and political topics, or offer specialized research on issues of interest since 1973:

Americas Watch, *Chile Since the Coup: Ten Years of Repression*, New York, 1983;

José P. Arellano et al., *Modelo económico chileno: trayectoria de una crítica*, 1982;

Jere Behrman, *Macroeconomic Policy in a Developing Country: The Chilean Experience*, New York, 1977;

Sergio Bitar (comp.), *Chile: liberalismo económico y dictadura política*, Lima, 1980;

Guillermo Calvo, "The Chilean Economy in the 1970s," in K. Brunner and A. Meltzer (eds.), *Economic Policy in a World of Change*, Carnegie Rochester Conference Series, 17, 1982;

Guillermo Campero, *Los gremios empresariales en el período 1970-1983: Comportamiento sociopolítico y orientaciones ideológicas, 1970-1983*, 1984; —— and José A. Valenzuela, *El movimiento sindical en el régimen militar chileno, 1973-1981*, 1984; —— and René Cortázar, "Lógicas de acción sindical en Chile," *Colección Estudios CIEPLAN* 18 (Dec. 1985);

Colección Mensaje, *Chile visto por Mensaje. 1971-1981*, 1981 (selection of editorials from influential Catholic review);

Raquel Correa, Malú Sierra, and E. Subercaseaux, *Los generales del régimen*, 1983;

Douglas H. Cortés and L. A. Sjaastad (eds.), *The Political Economy of Trade Reform in Chile* (*Cuádernos de Economía* No. 54-55) 1981;

Sebastián Edwards, "Stabilization with Liberalization: An Evaluation of Ten Years of Chile's Experiment with Free Market Policies," *Economic Development and Culture Change*, Jan. 1985;

Ricardo Ffrench-Davis, "El experimento monetarista en Chile: una síntesis crítica," *Colección Estudios CIEPLAN*, 9, Dec. 1982;

Manuel Antonio Garretón, *El proceso político chileno*, 1983; *Dictaduras y democratización*, 1984;

Arnold Harberger, "The Chilean Economy in the 1970s: Crisis, Stabilization, Liberalization, Reform," in K. Brunner and A. Melzter (eds.), *Economic Policy in a World of Change*, Carnegie Rochester Conference Series, 17, 1982;

David E. Hojman (ed.), *Chile After 1973: Elements for the Analysis of Military Rule*, Liverpool, 1985;

Lovell S. Jarvis, *Chilean Agriculture under Military Rule*, Berkeley, 1985;

Fred D. Levy et al., *Chile: An Economy in Transition* (World Bank Country Study) Washington, D.C., 1979;

Ricardo Lagos, *Democracia para Chile, proposiciones de un socialista*, 1985;

Jonathan Marshall, "Did Milton Friedman Really Ruin Chile?," *Inquiry* (Aug. 1983);

J. C. Méndez (ed.), *Chilean Economic Policy*, Santiago, (1979);

Tomás Moulian, *Democracia y socialismo en Chile*, 1983;

G. Munizaga, *El discurso público de Pinochet, 1973-1976*, Buenos Aires, 1983;

Phil O'Brien and Jackie Roddick, *Chile: The Pinochet Decade*, London, 1983;

Vincent Parkin, "Economic Liberalism in Chile, 1973-1982: A Model for Growth and Development or a Recipe for Stagnation and Impoverishment?," *Cambridge Journal of Economics* 7 (June 1983);

Política, Special Issue, Chile, 1973-1983, *Enfoques para un decenio*, 1983;

Joseph Ramos, "The Economics of Hyperstagflation: Stabilization Policy in Post-1973 Chile," *Journal of Development Economics*, Dec. 1980); *NeoConservative Economics in the Southern Cone of Latin America, 1973-1983*, Baltimore, 1986;

Thomas G. Sanders, "Chile's Economic Crisis and Its Implications for Political Change," Universities Field Staff International *Reports*, No. 4, 1983;

Antonio Schneider, "Supply-Side Economics in a Small Economy: The

Chilean Case," in Edward Nell (ed.), *Free Market Conservatism, A Critique of Theory and Practice*, London, 1984;

Patricio Silva, *Estado, neoliberalismo y política agraria en Chile 1973-1981*, Dordrecht-Holland, 1987;

Augusto Varas, F. Agüero, and F. Bustamante, *Chile, democracia, fuerzas armadas*, 1980;

Pilar Vergara, *Auge y caída del neoliberalismo en Chile*, 1984 (an excellent analysis of the ideological and policy evolution of the Pinochet government);

R. Zahler "El neoliberalismo en una versión autoritaria" in ILADES: *Del liberalismo al capitalismo autoritario*, 1983; "Recent Southern Cone Liberalization Reforms and Stabilization Policies: The Chilean Case, 1974-1982," *Journal of InterAmerican Studies and World Affairs 25*, Nov. 1983.

For insight into General Pinochet's political ideology and motivations, see *Pinochet: Patria y Democracia*, 1983; *The Crucial Day* (translation of *El día decisivo*), 1982.

Index